OBSERVATIONS
UPON
LIBERAL EDUCATION

NATURAL LAW AND
ENLIGHTENMENT CLASSICS

Knud Haakonssen
General Editor

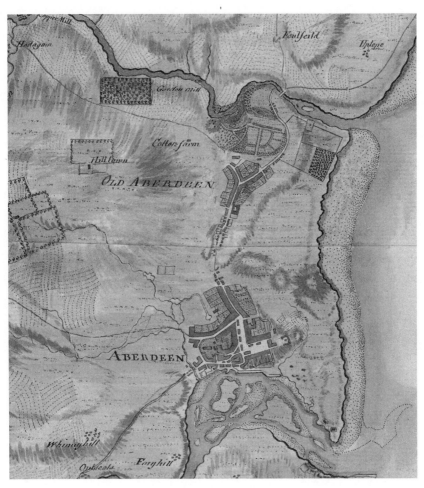

Map of Aberdeen

NATURAL LAW AND
ENLIGHTENMENT CLASSICS

Observations

upon

Liberal Education,

in All Its Branches

George Turnbull

Edited and with an Introduction
by Terrence O. Moore, Jr.

LIBERTY FUND

Indianapolis

© 2003 Liberty Fund, Inc.

Cover art and frontispiece are the Aberdeen detail of the William Roy Map, created from 1747–1755, and are used by permission of the British Library (Shelfmark Maps C.9.b.21 sheet ½).

07 06 05 04 03   C   5 4 3 2 1
07 06 05 04 03   P   5 4 3 2 1

Library of Congress Cataloging-in-Publication Data
Turnbull, George, 1698–1748.
[Observations upon liberal education, in all its branches]
Observations upon liberal education/George Turnbull;
edited and with an introduction by Terrence O. Moore, Jr.
p. cm.—(Natural law and enlightenment classics)
Originally published: Observations upon liberal education, in all its branches.
London: Printed for A. Millar. 1742.
Includes bibliographical references and index.
ISBN 0-86597-411-X (alk. paper). —ISBN 0-86597-412-8 (pbk.: alk. paper)
1. Turnbull, George, 1698–1748—Contributions in education.
2. Education—Philosophy—Early works to 1800.
3. Education, Humanistic—Early works to 1800.
I. Moore, Terrence O., 1967– II. Title. III. Series.
LB575.T87 T86 2003
370.11'2—dc21   2002034059

LIBERTY FUND, INC.
8335 Allison Pointe Trail, Suite 300
Indianapolis, Indiana 46250-1684

CONTENTS

INTRODUCTION

The Scottish Enlightenment was recognized at the time and is studied today as one of the great moments in the history of liberal thought. Scottish thinkers in the eighteenth century understood both the benefits and the hazards in the creation and preservation of a free and commercial society. Hutcheson, Hume, Smith, and others wrote extensive treatises concerning almost every aspect of the growth of commerce, learning, and a liberal constitutional order. Nonetheless, one great embarrassment for the Scottish Enlightenment, or so it has seemed, was the lack of any formal treatise written on education, despite the emphasis placed upon "education, custom, and example" in Scottish moral philosophy and political economy. Although there are passing references to education in the writings of the great luminaries, thus underlining its importance, the Scots seem to have put forth no treatise as comprehensive as Locke's *Some Thoughts Concerning Education* or Rousseau's *Emile*.[1] This seeming omission in the body of enlightened Scottish thought is in fact an illusion of modern editing and reading. For an extensive and illuminating treatment of education, sensitive to the means of inculcating the personal responsibility necessary for living in a free society, was provided by George Turnbull's *Observations upon Liberal Education*.

George Turnbull (1698–1748) was born in Alloa, Scotland, and began

---

1. John Locke, *Some Thoughts Concerning Education*, in *The Educational Writings of John Locke*, ed. James L. Axtell (Cambridge: Cambridge University Press, 1968). The most recent edition in print is John Locke, *Some Thoughts Concerning Education* and *Of the Conduct of the Understanding*, ed. Ruth W. Grant and Nathan Tarcov (Indianapolis, Ind., and Cambridge, Mass.: Hackett Publishing, 1996). Jean-Jacques Rousseau, *Emile, or On Education*, trans. Allan Bloom (New York: Basic Books, 1979).

his studies at the University of Edinburgh in 1711.[2] While in Edinburgh, Turnbull was an active member of the Rankenian club, founded in 1716 or 1717 by a group of young students dedicated to the writings of Shaftesbury.[3] After graduating with a master of arts degree from Edinburgh in 1721, Turnbull taught as a regent at Marischal College, Aberdeen. Although he is principally known as the teacher of Thomas Reid, Turnbull can be considered innovative in his own right. While at Marischal he promoted the study of Shaftesbury in the moral philosophy curriculum, became the first Scottish moralist to call for the experimental method in the investigation of morals, and went further than any other of the Moral Sense philosophers in developing the analogy between moral inquiry and the natural sciences. Turnbull did not, as is often thought, owe his ideas to Hutcheson; rather, he worked out many of the implications of Shaftesbury's thought simultaneously with the great moral philosopher at Glasgow.

Despite his initial success in Aberdeen, Turnbull left in 1727 and began to tutor young aristocrats on their continental grand tours. Yet his writing drew upon his experience at Marischal, and he gave more attention to the role of education in the maintenance of civic and religious freedom than anyone else among the Scots except perhaps David Fordyce.[4] Besides vari-

2. For biographical information on Turnbull, see M. A. Stewart, "George Turnbull and Educational Reform," in *Aberdeen and the Enlightenment,* ed. Jennifer J. Carter and Joan H. Pittock (Aberdeen: Aberdeen University Press, 1987). On Turnbull's educational philosophy, see Stewart and the following works: David Fate Norton, "George Turnbull and the Furniture of the Mind," *Journal of the History of Ideas* 36 (1975): 701–16; Earl R. Wasserman, "Nature Moralized: The Divine Analogy in the Eighteenth Century," *ELH* 20 (1953): 39–76; Paul B. Wood, *The Aberdeen Enlightenment: The Arts Curriculum in the Eighteenth Century* (Aberdeen: Aberdeen University Press, 1993).

3. See Anthony, Third Earl of Shaftesbury, *Characteristicks of Men, Manners, Opinions, Times,* foreword by Douglas Den Uyl (Indianapolis, Ind.: Liberty Fund, 2001).

4. Fordyce taught moral philosophy at Marischal College from 1742 to 1751. His best-known works were *Dialogues Concerning Education* (1745) and *The Elements of Moral Philosophy* (1754), ed. Thomas Kennedy (Indianapolis, Ind.: Liberty Fund, 2003). He also wrote the article on moral philosophy for the first edition of the *Encyclopaedia Britannica.*

ous works on rational Christianity, moral philosophy, and natural law,[5] he published *A Treatise on Ancient Painting* in 1740 and *Observations upon Liberal Education* in 1742, both concerned with education reform. In 1739 Turnbull was ordained in the Anglican Church. He became rector of a small Irish parish in 1742 and died six years later on a trip to the Netherlands.

In *Observations upon Liberal Education* Turnbull joined a discussion of the best means of educating young gentlemen that began in antiquity but was reinvigorated at the close of the seventeenth century by the English philosopher John Locke. In his *Some Thoughts Concerning Education* (1693) Locke irrevocably altered the scope of education in the English-speaking world. The pedagogical inheritance from the Renaissance throughout Europe had been the study of the classical languages. In their period of vibrancy, the classical schools of England, founded mostly during the Tudor and the early Stuart period, taught the Latin and Greek classics to young boys destined for careers in the church and the law. Locke himself had attended the prestigious grammar school of Westminster under the schoolmaster Richard Busby, a man famous for his classical erudition and notorious for his brutal methods of discipline. Despite the distinguished history of such schools, Locke accused late-seventeenth-century schoolmasters of beating children for failing to understand the arcane rules of grammar in languages the schoolmasters barely understood themselves. English gentlemen would be better served, according to Locke, by learning the language and history of their own country. In addition, the high numbers of unruly boys in English boarding schools, whom masters could only barely control by means of merciless beatings, turned these celebrated institutions of learning into schools of vice. Locke warned parents against compromising their sons' virtue for the sake of the

---

5. See George Turnbull, *The Principles of Moral and Christian Philosophy* (1740), ed. Alexander Broadie (Indianapolis, Ind.: Liberty Fund, forthcoming); *A Methodical System of Universal Law: Or the Laws of Nature and Nations Deduced from Certain Principles, and Applied to Proper Cases,* by Johann Gottlieb Heineccius, trans. George Turnbull (1741), ed. Peter Schröder (Indianapolis, Ind.: Liberty Fund, forthcoming).

dead languages. He advocated, instead, education in the home, under a polite and virtuous tutor, in more modern and useful subjects.

In addition to his critique of grammar schools, Locke provided the age with an epistemology that both alarmed and inspired moral educators. In Locke's view, the individual has no innate understanding of truth and beauty. Rather, the individual's ideas of the world are formed in early childhood according to his or her exposure to certain stimuli perceived by the mind simultaneously, a process Locke called "the association of ideas" and a concept on which Turnbull often drew. Simple elements that have no natural relation to each other, but are joined by social customs, become connected in the individual's imagination. Once the association is made, it is almost impossible to break. False associations made in early youth could have an adverse effect on the whole course of a person's life. Locke and subsequent philosophers worried about the "false associations" made by the culture at large that would cause youth to engage in pernicious pursuits. For example, Locke thought that children had no proclivity toward violence but acquired a taste for it when they read accounts of cruelties in history or when people laughed at the children's feeble attempts to hit others. Acquiring false associations in childhood, if unchecked, led by degrees to a course of ruin in adulthood, both to oneself and to others. Although originally used by Locke to criticize the schools, the appeal of this theory of association for enlightened schoolmasters and educational theorists became irresistible. It was simple. It placed a premium on the early upbringing and education of the child. And it took aim against the "false associations" of a culture that too often preferred luxury to virtue. As a result, education reformers throughout the eighteenth century attempted to demonstrate how children might be steered away from the false associations of the culture (and too often the home) and toward the true association of happiness with virtue.

Like all eighteenth-century education reformers, Turnbull owed a considerable debt to John Locke. He appropriated wholesale many of Locke's ideas on early instruction and the cultivation of good habits, specifically, on the dangers of parental indulgence, on the importance of self-denial, on the use of praise and blame, and on the best means of disciplining children. Turnbull also embraced the Lockean description of the ideal English gentleman. The child should learn to be natural in company rather than affected, industrious rather than lazy, and courageous rather than pusillanimous. Turnbull also followed Locke closely in his prescriptions for the teaching of English and foreign languages as well as British history and law. Despite these obvious borrowings, Turnbull's *Observations* cannot be regarded as merely a restatement and elaboration of Locke's educational writings. Locke proved too antiestablishment and anticlassical in his pedagogy and apparently too antinormative in his epistemology for Turnbull's more balanced view of human nature and education.

An instance of Turnbull's balanced approach to education reform can be seen in his handling of the most controversial educational issue of the century and the one with which he began his *Observations*. Every elite family in Britain had to decide whether to send its sons to school, usually one of the "public" boarding schools such as Eton or Westminster, or to educate them privately in the home by hiring a domestic tutor. Though Locke had made a strong case against corrupting the young gentleman's morals by sending him to a school, the accomplished schoolmasters of Britain were not without their own powerful arguments. Foremost they rehearsed the advantages of public education set forth by the great Roman schoolmaster Quintilian.[6] His *Institutio Oratoria* offered a systematic account of the rigorous oratorical training undertaken by the Roman youth and aimed ultimately at producing a Cicero. Renaissance education had largely been modeled on the *Institutio Oratoria,* and Quintilian's authority had by no means diminished in the eyes of eighteenth-century British schoolmasters. According to Quintilian, a boy's morals could be preserved in a public school provided that upstanding and watchful instructors were in charge. Moreover, a child's morals were as often corrupted in the home as in the school. Parents spoiled their children, and slaves introduced them to all sorts of vice. Even more important, a school offered youth a public setting that stimulated their minds through "emulation," that is, the spirited rivalry of many boys competing to be the best. The advantages of

---

6. Quintilian, *Institutio Oratoria,* trans. H. E. Butler, 4 vols. (Cambridge, Mass.: Harvard University Press, 1963).

emulation for producing a great orator and a public man were obvious. British schoolmasters adopted Quintilian's arguments wholesale; they had only to adjust "slaves" to "servants." Turnbull, however, saw the merits of both sides and hoped to effect a compromise. In his Socratic dialogue devoted to the issue, he concluded that smaller schools could preserve morality and also offer emulation, "rivalship," and "bustling."

As important as the educational setting, the curriculum was something that must be addressed by every education reformer. Turnbull devoted considerable attention to the subjects that should be taught, and even more to how they should be taught. Again he reached a compromise between Locke and the classicists. In doing so, he made some unique contributions to his age's understanding of what today is called "the canon," those arts and sciences that should be studied by all liberally educated individuals. Turnbull agreed that British youth should study their own history and language. At the same time he allowed for more training in the classical languages and classical history than did Locke.

For support of this more classical curriculum, Turnbull drew on the Frenchman Charles Rollin as well as Quintilian. After Locke, Charles Rollin was probably the most authoritative writer on education in eighteenth-century Europe.[7] Whereas Locke's experience in education derived from his office as private secretary and tutor in the house of Shaftesbury and later his observations of Damaris Mascham educating her children, Rollin was a schoolmaster through and through. While rector of the University of Paris, he turned his lectures into two of the most voluminous and popular works of the century, *The Method of Teaching and Studying the Belles Lettres* and *The Ancient History*. In the former work Rollin explained his methods of teaching the classics, methods that drew liberally from Cicero, Horace, Seneca, Xenophon, Plutarch, Plato, and, above all, Quintilian, authors who also make frequent appearances in Turnbull's *Observations*.

---

7. See his monumental treatise, *De la manière d'enseigner et d'étudier les belles lettres* (1726–28), translated as *The Method of Teaching and Studying the Belles Lettres,* 4 vols. (London, 1734). On Rollin's importance, see Albert Charles Gaudin, "The Educational Views of Charles Rollin" (Ph.D. dissertation, Columbia University, 1939), and Georges Snyders, *La Pédagogie en France aux XVIIe et XVIIIe Siècles* (Paris, 1965).

Rollin explained how youth should be steered away from false images of "glory" presented by the culture and instead turned toward true glory and a correct taste as found in the great works of history and literature. In short, Rollin paved the way for Turnbull by showing how the proper teaching of a canon of great works in school could achieve the same ends that Locke advocated in his system of private instruction. As much as a tribute to Locke, the *Observations* can be read as a defense of teaching the classics for moral purposes.

Turnbull's curriculum comprehended far more than the classics. Turnbull also embraced subjects that Locke either criticized or largely ignored, such as poetry, painting, and the natural sciences. Although today we take for granted scientific and aesthetic subjects in a liberal-arts curriculum, it must be realized that the rigorous linguistic basis of the classical curriculum left little room for "modern" subjects. Turnbull was one of the first educational theorists to open up liberal education to the study of the natural world as it had been explained by Newton. He stood virtually alone in his enthusiasm for art.[8] Unlike educators today, however, Turnbull did not compartmentalize or departmentalize such different "branches" of learning. As the metaphor of the tree implies, all forms of learning had a common origin and were connected. Invoking Plato and other ancient philosophers, Turnbull pronounced all knowledge as having "one common scope" whose purpose is to harmonize the human mind and affections. The lessons drawn from nature were the same as those to be found in the human, or "moral," world because a benevolent creator has set into motion laws of nature, both human and material. It is therefore the duty of human beings to live according to the designs of "God's moral providence" as revealed to us in history and through the "analogies" of the physical world. The one true purpose of philosophy, therefore, is to make men better. For Turnbull moral philosophers were, strictly speaking, philosophers who moralized.

Moral philosophers had an ally in human nature itself according to

---

8. Turnbull's aesthetic theories are explored in Carol Gibson-Wood, "Painting as Philosophy: George Turnbull's *Treatise on Ancient Painting*," in *Aberdeen and the Enlightenment,* 189–98.

Turnbull. Following Shaftesbury, Turnbull rejected the ideas of a "certain set of philosophers" who regarded human nature as "originally deformed." These unnamed philosophers were no doubt Hobbes and Mandeville, but also by implication Saint Augustine and the theologians inspired by him, especially the orthodox Calvinists in the Church of Scotland. To explain evil deeds in the world, Turnbull had recourse to Locke's association of ideas. Individuals would become vicious when they were exposed to false associations in childhood and formed habits accordingly. Yet he seemed as troubled as Shaftesbury by the underlying idea that morality is only the result of custom, habit, or education, as one reading of Locke would have it. Instead, Turnbull posited that human beings are equipped with a "natural furniture" of the mind that urges them to advance in knowledge and virtue. By natural furniture Turnbull referred to reason, the imagination, the moral sense, the passions or affections, and other capacities common to every individual. The benevolent "author of Nature" endowed human beings with these capacities so they could "exercise a very large power" by doing good in the world. Given proper instruction, people would normally imitate their benevolent creator and thereby attain real and lasting happiness. Turnbull's optimistic view of human nature allowed him to enlist for moral purposes certain parts of the mind that seventeenth-century philosophers had distrusted, such as the imagination. Of course, the "fancy" had to be regulated, but it could not be restrained completely. Rather, the imagination opened up to the spectator the beauties of nature and of poetic and artistic excellence. Like Shaftesbury, Turnbull held that the aesthetic and moral senses were closely allied. Pleasures of the imagination, as Addison had shown, could thus be used to harmonize the soul.[9]

9. The importance of Addison and Steele's *The Spectator* in creating a culture of politeness in eighteenth-century Britain has been traced in the various essays of Nicholas Phillipson. See especially "The Scottish Enlightenment," in *The Enlightenment in National Context*, ed. R. Porter and M. Teich (Cambridge: Cambridge University Press, 1981), and *Hume* (London: Weidenfeld and Nicolson, 1989). On this same theme in Shaftesbury, see Lawrence E. Klein, *Shaftesbury and the Culture of Politeness: Moral Discourse and Cultural Politics in Early Eighteenth-Century England* (Cambridge: Cambridge University Press, 1994).

By "liberal education," then, Turnbull meant the employment of the various branches of learning to show youth how to gain mastery over their "affections." The ability to regulate the passions and imagination granted youth a true "inward liberty" and strength. Teachers and moralists should therefore "cherish into proper vigour the love of liberty" in children but not allow it to degenerate into willfulness and vice. Such a liberty constituted a real "power," a command over the self and a power to do good in the world. This self-command in turn led one to true happiness and, according to Turnbull, moral "perfection."

There has been some dispute over Turnbull's originality and influence as a moral philosopher. As an educational theorist, however, his influence was more direct. References to the *Observations* and *A Treatise on Ancient Painting* in eighteenth-century schoolmasters' educational treatises suggest that Turnbull's advice was read, admired, and followed by enlightened teachers.[10] Perhaps the most important use of Turnbull was in America. When writing his *Proposals Relating to the Education of Youth in Pensilvania*, Benjamin Franklin drew explicitly on George Turnbull.[11] Franklin, of course, was one of the early advocates of a liberal, moral, and English curriculum in American schools. He was also a great believer in attempting to reach "moral perfection." Turnbull's *Observations upon Liberal Education*, therefore, was an important contribution to the theory and practice of education during the Age of Enlightenment, a period when the best minds in Europe turned their attention to making young people "happy in themselves and useful to others." The *Observations* should prove worthwhile reading to scholars of moral philosophy, liberal education, and the eighteenth century. In addition, as our own age struggles to reform schools and to form free and responsible citizens, concerned teachers and parents may wish to return to their enlightened moorings by contemplat-

---

10. James Barclay, *A Treatise on Education* (Edinburgh: James Cochran, 1743), 217–18. George Chapman, *A Treatise on Education*, 4th ed. (London, 1790), appendix.

11. Franklin identified the authors he consulted while writing the *Proposals* as Milton, Locke, Hutcheson, Obadiah Walker, Rollin, and George Turnbull, in that order. Franklin actually mistook David Fordyce for Francis Hutcheson. See Benjamin Franklin, *Writings* (New York: Library of America, 1987), 323–44.

ing and indeed emulating Turnbull's ambitious curriculum in virtue and learning.

Terrence O. Moore, Jr.

Editorial Note

George Turnbull left no stone unturned in supporting his observations on education with the best of classical and modern sources. He assumed a readership that was well versed in the literature of antiquity, ancient and modern history, and contemporary works on moral philosophy and education. Like many an eighteenth-century author, he did not always identify these sources precisely. Moreover, he was prone to make general references along the lines of "see Plato on this." A modern editor could potentially offer a thousand footnotes to this edition and still not consider his or her job complete.

My principle of editing has been less ambitious and, perhaps, less obtrusive. I have simply tried to make Turnbull more readable for a modern audience. To this end, I have followed three basic guidelines. First, I have attempted to identify all of the direct quotations in the body of the text. Many of these passages are taken from authors such as Locke, Rollin, and Quintilian. Turnbull was often unreliable in setting off quoted passages with both opening and closing quotation marks. To assist the reader I have supplied the missing punctuation, using intelligent guesswork in a few instances. Second, I have provided translations for all of the Latin and Greek passages, whether in the text or in the notes. Where possible, I have used the Loeb Classical Library published by Harvard University Press. All such identifications and translations added by me are enclosed in square brackets. Third, I have studiously avoided piling up my own footnotes on top of Turnbull's. The general quality of some of these notes is an important aspect of Turnbull's style. Furthermore, he seems to invite readers to take on whole texts, especially those of ancient philosophers, rather than to consult them on specific points of interest. A thorough acquaintance with Turnbull will, no doubt, enlist many of today's readers to study the ancients on the all-consuming topic of education.

ACKNOWLEDGMENTS

Like so many other students and scholars of the Scottish Enlightenment, I owe a considerable debt to the teaching and conversation of Nicholas Phillipson. If the chief purpose of the historian is to make a period of the past come alive for modern students, then Dr. Phillipson has fulfilled that office with conspicuous wit and learning for many decades. Professor Knud Haakonssen has been an exceedingly patient and helpful general editor. I am deeply grateful to my friend Professor Erik Gunderson of The Ohio State University, who has identified and translated a number of obscure classical passages at a moment's notice. Finally, I am most thankful to my wife, Jennifer, who has endured my working on Turnbull over weekends and holidays in our first year of marriage while during the regular workweek I was setting up a classical school that is not unworthy, I hope, of Turnbull's ideal.

OBSERVATIONS
UPON
LIBERAL EDUCATION

OBSERVATIONS
UPON
Liberal Education,
In all its Branches

CONTAINING

The Substance of what hath been said upon that important Subject by the best Writers Ancient or Modern; with many new Remarks interspersed:

Designed for the Assistance of Young Gentlemen, who having made some Progress in Useful Sciences, are desirous of making further Improvements, by a proper Prosecution of their Studies; as well as for the Use of Parents, who would give right Education to their Children, and of those who are engaged in the Business of Education, whether in a more Private or public Manner.

IN THREE PARTS.

By George Turnbull, LL. D.
Chaplain to his Royal Highness the Prince of Wales.

Gratum est, quod patriae civem, populoque dedisti,
Si facis, ut patriae sit idoneus, utilis agris,
Utilis & bellorum & pacis rebus agendis.
Plurimum enim intererit, quibus artibus, & quibus hunc tu,
Moribus instituas.——JUVENAL Sat. 14.[1]

LONDON:
Printed for A. Millar, at Buchanan's Head, over-against
St. Clement's Church in the Strand.

MDCCXLII.

1. [Juvenal, *Satires,* 14.70–74: "It is good that you have presented your country and your people with a citizen, if you can make him serviceable to his country, useful for the land, useful for the things both of peace and war. For it will make all the difference in what practices, in what habits, you bring him up" (Loeb translation by G. G. Ramsay).]

I

Right Reverend Father in GOD,

THOMAS,

Lord Bishop of Derry,

MY LORD,

Proper care about education being a concern of the highest importance, with relation both to private and public happiness; to the flourishing of liberty, learning, virtue, religion, of every thing, in one word, that is good or great in human life: And the thoughts which I have here laid together upon this subject, in the best order I was able, not being advent'rous conjectures, hazarded into the world upon no better authority than a presumptuous confidence of my own opinion, but observations transmitted to us from the more thinking and wiser part of mankind in almost all ages and nations of the world, as Truths or Facts confirmed in their experience: Permit me, my Lord, most humbly to dedicate these discourses to your Lordship, who are so universally acknowledged to have all the interests of mankind most sincerely at heart, and to be very distinguishedly qualified to serve them, by that happy concurrence of knowledge of the world, good-breeding, and polite taste, with extensive, solid erudition, true goodness, and genuine piety, which makes the perfect character, that education ought to have in view, and should be adapted to form.

The main drift, my Lord, of these discourses, being to turn education from words to things; to recommend the moral culture of young minds that is requisite to prepare them for philosophical or religious lessons; to delineate the true philosophy which ought to be the principal subject and scope of their instruction; and to shew what advances may early be made in real knowledge, without neglecting useful languages or exercises, if proper methods of insinuating the love of it into youth, and of initiating

3

them into the pursuit be taken: Even the philosophy which gives just ideas of providence, and the administration of the world, by pointing out the wise and good final causes every where pursued in it, and the many beneficial arts to which the knowledge of nature's general laws leads; and from thence enforces just and full conceptions of human duty, dignity and happiness:—This being the end proposed, whatever failures there may be in the execution, the design is laudable in itself; and is therefore sure of finding your approbation: And it is a most sincere satisfaction to me, to have a proper opportunity of publicly declaring the high value I put upon the share in your esteem with which you have long honoured me, and my most ardent ambition to preserve it.

> *I am,*
>> *My LORD,*
>>> *Your Lordship's*
>>>> *Most obedient*
>>>> *Humble Servant,*
>>>> GEORGE TURNBULL.

THE CONTENTS

Introduction

The observations in the following discourses are all taken from experience; so moral rules, as well as physical ones ought to be—The general scope of them—A Letter to the Author, containing several excellent remarks upon education.—The reason why so many authors ancient and modern are quoted in these discourses—'Tis here proposed to give the substance of all that hath been said by the ancients or moderns, on the subject, such as Socrates, Plato, Xenophon, Aristotle, Cicero, Plutarch, Quintilian, Milton, Locke, Montaigne, Mr. de Fenelon, Rollin, Nicol, &c.—Why in two Pieces of this collection the character of an ancient, narrating conversations about true philosophy and liberal education is assumed,

PART I

temperance, and all the virtues early in young minds, wherein the use of rewards and punishments is fully considered,   p. 44.

The great arcanum in education consists in forming self-denial and mastership of the passions, without weakening the vigour or activity of the mind, and how this may be done, explained at some length,   p. 49.

There is but one lesson education has to teach or inculcate, love of virtue, and just notions of what it requires in all the various relations and circumstances of life—How it ought to be taught—How all the arts ought to be rendered subservient to this lesson—And how naturally they all tend or conspire to recommend the love of virtue, natural philosophy, geometry, poetry, and all the polite arts, their natural union,   p. 52.

No hood-winking or blinding arts to be used in education—Youth ought to be warned and armed against the vices and snares with which they will find the world to abound so soon as they enter upon it,   p. 64.

'Tis not enough to give rules to children, many good habits may be formed by right practice before rules can be fully comprehended—Yet we cannot begin too soon to reason with them—And they ought always to be treated in a rational way—Praise and blame the properest handles for moulding youth into a right form and temper, the force of honour and shame in human nature,   p. 67.

A conversation upon giving a right turn to all the natural dispositions or principles in human breasts—Reflexions upon several methods by which children are corrupted—Wherein true virtue consists—And how it may be early formed and strengthened—A great difference between the cravings of nature and of fancy—Children ought to be taught where to place their happiness—And for that effect to distinguish between external and internal goods, and things subject and things not subject to human power—This distinction explained, and the importance of attending to it inculcated—What are the motives that are most consistent with virtue, and have greatest influence upon a good mind—Virtue ought to be represented as conformity to the Divine Mind, which he will reward and make happy in the final issue of things, this opinion renders the cause of virtue triumphant,   p. 69.

Thus were virtue and science taught by the better ancients; their care about bodily health and vigour—The best preservatives of these are temperance and exercise—Two ancient fables illustrating this subject; the happy effects of ancient education, p. 82.

Education ought to be suited to the form of government established in a state; so it was among the ancients—It ought to instruct in the nature and end of government and laws—How difficult a science politics is; men could not, previously to very long experience of human affairs, form just ideas of the best civil orders and constitutions—Reflexions on this subject—All civil constitutions liable to diseases—The excellency of mixed monarchy: The sentiments of ancient republicans on that head, p. 86.

PART II

Adversity necessary to awaken a mind which hath been depraved by wrong education; or hath through neglect of education fallen into bad habits—Our dependance upon the care taken of our education, or upon the examples and instructions we receive from our parents and others about us—Providence vindicated in this respect—Here, by the by, some false notions concerning education are refuted—None of the affections natural to man ought to be opposed or crushed; they are all capable of great improvements, and how they ought to be guided and turned—A digression into the vindication of providence with regard to the distribution of happiness in this world—How men are furnished by nature for happiness, and whence inequalities in that respect amongst mankind proceed, p. 93.

The force of education considered and exemplified; what right education is able to do, p. 107.

A conversation about man, and his natural furniture for acquiring knowledge and virtue, and thereby true happiness, in which the ways of God to man are fully justified, and human vices and miseries are traced to their real causes or sources, p. 108.

The doctrine or lesson to be taught and inculcated by education is, That the Author of nature is wise and good in all his works, and hath made us capable of attaining to a great degree of moral perfection and happiness, by imitating him in wisdom and goodness, or by making the good of our kind the end and rule of our conduct—And how this lesson ought to be taught and inculcated, by instructing youth in the good final causes pursued by the Author of nature throughout all his works, in the material world, and in the moral world,   p. 127.

How all the arts will naturally enter into and contribute towards illustrating and confirming this lesson,   p. 129.

Of several dispositions in human nature, and the culture due to them, as curiosity, or the love of novelty,   p. 134.

Of the admiration with which great objects strike the mind, and how this passion ought to be educated, and how guarded against; the errors or extravagancies it may run into,   p. 136.

A conversation about the human mind, in which the social affections are considered, and the selfish or interested philosophy is refuted,   p. 145.

A Recapitulation of what hath been hitherto delivered concerning education,   p. 158.

A dialogue about the chief end of education, in which instruction in final causes, virtue, and the arts of government are shewn to be the principal scope liberal education ought to have in view; and the philosophy Socrates taught is briefly delineated.   p. 159.

PART III

An Essay on Liberal Education

Chapter I

Instruction in the science or art of right living, is the chief lesson in education, to which all others ought to be rendered subservient; and what this science is, and what may justly be called false learning.

Instruction in the nature of human perfection and happiness, and in the right conduct of life, the chief end of education—So a Roman satyrist teaches us—How he commends the instructions he had received early from his tutor—The several parts of this true philosophy delineated—And the general way of teaching it pointed out, p. 171.

The use of setting characters which contrast one another before youth, to give them just ideas of virtue and vice; to give them just ideas of the perfection belonging to and aquirable by human understanding, if rightly employed—And to human will or temper—

A beautiful character drawn by Horace—How his father taught him what to admire and imitate, and what to avoid and abhor, and the natural effect of such discipline, p. 175.

How Cato taught and formed his son by setting characters before him, and early acquainting him with history, the history of his own country in particular, p. 180.

The knowledge of human nature, and of human life and duties, which is best taught by characters and examples, more fully delineated—The proper method is to lead from wise final causes in nature to the consideration of the good final causes we ought to pursue in our spheres, in imitation of and conformity to the Author of nature—The transition from the one to the other, is natural and easy—Of the use of natural knowledge to extend human power; it is the only way of enlarging our dominion—Of the moral use of it, and the error of philosophers in stopping short of final causes in their lessons upon the material world, or physics, as they are called—The advantage to society of giving youth a turn towards the study of nature, and the cultivation and improvement of mechanical arts—When youth have a clear notion of the use of ingenious, benevolent industry, it will be easy for them to conceive what must be the chief end of civil government, even to encourage and protect ingenious benevolent industry—If proper methods be taken, young people are not incapable of this kind of instruction, p. 181.

However difficult it may be, nothing really useful is done by education but in proportion as youth are improved in this knowledge—But it will not be found so difficult as is imagined—Excite youth to attend to the benefits arising to society from ingenious arts; and to the general properties of bodies and laws of motion on which these depend—And shew them how general properties of bodies and laws of motion are inferred by induction from particular experiences—Trace phenomena with them into their general laws, and shew them what human art hath done, or may do, for the abridgement of human toil, and the conveniency of life, in consequence of these general laws—And thus they will see how human power, in the natural world, may be extended and enlarged—They will see that knowledge is power—Thus they will be able to comprehend what human power means, and how far it extends—Let the final causes of the general laws of matter and motion be pointed out to them, and the wisdom and goodness they discover; and hence lead youth to consider the texture of the human mind, the powers and affections with which it is endued, their uses, and the virtues or improvements they are capable of by due culture; and thus they will comprehend what our moral power means, or our power to improve our understandings, discipline our affections; and govern our actions; and what power over the understandings and affections of others means,   p. 186.

It will not be unpleasant to observe to them the analogy between our natural and our moral power; but it will be of greater use to engage them to attend to this important truth, that the discipline of our minds depends more upon us than the culture of our gardens.—Moral duties quickly discover themselves to all who set themselves seriously to enquire what is right or wrong; and practice in examining and controuling the appetites and affections, will soon render them very orderly and regular,   p. 189.

Philosophy ought to be accurate and exact in developing to youth all the powers and affections of the human mind; but some of its natural determinations deserve our very particular attention: Our determination to distinguish involuntary from free actions, without which we could have no ideas of merit or blame—The reality of this distinction proved—Our determination to approve free actions which are beneficial to the public, and to disapprove free actions which are hurtful to the public—Our determination to receive pleasure from uniformity amidst variety even in material objects.—The Uses of these natural determinations of the human mind,   p. 191.

An observation upon the passions, and the manner in which they are engendered not commonly attended to in discourses upon them—Youth ought not to be perplexed with subtleties: But it is necessary to shew them the origin and formation of the passions, in order to teach them how to regulate them,   p. 193.

Let youth be led from the contemplation of final causes, whether in the natural or the moral world, to the admiration and love of the supreme Cause and Author of all things, and to views of human duties resulting from our relation to him,   p. 198.

All science which stops short of such conclusions, is justly pronounced vain philosophy—Of what use is mere knowledge of words?—Many useful sciences depend upon mathematics; but can that science alone teach how to govern the mind, or how to steer a wise and safe course through life?—Even natural philosophy, if it stop short of final causes, and the moral conclusions which evidently result from thence, is a very defective and imperfect science—But the most dangerous of all the pretended sciences, is that which seems to have the human and the supreme Mind for its objects, and yet produces nothing but idle jangling and sophistry; no solid rules or maxims for practice,   p. 199.

Chapter II

Concerning the formation of good habits in young minds; the proper methods of cultivating virtuous dispositions; and the practices by which the vices are early engendered and strengthened, and of the best means for correcting and reforming them.

The culture of virtuous habits in the mind is as pre-requisite to instruction as the due preparation of ground is to sowing good seed—And 'tis not vice but virtue, on the contrary, that in any proper sense can be said to be natural to the human mind—Nor is it to be wondered at that vices sprout up so early in young minds, if we attend to the common methods of education,   p. 206.

Reflexions quoted from Mr. Locke on this subject, which are further confirmed from other considerations, where rewards and punishments are treated of,   p. 208.

Hence it appears, that education must begin very early, otherwise it will be but weeding or cleansing-work, with further observations from Mr. Locke on this head,   p. 212.

Our Saviour's parable of the sower applied to illustrate the necessity of preparing young minds for receiving instruction by previous moral culture and discipline, early begun and steadily pursued— Some general rules with regard to this culture,   p. 221.

Reflexions upon the choice of preceptors or tutors, two letters of Pliny the younger on this subject,   p. 233.

The exact care of the ancient Greeks and Romans about the first habits of their youth—A short account of the first part of Cicero's education—The neglect of education in modern times censured,   p. 226.

But since bad habits are nursed, or at least are suffered to grow up without controul, 'tis worth while to enquire if there be any methods of curing or reforming them.—Horace assures us there is, but it is a painful and difficult art—The first step is to gain the patience of hearing counsel—Reflexions of Mr. Locke on some diseases of the mind, and their cures—Upon cowardice or timorousness—Upon listless carelesness and sauntering, one of the worst of habits—Gentle admonitions, soft irony, shame and praise, are the proper handles for reforming and amending youth by,   p. 228.

But if all other methods fail, corporal punishments must be applied; these ought to be used only to correct obstinate vices; the necessity of employing them for that effect: This subject to be more fully handled in the next chapter.   p. 238.

Chapter III

Of teaching languages; and of the exercises and their uses; together with some observations of the ancients upon punishments and reproofs confirmed by examples.

Mr. Locke's Sentiments about teaching languages confirmed—Of the proper time and way of teaching grammar—Of all grammars, that of our own language, ought chiefly to be minded—The great error in modern education is, that it consumes all the best years of youth for learning useful, real knowledge, in teaching them nothing but words—What progress may be made very early in useful sciences, without neglecting the learned languages—A turn towards verbal criticism how pernicious to youth, called by providence to apply themselves early to higher studies,   p. 240.

Grammar, which, tho' the first, is the most difficult part of rhetoric, cannot be understood till youth have minds very well furnished with various knowledge, and have been well practised in reading good authors—How the Greeks and Romans studied their own languages,   p. 244.

There is time enough to teach all the learned or useful languages, without neglecting the more substantial parts of education—Of a right choice of books, even in teaching words or languages, p. 246.

Reflexions from the ancients, confirmed by the experience of several moderns, upon the importance of right education—Upon punishments and rewards—Praise and blame, reproofs and admonitions—Of good example in masters—Of the arts of engaging youth to the love of knowledge and study,   p. 249.

The chief thing is, that the master take proper methods of gaining the affections of his pupils—How this may be done—Encourage their curiosity—Take fit opportunities of engaging their attention—Diversify study—Make it easy and pleasant—These observations, taken from ancient writers; and confirmed by Mr. de Fenelon, Mr. Nicol, and Mr. Rollin, as likewise by our Milton and Locke,   p. 274.

Some reflexions to confirm Mr. Milton's opinion about teaching logic and rhetoric,   p. 277.

Examples to confirm what hath been said—Plato's account of the education of princes among the ancient Persians—Xenophon's account of the Persian education—The education in the schools of Apollonia, whither Julius Cesar sent Octavius to be formed, and where Mecenas likewise was bred,   p. 278.

An Account of the finishing part of Cicero's education, and its happy effects—When he went to travel—The design of travelling,
                                                                                        p. 282.

A letter of Pliny upon study, from which masters may learn useful hints for improving their pupils in eloquence and stile,   p. 291.

Of the liberal, manly exercises that ought to be joined with teaching—The design and use of the exercises, not only to give health, vigour and grace to the body, but strength and activity to the mind—Observations of Plato upon the different effects of the softer studies, and the rougher exercises, and the necessity of uniting them in education,   p. 293.

Children ought to have recreations, but care ought to be taken of their choice of them, and their behaviour in them—Let them be inured to act generously; or let due pains be taken to give them a liberal cast of mind, and a graceful manner of doing every thing—Of good-breeding, and wherein it consists, and early care about it—The necessity of good example in this case particularly—Of dancing,   p. 296.

Reflexions by Mr. Simon upon the urbanity or politeness of the Romans, and their care about it in education,   p. 306.

Chapter IV

The true philosophy, and the proper methods of teaching it more fully described; where the Socratic method of teaching, and instruction by fables, parables, or allegories, are considered.

An apology for the minute detail the author was obliged to enter into in the preceding chapter—The character of the true philosophy, which alone can produce good and useful citizens, from Tacitus—from Lucan—from Socrates—from Cicero—How the latter refutes the selfish narrow-minded philosophy of Epicurus,   p. 315.

A definition of the true philosophy which ought to be the main scope of education—The history of nature and the history of mankind the chief subjects of education—How masters ought to proceed in teaching this philosophy regularly, by beginning with natural philosophy, and laying open the wise and good final causes nature pursues in all her works—How pleasant and engaging this study is,   p. 318.

But let not philosophy stop here, but proceed to the consideration of the human mind—The transition from the one philosophy to the other is easy and natural; they make in reality but one science,   p. 320.

Natural philosophers censured for leaving out final causes in their lessons upon physics, and not proceeding to the moral conclusions to which a just view of nature's wisdom, harmony and goodness naturally leads—The happy effect of true Theism upon the mind—Virtue not compleat without piety—And moral rules of conduct cannot have their due, their full force, unless they be considered as laws of our Creator, who loves virtue and will reward it,
                                                            p. 323.

What perfect providence must mean—Frequent occasions will occur in teaching the philosophy of nature, and developing the human mind, of taking off all seeming difficulties or objections against providence—Virtue the best possession—Efforts to acquire and improve in moral perfection and happiness never prove abortive—External goods not partially distributed, but purchased according to the general law of industry—The absurdity of supposing virtuous industry alone to be successful—This life, our entrance upon being, and a very proper school of education and culture for various virtues—Hence it is that human life is so chequered—But it is to be succeeded by a state of rewards and punishments, in which men will be placed according to their improvements and deserts—How useful and comfortable this belief is,   p. 326.

But general lessons upon virtue are not sufficient—Education must be particular, in order to prepare for the various duties and offices of life—Now reading history with pupils will afford proper examples for explaining all the springs of action in the human breast, all the human powers and passions, and all their improvements and virtues—All the ruling passions and distinguishing characters of men—All the different consequences of actions—All the various relations of human life, and all the duties belonging to them—All the corruptions of mankind, and all the snares and temptations of the world—All the rules of private conduct—And all the rules of conduct in public life—The laws of nature and nations relative to public affairs and independent sovereignties—The progress and connexion of human affairs from the beginning of the world—All the truths which the Bishop of Meaux, Mr. Rollin, and others, have shewn us to be the lessons of history,   p. 329.

When it is proper to read Justinian's institutes with young people, and practise them in examining a body of particular laws by the principles of equity—And when to read with them Grotius, Puffendorf, or other writers on the laws of nations—History will prepare for this kind of reading, by giving opportunity of discoursing upon every subject in morals—And 'tis better to take occasion to discourse on moral truths from examples, than to give formal lessons upon morals, to confirm which examples will seem to be haul'd in and warped to particular purposes—The advantages of this education in retirement as well as in active life,   p. 336.

'Tis impossible, in a discourse of this kind, to point out all the important truths history read in order will furnish occasions of illustrating and enforcing—It will give occasion to explain all the various kinds of civil government, and the best ends of civil laws and policies—And to shew the fatal consequences of luxury to states—The reflexion of Scipio upon the fall of Carthage—His education, and its happy effects,   p. 339.

It is such education only that can qualify youth for public service—Every science requires previous acquaintance with the history of mankind—Moral philosophy requires it—The primary philosophy requires it—The most useful part of logic, which is, the nature of moral evidence, may be best taught in reading history, by examining into the evidence of particular facts—Logic, considered as a review of the connexion and unity of the sciences, supposes acquaintance with history, and with all the particular sciences, p. 345.

In fine, without such instruction in natural and moral knowledge as qualifies youth for a proper prosecution of these studies by themselves, education, whatever it does, neglects its most useful purpose—We have not left out religion, because we have considered it, as the principal end of instruction in the order, harmony, and wisdom of nature, to lead youth to the love of the Creator, and to a sense of his will concerning our conduct—Now a just notion of God, and of human duties, will prepare and dispose for the reception of the Christian doctrine—Several observations on this head,

p. 350.

History will afford to teachers frequent opportunities of shewing the necessity of a public religion, and the mischiefs of superstition, and of evincing the excellency of the Christian religion considered with regard to the ends of a public religion, above every other that hath ever appeared in the world—Benevolence is the perfection of man, and it is in a particular sense the law, the new law of Christ,

p. 354.

In short, there is no moral or political truth which a judicious reader of history will not find frequent opportunity of explaining and confirming to young people—And both in natural and moral philosophy, facts ought to go before reasonings or conclusions, which can only be inferred from facts—Besides, it is fit youth should see mankind as they really are, in the worst colours they have ever appeared—But notwithstanding all the wickedness that hath ever abounded in the world, men are made for society, and have a social disposition deeply inlaid into their frame—What it is to be made for society, and men are so made,   p. 355.

In reading history, youth ought to be taught to attend to the rise and progress of empire, the generative principle of dominion, and the natural cause of changes in it—To observe how men are made for civil coalitions—And to the advantages of good civil orders and constitutions—Several reflexions on this subject,   p. 359.

History-lessons ought not to stop short till youth are brought home to modern times, and their own country, and are instructed in its history, government, laws and interest—But it is best to begin with ancient history, and descend regularly and gradually to modern times, that youth may see the connexion and suite of human affairs,   p. 360.

But after all, the chief lesson is to teach them wherein true merit consists, viz. in wisdom and virtue—In what sense virtue is its own reward explained,   p. 362.

All the arts ought to be called on, in their proper places, to recommend virtue—Great use might be made of poetical fictions—

Great use might be made of fables, parables and allegories—Their antiquity—Whence their aptitude to instruct or insinuate moral truths agreeably, proceeds, p. 365.

Of the Socratic method of teaching—Of the fitness of instructing youth by the familiar way of conference—The admirable success of Socrates in that way of teaching—The invention of youth ought to be improved by practising them in finding out truths by themselves—In resolving questions—about morals in particular,

p. 370.

History gives proper opportunities of explaining ancient customs, religious or civil—When these occur in history, then is the proper place for medals, basso-relievo's, and other ancient monuments or prints of them—Any other way of teaching antiquity is dry and insipid, p. 372.

It will likewise afford the best occasions of explaining the chief rules of oratory; for then is it the proper time to discourse of them when youth are agreeably affected by the beautiful speeches that occur in historians—How preposterous it would be to speak of rules till the effects they are designed to produce, and which the observance of them produces, have been felt—Reading history will give occasion to point out the invention, rise and improvements of all arts, and consequently, of trying different genius's, and inviting them to discover and exert themselves—Modern education too stinted—Observations on this subject—How schools ought to be furnished to serve this important business—The instituto at Bologna how adorned, p. 372.

Education ought to be large, whatever particular profession one may afterwards betake himself to—The advantages the Grecian youth had in this respect—The practice of their great men in laying themselves out to be useful to youth of promising parts recommended, p. 376.

Chapter v

Of instruction in poetry and her sister arts, painting, sculpture, music, and architecture; and the place which these arts ought to have in liberal education, in order to form elegant taste, which is one of the best preservatives against luxury, being naturally assistant to and corroborative of virtue.

The author hath hitherto been labouring to prove a very plain truth, That science, or real knowledge, and not mere words, ought to be the principal scope of education—What is meant by real knowledge—All the objects of human enquiry may be divided into these two, science and languages—What science comprehends—What is meant by languages—The didactic stile, oratory, poetry, painting, sculpture, fall under the idea of languages—This illustrated, by shewing painting to be a language, the truth and propriety of which it is well worth while to understand,   p. 381.

Previous to instruction, care ought to be taken to form good habits—To form the deliberative habit—What this means—It is freedom of mind—It is mastership of one's self, and the foundation of virtue,
                p. 382.

In instruction what rules ought to be observed—Youth ought to be taught to reason from facts alone, and not from imaginary theories and feigned hypotheses—And to reason first and chiefly about things relating to life and practice—And they ought to be taught to keep a just view of human nature before them, and to consider man neither as a merely sensitive nor a purely moral being, but as he really is a compound of moral and sensitive powers nicely blended together—Errors arising from not considering man in this view—Hence vague, loose, unmeaning raillery against luxury, in which several useful, as well as ornamental arts, are confounded with it,
                p. 384.

But having said enough of science, we proceed to consider languages as above defined—First the didactic stile, how masters ought to study clearness and perspicuity, and how youth will learn this stile from masters who excel in it, while they are taught by it—But youth ought to be employed in teaching what they know to others—The advantages of so employing them—There is another eloquence that ought not to be neglected in education, which is the concise stile, in which men ought to talk to men—How youth may be improved in this—How the rules of oratory ought to be taught—They are all founded in human nature, and teaching them aright, is developing human nature, because it is shewing how and by what the passions of men are affected—Observations on this subject,   p. 386.

The same is true of poetry—Observations from Plutarch upon reading the poets with youth—Further reflexions on this subject—

Of the common commentaries upon classic authors, upon the Greek and Roman poets in particular—Mr. Pope's notes on Homer a true model of criticism,   p. 391.

Painting and sculpture considered—Their ends, their rules, their connexion with natural or moral philosophy—The author is shorter on this subject, having elsewhere treated of it at large,

p. 397.

Of instructing youth early in drawing—The advantages of it—How youth ought to be inured to view and examine pictures and poems—By what rules or questions both ought to be tried, and of the false taste in painting corresponding to verbal criticism in classical reading—Upon the necessity of improving the imagination of youth—Our eyes and ears were designed by nature for improvement, being capable of very noble improvements—What genius and wit means—How the imagination may be improved and refined—The fancy will ever be pursuing some species of beauty, some Venus—The advantage of directing it early towards the true Venus, the true beauty—This is the only way of securing it against straying, wandering and seduction,   p. 400.

An important rule of nature to be attended to in teaching the arts which imitate nature, *viz.* the connexion in nature between beauty and utility—This rule must be attended to by all artists, if they would gain the end of their arts, which is to please an intelligent eye—Reasonings from Vitruvius, Cicero, Quintilian, on this subject—Nature's beauty proceeds from her steady observance of this rule, *Natura nil frustra facit,* and art must imitate nature,   p. 405.

The polite arts have been condemned by some moralists as a part of the luxury which hath always proved so fatal to states—Reflexions on this subject—The argument from abuse considered—Poetry and painting have always flourished together—They lend each other mutual aids and charms—They only lend their ornaments to virtue with willingness—When they are prostituted to bad purposes, the force, the constraint, the violence they suffer appears—They have flourished best in virtuous times—Their genuine uses and ends described,   p. 408.

They cannot be cultivated in poor indigent states, 'tis only in times of ease and opulence there is leisure or spirit for cultivating them—But affluence soon corrupts men—Philosophy itself hath always been first corrupted before the polite arts have been prosti-

tuted to serve vice—These arts declined at Athens with public virtue—Rome was very corrupt before they were known in it; and
therefore they soon declined there—Under the bad Emperors, after
the dissolution of the commonwealth, good taste sadly degenerated—It revived again with liberty and virtue under a few good
ones,   p. 412.

These arts had no share in the ruin of Carthage—Nor in that of
Sparta—How both these states fell—Nor in the ruin of the Persian
empire—How it fell—A private man may bestow too much time
and expence upon pictures, &c. but this no objection against the
good uses that states may employ the arts of design to promote—In
the character of Atticus elegance is distinguished from luxury—
Expensiveness in the materials is ruinous to good taste; so Pliny observes—Whatever abuses have been made of the polite arts, they
may be well employed, and there is a real distinction between tasteless waste or prodigality, and elegant use of wealth—The way to secure a state against bad taste and gross voluptuousness, is by right
education to form early in young minds love to virtue, and good
taste of true beauty and decency in the arts of design,   p. 414.

Conclusion

In which a few obvious reflexions are offered to shew what preparation is necessary to qualify one for travelling to advantage. p. 418.

Plutarchus Plasmatias:

BEING A
RECITAL OF CONVERSATIONS,
IN WHICH

The Sentiments of the best Ancients concerning Philosophy and Liberal Education are fairly represented.

Nunquam aliud natura, aliud sapientia dicit.

—JUVENAL[2]

---

2. [Juvenal, *Satires,* 14.321: "Never does Nature say one thing and Wisdom another."]

Observations upon Liberal Education

❧ INTRODUCTION ❧

Having been long engaged in the important business of Education, as it was my duty, so it hath ever been my chief employment to collect all the instructions relating to this art I could, from ancients and moderns.—And whatever I have been able to learn from the experience of others, or my own, concerning this matter, is now offered to the publick, because the subject is of publick, of universal concern.—I say from experience, because, as with regard to the culture of plants or flowers, sure rules can only be drawn from experiment; so, for the same reason, there can be no sure rules concerning education but those which are founded on the experimental knowledge of human nature.—And here every conclusion is deduced from internal principles and dispositions of the human mind, and their operations, which are well known to all who have carefully studied mankind; and is therefore confirmed by experience, in the same manner that natural philosophers establish their physical doctrines, upon observations evincing certain properties of bodies and laws of motion.

Every question of any moment relating to liberal education is here treated of at due length, as may be seen by casting an eye over the contents. But tho' this essay be divided, for method and order's sake, into chapters, yet all the questions belonging to this subject are in their nature so closely connected, so interwoven, that to judge how any one of them is handled, the whole must be read. In every article, brevity and conciseness have been studied, as much as was consistent with the perspicuity, distinctness, amplification, and variety of illustrations, an argument of so complex a nature, and such vast importance, required.

The design of this Treatise, to give a general idea of it in the fewest words I can, is to shew, "How greatly private and publick happiness depend upon the right education of youth: And that human nature is so far from being incapable of arriving very timeously at a considerable degree of perfection in wisdom and virtue, that young minds, by suitable methods of education, may indeed be very early formed to the sincere love of virtue; and may make great improvements in the more useful arts and sciences, as well as in languages, with much less difficulty, and in much less time, than is commonly imagined: And to delineate and recommend these methods of instructing and forming youth."

This is the shortest account I can give of the intention of these discourses on education.—But because a fuller view of our scope may be necessary to engage severals whom it greatly concerns, to read so large a treatise upon a subject every one is too apt to think himself sufficiently master of:—Or rather, because the true end of education, and the properest methods of pursuing that end cannot be better described, or more warmly and strongly enforced in so narrow a compass, I shall here insert a Letter from a Person of eminent learning, taste and virtue, (in answer to one wherein I had desired to know his sentiments concerning education, and but barely hinted my design of revising some observations I had been led to on that subject by experience, joined with reading, in order to publish them) that briefly chalks out the same manner of liberal education which it is the design of these discourses to illustrate and recommend. In reality 'twas the exact agreement of this Gentleman's sentiments with those I had long entertained concerning this momentuous affair, that fully emboldened me to submit them to the publick judgment.—And there are few living names that would more forcibly, or more universally call up attention, or give greater weight and authority to any performance, were it not better to avoid all appearance of endeavouring to prepossess readers, and to give up every opinion delivered here to the freest, the severest trial.— But 'tis reason alone, and not authorities, that ought to determine a reader's judgment and assent in matters of science.—And therefore, let it be just suggested here in general, that no author of the most established fame is quoted in these discourses, to overawe by his venerable name, but merely because his reasonings appear to us solid and conclusive; and we think it highly criminal in an Author, to purloin to himself the honour that belongs to another. The ancient fable of the Jay strutting in borrowed feathers, elegantly points out both the guilt and the danger of that sort of pilfering.

A LETTER, &c.

Dear Sir,

When I received your obliging letter, I was confined to my chamber by a fever, and had not spirits, or an opportunity to thank you for it. Nothing certainly can be of more service to mankind than a right method of educating the youth; and I should be glad to hear —— —— to give an example of the great advantage it would be to the rising age and to our nation.

When the publick schools were established, the knowledge of *Latin* was thought learning; and he that had a tolerable skill in two or three languages, tho' his mind was not enlightened by any real knowledge, was a profound scholar. But it is not so at present; and people confess, that men may have obtained a perfection in these, and yet continue deeply ignorant. The *Greek* education was of another kind. Their children at first were initiated into some parts of *mathematicks,* to learn in their years of docility and attention, an habit of reasoning; and open their views by some of those practical arts which depended on that science. They then advanced to their *graphicks,* writing and designing: They accustomed their eye to the truths of proportion, and led it into a taste of sculpture and architecture, by pointing out to its admiration the noble performances which they saw all around them. Next they learn'd *musick;* which did not then poorly mean the doctrine of inarticulate sounds, but all the powers of harmony in their language, all the magic of numbers and of rythm, the simplicity and force of composition in their various kinds of writing, as well as how to assist verses by instruments and notes, or by the mimickry of action and dancing, or the melody of singing, in a manner that heightned the force of sentiments and poetry, and did not bury and stifle the sense under sweet sounds, as

Heliogabalus did his guests, under roses and jasmines. Under this branch they comprehended even the *rhetorick* of their own tongue; and studied to write it more accurately than we do *Latin* and *Greek*. But where is *English* taught at present? Who thinks it of use to study correctly that language which he is to use every day in his life, be his station ever so high or ever so insignificant. It is in this the nobility and gentry defend their country, and serve their prince in parliament; in this the lawyers plead, the divines instruct, and all ranks of people write their letters and transact all their affairs; and yet who thinks it worth his learning to write this even accurately, not to say politely? Every one is suffered to form his stile by chance; to imitate the first wretched model which falls in his way, before he knows what is faulty, or can relish the beauties of a just simplicity. Few think their children qualified for a trade, till they have been whipt at a *Latin* school for five or six years, to learn a little of that which they are obliged to forget, when in those years right education would have improv'd their minds, and taught them to acquire habits of writing their own language easily under right direction; and this would have been useful to them as long as they lived.

During their learning these three, the *Greek* children were refreshed and amused by their *Gymnastick* art, which could not be learned too early, or continued too long. It comprehended every exercise which could give strength and agility, grace and firmness in their motions, and a manly intrepidity of behaviour in every circumstance of life. When the minds and bodies of the youth were perfected in these, they were carried to *philosophy,* to learn what they were, whence they were, and for what end: to learn wherein their own happiness, and their merit towards each other consisted: what would make them dear to their friends, and adored by their country: *to do justice, and to love mercy.* And if, alas! their bad religion had not betray'd them to neglect to instruct them in the proper humility to the Creator and Governor of the universe, nothing could have been more worthy and compleat. Had they taught them every morning to have offered up a hymn like Adam's, in transport of gratitude and contentment,

These are thy glorious works, Parent of good,
Almighty, thine this universal frame,
Thus wond'rous fair, thyself how wond'rous then!
&c.———
Hail, universal Lord! be bounteous still,
And give us only good.———[3]

Reason could have added no more, and all further improvements must have been deferred till the world had received new light from the Gospel. Tho' in this particular Greece was deficient, Persia seems to have enjoyed the blessing, if we may credit Plato, by the authority and laws of Zardush. The education of the old Persians, as described by Xenophon, which afterwards was perfected by the religious institutions of Zoroastre, seems to have been the noblest method which had ever been established in the world; as that monarchy (which was originally of a King governing by laws) was, on the whole, the wisest government then on the earth, excepting one only, resembling ours sufficiently: I wish our education equally resembled theirs. They took care to educate the heart as well as the understanding: but who thinks of the strange task at present! I once saw a picture, or a basso-relievo, in which Minerva was teaching Cupid to read, and a satyr pointing and laughing at the idle labour. But yet I think the most impetuous of passions may be guided by wisdom, and educated to decency and self-denial; to a detestation of selfish indulgences, when they conduce to the misery of others, and to a love for all the generous feelings which belong to the human heart. But this must be begun early, pursued prudently and steadily, and supported by principles of rational honour, and truly God-like religion, not learn'd by rote, but by evidence and degrees, which shall exalt the soul to an affection rather than dread of the supreme Lord of all things, and to a conviction that his laws lead us both to happiness here and hereafter; and that all his restraints are from indulgences which would

3. [John Milton, *Paradise Lost*, 5.153–55, 205–6.]

make ourselves or our neighbours wretched. The final causes seen, on the slightest view of nature, will inspire unprejudiced minds with an evidence that will not only give light but transport. History will soon teach them into what corruptions and idolatry, into what errors man was fallen, which sanctify superstition, and dishonour not only God but human nature; which turn the attention from virtue, to rest in all the Proteus-ingenuities of religious flattery; and by teaching us this, shews the infinite goodness of God in so loving the world, as to give his only Son, to purchase a peculiar people, and by his doctrines, institutions and motives, enable them to do good works: and hence, by degrees, you may teach them the excellency and use of revelation, and all the sublime indisputable truths of genuine Christianity.— That all who can, or think they can choose, by their own search and enquiries, the best means of making themselves acceptable to God, have the right to use their own reason for this noblest purpose: But that the laws ought to provide instructors and publick worship for those who cannot, and think they cannot guide themselves, which will be the greater number in every nation: and therefore such public establishments, even when not submitted to, ought to be reverenced, not to weaken their authority over those who are placed by God under the Conduct of the laws in religious, as well as civil affairs. It is true laws may, and in fact have misguided mankind in many countries. But so have private enquiries; and this consideration should make us humble and charitable, and open to information, whichsoever guidance we follow. This should stifle the spirit of imposition and anathematizing each other, and soften us to modesty and mutual forbearance: And then, if our differences have this blessed effect, they will be of more service to mankind than truth itself, in all those points about which sincere Christians can be supposed to be mistaken. Rites and outward performances are to real essential religion, as words and languages are to reason. One may be more beautiful and harmonious, and significant than another, but the worst will assist an honest mind in cultivating his understanding, and becoming a man of sense and prudence tolerably well; and he may be contented.

You see, Sir, my opinion of education enlarges the task you have undertaken much beyond the expectation of those who send their children to school. But I do not hope a private man can accomplish this whole scheme; but by having it in view he may approach towards it. Particularly, I should think teaching them to write and speak correctly and fluently in their own language, is the most important instruction. One exercise should be daily to write a page of English, and after that to examine every word by the grammar rules, and in every sentence they have composed, to oblige them to give an account of the English syntax and construction. Thus an habit would soon be acquired, and they would do it of course. All affected words and harsh transpositions should be noted; every phrase not used in good company exploded; harsh metaphors, which have neither a peculiar light or force, be discarded: Metaphors are a kind of embroidery, which do admirably on proper occasions, but shew a tawdry mind, if it scruples to appear, unless dressed in such finery. Another exercise should be obliging them to speak every day their unwritten thoughts on any subject in English. Let them read an oration in Tully or Livy; let them read it to themselves in Latin as often as they please, then shut the book, and speak the sense of it *extempore* in unpremeditated words. A little use will make it most agreeably easy: and what a habit is this for a man of quality? Begin with a fable of Phaedrus, thence to a short speech in an historian, you'll be amazed how soon they would enter into the spirit of Cicero, and plead the cause of Ligarius with his ardour, and feel what they utter. This is the ambition I would have you pursue: afford to gentlemen this distinguishing, this necessary education, and become thus a nursery of state orators.

Another task, I fear, will employ all instructors, that is, the business of a weeder. How rich soever the soil, I fancy it comes full sown from the nursery. I have seen children shew pride, revenge, nay, and falshood too, before they could speak: it is no blunder, but a strong truth: and unless these weeds are cleansed away, they will choak the best instructions. I need not advise you to give them a taste of our best poets, and make them read aloud gracefully: an accomplishment that many men, who do not want good ears, cannot perform, because they are either unexperienced and bashful, or ill taught. Books of Prints, to give them a notion of the elegance of simplicity and proportion in architecture and designing, without much trouble, open the mind wonderfully. A notion of the universe, the magnitudes, order, distances, and relations of the heavenly bodies to each other, will amuse the youngest minds, and incite them to enquire into the final causes why each is placed where it is, or why formed of such a magnitude, and afford opportunity for chit-chat lectures which never are forgotten. I write in an hurry, have neither health or leisure to meditate before I scribble, or to review it when on my paper. You know my way of thinking, my writing is as much *extempore* and as careless. When I see you, an hour's conversation shall add many other hints————

This letter, tho' the writer had not seen the following discourses on education, is almost as just an abstract of them as if it had been intended for such. And whoever thinks it worth while to see the methods of education which are there briefly hinted, more amply explained and urged, will, we hope, find full satisfaction, by a careful perusal of this treatise. Every thing with relation to the liberal formation of youth, is perhaps fully enough discoursed of in the essay itself. But the other two pieces, in which ancient personages are introduced conversing about education, are added; because this hath generally been reckoned a more lively and agreeable way of representing the sentiments of the ancients upon any subject, than mere narrative.—These pieces were originally wrote for the satisfaction of a friend, who desired to know the opinion of certain ancient sages with respect to education, and proposed that in answering his question, the character of some ancient reciting conversations upon the subject might be assumed. And because[4] nothing here is fictitious but the plan, for which liberty there is very good authority amongst the moderns as well as the ancients, they are sent into the world in the same form, for the very same reasons that it was desired they might be wrote in it; namely, for the reasons often given

4. Marginal notes are added, to shew that nothing is put into the mouth of any ancient personage without good authority.

by Plato and Cicero in their dialogues, or recitals of conversations, for choosing that method of delivering their philosophy.[5] "Quasi enim ipsos induxi loquentes, ne, inquam & inquit, saepius interponerentur, atque ut tanquam a praesentibus coram haberi sermo videretur.—Genus autem hoc sermonum, positum in veterum authoritate, & eorum illustrium, plus nescio quo pacto, videtur habere gravitatis."[6]

Finally, in them several material points relating to education are more minutely canvassed than in the Essay, because dialogue way of writing affords more room than any other for stating objections, and setting things in a variety of lights. And all I have further to add in this introduction is, That the whole is most sincerely intended for what will readily be owned to be the best and most important of ends, the assistance of those who are concerned in the education of youth in that momentous task, and the direction of young gentlemen, who having made some advances in useful knowledge, are desirous of making further improvements by a proper prosecution of their studies.

5. See Cicero de amicitia & de senectute, his introductions to these pieces, and Plato's Theaetetus.

6. [Cicero, *De Amicitia*, 1.3, 4: "For I have brought upon the boards the very men themselves, so to speak, in order that the words 'say I' and 'says he' might not be scattered too thickly, and that the discussion might seem to be held as it were by men present face to face. . . . Now this kind of discourse seems in some strange way to have more weight, if it rests on the authority of men of old, particularly such as are famous." Translation from *Cicero: De Amicitia* (London: University Tutorial Press, 1897).]

Plutarchus Plasmatias
to
His Friend *Fundanus,*
Concerning Education

In the better days of Greece, and long afterwards, the education of youth was reckon'd a most honourable employment: For while virtue was in repute, employments were honoured in proportion to their usefulness. Hence many of noble birth and easy fortunes, disdained not to become preceptors,[7] and take youth under their tuition. In every city there were many schools, under the inspection of men of great probity and prudence, who confined themselves to a small number of pupils, well-knowing that it is much easier for one gardiner to take proper care of a very large garden or nursery of plants and flowers, which yet an expert honest gardiner will not undertake, than for one person, however great his abilities may be, to bestow all the due attention and suitable culture upon a great number of young minds, which variety of natural genius's and dispositions must require. Some indeed read lectures, or discoursed to great numbers promiscuously in publick assemblies: but those succeeded best in the formation of youth, who restricted themselves to such a flock as they could constantly have within their sight, and be fully and familiarly acquainted with.

7. This fact we learn from Plato himself, and from Cicero, who often tells us so in his books of oratory, and his philosophical works. See many besides Plato, Isocrates, Aristotle, Theophrastus, Isaeus, &c. named in Plutarch's account of the ten orators. See the note (*r*) upon the English translation of Plutarch's discourse to shew happiness not to be attainable, &c.

It was disputed in the days of Socrates, whether private or public education ought to be preferred. For certain sophists, who studied their own private profit, more than the real advantage of their scholars, pled strongly for the great benefit arising from being bred amidst many rivals in numerous schools. But Socrates is said to have determined the matter, as he generally did, by shewing that the right way lay in the middle between private and public education; whereas the debate was generally stated as if there were no midway between the two.

Socrates thus addressed[8] Callias.

Soc. You have two Sons, Callias, have you not?

Cal. I have.

Soc. If these sons of yours were calves or colts, would you not take care of them, and commit the charge of bringing them up to one well-skilled in agriculture, horsemanship, and breeding of animals? But being young men, have you no thoughts of setting one over them to form and educate them? No doubt you have: and consequently you have been looking about for one well versed in the arts of human and civil life? Now I would gladly know if you have found a fit person for this trust?

Cal. I have.

Soc. Who is he pray, and of what country?

Cal. Evenus is the person, a Parian. He has long professed the art of teaching and moulding youth, and is reputed to be a perfect master of it.

Soc. He is a happy and useful man, if he be indeed qualified for this great work, and sedulously applies himself to it. How happy and valuable should I think myself if I thoroughly understood it? But what is his price?

Cal. It is not in reality high, tho' many think it so. But perhaps you wonder he should take a hire.

Soc. You mistake the matter much. For had I money, I should think it, even at my age, very well bestowed in the purchase of wisdom. I know no profession that better deserves a high reward than that of a preceptor. And tho' one may go about instructing in virtue and true wisdom in public

---

8. In Plato's apology for Socrates, Socrates refers to a conversation of his with one Callias about the education of his sons, which begins in this manner. In it he names with respect several persons who professed education.

places,[9] those who are disposed to learn from him, without taking money; yet it cannot be expected that those who receive youth into their houses, which must be done in order to take all the care of them that is necessary for sowing the seeds of wisdom into their minds, and training them up in virtue;—'tis not to be expected, I say, that any should do this at their own expence. You know how greatly I value many who profess this art, and how much I think the state obliged to them; since it is by the right education of youth that the foundation-stones of public and private happiness are laid.— But what number may Evenus have under his tutorage at once?

CAL. He has a vast reputation, and his house is always full. He has at present above threescore pupils. But you seem to sneer—perhaps you prefer private to public education, and think one or two boys task enough for any one preceptor. So I once thought. But Evenus soon brought me out of this error. The question however has been so much debated, that I should be glad, Socrates, if you are not in a hurry, to hear you upon the subject.

SOC. I am not in so great a haste as to leave you till we have canvassed this important matter a little: on the contrary, I am very glad you have proposed it. For I lately found our Friend Hippias very pensive, and in great doubts what to do with his son. And having urged him to vent his anxiety to me his old acquaintance, in whom he had oftener than once placed some confidence, he told me, his son being now seven years of age, he was at a great loss what to do with him. For, said he, if I keep him always at home, he will be in danger of becoming my young master; and if I send him abroad to a school consisting of troops of boys, assembled together from parents of all kinds, how is it possible to preserve him from the infection of that rudeness and vitiousness which must prevail in all such moatly medleys. In my house he will perhaps be kept more innocent, but he will go out of it more ignorant of the world, and therefore very unfit for it. Yet launch into it he must. Wanting here at home sufficient variety

9. Socrates went about teaching in this manner himself without taking money: so did many others. But not a few received hire for their lectures. This we learn from several of Plato's dialogues.

of company, and being constantly used almost to the same faces, he will, when he comes abroad, be a sheepish or conceited creature.

CAL. There indeed is the difficulty, and how, pray, did you advise him?

SOC. What do you think, Callias?

CAL. I see the emulation of school-fellows puts life and spirit into young lads. Being abroad, and inured to bustle and shift amongst many boys of his own age, makes a young man bold and fit for justling and pushing when he comes into the world. Does it not?

SOC. We shall consider this afterwards. But let me first tell you how I answered Hippias.

CAL. Go on then.

SOC. Which do you, Hippias, said I, think most necessary to the happiness of your son, virtuous habits early established and well confirmed, or that which is called learning, suppose by Anaxagoras, who says he can unfold all the mysteries of nature, and explain her most secret operations; or by Palamedes, who places it in being able to call every thing into doubt, and to make either side of any question appear equally probable by his eloquence?[10] Hippias having answered in his grave austere way, that he hoped I knew him better than to suspect him of preferring oratory, mathematicks, or any science, however ornamental, or even useful it may be, to virtue; I replied, you can then be in no doubt whether you should hazard your son's integrity and virtue for a little literature or scholarship.—No,

---

10. Most of the arguments for and against public education here used are to be found in Quintilian, who prefers public to private education. Our Locke takes the other side of the question. From him we have borrowed several of the reasonings and phrases here used. We likewise find some of the same sentiments in the younger Pliny about education, and the choice of a tutor, and on erecting a public school. But most of the sentiments are as old as Socrates, and are put into his mouth by Plato in his dialogues about laws, and those about a republick. There he, oftner than once, blames the wrangling arts; and calls teaching young lads these arts, teaching them to bark like dogs. Virtue is the great good, and ought to be the chief aim of education, and indeed of laws; but without proper care, says he, about education, laws will be of very little use. So Xenophon in his Cyropaedia, and so Plutarch in his treatise of education, and his Lacedemonian customs. [The home vs. school debate raged throughout the eighteenth century, with Locke and Quintilian being the principal authorities. See Quintilian, *Institutio Oratoria*, 1.2, and John Locke, *Some Thoughts Concerning Education*, §70.]

nor for a great deal neither, said he.—Well then, said I, you are certainly resolved not to part with your son till you can find a school where it is possible for the master to look after the manners of his scholars, and he can shew as great effects of his care and skill of forming their minds to virtue, as of their tongues to wrangling and disputation.—I am, said he.— Where lies your difficulty then, replied I? For may not the figures of rhetoric, the measures of verse, the refined subtleties of logic, and every other so much boasted of science be taught at home? Cannot you find a preceptor able to take this part of the task, at least, off your hands, while you yourself are his tutor and guardian with respect to what you acknowledge to be principal? But one thing more I must ask you, Hippias, on this head. What is this sheepishness and softness you are so much afraid of? What is this timorousness you dread so much? May it not be avoided at home? Or why is it, do you think, to be so carefully guarded against? Is it not principally for the sake of virtue, that is, for fear lest such a yielding tame temper should be too susceptible of vitious impressions and influences, and expose the raw novice too easily to be corrupted?—Truly, said he, it must be owned, that the chief use of courage is only for the preservation of virtue. He who cannot resist the assaults of vice, and bad example or persuasion, does not deserve to be called brave. For magnanimity consists in a bold undaunted adherence to truth and right.—You have said well, Hippias, I replied. But if so, it must be very unadvisable to risk a boy's innocency for the sake of his attaining to confidence, and some little skill of bustling for himself among others, by his conversation with ill-bred and vicious boys.—Now, as for you, Callias, why is it that you are so anxious your sons should acquire a manly air and assurance betimes? Sure it is not merely that they may be sturdy and obstinate.

CAL. That is far from being my view.

SOC. And I am persuaded, that as it is not malepertness, so neither is it cunning you would have them learn by wrangling and rooking with playfellows of various tempers and humours. This certainly, Callias, is not the skill of living well in the world, and of managing, as an honest man should do, his affairs. So far are tricking on the one side, or violence on the other, from having any affinity to those good qualities which make an able or useful member of society, that if your sons should acquire such habits

from bad companions, must you not undo them again, or give them up
to ruin? Besides, what is so becoming youth as modesty and submission?
or how else are they rendered docile and pliable to instruction? Believe me,
Callias, conversation, when they come into the world, will add to their
assurance, but be too apt to take away from their virtue. And therefore that
which requires the greatest care and labour in education, is to work deeply
into young minds the principles and habits of probity. With this seasoning
they should be so prepared for the world, that it may not easily be rubbed
out. If confidence or cunning and dissimulation come once to mix with
vice, and support a young man's miscarriages, is he not only the surer lost?

CAL. That, Socrates, is undeniable.

SOC. Must it not then be very preposterous to stock them with confidence, before they are well established in the knowledge and love of virtue?
In fine, my friend, either wisdom and virtue are the main thing in the institution of youth, or they are early to be inured to dissimulation and pertness. There is no middle. But if the former be the principal point, youth
must be formed, where their manners can be carefully look'd after. Now,
let a master's industry and skill be never so great, it is impossible he should
have a hundred, or even the third of that number under his eye any longer
than they are in the school together: nor can it be expected, that he should
be able to instruct them successfully in any thing but their books; the
forming of their minds and manners requiring a constant attention, and
particular application to every particular genius and disposition, which is
impossible in a numerous flock, and would be wholly in vain (could he
have time to study and correct every one's particular defects and wrong
inclinations) when the lad was to be left to himself, or the prevailing infection of his fellows, the greater part of every four and twenty hours. 'Tis
virtue, Callias, direct virtue, which is the valuable but the hard part to be
aimed at in education; and not a forward pertness, or any little arts of
shifting. All other, even good accomplishments, should give place and be
postponed to this. This is the solid and substantial good which tutors
should not only talk of, but which the labour and art of education should
replenish the mind with, and deeply root there: nay never cease inculcating, and fixing by all proper methods, till the young man, having a deep
and abiding sense and relish of its excellence, places his strength, his glory,

his pleasure in it.[11] But tell me, pray, whether a master, with the eyes of Argus, can watch over fifty boys, with all the assiduous vigilance necessary to form and nourish this noble disposition in their minds.

CAL. You then prefer private education at home: yet we seldom see such make their way so well thro' the world, as those who have been justled and tossed about in a public school. The contests and collisions of many lads, one against another, wonderfully sharpen and brighten genius.

SOC. No matter what name you give the education I am pleading for. But I have not yet said, whether I would have lads bred at home by a skilful preceptor, or abroad at some school with a[12] few other condisciples, under an expert good master. All I have hitherto contended for is, that they ought to be educated where the principles and habits of candour, benevolence, temperance and fortitude of mind may be early learned; not the definitions merely, but the habits of them; and where they run no risk of learning waggeries or cheats, and pertness or roughness. And this is as true, as it is, that the former, not the latter, make an able, as well as a good man. And yet, Callias, if you will insist upon the vast benefit of assurance, I am willing to put the whole matter upon this single point. Take a boy from the highest form in Evenus's numerous school, and one of the same age, bred as he should be in his father's family, our friend Pointias's son, for example, who is not yet ten years old, and bring them together into good company, and see which of the two will have the more decent manly carriage, and address himself with the more becoming genteel assurance to strangers. Here, I imagine the school-boy's confidence will either fail or discredit him, whereas we have often seen the other make a very agreeable charming figure in the company of strangers. But if the confidence and assurance acquired in public schools be such as fits only for the conversation of boys, had he not better be without it? Let me use one argument more with you, Callias. Does that retirement and bashfulness which our daughters are brought up in, make them less knowing or less decent

---

11. [This passage is taken from Locke, *Education,* §70, almost verbatim.]

12. Quintilian sometimes seems to be in suspense between this way and more public education. But he affirms care about the morals of youth to be the main thing, and that nothing ought to be preferred to it.

women? Conversation, when they come into the world, soon gives them a becoming assurance: and whatsoever there is beyond that, of assuming and rough, may in men be well spared too. For courage and firmness, as I take it, are very different from boisterousness and rudeness.

CAL. How then would you have young men able to stand upon their own legs, so as not to be dupes and bubbles when they come into the world, which is so over-run with tricksters and crafty artful knaves of various kinds?

SOC. How young men should be fitted for conversation, and entered into the world, we shall enquire on some other occasion. A young man, before he leaves the shelter and guard of his father or tutor, should be fortified with resolution, and made acquainted with men to secure his virtue, lest he should be seduced into some ruinous course, before he is sufficiently apprised of the dangers and snares of the world, and has steadiness enough to resist temptation. But what is done in public schools thus to prepare them for the world?—But of this, I say, another time. Now, I would only ask you what you meant by saying education must be either private or public?

CAL. Is there any difficulty in understanding this? Is there any middle between private and public?

SOC. Is there no difference, Callias, between a vast extensive garden and a small one;[13] or between a moderate flock of sheep and a very numerous herd?

CAL. There is certainly.

SOC. What do you then say of a few pupils, suppose eight or ten, and

13. Thus commonly does Socrates decide disputes; and this appears, from the conversations he is represented by Plato to have had with the Sophists, to have been his opinion. Isocrates at first had but nine scholars. But he had afterwards a greater number. He addicted his whole life to the education of youth, and after his death statues were erected to him with very honourable inscriptions, as Pausanias tells us. See Plutarch of the ten orators; and see what Isocrates says of Athenian education in his Areopagit. We may see this doctrine in Cicero. And whence had he his Philosophy? We meet with it often in Plato and in Aristotle. And yet more frequently in the writings of certain Pythagoreans. But no where oftener than in Plutarch's moral tracts, from the mouths of ancient sages there introduced speaking.

three or fourscore? Will there be no emulation, no rivalship, no bustling or collision, but where there is so great a number of competitors, that their emulations and justlings cannot possibly be attended to with sufficient care, in order to make a proper use and improvement of them to the real advantage and good of each different temper and genius?

The rest of this conversation is not preserved to us. But for these reasons, young pupils were sent very early in ancient times to masters of eminent wisdom and virtue, and well acquainted with the world, who, with the help of proper assistants of their own choice, and under their superintendency, took some ten, some twelve, some seventeen, none above twenty, under their inspection. And upon them did parents devolve the whole care of their children's education, with full confidence and satisfaction. Here they were safer from the infection of servants than they could possibly be at home with their fathers, who being engaged in business, were obliged to leave the care of their children, in a great measure, to low domestics, or at least could not keep them intirely from their company, which soon effaces the best lessons parents can give. For those masters making education their sole employment, and confining themselves to a small number, could easily watch over and direct all the motions of their pupils, and keep them from whatever company and conversation they thought improper for them. But this was done without force or restraint, with due regard to that love of liberty which is natural to the human mind, and the foundation of magnanimity.

Liberty, said one of these masters, I think it was another Parian, whom Socrates is said to have highly esteemed, is man's noblest birth-right: the child who loves it not must needs have a very mean dastardly spirit, incapable of nourishing generous seeds: the noble virtues cannot be reared up to any perfection in such a cold, lifeless soil. The whole business therefore of liberal education, and it is called liberal for that very reason, is to cherish into proper vigour the love of liberty, and yet guard it against degenerating into the vice which borders upon it, wilfulness or stubbornness. The great secret of education is to render young minds pliable and submissive, not to commands and threats, or violence, but to mild persuasive reason; willing to do what is right, and for that reason eager to be informed in what is such, and yet at the same time impatient of violent restraint: too manly

to be driven like beasts, and yet too rational to refuse to hearken to persuasion, or to oppose what is enjoined them, merely because it is fit for
them, and as such. Now, in order to form this temper, youth must be accustomed to rational treatment, that is, to do the things that are good for
them, because they are so without feeling any compulsion or restraint laid
upon them. "I never command, said he, and I always gain my point. For
when I would have any of them under my care to do any thing, I am sure
that it is proper for them; and I am as sure that I can easily make them
perceive it to be so by asking them a few simple questions, in a mild loving
manner, about it. It is not implicit respect to me, but regard to reason I
aim at establishing in their minds. And he who is taught to know no master but reason, will soon love the teacher who hath thus made him free, in
proportion as he loves reason, and tastes the endearing sweets of the true
liberty which reason and virtue alone can give."

Those sage preceptors well knew, that the desire not of liberty only, but
of dominion, is natural to mankind, and a passion that ought not to be
erased but cherished. This desire is, perhaps, the original of most vicious
habits that are ordinary and natural. But without it, how listless and dead
would the human mind be? Upon this stock only, can all the great or heroic virtues be grafted. And therefore, kind nature hath not implanted it
in our breasts, to be eradicated by a tyrannical father or schoolmaster, but
to be nursed and directed into the laudable ambition and true greatness of
soul of which it is the seed: into the noble desire of acquiring authority by
superior wisdom and virtue; and into the virtuous pride which consists in
foregoing pleasure, or suffering pain with chearful constancy, for the satisfaction and merit of doing great and generous deeds.

This natural love of dominion and power discovers itself early, and that
chiefly in these two things. We see children, so soon almost as they are
born, long, I am sure, before they can speak, grow peevish, and cry for
nothing but to have their wills. They would have their desires yielded to
by others, those especially they come to consider under certain distinctions, which parents are generally not remiss in teaching them to make.
And how very early does their desire of property and possession appear?
How soon do they begin to please themselves with the power which that
seems to give, and the right they thereby have to dispose of things as they

will? He who has not observed these two humours working betimes in children, must have taken very little notice of their actions. And he who thinks, that these two roots of almost all the injustice, oppression, and contention, which so sadly disturb human life, are to be intirely rooted out, hath not reflected, that this love of dominion is a necessary spur to industry and improvement, and the chief spring of all our motions. Ancient masters did not therefore dream of weeding it out, but carefully applied themselves to give it a right turn, and to improve it into the noble virtues of which it is the natural principle or stock.

Now you may easily perceive, that beating or corporal punishment of any kind, was seldom used in such academies, or where it was the design of education to render the mind free, active and great, nothing being more diametrically opposite to such an end. Blows, often repeated, may produce a timorous, slavish mind, and miserably deject or debase the soul; or they may beget an inclination, a longing in young people, to have it in their power to tyranize in the same manner over others in their turn. 'Tis reason alone, i.e. accustomance to listen to and obey reason, that can form a truly rational temper, or establish reason as a governor in the mind. There is indeed no danger of misconduct, but where reason does not preside, and is not regularly consulted. And in order to bring this about, young people must from their infancy be inured to consult reason, and to feel the pleasure of governing themselves by it. The rod, which is the only instrument in government that tutors or schoolmasters generally know, or at least use, is a very short compendious way, which may at once flatter their pride, love of power and laziness, but it is the most unfit, nay the most dangerous of any that can be used in education. For extravagant young lads, who have liveliness and spirit, come sometimes to think, and taking once a right turn, seldom fail to make able and great men. But timid, low and dejected minds, are hardly ever to be raised, and so very seldom attain to any thing that is laudable, but generally prove as useless to themselves as to others. The principal rocks upon one or other of which education commonly splits, are, over-indulgence, which of course renders some favourite caressed passion too strong for reason during one's whole life; or over-severity, which either dispirits, or begets stubbornness and a cruel disposition. And therefore, to avoid the great danger that is on either hand, must be the principal art in education. And what is this! but to keep up a child's spirit, easy, active and free, and yet at the same time, to inure him to self-command, or to take a pleasure and pride in restraining himself from many things he has a mind to, and in undergoing many things that may be uneasy to him for the superior pleasure of doing good, and gaining at once the approbation of his own reason, and the love and esteem of his parents, masters, and all good and wise men.[14] But corporal punishments cannot possibly contribute any thing to this excellent end. This kind of correction conduces not at all to the mastery of our propensity, to indulge present bodily pleasure, and to avoid present corporal pain by any means. It rather encourages and strengthens this inclination, which, in spight of the best care, must grow up with us to a considerable degree of strength. And by cherishing it, the source whence almost all the irregularities in life flow, is fed. For by what other motive, but of sensual pleasure and pain, does a child act, who drudges at his task against his inclination, or abstains from any unwholesome fruit, for instance, he likes, only out of fear of being drubb'd? He in this instance only avoids the greater present corporal pain, or prefers the greater present corporal pleasure. And is there any virtue in being influenced by such views? What can this do but invigorate a passion, which it is the business of education to destroy, or rather to prevent? Will this method beget an inclination to be actuated and guided by reason, and a higher relish for the approbation of a considerative mind, reflecting upon reasonable conduct, than for any joys mere sense can be gratified by? This sort of chastisement naturally creates an antipathy against that which it is the preceptor's business to cherish a liking to. For how obvious is it, that children soon come to have an aversion to things, whatever pleasure they at first took in them, when they find themselves teazed, chid, or tormented about them? Nay, who is there among grown up men that would not be disgusted with any innocent recreation, if he should be forced to it by blows, threats, or abusive language, when he had

14. Every one who is acquainted with the ancients, knows this was the doctrine of Socrates, and all the better ancients, concerning virtue, and the discipline necessary to form it. Epictetus indeed places all virtue in bearing and forbearing. But the doctrine is much older.

no mind; or be for ever so used, for some circumstances in his application to it? If we consider the power of habit in any one instance, we will not wonder, if aversions so formed, are never, or at least not easily overcome. The very sight of a cup out of which one has often taken a nauseous potion, turns his stomach: let it be ever so clean, or made of the richest materials, and garnished with the most precious jewels, yet every thing offered in it will nauseate him. Again, such a sort of slavish discipline creates a servile temper, a soil in which no virtue can grow up to maturity; a soil, on the contrary, in which envy, revenge, and many other abominable vices naturally sprout up and pullulate. The child may submit, and dissemble obedience whilst the rod hangs over him; but when, that being removed, he can promise himself impunity, he will give, with double gust of pleasure, full swing to his disguised inclination. Generally speaking, no passion can be altered by this method, but is rather increased and corroborated. And hence it is, that after such restraint it usually breaks out with greater violence. But if any disease is thus cured, how is it, but by bringing in a much worse one in its room, which is either, low spiritedness and inactivity for want of conscious capacity, which is ever active, or a secret burning to get loose, in order to give full indulgence to appetite, and make large amends to himself for all his suffering in this rigid way, by equal austerity, or rather cruelty to others, as far as his power can reach. Thus did the famous Lockias reason, who had so accurately studied human nature, that he is said to have had a glass by which he could spy into the inmost recesses and windings of the human heart.

And Socrates is said to have had this conversation with a father who had been just whipping his son.

Soc. You love hunting, Ctesicles, I know, and your dogs are famous. You must certainly have some particular secret for breeding them.

Ct. They are indeed the best I know. I could tell you many surprizing things of them.

Soc. Another time I shall be glad to hear them; for I do not think the instincts, the sagacity and docility of brutes unworthy the notice of a philosopher. One thing only at present I would gladly learn from you. Does it cost much whipping to give them a good nose, or much travel. For if it does, I am afraid I should never succeed in their education. So effeminate am I, that I cannot bear the cries even of an animal.

CT. It is good for you then, Socrates, you did not come here two minutes sooner.

SOC. You was giving some instructions with your rod to some of your dogs, I suppose.

CT. Ay, to a whelp worse to breed than any one of the race that is properly so called.

SOC. You don't mean one of your children surely.

CT. They, you think, want no correction; or correction, you perhaps imagine, is proper discipline for brutes only. But let me tell you, that if you think so, you must be a novice indeed, as wise as you are said to be.

SOC. The oracle called me so, but why I have not yet found out—,[15] unless it be for my sincere disposition to learn wisdom from every one who can teach me.—And as you have now exceedingly raised my curiosity, so I hope you will satisfy it.

CT. What would you know from me?

SOC. Only why you whipp'd your boy? whether it was to whip him into the love of knowledge, or the love of virtue? For I think these two are called the goals at which education aims.

CT. I am no stranger, Socrates, to your odd way of perplexing and confounding our celebrated pretenders to science and rhetorick, but you must not think to catch me in one of your subtle nets.—I never imagined one could be whipp'd into a liking for any thing, but I think one may be whipp'd out of a liking to a thing.

SOC. Ay, I am of your mind, out of a liking to learning, virtue, or any good thing, before the pleasure of it hath been much felt, or the excellence of it hath been fully perceived.—But sure it was not for any such end you were just now plying your rod so heartily. What then, pray, was your end, since you say one cannot be whipp'd into a liking to any thing.

15. We find Socrates frequently speaking in this manner about what the oracle said of him. See Plato's apology for Socrates in particular.

CT. Strange that you will still endeavour to puzzle the matter. Did not I plainly tell you, that I know the whip can only beget disliking and not liking.

SOC. I wish you would be as plain as you pretend to be, for you really puzzle me.

CT. As how? Can't you conceive how a sound beating may cure a liking and beget a dislike?

SOC. So dull am I, that tho' I can easily understand how the whip may produce a dislike to any thing to which one is compelled by stripes, yet I cannot comprehend how one can be made to dislike without liking: dislike the rod, for example, or the hand that employs it (for hardly can one, however young, hate the rod itself) without liking to escape or elude it, or rather the hated hand that makes it so bitter.

CT. Why, this is the very thing I use it for.

SOC. You want therefore your child should make it his chief good to avoid the whip, or rather to get rid of the whip's master. You do not aim at his hating lying, dissimulation, sauntering, or any other vice, but at his hating the whip.

CT. Indeed, Socrates, you are very dull, or would appear to be so. If he hates or fears the whip, will he not hate and fear the vices that expose him to the danger of it?

SOC. Tell me then, pray, Ctesicles, does one hate theft, who would steal with all his heart, if he thought he could escape hanging or scourging? Or is the boy in a fair way of learning, by the discipline of the rod, without any other instruction, to hate any vice for any other reason, but that it exposes to the risk of punishment?—But I suppose you had found all other methods fruitless, and it was stubbornness you corrected him for.

CT. Perhaps you would not approve of the method even in that case.

SOC. I shall not scruple to tell you my mind about the matter, if you will but satisfy me first as to this one thing; which is, whether you think any of the virtues, candour, temperance, or generosity, can be established in the mind by whipping?

CT. Did I not already tell you, that one cannot be whipped into liking, but only into disliking?

SOC. And can the vices be whipp'd out by the root, so as never to sprout again, unless the soil be sown with the virtues, and these grow up in their room? Can the field of the mind be quite bare and empty?

CT. There is no keeping you from your allegories.

SOC. Be not angry. I was just coming to your point. I was going to answer you in the words of a father, who is no less estimable for his own virtues, than for the many excellent citizens he has formed, by his proper care of his children. Four of them are now men able to serve the state in any capacity, whether in peace or war; and the other three have yet a more promising appearance than their brothers had at their age.

CT. Now you excite my attention. Pray tell me the story.

SOC. I shall not trouble you with the circumstances which gave rise to the discourse; for that might tire you. But his final observation was this: "That beating is found to do little good, where the pain of it is all the punishment that is feared or felt in it. For the influence of that quickly wears out with the memory of it.—But yet there is one fault, continued he, and but one, for which children should be beaten; and it is stubbornness or obstinacy. And in this too I would have it ordered so, if it can be, that the shame of the whipping, and not the pain, should be the greatest part of the punishment. Shame of doing amiss, and of deserving chastisement, is the only restraint belonging to virtue. All others may take place with the most vicious inclinations. If you would produce a truly ingenuous temper, it is shame for a fault, and the disgrace that attends it, rather than bodily suffering, children must stand in awe of. But stubbornness, and an obstinate disobedience, must be mastered by force. For this there is no other remedy. By this vice I mean, sturdy refusal to hear reason; for I suppose the parents or tutors never to command merely for the sake of commanding, but to deal rationally with their children or pupils, as they must do, if they would make them rational, i.e. virtuous and manly enough not to be over-ruled by arbitrary force or power, if they can shake off the chain."

CT. Don't you perceive, Socrates, how easily I might retort your own quibble upon you, and say, how can the whip produce a liking to reason?

SOC. I told you from the beginning the observation was not mine. But if you attend to it, you will see, by this very instance given, that it is no quibble. I said the whip did no good when it merely produced a dislike to it, and no liking to something contrary to the vice that deserved the whip.

Now here in the case of stubbornness, and in that case only, the whip may banish stubbornness and produce pliableness; and all that reason wants is to have a fair hearing. So that the rod applied in the case of obstinacy may beget a disposition, a willingness to hear reason, rather than be whipt for not hearing it: and reason, when it can once gain attention, will soon give such pleasure, that listening to it will be liked more than the whip can be feared by any one used to it. For by use the whip soon loses all its terror. But reason, by practice, becomes daily more sweet and agreeable. Besides, in the case of stubbornness, or wilful headstrong refusal to hearken to reasonable conversation and instruction, there remains no other cure but the rod. Whereas, if docility be not wanting, there can never be occasion for any thing but information and reasoning, and the rewards of love and praise due to improving minds; the strongest relish of which will never diminish regard to virtue, or a sense of its intrinsic beauty, amiableness and excellence. If you once get into children love of credit, and an apprehension of shame and disgrace, you have put into them the true principle, which will constantly work and incline them to the right.

CT. Your notions are uncommon; the practice of the world, founded upon experience, the best guide, seems to be against them: yet they are very specious. I will think of them.

SOC. If experience be not on my side, I must be wrong. But I am sure, Ctesicles, whether you agree with what hath been said upon better authority than my own, or not, you will grant to him and me, that for all their innocent folly, playing and childishness, children are to be left perfectly free and unrestrained, as far as is consistent with respect to those who are present, and that even with the greatest allowance: and that if these faults of their age, rather than of the children, were left to time and good example to correct and cure, children would escape a great deal of useless, misapplied correction, which, surely, good parents or masters can't have pleasure in.

CT. I never use the rod for any thing but vice.

SOC. Well, Ctesicles, so far you are right. But what do you think, is one virtuous, or so much as secure against vice, till he cordially loves virtue, and could not be whipt into any vicious compliance? Surely, you will not say he is. You feel a nobler and purer principle of honesty in your own heart. And therefore, if I should grant, you may scourge into the hatred of vice, yet I would willingly know what you do to beget the love of virtue? I know some reward virtue by sugar-plumbs; what is your way?

Cт. Why, by giving them that or any thing they like.

Soc. Is it temperance, self-denial, or the power of abstaining from bodily gratifications, when duty commands, that you thus reward to strengthen it?

Cт. I know not what to make of you. As it seems to me, you would neither have rewards nor punishments used in education.

Soc. Surely you would not have rewards and punishments employed to educate virtuous habits, which directly tend to destroy them. Tell me, pray, which would you have your sons to like best, virtue and knowledge, or sugar plumbs?

Cт. You are merry, Socrates.

Soc. I am very serious. For how can that be considered as a reward for doing any thing, which is not better liked than the thing it is given in re-compence for? "Do this and I will give you a sugar plumb." What does it mean, but put yourself to pain for a moment, and you shall be abundantly recompensed by what I am to give you afterwards.—How Socrates went on we know not, the remainder of the conference not having been trans-mitted to us.

But this seems, my good friend, to be certain, that every affection in the human breast, which is implanted there by nature, is of great use; and that we may nurse any young affection into virtue or vice, as we please; whereas you cannot extirpate or crush any one of them nature hath inlaid into our frame, without rendering man a much more imperfect creature than he is furnished and equipped by nature to be. And in particular, as love of lib-erty and dominion is a very necessary one, so a sense of shame and a sense of honour are of indispensible utility.

Eutyphron, a noted preceptor, who had formed many great princes, pa-triots and heroes, was wont to say, "That he who knew how to reconcile this seeming contradiction, had, in his opinion, got the true *arcanum* of education, *viz.* 'To form self-command or self-denial, and mastership of the passions, without weakening the vigour and activity of the mind, or destroying that love of power, dominion and authority, without which there can be no greatness of mind; nay no incentive to industry and improvement.'" And indeed, at first view, it seems to be a very difficult, if not impracticable task. But if we look more deeply into the matter, it will no longer appear a paradox. For what is the true principle of fortitude, generosity, patriotism, philanthropy? Whence proceed great actions, or what alone renders capable of them? Is it not such mastery over the appetites and inclinations as emboldens and enables one to resist the importunity of present pleasure or pain for the sake of what reason approves: such resolution and firmness as strengthens us to oppose terror or desire, till reason hath pronounced the action proposed, at least not unbecoming, and to look down with brave and generous disdain upon any thing that competes with honour and integrity? This temper ought therefore to be formed betimes: this habit, which is the only solid foundation of virtue, and happiness, virtue's gift, ought to be wrought into and settled in the mind, as early as may be, from the very first dawnings of apprehension in children; and to be confirmed in them by all the care imaginable, of those who have the oversight of their education. So only are habits formed: so alone is any disposition rendered natural to the mind. But how can this be done otherwise than by accustoming children betimes not to have things unless they be proper for them, and only because they are so, and not in compliance with their wilfulness and peevish fretting or crying?

For this reason, the youth under his care were early taught the beauty, the dignity of self-dominion, and rule over their passions, and inured to the practice of it, and to placing their whole ambition in excelling others in wisdom and virtue, and in meriting thereby the esteem of all good men. They were taught to yield to reason, and to conquer by reason; and to take high delight in the ability of doing good; but to look upon compliance with vice as sinking and degrading the man. And thus their natural love of power took an excellent turn. They felt themselves grow in capacity, power and liberty, in proportion as they advanced in wisdom, and were able to resist pain or pleasure. And this inward force they could not feel without a sincere triumph of reason and conscience, that needs only to be felt to be preferred before all the gratifications of mere sense. By practice in self-denial and liberality, they became strangers to all fear, but the fear of incurring guilt, by acting contrary, or not sufficiently attending to the counsels of reason. They looked upon injustice, ingratitude, intemperance, ungenerousness, and the other vices of the mind, as the greatest evils man ought either to fear or be ashamed of. To dread any thing more than sin, was in their eyes errant cowardise. For thus they used to reason with themselves. "Is not my honour, my integrity, my principal good?—What remains to me worth enjoying in life, if that be impaired or sullied? Shall I then tremble at a wound in my body, and not be afraid of a wound in my better part?—If my reason be my dignity, then, surely, when I suffer my palate, my belly, or any of my senses to get the ascendant over my reason, and betray me into disobedience to it, or neglect of its authority— what do I but basely desert or betray my trust, and give up for a pitiful bribe all that ought to be dearest and most valuable in my estimation!" Indeed virtue must be an empty sound, or this is the chief lesson education ought to inculcate: "That no external evil is to be so much feared as the smallest immoral indulgence."[16] And never was there a truly great man, who had not his mind early seasoned and deeply tinctured with this noble sentiment. This produced an *Epaminondas* and a *Pelopidas,* a *Scipio,* a *Cato,* &c.—No other lesson could have formed such truly generous heroic minds, who thought of duty, and of that alone, in all their undertakings. But why do I say lesson? It was not by bare lectures, but by discipline and practice this God-like temper was produced. The youth in the ancient schools, which formed legislators, politicians, heroes, patriots, men equally fit to fight against tyranny, and to oppose luxury and corruption, which have done more mischief in free states than ever despotic power was able to do to mankind, without first introducing them.—Such noble souls were not only taught to distinguish right from wrong, but steadily inured to abstain from every appearance of evil, and to place their supreme

16. Lest any should think none of the ancients ever talked of virtue in this manner, because Epictetus, or even Plutarch, may be reckoned perhaps too modern, I would refer them to Plato's apology for Socrates. The essence of virtue was placed by them in what cannot be better translated than self-command, and Socrates expresly says, that vice alone ought to be feared: the smallest vice more than the greatest natural pain.

delight in being as useful as their power could reach. Their masters, whose examples were ever in their eyes, were patterns to them of every virtue, of temperance, of fortitude, and of vigilant active benevolence. And no day passed in which some new example of some one or other eminent moral excellency was not set before them from history, to add new spurs to their noble ambition.—But this was not all. Hardly did any day go over their heads, in which some opportunity was not found out to try and exercise their virtue, that one, at least, which is the foundation, and may justly be called the mother of all the virtues, self-command, and the habit of duly consulting reason what ought or ought not to be done. For it is by no means a difficult matter for a wise master, who has the care of a small number of young pupils, to devise several such trials, or to make occasions for them.

This was the method generally used in these schools; and what was the effect of it? The seeds of virtue being thus early sown in the mind, and the growth and progress of them being duly watched over, and pursued with proper culture, all the virtues soon sprung up in them to great vigour, and the soul was betimes formed into a temper able to withstand all the snares and allures of the world. "Train up a child, said he, in the ways you would have him to persist in, and he will never desert them. For custom, saith the proverb in every one's mouth, is a second nature." The vices of others, to a well-form'd mind, will only afford materials for the exercise of its virtues, its prudence, its compassion, its fortitude and generosity. And what signify a sprightly imagination, eloquence, erudition, if the soul hath not a truly liberal and generous cast? What is courage without regard to justice and the rights of mankind, but brutality? Or what are oratory, wit, and learning, without love to equity, liberty and truth, that no temptations can shake, intimidate, or cool, but very dangerous weapons in very bad hands? A quick sense and warm love of right, are qualities without which all other accomplishments are really noxious. Let therefore education have virtue chiefly and continually in its view.

Cebes, master of a school at Athens, being asked what he taught, said, I have but one lesson to teach. For tho' it may seem to consist of many parts, yet it is but one, even as a tree with all its arms, leaves, and fruits, is one. And it is justly called in one word *philosophy*, or the medicine of the mind. "It shews what is honest[17] and dishonest; it distinguishes just from unjust, and teaches us what we ought to avoid with all care, and what is truly worthy of our desire and pursuit: It informs us how we ought to love and honour God the supreme Being, the Author of all things; what reverence is due to parents; what respect we owe to the wise and good, to experienced sages; what regard to the laws and magistrates, and how we ought to behave ourselves towards our friends, and how towards strangers; our duty to our wives, to our children and our servants: That we ought to worship and imitate God with pious love and veneration; that we ought to render filial honour and obedience to our parents; pay great deference to our superiors in age and wisdom; chearfully obey the laws of our country; love our friends; be faithful to our wives; embrace our children with cordial and sincere affection; and treat our servants not only justly but tenderly, with great lenity and mildness: And which is principal, not to be elated by prosperity, nor depressed by adversity: Not to dissolve in pleasure, nor to be transported into cruelty by anger and a desire of revenge. For such a temper of mind is the greatest of goods, the only unchangeable immortal inheritance. To moderate our affections amidst affluence, and make a generous use of power and wealth in flourishing circumstances, teeming with temptations, is truly manly. To live without envy, is self-command: To derive happiness to ourselves from the happiness of the deserving, is true generosity: To overcome pleasure by reason, and to keep our rebellious appetites in due order, is wisdom: And to be proof against the transports of passion is real greatness of mind; a very rare excellence

17. This excellent description of philosophy, or the medicine of the mind, occurs in Plutarch's discourse on Education. And it is so described numberless times by Socrates in Plato and Xenophon, and by Cicero.—There was a Cebes contemporary with Socrates, but whether he be the author of the allegorical picture called Cebes's is disputable. The manner of teaching philosophy here delineated, is agreeable to the character of that piece, and is as old as Socrates. [A number of the works attributed to Plutarch throughout the eighteenth century are now generally thought not to have been written by him or are still disputed. The works in question are "The Education of Children," "The Ancient Customs of the Spartans," "On Affection for Offspring" (probably Plutarch's), "Of Fate," and "Lives of the Ten Orators." All of these essays can be found in the Loeb edition of *Plutarch's Moralia,* trans. Harold North Fowler, 15 vols. (Cambridge, Mass.: Harvard University Press, 1960).]

indeed. These, I think, are perfect men, who know how to mix philosophy with action, and to govern their conduct in public and private affairs by it. Such, in my opinion, have attained to the two greatest goods in human life, which are, to be useful in society, and to enjoy, at the same time, a philosophical tranquillity and sedateness of mind. For there are three ways of life. One consists in action, another in contemplation, and the third in voluptuous indulgence.[18] He who gives himself up to pleasure is a dissolute slave, and lives like the abject, groveling brutes, whose apprehensions and appetites rise not above their senses. One who devotes himself wholly to speculation, and never acts, must make great discoveries not to be very useless in society. And he who without acquaintance with true philosophy, will meddle with public business, undertaking what he does not understand, may easily err, or be deceived, to the irreparable detriment of millions. The chief business of education therefore, is to prepare one for useful activity in such a way that he can, and will pleasantly give himself to philosophy, as often as times and circumstances permit him to retire to her. Thus did Pericles, Archytas, Dion of Syracuse, and the Theban Epaminondas (with the two last of whom Plato was so familiar)—Thus did those great men live and serve the public." Nor need I, I think, say any more about true learning, or right education. This is the substance of what I teach: Nor is there any thing wanting to render this lesson compleat, either with respect to private or public usefulness and happiness. It is one whole, no part of which can be severed from the rest, without tearing and maiming that part itself, as well as the whole body: No more than a member can be taken from a poem, a tune, the human body, or any thing else in nature or art that hath unity, can this lesson be disjointed and broke into pieces. And conformity of life to this philosophy renders conduct uniform and consistent; one perfect, beautiful whole, in the same sense that any thing natural or artificial is such. For as whatever is beautiful is such, by a strict coherence and dependance of various parts[19] uniting in one end, so that the smallest alteration or diminution would render it deform'd; in

---

18. All this is to be found in Plutarch's abovementioned description of philosophy.

19. This description of beauty occurs also in Plutarch's discourse on hearing.

the same manner is a life directed by a principle of virtue, always consonant and harmonious: All its different parts and several offices flow from
the same motive, conspire to the same end, and mutually illustrate and set
off one another: Being fitly measured and approportioned; having a close
and intimate connexion with one another, and with one common scope;
and bearing a proper relation to times and circumstances, the whole piece
is beautiful to behold. But whatever is contrary to virtue is disorder and
dissonance. And a vitious course of life is a continued train of irregularities, contrarieties and discords. Pythagoras[20] therefore said well, "That order and beauty or harmony is the chief good. God is perfect harmony; nature, his workmanship, is a perfect whole, compleat harmony as God its
author. And every intelligent being, in proportion as he loves and imitates
God and nature, is harmony: The inward motions of his mind are well-
tuned, and his outward actions are in concert with them. But harmony,
said he, is and must be happiness. Perfect melody is compleat pleasure.
And every dissonance in heart or life is proportionable pain."—And therefore, in general, as much harmony as there is in life, just so much true happiness is there in it. As well may we expect to receive satisfaction from a
poem, or a picture, as from an action without it. Were not nature all con-
cord and proportion, the contemplation of it could give no more pleasure
to the understanding than discord to the ear.—And as if the temper and
life be not justly modulated and regulated, according to the rules of harmony, it must needs be a very displeasing, offensive object to our reflection
and contemplation; so neither can the actions or motions which are irregular, be otherwise than harsh and of uneasy feeling. For this, believe me,
is universally true in nature, "That whatever motion is not justly commensurate, is awkward and grating. Then only does a machine, a musical instrument, or any frame, natural or artificial, work easily, smoothly and
pleasantly, when all its parts are in exact symmetry and proportion, and
when every thing is in its proper place and tone, and readily performs its
functions without too much sluggishness or tardiness on the one hand, or

---

20. Plutarch himself gives this account of the doctrine of Pythagoras in different
places of his works. But see the writings of some scholars or disciples of Pythagoras,
collected by Mr. Gale.

precipitance and impetuosity on the other."—Have you not seen, my friend, some antique gems on which the signs of the zodiac and the planets are represented as keeping time to one playing upon a musical instrument?

So soon as Cebes made a pause, for he talked with great warmth, he was asked, But how can this be the only lesson you teach? Do not you instruct your pupils in all the arts and sciences?

To this Cebes replied. And what science does not this lesson comprehend? Call it again to mind, and see what you think wanting in it?

Why, it was answered, I can neither find geometry, nor natural philosophy therein, much less can I find dialectic, rhetoric, or poetry, not to mention the arts of war.

Perhaps then, replied Cebes, you imagine I have no more to do but to con this lecture over and over again I have now given you.—Must I not, in order to explain and enforce it, not only define, but bring examples.— Now try how you can conceive this to be done in a variety of ways necessary to engage attention, and set forth what I would recommend to my pupils with due energy, or in a manner that will sink my instructions deep into their hearts, and firmly rivet them there.—Let me know how this can be done without uniting all the arts and sciences in the cause of virtue, or making them all contribute towards impressing the precepts of integrity and piety upon tender minds.

I confess, said the interrogator, I am at a loss to understand you.

You are then, answered Cebes, a stranger to the truth and force of that maxim which was always in the divine Plato's mouth. "That all the sciences which belong to man have one common scope, which is to harmonize the mind or affections; and all conspiring to this noble end in various manners, have a strict union and connexion, and make one most harmonious system.[21] For this reason do poets and painters represent the muses

---

21. This unity of the arts and sciences was Plato's doctrine. Cicero speaks of it with high applause. Plutarch often has recourse to it in his discourse upon hearing the poets, in particular, and he records some excellent sayings of philosophers and painters to this purpose. See Turnbull's ancient Painting, cap. 7. [George Turnbull, *A Treatise on Ancient Painting* (London: Millar, 1740).]

and graces in harmonious dance to the music of Apollo, and mutually aid-ing and adorning one another. The representation is as old as Homer."[22]

But so willing do you appear to be instructed, that I should indeed act a most incongruous part to your intention, and to my own profession, if I could grudge to explain myself more fully to you upon this important sub-ject, the best method of instructing youth by one and the same labour, in virtue and the sciences, or good taste of life and composition. And in truth, all I have to say may be comprised in one sentence, viz. There is but one beauty in nature, in life and art, and that is virtue.

Being told it would be intirely obliging if he would be so gracious and condescending as to be more particular, he is said to have discoursed much to this effect.

The design of philosophy, I said, is to distinguish right from wrong, just from unjust, the becoming from the base and unfitting in life and manners. Without this knowledge, 'tis plain, we cannot direct our affec-tions or actions aright, no more than we can sail without skill in naviga-tion. What else then is the first thing to be learned or rather acquired in life, but knowledge and resolution how to live as becomes men, i.e. cour-age to govern our pursuits by reason? But how can this first and essential lesson be taught and sufficiently inculcated, without describing, or rather painting out to the view of my pupils the character of the rational man, and fully delineating the methods of fore-thinking and after reflection or examination, by which the empire of reason is established and kept up in the mind? Can this be done without bringing examples, and thus setting the rational man, as it were, before the eyes of my scholars, in his closet soliloquies before and after action, and in public councils, now debating with himself, and now consulting with others, and that in very various circumstances? Now here, may I not, nay ought I not, sometimes to fetch instances from imitation or fiction, as well as from real life or history?

He was answered, that the thing was self-evident.

22. He alludes to such a picture in one of his Hymns, that to Apollo in particular—αυταρ ὁ Φοιβος Απολλω εγκιθαριζει, &c. [*Homeric Hymn to Apollo,* line 201: "But Phoe-bus Apollo plays the harp."]

Well then, continued he, when I come to particular virtues, 'tis but a continuation of the same lesson; for it is but shewing what reason, if it is consulted, will prefer in this or t'other situation. And therefore, whatever virtue be the subject of the lesson, suppose justice, benevolence, gratitude, temperance, or any other, I am still obliged to define and to exemplify. And as contrast gives relief in picture; so for the same reason, to heighten each virtue, and set it forth with all its charms, not only must it be represented in various trials; but its opposite vices must be placed over against it, i.e. they also must be described and characterized.

You know, how Theophrastus makes every virtue and vice speak and act. You know painting true characters is the great business of poets. And you will as readily own, that developing the motions of moral causes, and the springs and processes of events, drawing just and lively pourtraits of minds, and tracing actions to the ruling passions which did, or would naturally have produced them in certain conjunctions, is the great excellence of historians. But if you keep this reflection in your view, you can't sure be at a loss to find out how, by teaching virtue from descriptions and examples in history and fiction, one is naturally, at the same time, formed into a good taste of life, and of writing, as far as true design and just drawing are concerned.—And what, pray, remains, to compleat a thorough intelligence of good composition in the best kinds, besides skill to distinguish, whether the circumstances in which characters are placed, and the consequences of their determinations and actions be natural? And here, no doubt, you prevent me, and see this knowledge must necessarily be acquired by that due attendance to the operations of the human passions and their effects, the exhibition of which, in well chosen examples, must make a principal part in lessons upon virtue and vice, or the conduct of life. For imitation to please must be like: And what is like or agreeable to nature, is nature itself. There cannot be one nature for life, and another for fiction, which is the imitation of real life. The only difficulty in all this matter, is to make a proper choice of examples at first, and a just progress from simpler to more complex ones, in proportion as the minds of pupils open and enlarge, which, believe me, they do much faster than is generally imagined.

Now, my friend, if you understand what has been said, as I perceive by your countenance you do, I think I may venture to add, that a good picture of any great action, may not unfitly be joined with description, and historical or feigned examples. This is not multiplying lessons, but duly diversifying the same lesson, if the subject of the picture be the same in kind with that of the example and description.—Nor is it really any thing new to say, That a picture is quite natural, and properly shaded and contrasted, when one hath conceived what is meant by nature and consistency, or truth of description and character in writing; or *vice versa,* if beginning with the picture, and having observed the conformity in it to nature, and the mutual references in it of all the parts to one main good end, we have pronounced it an excellent imitation—If, I say, after this, we should then talk of truth, beauty, and unity in writing, it would be nothing new.—And whether we are considering imitation by words, or by the pencil, or in a real character in history, which ought to be like, as a portrait in painting is like, i.e. be a strong likeness in a judiciously chosen attitude—of whichsoever of these we are talking, 'tis nature, human nature we have still before us, as our standard to judge by, that is to say, what we feel within to be natural. The lesson therefore is a part of the science of man. It is about the natural operation of some human passion: It is about the natural conduct and effects of some virtue or vice.—It is therefore some rule relative to the conduct of life, as well as to the arts that imitate men and manners, and relative to them only, because it is true in fact, or real life.

I must give you, my friend, a whole course of lectures, if I would shew you fully, that without deserting my one subject, I must naturally be led to discourse of every part of nature, i.e. to unfold the chief principles and truths in every science. For every science has it not some part of nature for its object; and are not all the parts of nature closely linked together? Is not nature one?

But if you are not fully satisfied already, one or two instances, I fancy, will do it.

He was intreated to go on, and having told them they must resolve upon patience, and to hear a lecture, he thus proceeded. "To act steadily under the direction of reason, is the perfection of man, because it is the perfection of reason. It is therefore to imitate the supreme Author of all intelligence and reason, who must be perfect reason.—But how do we, or can we know how he acts?—Just as we know how men act, viz. by attending to their actions.[23] What then do you call the actions of the supreme Being? All that we call, in other words, the operations of nature, the growth of flowers, plants, trees, animal bodies, the implantation into us, and all intelligent beings, of our perceptive, retentive, thinking, comparing, judging faculties, and all our affections, capable of being improved, according to laws of his appointment, to so great perfection, as we may see in the history of a Socrates, a Plato, a Xenophon, an Epaminondas, a Leonidas, an Aristides, and many other glorious examples of eminent wisdom and virtue.—But what can we learn from these actions of the supreme Cause? That he always, in every frame, pursues some good end by the best, that is, the simplest reasons: And this is wisdom, love of order, and benevolence. This, in one word, is acting by the best reason."

I see, said the auditor, how you may easily go on in this way at various reprises, at once developing nature, and recommending piety and virtue, i.e. teaching natural and moral philosophy with one breath.—What, pray, is your other instance?

Do you, said Cebes, choose one for me.

Let it be, replied the other, love to our country, and the deference we owe to magistrates and laws.

With all my heart, said Cebes: For this also is piety; and thus he went on. "We have seen who may be called a reasonable man. Now what will make a reasonable body of men? Will any number of men be such, if reason do not preside among them; that is, if they be not united by reason in the pursuit of an end, reason approves, by reasonable means?—But will not the common good be the end of this union? And will not the rules or laws of this society be directions that point out the paths leading to this excellent end?—What then will their united power be employed for? Will it not be to accomplish this end, and to prevent acting contrary to it, which is, acting contrary to the common interest, and the common guide,

---

23. We have a discourse of Socrates much to the same purpose in Xenophon's memorable things of Socrates. And Cambyses's lesson to Cyrus is remarkable to this purpose. He teaches him the absurdity of praying to God for success, if one does not use the means for obtaining it, &c.

reason?—Are not then a reasonable mind and a reasonable society pictures one of another? And are not both pictures[24] of the supreme Being and his government?"

You need go no further, Cebes, said the person to whom he principally addressed himself in this conference; for tho' I would never tire hearing you, yet I am unwilling to fatigue you. I now understand what you mean by your unity of the philosophical sciences. But here, methinks, your other unity of teaching would fail you, would it not? Or how can truth and beauty in writing and painting have any place in this lecture?

Have not, replied Cebes, Sparta and Athens been described justly and elegantly? They have, you know. And you are no stranger to many beautiful descriptions in miniature, of the end of civil government, and of the happiness resulting from what Aristotle somewhere calls, *The empire not of men but of laws; and the kingdom of God.*—You are, I say, no stranger to many beautiful descriptions of this kind in the works of our philosophers, nay, and our poets too.

Here the interrogator stop'd him, saying, he wondered at himself how he came to ask so odd a question. For now Cebes, said he, I see likewise how the picture of Theseus founding the democracy at Athens, or of Lycurgus taking leave of his Spartans, and going to consult the oracle about his newly modell'd state, and many other excellent pictures[25] I have often highly admired, naturally belong to this lecture. Strange! that I should have so often felt the moral effects of these wonderful pieces, and yet never till now have adverted to the moral use that might be made of them in education.—But tho' I should betray my ignorance or want of reflection once more, I must ask you, how writing or painting can be made subservient or introduced into the first lesson?

Cebes answered, Do you not here also prevent me? Would there be any harm in having pictures of flowers, trees and animals by us when we are talking of their wonderful structures, and the wisdom of nature displayed

24. This Socrates often says in Plato's books of laws and of a republic. Plutarch says much the same things about God and good government, or good magistracy, in his discourse to an unlearned prince.

25. There are such ancient pictures, as we learn from Pausanias, Janius de pictura veterum, and Turnbull's treatise on ancient painting.

in their contrivance, growth, instincts, and the provision made for their appetites?

Here Cebes was interrupted by a third person, who being surprised to hear him talk of flowers, trees, animals, appetites, and instincts at one breath, said, smiling—Sure Cebes, you do not ascribe sense or feeling, appetite and passion, to trees and plants?

Cebes replied, That he would not positively justify the way of speaking, but that there was however an analogy between vegetable and animal bodies, which highly delighted him, and to which poetry owed no small part of its charms.—And then he proceeded.—But, as I was saying, there can be no hurt, surely, in having good pictures of natural objects before us, while we are searching into their contexture, and admiring the wisdom and goodness of the Creator in adjusting every fabric to its end and use, and in making all the various parts in each frame so accurately subservient to what is principal in it; and we are thus enforcing upon our minds, from the divine example, the great rule of our actions, public good.—And yet this is not all the use I make of painting on such occasions. For what we call wise contrivance in the structure and oeconomy, suppose of any animal, we call good taste, harmony and beautiful disposition, true arangement, unity and just ordonance in painting. There likewise must be something principal, and a just subordination of parts to it, or there can be no unity, no harmony, and consequently no beauty. But when this is accomplished, the piece is compleat: It is a perfect creation, or a regular beautiful whole in itself. When we meet with what we call a fine landscape in nature, what is it but a piece of nature, which by itself makes something perfectly satisfactory to the eye? And a good landscape in painting, tho' copied upon the canvass from the imagination, is, in like manner, something compleat in itself that fully charms the eye. But what has this effect in nature or in art, but one good, principal end, to which a proper variety of parts justly and harmoniously conspires? Now hence poets and painters are called creators.—I believe, said Cebes, I have said enough at present. And therefore I shall conclude with a short saying of one of our philosophers: "That all the arts and sciences, poetry, oratory, painting, statuary, &c. are imitations of nature, and but so many different languages for expressing and enforcing upon the mind some truth, i.e. the knowledge of some connexion in nature. They are learned from nature, but being got, they are glasses in which we may see nature reflected or doubled. And often to compare the original and image together, is the pleasantest and surest way of understanding both." As I would never, therefore, present a copy to my pupils to be considered by itself, or without directing them how to refer it to the original from which it is taken; so, I would never have them look into any original without bringing some imitation to be compared with it, if one could be got.—But what is this but in other words to study nature, and imitations of nature at the same time; or to compare real with descriptive and painted life, in order to acquire by our labour a good taste of both.

The interrogator said, he thought he could now comprehend the whole scheme of teaching, that at first appeared so dark and mysterious to him, if Cebes would but be so good as to shew him how geometry could come in and mix with morals.

To which Cebes briefly replied, "You have seen how amicably natural and moral philosophy must meet and unite. Now what is geometry, but the knowledge of the numbers and proportions, according to which, nature, justly called, the most perfect geometrician, works towards her good ends in every thing? It must therefore be the key, as it were, that opens nature to us, and disclosing her secrets, shews us her harmonies, her analogies and general laws.—Let me only add, that I follow Plato's method, and begin early with geometry, in order to purify the mind, as well as to enlarge and strengthen it."[26]

In ancient schools, the science of life was the lesson, and all the arts and sciences were taught by rendering them subservient to this lesson. And indeed what else is their business, or wherein does their excellence and beauty consist, but in singing the praises of nature, and displaying the wisdom and goodness that reigns throughout all her works; and in celebrating great men and truly glorious actions, unfolding the generous motives

---

26. This is known to have been the method in Plato's school. Quintilian commends the practice, and gives good reasons for it. But of this afterwards.

whence they proceed, and painting out their blessed effects within the good man's own breast, and in society?[27]

In ancient education no hood-winking or blinding arts were used, but vice itself had fair play, and was represented in its genuine colours. None of its tempting allurements, by which it seduces its votaries, were hid or disguised. But the youth were taught to compare the pleasures of sense with those of reason and virtue in an equal balance. To this end did Prodicus devise that instructive allegory so well told by Xenophon, and which hath been so often put into numbers by our poets, and into colours by our painters; the well known story of Hercules's choice, which I need not repeat.

We are told of the same excellent Lockias, whom we have already commended in particular, that he hid no vice from his scholars. He thought it necessary to shew them the follies and corruptions of mankind, as they were described in history or by poets, in their dramatic pieces more especially, which are, in a peculiar sense, imitations of men and manners. This he thought requisite, in order to point out the vitious, as well as virtuous turns every affection belonging to man may take, and thus give a fair and full view of human nature. " 'Tis not only safer, said he, to begin with exciting aversion and abhorrence against vice in young minds, by a fair representation of its vileness and of its fatal consequences, than by raising their admiration: This is not only, said he, the most effectual way of securing them against all temptations to indulgences in pleasure, which have equally base and pernicious effects, as all who have studied human nature have agreed.—But how else, said he, can they be prepared for launching into a contagious world, and learn how to steer their course through its snares and dangers, without being made acquainted with them. The sailor, in order to avoid rocks and shelves, must know how they ly. To go into life

---

27. See a fine Idyllion of Theocritus to this Purpose. Idyll. 16. The muses sent by Juno to discomfit the Syrens, plucked their wings, and hence, says Pausanias, their statues are crowned with feathers, or hold feathers in their hands. The syrens sung sweetly, and gave by their enchanting voice false charms to vice. But the muses exerting all their vigour, soon got the better of this only dangerous rival. Such statues of the muses are yet preserved.

without any knowledge of its temptations and perils, is like venturing to sea without a sea chart. If young men are bred up in ignorance of what the world really is, is it any wonder, that soon finding it quite another thing than what they were taught it should be, and so imagined it was, they are easily persuaded by other kind of tutors, which they are sure to meet with, that the discipline they were kept under was but the restraints of school-boys, or the austere formality of education; and that the freedom of men is to take their swing in a full enjoyment of what was before forbidden them? Shewing youth the world as it really is, before they come wholly into it, is the only way, I think, of preventing this mischief. It is not possible, now a-days at least, whatever it may formerly have been, to keep a young gentleman from vice by a total ignorance of it, if he is not cloister'd for life, and never suffer'd to peep out of the cell in which he is mewed up. And therefore he should be early shewn the prevailing vices of the world, of his own country, and of the age he has fallen into, in particular. He should be informed of the traps that are laid for youth, and the arts that are used to seduce and corrupt them, and have the tragical or ridiculous examples set before him, of those who are ruined, or in the way to it by these guileful ruses. The plainest, easiest, and most efficacious way of teaching young people, is to exhibit to their eyes examples of what you would have them to avoid, as well as of what you would have them to do.[28] Virtues and vices can by no words be so forcibly set before their understandings as the actions of others will shew them, when you direct their observation to this or that good quality in the examples you lay before them, by some proper reflections on their beauty or unbecomingness, their merit or vileness, and their good or bad consequences. These are the lessons that sink deepest into the mind, and make the most vivid and lasting impressions upon it.—Besides, said he, could you secure their virtue, without letting them know that they will hear it called an empty name, a political trick and imposition to restrain man's natural liberty, and confine

28. Our Lock reasons thus. Some phrases, and many sentiments are here taken from him. But the rule is as old as Plutarch, at least. See his treatises on education, upon knowing a friend from a flatterer, and how one may know what progress he makes in virtue, and how one may profit by his enemies.

our enjoyment of life within very scanty and severe bounds, yet you cannot secure them from being dupes to the birds of prey that are ever upon the wing hunting for so easy a booty, as such an honest novice must be to the cunning sharpers of various sorts, with which the world abounds. Those who have wicked ends to promote, well know how to put on very deceitful appearances of different kinds, as may best serve their knavish purposes. Youth therefore ought to be learned to pull off the masks with which artful men may cover their designs, and be taught not to judge by the outside, but to discern through it into the filthy views that so often lurk under the most specious semblances.

"This skill in men and manners, is not the product of a few superficial thoughts, or even of much reading, but is the effect of experience and observation, in a man who has lived in the world with his eyes open, and conversed with men of all sorts: And to instil this knowledge into young minds with due precaution, to open this scene to them gradually, with a gentle and wary hand, and thus conduct them, as it were by the arm, into a world of dangers, by proper degrees, or step by step, requires great prudence, great dexterity. But he who thinks not this knowledge of mankind of more moment to his son than abstract speculations about the essences and modes of spirit and matter, than all the languages and all the learned sciences, forgets that the art of living right with men, and of managing one's affairs with prudence, is the most necessary of all arts and sciences.

"Oh! my friend, said he, to one who desired to hear him on this subject, how large, how extensive, how profound, how difficult is this lesson, for it must comprehend all the dangers, temptations and snares that environ a young man from his first entrance upon the stage of the world, from all the several degrees, tempers, callings, professions, designs, and clubs or factions of men! A virtuous youth of birth and fortune must be prepared to be flattered and caressed by some, and ridiculed, affronted and shocked by others: He must be warned who are like to mislead, who to undermine, who to sooth and cajole, and who to banter and oppose him, and taught to distinguish the plain upright friend from the smooth officious villain.— But he must be taught thus to beware of the designs of men he hath to do with, and to distinguish realities from pretences and appearances, without contracting a too suspicious temper. For it is indeed hard to decide on which side the greater danger lies, in being too ready to confide, or too jealous and mistrustful. Both are extremes carefully to be avoided in forming youth: yet hood-winked they must not be, but accustomed to distinguish men, and to form right judgments of them, and to conceive of the world as they will really find it to be, so soon as they come into it. And therefore examples from history, from present times, and from just imitations of human manners, of men and things as they are, must be fairly set before them. In these faithful mirrors are they often to be shewn by a prudent teacher gradually, the whole of human life, all the various characters of mankind, all their different ruling passions, and all their different pursuits and arts.—And why indeed should we fear to shew virtue and vice together, or to set the one over against the other? Are not all the charms on the side of honesty and worth, till the mind is sadly corrupted by bad example; or till some appetite that might early have been directed into a very proper course, hath taken a very wrong one, and by indulgence is become too strong for precept, for reason, nay almost for suffering itself and fatal experience to conquer?—I say for fatal experience itself to subdue or reform. For have all the bad consequences Curio has suffered by his intemperance and debauchery been able to render him chaste and sober? And so is it with ambition, avarice, and every vice. Such is the fascination of habit. But what does this teach us, but that the great business of education is to form betimes good habits[29] in the mind, that thinking and acting aright may by practice early become natural to young people. Accustom them to a graceful air in walking, in speaking, in the whole of their deportment, in all their motions from their childhood, and it will never leave them. And for the same reason, if we inure them to think well before they act, and to act prudently and virtuously, they will ever continue so to behave, as it were, by impulse: The first thoughts and motions of their minds on every occasion will be virtuous.

"They are strangers to human nature, continued he, who think it suffi-

---

29. Quintilian says fine things about imitation and habit. *Imitatio in mores transit,* &c. [Quintilian, *Institutio Oratoria,* 1.11.3: "imitation passes into habit."] But what is virtue according to all the ancients but the habit of self-government by reason? And how are habits formed but by repeated discipline and exercise?

cient to give rules to their children: many good habits may be formed by exercise or practice, before precepts can be understood or retained: And rules without practice can never form habits. These can only be acquired by repeated acts. Therefore, what you think necessary for them to do, inure them to do it by frequent practice, as often as proper occasions return; nay, as much as is possible make occasions. By this method may the mind be made liberal, humane, compassionate, grateful, obedient and pliable to reason, long before the easiest reasonings can be fully comprehended.— Yet mistake me not, as if I were for delaying reasoning with children so long as is commonly done. They love and are pleased to be treated as rational creatures, much sooner than we are apt to imagine. And this is a noble pride that ought to be carefully cherished in them, and indeed made one of the principal handles for turning them into a right mould. Reason is called forth, strengthened and perfected by reasoning. And why is it, that it is so long of beginning to dawn in most children, but because we think it too early to draw it out, or invite it to disclose itself? As often as the kind experiment has been tried by such as understand *how to make the young idea shoot,* it hath been found that reasoning is understood by children almost as early as language. I do not mean that an infant should be argued with as a grown man, nay nor as one of six years old. Every thing in nature opens and expands itself gradually, and in proportion to the friendly aid it receives from art and culture. But when I say they should from the beginning be used to hear and obey reason, and so be treated like rational creatures, I mean, that they should always be made sensible, by the mildness of their managers, that it is not out of caprice or passion they desire or forbid them to do, but because it is useful and good for them so to do. This they are capable of understanding. And I think there is no virtue they should be excited to, nor no vice they should be kept from, of the fitness or unreasonableness of which they may not be convinced by arguments suited to their capacity and apprehension. To gain and preserve the parent's and the tutor's favour and love, and to avoid their displeasure, or falling into discredit or disgrace with them, are motives that will be intelligible from the earliest dawn of understanding. And this is always a very proper one to work by, while the instructor aims at nothing but establishing virtuous habits in their minds; that in particular, which is the foundation of all the rest, a liking to hear and act agreeably to reason, and desire to gain the love and esteem of the wise and good. Above all, let the examples they have ever before their eyes be such as we would have them to be. For by imitation do children learn not language merely, but whatsoever turn they first take of body or mind. By this means may they be insensibly moulded into any form. Had not nature made imitation natural to us, and given it a great power in forming our inward as well as our outward man, how very slow would our progress in any acquirement have been? But if kind nature hath thus framed us, let us follow nature, and make a proper use of this disposition and propensity, to form young children early and insensibly, without any pain to them, and with very little trouble to ourselves, into the inward temper and outward carriage we would have them betimes attain to. For whoever was so wicked, as not to wish his children to be good? And this is the only way of rendering them such, viz. by taking due care to practise and train them up in the good ways wherein they ought to walk. Teach them to relish no pleasure but what reason gives them, as it were out of her own hand: Teach them to make her their counsellor and their comforter; for she will lead them in the paths of honour, and fill their minds with consolation and joy that never cloys, and instead of enervating, invigorates the soul."

But this method of nursing and educating virtue I find yet more fully illustrated by another conversation between our much loved Damocles and a friend of his, who had a more than ordinary share of those excellent and sweet affections, which are commonly called, in a peculiar sense, natural ones. Damocles having often asserted, that most vices were the early effects of bad education, and that by suitable care and discipline, any virtue might be taught and brought betimes to great vigour and perfection, almost in any mind, a certain father, called Strephon, very sollicitous about the right instruction of his son from his earliest years, is said to have thus accosted him.[30]

Damocles, you know I have been married for some time without hav-

---

30. In Plato's Theages a father, Demodocus, is introduced expressing great concern about the education of his son, as we shall see afterwards.

ing children, and that I was not a little uneasy on that account, but little did I foresee what an unknown anxiety was to sprout up in my breast, so soon as I saw a son come into the world.

DAM. I congratulate you, Strephon. Heaven has granted you your desire, and I hope now your prayer has been heard, you shall have all the contentment you promised yourself when it should.

STR. O Damocles, how ill do we mortals judge for ourselves! I was extremely impatient to be a father, but now that I am, I feel I have brought a very heavy burden upon me. For the public has a right to expect from me I should use my best endeavours to make my son a good citizen. And the child I have been the instrument of bringing into the world, has a right, as a rational creature in embrio, to claim my care to make him betimes really such. For this task hath nature left to parents. This, to me, is the language of his eager looks, and of all his melting groans and cries. Nature appears to me to call upon me by all these heart-moving signs shall I say, or voices, to think seriously of the important trust and charge I have brought upon myself. In this deep concern do I come to you, Damocles, for advice. Is it indeed possible that a child may be made early virtuous, and that all the vice in the world is chiefly owing to neglect of education, or wrong management of children in their tender, docile, pliable years? I have often heard that Socrates was wont to say, "That if a right course were taken with children, there would not be so much need of chastisement as the general practice has established: But tho' we are generally wise enough to begin with other creatures we would make good for somewhat, when they are very young; yet our own offspring we sadly neglect in this point, and having taken a great deal of pains to make them ill children, we foolishly expect they should be good men." But what can this course be? Socrates is no more: And to whom can I go but you, Damocles, who hath indeed had wonderful success in training up children in wisdom and virtue? The progress of some of your young pupils is in truth astonishing.

DAM. I do not boast of any particular secret in this business. But if children are sent to me uncorrupted, it must be my fault if they become such under my inspection. 'Tis difficult to amend, but it is, I think, very easy and very pleasant to form good habits. I know a certain set of philosophers have represented mankind as originally deformed, as coming into the world with very depraved minds, with a strong biass to vice, and a violent aversion to virtue, which the best education cannot totally overcome; as if habits could precede exercise, nay thought itself.—But setting aside all other reasons, by which I could easily shew the absurdity of this doctrine, I have never found in experience children not to be, at least, very susceptible of good impressions, when due care is bestowed to convey them into their tender minds: And indeed I have often wondered, considering the common mismanagement of children, that there are any footsteps of virtue left in the world.

STR. You call up my attention wonderfully. This I have often heard was your common doctrine. Pray let me hear you fully on this subject. I wish it were so as you say, and that I knew how to avoid these fatal mismanagements.

DAM. I desire to know what vice can be named which parents and those about children do not breed and nurse up in children's minds.

STR. You mean by their bad example. Don't you?

DAM. No, Strephon. That is indeed encouragement enough. But I mean downright teaching them vice.

STR. Can the worst of parents be so abandoned as to take pains directly to instruct children in vice, and recommend it to them?

DAM. Alas! Strephon, the best of parents do it, but it is because they do not reflect what they are doing.

STR. As how, for I am all attention. I would, methinks, sooner cut my dear infant's throat, than have the least share in corrupting his mind. There is, in my sentiment, no comparison in point of guilt between the two, both monstrous crimes. But how is this done by the best of parents?

DAM. I will give you one or two familiar instances of it, which yet you may perhaps have not attended to. Do not very good parents instil revenge and cruelty into their infants before they can go? "*Give me a blow that I may beat him,*" is a lesson repeated to children every day. And it is thought nothing, because their little hands can do no hurt. But let me ask you, must not this lesson corrupt their minds? Is not this not only recommending the way of force and violence to them, but actually setting them into it, and practising them in it? Reflect a little how habits are contracted, how temper is formed, and then tell me whether it be strange that those who have been thus taught, practised and applauded when little, for striking and hurting others by proxy, and thus encouraged to take delight in doing harm and making others suffer, are prepared and prone to do it when they are strong enough to make their own weight felt, and to deal blows to some purpose. What say you Strephon?

STR. You confound me, Damocles. How was it possible I should never have made this obvious simple reflection to this moment? But go on, I beg you.

DAM. The coverings of our bodies, which a child ought early to be taught to consider merely as designed for modesty, and defence against the injuries of the weather, are they not made a matter of vanity and ostentation? A child is set a longing for some new finery, and when master is trimm'd with his embroidered suit, and his hair nicely dressed, how can his mother do less than lead him to the glass, and teach him to admire himself, calling him her prince, her charmer, and telling him how all the ladies must fall in love with him. We wonder how children come so early to like pageantry and show: And yet all children are taught to be proud of their cloaths before they can put them on. Is it strange they should continue to value themselves upon their outside, and to like dress and gawdy apparel when their parents have so early instructed and inured them to do so? Strephon, if we would reflect as we ought upon these very common practices, consider the force of early impressions, notions and habits, and withal call to mind that hunger and thirst, and a very few other appetites excepted, all the rest presuppose some previous idea of good or ill.—If we would, I say, duly ponder all this, we would not rashly charge nature with the perverseness and dissoluteness of the world, but be able to account for all the vices of mankind without blaming her, who will be found indeed to have provided us with no appetite or affection that is not necessary to us, necessary to make us capable of some noble acquisition or virtue.

STR. Enough, Damocles. To this source can I now trace luxury and voluptuousness in all its branches, avarice, false ambition, and indeed every vice. For now that you have by these few hints led me into reflection upon the necessary effects of our common ways of treating and breeding children, upon the common method in particular of rewarding them with sweetmeats, palatable food, strong drink, and the like things, which ought never to be represented to children as the greatest goods, nay as any goods at all, in comparison of wisdom and virtue.—When I reflect on all this, I begin to see plainly that there is hardly any irregularity or vice which children are not taught, which is not recommended to them, nay, which is not inculcated upon them. And in truth I wonder the more, this useful observation never occurred to me, that I have often found fault, and I think with good reason, with the lies, the equivocations and excuses little different from lies, not barely commended in children, but actually put into their mouths. Their cunning and archness we applaud as if it were wisdom. Their violence we praise as if it were spirit and courage. And when children are trained up in this way, 'tis indeed no wonder we find so much hypocrisy and so little true virtue in the world.[31]

DAM. I find, I need not insist longer on this subject, and therefore I hope by this time your anxiety is much allayed; for you see that it is not so difficult a matter as you may have apprehended, to train up a child in the way of virtue; or at least not to corrupt him. One thing only, because of your very laudable concern, I must tell you, which very probably hath already occurred to yourself, and that is, to beware of servants: For in vain will you strive to form your child well, if they are every day giving him quite opposite lessons. If you cannot be sure of keeping him intirely from them, pray let him go from you betimes, into a house where education is the business. I speak not for myself, because you know I must now retire from my business, should I call it, or the pleasure of my life. My infirm state of health calls upon me to quit what it disables me from doing. Take

31. So Quintilian, Inst. lib. 1. cap. 2. Quid non adultus concupiscit, qui in purpuris repit? nondum prima verba exprimit, jam coccum intelligit, jam cochylium poscit.— Gaudemus si quid licentius dixerint, &c. [Quintilian, *Institutio Oratoria*, 1.2.6–7: "If the child crawls on purple, what will he not desire when he comes to manhood? Before he can talk he can distinguish scarlet and cries for the very best brand of purple. . . . We rejoice if they say something over-free" (Loeb translation by H. E. Butler).] See Juv. Sat. 14. Pleasure and pain, according to Socrates, are the enemies virtue has to struggle with and conquer. Virtue signifies strength of mind able to resist temptation from the side of bodily pleasure or suffering.

my parting advice, which is, to watch over the associations of ideas (I may speak to you in this philosophical stile) which form, which the occurrences in childhood must form in every young one's mind; lest by this means any thing become a more honourable, pleasant, attractive idea than virtue and honesty. This is the sum of wisdom, and the sum of education.

STR. This lesson I shall never forget, nor the conversation that introduced it, and the friendly virtuous warmth with which it was pronounced. But pardon me, dear Damocles, we must not part yet. The substantial part of my question still remains to be considered. And that is, how virtuous habits may be early formed. It will but cost you a few words to satisfy me, if this be as easy to comprehend as the negative part (may I not call it so) we have gone through.

DAM. A hint of any thing is enough to you. And so it is indeed to all those who love truth and virtue. If we have but a heart good enough to desire to find wisdom we shall soon find her. Do you therefore ask me any question you please on the subject. Name me any virtue you would have early formed in your child, and I will tell you what I take to be the properest method of doing it: For it is but applying to a particular case the rule we have already fixed upon, which is, that it must be done by instruction, joined with discipline or practice, the latter of which is the chief part.

STR. I would rather have you to go on, and to choose any instances you think properest.

DAM. Let it be as you will. Only tell me what you take to be the cardinal virtue, the foundation, the mother of them all?

STR. I think it is the noble strength or fortitude of mind which the word itself originally signifies.

DAM. You are right. And that means a mind vigorous enough to make any appetite listen to reason, and take its directions from that faculty, which surely, has an original indefeasible right to govern all our motions and pursuits. This nursing mother of the virtues is called *temperance,* and she was properly painted like the parent of the Gods, old reverend Cybele, drawn by rein'd lions, patient of the bit, and on her head a turret-like attire, the image of defensive power and strength of mind.—But surely I need not tell you, that such a temper will never be acquired, if the child's cravings, much less, if his wilful, peevish cravings are readily complied with on the one hand; nor if he is teazed and crossed on the other without reason, or in a capricious arbitrary manner.

STR. This I am convinced of. Temperance consists in bearing and forbearing in obedience to reason. Youth therefore must be taught to bear and forbear, but still for good or satisfying reasons. But what if they are stubborn, and will not be satisfied by good reasons?[32]

DAM. There is little occasion to apprehend that, if they are early taught and inured to know, that what is good for them, if it can be given them, will never be refused them, and that nothing is ever forbidden them that is not really unfit for them. Teach them to moderate their desires, and to suspend giving satisfaction to their fancies and appetites till the reasonableness of them hath been considered, and never cross them when they are modest and reasonable in their demands, and there will be very little, if any necessity for the rod, which most parents use so liberally, after their children are grown up to a certain age, to correct faults of their own production. The patience of thinking being once gained, it will be easy after that to teach children any lesson, or to form not merely the ideas, but the principles and habits of liberality, or any other virtue in their minds. But how is this habit to be engendered and settled in them, but by accustoming them to submit their desires from their very cradles, and never yielding to their impatience. If they were thus used from the beginning, children would no more cry for other things than they do for the moon. This may seem harsh doctrine to fond parents. But let them consider how this practice will prevent the necessity of punishment, when the conquest will be very difficult. For appetites become strong and restive, in proportion as they are humoured and indulged. And at whatever times we ourselves would attain to the mastery of our desires, the first step must be, to be able to stop them, and keep them in silence. How happy therefore must it be for children, during the whole course of their lives, to have early and insensibly, while their affections were young and pliable, acquired the habit of staying the impetuosity of their fancies, and of deliberating with them-

---

32. It is said of Cato, that in his childhood he used to ask a reason for every document given him.

selves and advising with others about what is fit to be done or not done, before they take their resolution, and proceed to action! In fine, the great secret of education lies wholly in considering what influence any action of a child, or any indulgence to his desires, will have upon his mind: What habit it tends to produce, and how that habit will befit him, or whither it will lead him when he is grown up. For however small or trivial an action may appear in itself, yet custom is not a light thing, but of the last consequence. Strange! that the power of habit should be every day acknowledged by every one, and yet children should be treated as if there were no such principle in human nature; as if repeated exercises had no aptitude to settle habits, or as if habits could be as easily laid aside as one's cloaths. These things, Strephon, are too plain to need any further confirmation to you. Have you any thing else to ask?

STR. Forgive the weakness of a father, who fears he shall hardly be able to keep your excellent lesson in his view when his child frets and cries, and shews great uneasiness. I must beg you to explain a little further upon this article, of not yielding easily to children's demands or complainings. For methinks, you can't mean that a child should not be allowed to express his wants and pains to his parents.

DAM. There is a great difference, Strephon, between the cravings of nature and those of fancy. And therefore parents ought to distinguish between them. There are natural wants, which reason alone, without some other help, is not able to keep from disturbing us. The pains excited in us by the necessary demands of nature, are designed to be monitors to us of the mischiefs of which they are fore-runners. And therefore they must not be totally neglected, or even suffered unnecessarily to give us too great uneasiness, or to put us in imminent peril. The pains of sickness, hunger, thirst, cold, heat, want of sleep or rest, are what all men feel. The best disposed minds must and ought to be sensible of these uneasinesses: nay, it is duty to seek their removal by proper methods. But how? Not with too great impatience or over great haste, but with deliberation, patience, and sedate thought about the fit means of redress or relief. A person who cannot bear up, even under these necessary uneasinesses, to a considerable degree of fortitude and constancy, is far from being so firm and hardy, as adherence to virtue, as regard to the public, as compassion, as friendship, as several good offices of life will often require at his hands. What therefore must be the consequence of this truth with respect to education? It is indeed fit that children should have liberty to declare their wants to their parents, and those who have the oversight of them, and that they should be tenderly hearkened to. Austerity in refusing to hearken to them, far from serving any good purpose, must have this very hurtful effect, that it will quickly cool the affection which should be between them. But are not those two very different things, to say, "I am hungry," and to say, "I must have such a particular good thing, or I won't eat." Parents are bound to supply the necessary wants of their children, but children ought not to be allowed to choose for themselves, but should be inured to leave the choice and ordering of their food and cloaths, and every thing, to their parents or tutors. In truth, the more our children can be brought by mild discipline to endure pains, arising even from the necessities of nature, the better for them. Such endurance will make them stronger in body, and which is still better, stronger in mind. But whatever compliances the necessities of nature may require, the cravings of fancy ought never to be gratified; unless we would teach and encourage fancy to be ever inventing new wants. For in proportion as it is humoured and indulged, does it not become more impatient, more exorbitant and insatiable? Consider well, Strephon, how few the wants of nature are, in comparison of those of indulged, wanton, capricious fancy; and whence it is that virtue receives the fiercest assaults; nay, how far superior in number, as well as in force, imaginary evils in life are to real ones, and you will, by no means, think the discipline I have been recommending, cruel, tho' it were to cost children a great deal more pain than it can possibly do, if early begun. Take care to prevent the false associations of ideas that inflame the desires from which virtue runs the greatest risk; and you will by this means reduce the wants of children into a very narrow compass; you will early lead them to place their chief happiness where it is only to be found, i.e. in things wholly within their own power, the eternal goods of the mind. Wisdom and virtue are immortal as the soul, and nothing else is such. I remember, continued he, my tutor used to say, "That the great business of education was to teach youth early to distinguish between objects of industry, and objects quite beyond our power, and therefore objects of resignation to the divine will. Till the goddess Minerva, said he, had driven away the mist that overcast the eyes of Diomede,[33] and had cleared his sight, his bravery stood him in very little stead, for he could not distinguish between gods and men, but promiscuously attacked whatever opposed him." We cannot, without long and costly experience, except by the early help of a wise teacher, discern what things are the proper objects of our pursuit, care and industry; and what things nature hath put beyond our power to obtain. Education ought therefore to open the eyes of youth, dispel the mist which hinders us from observing this essential, important difference of things, and thus direct our labour and resolution towards the objects wherein they can have success; and teach and inure us to submit the things above our reach or power to the kind will of heaven, which manages all these to the best end, the greater good of intelligent beings. The former are men's, i.e. they are human things, things subjected by the laws of our nature to human power and industry: The latter are God's, i.e. divine things, objects not subjected to our command, but which the divinity hath reserved the disposal of to his own wisdom, that alone can comprehend the universal good the disposition of them is to promote.

STR. The similitude is admirable and full of instruction. For indeed if one does not keep this difference of things in his view, he cannot possibly direct his industry aright; that industry to which, it must be owned, heaven is not niggardly: For, as every thing we do, or can obtain, is done and obtained by it alone, so it hath abundant room to exert itself: It is able to make large conquests, or to acquire a very extensive and glorious dominion, if it be rightly applied and directed.

DAM. You fully comprehend my meaning. And if this be the rule in life, ought it not also to be the rule in education?

STR. It ought, and I can now see, how happy and wise due attendance to it in the instruction and discipline of children would very early make them, with much less trouble to themselves, or their parents and tutors, than the correction of any one passion costs, which, if suffered to prevail,

---

33. Socrates applies this story very pleasantly, much to the same purpose, in his discourse with Alcibiades about Prayer, in the second Alcibiades, near the end.

would be of very fatal consequence. I can now see, how the love of liberality, justice, and every virtue, may be early formed in young minds, by practising them in these virtues, and giving them just notions of their beauty and excellence.

DAM. You have yourself laid down the principle that ought always to be kept in view, and by which education should be directed, in your excellent definition of virtue, when you said it consisted in bearing and forbearing as reason dictates. Whence can virtue be in danger but from pleasure or pain? But if that be the case, then to breed virtue in a young mind, can be nothing else but to nurse the habit of hearkening to reason, and of not suffering pain or pleasure to lead us as they will, without controul. Now to do this, it is evident that the mind must be early accustomed to look upon every immoral indulgence as more contrary to nature, and a greater evil than any bodily pain.

STR. Alas! Damocles, how few arrive at this pitch of fortitude!

DAM. And whence is it so rare, but because men are not thus educated, but contrariwise, are taught and inured to prefer bodily pleasure to virtue, and to dread the smallest corporal pain more than the greatest vice? Let us not charge human nature with incapacity of such virtuous strength and resolution, as we have been discoursing of. For upon what pains and dangers do not men rush to gratify avarice, ambition, or revenge? Do not these passions by their strength often get the ascendant of self-love? Or why else do we so often wonder that men should run with their eyes open to their manifest ruin? But if persons can expose themselves to hunger, want of rest, nay, poverty, shame, racking torments, and even to death itself, commonly thought the greatest of evils, in pursuit of some imaginary good, that cannot stand the test of cool examination; how can we pronounce it impossible to beget by proper institution and discipline in young minds, true courage, even that which fears nothing so much as acting contrary to reason and virtue? We know it hath been attained, and that maugre the worst education, the most inveterate evil habits. And we know that falsely directed courage is not uncommon. The human mind must therefore be capable of true fortitude and magnanimity. But, Strephon, you will easily perceive, that in order to form this habit in the mind, children must not on the one hand be taught and inured to look on bodily pain as the greatest evil, or punishment; and therefore they must not be beaten for their faults; nor upon bodily pleasure as the greatest good, as the greatest reward; and therefore bodily gratifications must not be the recompenses of their good behaviour. For such discipline is diametrically opposite to the lesson and habit we have agreed is the main thing.

STR. How then, Damocles, would you have no rewards or punishments used?

DAM. In order to find an answer to this question, you need only ask your own heart, Strephon, what are its motives to good actions? What, for instance, makes you so concerned to do your duty to your son, and to give him a good education; to place more satisfaction in this laborious task, than in the pursuits of pleasure most other fathers indulge themselves in, without any thoughts about, not to say the public, even their own offspring? What motives do you think consistent with virtue?

STR. He alone is truly virtuous, who sincerely abhors moral evil as such, and places his supreme satisfaction in acting conformably to his reason and moral conscience.

DAM. Are there no other motives, which may concur with this principle, that is indeed the genuine spring of truly virtuous deeds?

STR. I know but one, and that is the desire of the esteem and love of wise and good men. This, I think, is very near a-kin to the love of virtue for its own sake, if it be not inseparable from it. It seems to me to grow up and strengthen in the mind, as virtue waxes stronger and more ardent.

DAM. Well then, Strephon, only consider what must be the natural effects of the rewards and punishments we use with children, and you will easily discover what they ought to be. Will not what is used as a reward be esteemed a great good, and what is used as a punishment be esteemed a great evil?

STR. They will, and therefore we ought to employ no rewards which ought not to be considered as goods, and no punishments which ought not to be considered as evils, and be motives.

DAM. What then are we to make use of as motives to excite children to virtue, besides the excellence of virtue and the deformity of vice?

STR. None other but what I have named as the only other motive consistent with virtue, viz. good reputation and disgrace.

DAM. And hath not nature implanted in all young minds a desire of esteem, and a sense of honour and shame, which, if rightly used, are very proper handles for turning children towards the sedulous improvement of their minds in wisdom and virtue?

STR. Of this I am very sensible. But perhaps you may have thought of some other motives besides those named.

DAM. No, Strephon, I know no other but those you have mentioned, duly extended.

STR. What do you mean by the ideas of the excellence of virtue and of good reputation duly extended?

DAM. Extend your thoughts, Strephon, from good men to the Author of all good, the Father and Governor of the universe, and then you will be at no loss to comprehend my meaning. For is not his approbation and love a noble, an invincible incentive[34] to steady perseverance in goodness? And if you dwell a little upon this great and comfortable thought, it will quickly lead you to another, which renders the cause of virtue compleatly triumphant, viz. That under his government, virtue must be a perpetual progress from perfection to perfection; and therefore virtue, when arrived by proper culture in this its first state of education and trial, to great maturity, will not be wilfully destroyed, but on the contrary, as it is in its own nature an immortal good, the seed of eternal and never-fading bliss, so it will be taken due care of and properly placed.

STR. You have indeed by a few words raised my mind to a very chearful sublime idea; a prospect, that while it is before the mind, makes all the temptations vice can offer dwindle into mere nothings. And this sure is a delightful view of nature, that ought to be early disclosed to young minds. O, Damocles, my child shall early know who taught me to instil into his mind those great and comfortable ideas, and to work into him those glorious habits you have taught me in this short conversation: He shall no sooner love me, than he shall love you, the source of all his happiness: And by pursuing the methods with him you have delineated to me, I foresee he

34. This is the doctrine of Socrates in his Phaedon, Alcibiades, Crito, &c. See likewise his Apology by Plato.

must very early be much wiser and better than I was, till my care about him happily sent me to you.

Thus were virtue and science taught. I might now tell you the health of young scholars was taken care of by discipline, then imagined equally necessary for the body and the mind. Indeed so equally are these two yoked by nature, that they do not require two different regimens, but one and the same course is best for both. As the mind is in a bad state, when its wanton, petulant and luxurious imaginations irritate the body, and make it feel wants, which, when left to itself, it would not feel, or as often as it so feels them, might be easily supplied: So the body is then in its soundest and pleasantest temperature, when it most easily and readily obeys the commands of a well-regulated mind. We are apt to throw the blame of several irregularities and disorders upon our bodily constitution, and to call many violent appetites, cravings of our material part, which are really vices of the mind, and do not take their rise from any wants or uneasinesses in our bodies, but from the dissolution, impurity, and tumultuousness of ill-disciplin'd affections. In truth many more ills are brought upon the body by the mind, than by the body upon the mind, viz. by not following the prescripts of reason in bodily indulgences, or not taking the proper care of our body, which it is the duty of our mind, the governing part, to do. So that Democritus had good reason to say, "If the body should bring an action against the soul for damages, the latter would certainly be cast." Plato recommends teaching youth early to know, that body and mind are like two horses in a yoke, that should draw pretty equally; and to consider, that as it is the chief good we can have from the body, if it be no obstacle to us in the study and practice of virtue; so while our body is preserved in that state, our soul performs its duty to it, and best secures it against the most painful feelings to which it is obnoxious. We are to remember how little the mind can be useful to itself or others, when we have brought sickness or disease upon the body by neglect of it, or which oftner happens by fondling and cockering it too much. Let us not therefore oppress or fatigue it, or exact greater abstinence or harder labour from it than it can bear, but keep in mind the fable of the camel and the ox.[35] "They belonged to the same master, and had been constantly employed for many years to work together. But the camel, on a certain occasion being wilful or peevish and restive, refused to draw equally with the ox. Upon which the ox sagely told him, if he did not, he would soon repent it; for he should quickly have the whole drudgery to perform alone, and without his help: And so it soon happened. For the ox died of his over-fatigue, and the master ever after made the camel do the work of both."

This story did Speusippus tell his scholars, when they happened to be over sedulous in their studies to the neglect of their bodies. But he had much oftner occasion to have recourse to some other apologue like this. "A certain sprightly horse continued in perfectly good plight, while he was exercised, rid out, or put to moderate work. But coming, unhappily for him, to be the favourite of his master, he was kept at home, spared, as it is called, and put to no drudgery but that of eating and kicking about in the stable, and thus he soon became very miserable, quite lifeless and dispirited, and loathing his food enjoyed no manner of satisfaction: tho' perhaps often envied by his companions in the neighbouring stalls, when they came in fatigued; yet he well knew them by sad experience to be much happier than he, and earnestly longed to be no more the darling but rather the drudge. The fond master perceiving a fatal change, but not discerning the cause, tho' in every other stable but his own he was very apt to give the lesson he never thought of applying at home, had recourse to physic, till the poor animal, formerly fit to attend and obey his master in every exercise, to the admiration of all who saw him, turned first vitious, and at last quite languid and stupid. And the master, in danger of losing his minion, curses the air, the season, the food, the doctor, and in fine, blames every thing but himself, the sole cause of the dismal catastrophe, which cuts him

---

35. Most of the things here said on health are to be found in Plutarch's discourse on that subject. There we have the fable of the camel and ox. Plato used to compare the ruling passion in the mind to a horse; and he sometimes compares the body to a horse, and reason to the rider.

to the heart, and yet perhaps will not hinder him from killing or spoiling the next unlucky favourite with the same cruel fondness."

But of health perhaps we may write on some other occasion, and there gather together the most remarkable observations and rules among the ancients about preserving it sound. I shall now therefore dwell no longer on this head, than just to take notice, that few diseases steal upon us, to use Hesiod's phrase, unawares and dumb, Jupiter having denied the use of speech to very few of them. Most illnesses have their harbingers, which going before them, loudly announce their approach. And youth ought to be taught and inured to attend to the heaviness and languor, the weariness, oppression and nauseating, and other symptoms which predict the coming danger, if proper precautions be not taken to obviate it: And to observe what are the causes of them in themselves and others. This will quickly teach them the necessity of sobriety, temperance and exercise; for from some defect or excess in diet or labour, do obstructions or unwholesome humours, and most other bodily disorders of the worst kinds proceed. " 'Tis a greater shame, said an old physician, for one grown up to man, not to know his constitution, so far, at least, as to be able to discern what is contrary to his health, but to be obliged to consult a doctor what he may safely eat and drink, for instance, than not to know what is bitter, sour, or sweet, weak or strong, without asking his cook. The latter only indicates want of palate, but the other want of observation and reflection." The necessity of exercise to health is obvious. The utility of health consists in its enabling us to be active and useful. And by activity is health preserved. As well may one think of preserving his voice by not speaking, or his eyes by not making use of them, as of maintaining the vigour of his limbs by indolence and abstinence from action. The exercise of the voice, in particular, in reading aloud or declaiming, hath been found by experience to be a very useful one to the breast and lungs of youth, as well as for preparing them to speak in public.

The other great rule about health is sobriety. As the mind is strengthened, and gains the mastery over its appetites, by refusing to listen too readily to bodily cravings, and duly chastising the fancies; so the more the body is used to abstemiousness and hardship, if there be no affectation of excessive austerity, the more the body is braced and invigorated. What

Simonides said of Silence, we may well apply to temperance and abstinence. "He had often, said he, repented speaking, but very seldom being silent." We may often have reason to repent of indulgence, but very seldom of moderation, or even of abstemiousness. Let us often reflect upon what Lysimachus said, when he and his army were reduced by thirst to surrender themselves to the Getae, after he had greedily drank a glass of cool fresh water, "Good Gods, said he, for how transient a pleasure have I lost the greatest of blessings, liberty!" This we have good reason to say, when we have brought any disorder or illness upon ourselves by a debauch, or any irregularity. Let the examples of others be set before youth, to warn them against dangers of this kind. As Plato, when he observed an error in the conduct of any person, used to retire and narrowly examine his own heart, whether there were any disposition or tendency in himself to such a fault: so let youth learn from the follies of others what they ought to avoid, chiefly indeed with respect to vice or misconduct, but likewise with regard to bodily disturbances. For is it not duty to ourselves and to the public, to guard against whatever may incapacitate us for being serviceable by our honest, well-directed industry? And must not the instruments and utensils be found and in good condition, as well as the head that is to employ them? Above all, said the same philosopher, let youth, if they would have sound minds in sound bodies, which two comprehend the whole of human felicity, be used to plain diet, and to look upon the art which racks its invention to contrive provocatives of appetite, with the same abhorrence the most voluptuous persons hear stories of the love-potions and charms practised by lewd women to inflame the blood of their galants. For at bottom where is the difference?

By such care as hath been described, from these schools came robust vigorous bodies, fit for any honest or useful labour, and equally strong minds to govern them. Young men entered upon life fit for it, and not novices to the world, in consequence of these excellent methods of education, so different from what are now established into practice, that the whole tribe of tutors and school-masters will hiss at the scheme, if they have as little wit as virtue, and if more of the former than the latter, endeavour to make appear ridiculous. Before I leave the subject, I will give you, my friend, a specimen of the railery I have heard thrown out against such methods of education. Mean time I tell you, till virtue can be made the object of true ridicule, this plan of education cannot be dressed in a fool's coat, or be turned into a jest. For virtue is its scope, and virtue can only be taught and formed by virtuous instruction, united with virtuous discipline and practice. If there be any such thing as truth, that must be true. There are several diseases of the mind I have not yet considered, such as timorousness, and which is the worst, the most dangerous of all bad habits in youth, sauntering. But I should weary you, did I not as often change the scenes as the unity of my subject permits me. And therefore, before I proceed to treat of them, I shall just observe, that what Plato and Aristotle have so much recommended, and did themselves put in practice in teaching (for they were both professed educators of youth, and gloried in the employment) was generally taken care of by all the other best masters among the ancient Greeks in education.

"'Tis ridiculous, said they,[36] not to suit education to the form of government established in the state. For if the manner of education be not congruous to it, the state builds with one hand and pulls down with the other." And accordingly from the schools throughout Greece, the youth went early into the world, fit not only to manage their private affairs, but qualified for the highest trusts and employments in the public service: well acquainted with the constitution and laws of their country, and highly enamoured of the liberty and happiness, which, whatever civil government hath not for its aim, is not government, but tyranny and oppression. Under tyrannies education was ever neglected, not merely because the more ignorant and dissolute men are, they are the better, i.e. the tamer and more submissive slaves; but because, as Alcaeus was wont to say, tyranny is sagacious enough to know, that arguments are nowise its proper weapons: You may subject minds to it, but you can never persuade into the love and approbation of what is so directly repugnant to virtue and human happi-

---

36. So Aristotle expresly Pol. 5. 9. [Aristotle, *The Politics*, 5.9.11–12.] That the best laws are of little advantage, unless the subjects are early formed and instituted suitably to them, &c. So Plato who uses the very phrase here made use of, pulling down with one hand, and building with the other.

ness. The picture of it may please by its likeness, as the images of the deceitful crocodile, or the savage tyger do. But the better drawn such pictures are, the more will they raise our abhorrence of the original monsters themselves. The liberty and general good aimed at by the constitutions of Sparta and Athens, however different these constitutions were, made pleasing representations. It was no difficult matter to breed an early liking to them in a breast where there were any seeds of public spirit. But the tutors of youth in those days did not satisfy themselves with making general panegyrics upon this or the other form of free government, but taught their pupils to attend carefully to the various changes different forms of government had passed through, and to distinguish the internal and the external causes of such revolutions. From such masters had Polybius learned to do more than pass right judgments upon the past, that is, to foresee changes and revolutions yet hid in their causes, and to foretel them, as, you know, he did with respect to Rome, at a very considerable distance of time before the causes, whence the fatal change of government sprung, began to develop themselves, and shew their direful prognostics, or were, so to speak, yet come to a head. This foresight into distant times has nature granted to us, i.e. put within our power to acquire, if we will apply ourselves to get it by looking carefully into history. For perhaps the moon and planets are not more regular in their motions, to the eyes of an astronomer, than human affairs are to those, who being conversant in ancient history, know how to discern futurity in the past, in consequence of the likeness of man to man, and of the sameness of human nature in all ages, i.e. the sameness or likeness of causes in moral productions and events. This is true political wisdom. And this wisdom were youth early taught how to learn from history, and the comparison of times and events.—"Such circumstances happened at a certain period, and such was the successful expedient or cure, or such was the fatal mistake and misapplication, and such were its direful consequences; and when these or the like circumstances shall again concur, the effects will be nearly the same." This was a lesson duly[37] inculcated by ancient preceptors upon their pupils from his-

---

37. See what Dion Cassius says of the school at Apollonia, where Augustus and

tory and experience, so soon as they had imbibed just notions of the end of government, the design of magistracy and laws, and of the true grandeur and happiness of man, and of society, which is but a greater one; and by this means a clear idea of internal security in a civil constitution against mal-administration, by a just division and balance of power.

Now that I am upon this subject, I can't choose but tell you; for at this moment the amiable, venerable sage is full in my view.—I cannot, I say, forbear telling you, how my own tutor, who had survived several revolutions in the Roman state, and was throughly acquainted with all that history hath preserved to us, concerning ancient republicks or monarchies, and their struggles, commotions and vicissitudes—how he used to talk to his pupils on matters of government, which we observed to warm him more than any other subject.

"I know, said he, all that happened to Sparta, to Athens, to Carthage, to Syracuse, to Rome in particular. I have studied their respective constitutions, I will explain them all to you, and impartially compare them with you in the course of my lectures. And let me tell you, I do not wonder men were so long of understanding, or being able to find out the best model of civil society. For how can men, how indeed can any creatures, learn causes and the effects of causes, but from observation and experience? As costly as the teacher is, there is, there can be no other. And tho' the more complex the lesson be, the more danger there is in mistaking and judging wrong, yet a complex lesson must be as difficult as it is complex, and therefore it must require long and various experience to teach, i.e. to illustrate and confirm it. The happiness[38] of mankind depends greatly upon their falling into rightly modelled society or good government. Men can do very little singly, or without confederacy and union. Yet if civil union be not rightly constituted, it were better to live disunitedly, or without any other

---

Maecenas were sent to be educated, even at that time, and judge from hence what the Greek schools were before. And call to mind what is said of Isocrates's lessons, and his manner of teaching, and what he himself says of education in general, and of education in the schools of Athens in particular, in his Areopagit.

38. There is a very remarkable reasoning to this purpose, in Hippodamas Thurius, a Pythagorean philosopher. This author is in Mr. Gale's collation of Greek tracts. "In order to be happy, one must live and die, says he, in a well constituted government," &c.

links but the links of humanity or pure nature. But the best form of social union is the most complex and difficult of all lessons. It is a lesson which many dismal catastrophes in human affairs alone can teach. As many revolutions of the moon are requisite in order to learn such a knowledge of that planet's motions as men can render subservient to their uses, in navigation and otherwise, so many vicissitudes and revolutions of various kinds in different states, are absolutely necessary to shew men to men, and to develop fully to them the nature and operations of moral causes. The lesson is in itself difficult, setting aside all other considerations, as how, for instance, the passions of men blind them or shut their eyes, and hinder them from discerning truths, again and again confirmed to them by the most evident and indisputable experiments.—But as complex and difficult as it is, yet the sagacious penetrating Aristotle,[39] tho' born and bred up in a republic, was able, by his skill in political history and theory, to see there was another form of government, the world had not yet seen, which alone can stand firm and unshaken, and which when once rightly poised and fixed on its basis, will never totter.—A government compounded of democracy and monarchy, so as to make a perfect equilibre. And, said he, raising his voice, and with a warmth like one inspired, surely after long experience of the changes in ancient republics, and of the dismal consequences of absolute monarchy, there shall at last arise, in some happy country well situated for extending with commerce, the knowledge of liberty, and of all the blessings that attend it, over the world.—Surely the true mixture of popular and regal government, shall at last be found and settled in some fortunate isle. And the happy constitution is in itself eternal. It will not, it cannot in the nature of things arrive any where at compleat perfection all at once, but the idea being once formed, and the rudiments, as it were, of this glorious work laid, various struggles between king and people, and between the different ranks and degrees of subjects, will gradually justle the blessed composition into durable tranquillity and fixedness. But when I say tranquillity, I mean only as great tranquillity as is com-

---

39. So likewise Polybius, so Dionysius Halicarn, so Zeno in Laertius, so Cicero apud Non. Marcell. so also Tacitus. The passages to this purpose have been quoted by most modern political writers, and need not be again repeated.

patible with human passions and mortal affairs. For even after this happy government is fairly settled, as it were, upon its centre of gravity, the noble spirit of liberty, which is the soul that must preserve and actuate this whole, will not seldom boil, and produce very violent effervescences and commotions. Contests about power in the administration, the natural effects of abounding genius and capacity for rule, and perhaps necessary to keep the cord strait and duly balanced, will not unfrequently be in danger of cracking it. Nothing on earth can be perfect, or remain long undisturbed. But this government, whenever it happens to be once fairly and fully established, tho' it may be often shaken and convulsed by the winds of contention and faction, yet will shew itself to be by its product the best and most durable, as well as the most beautiful tree in the garden of the world. It will bring forth in great abundance the noblest souls, the greatest virtues, the most perfect arts, and the widest commerce, that ever blessed or adorned any state.—What was exceeding remarkable is, that here, he with a spirit yet more agitated and prophetic-like, cried out—I see the fortunate isle, and the happy time—But the prelude is awful and tragical.—Before this can happen, a race of domestic kings, blinded, by superstition or the lust of lawless power, to their own interest and glory, as well as that of their people, by opposing this glorious purpose, providence, in good will to mankind is resolved at last to compleat and finish, shall fall victims to their base, ungenerous aims; but these fatal examples shall teach future kings the true maxims of government, and their deserved extirpation open the way for a new royal line, of the people's free choice, who holding their prerogatives by the same tenure the people hold their rights, and greatly proud of this only honourable, because only lawful title to empire, will seek no other glory or happiness, but that of making liberty and happiness universal; and they shall be called, in future history, by a truly glorious, but yet unknown name, a race of patriot kings." He said, that once, after long meditation upon this happy frame of government, falling asleep, he had in a vision an obscure glimpse of the aera and name. But to interpret this sign none could be found.

The End of Part I.

Plutarchus Plasmatias:

BEING A

RECITAL OF CONVERSATIONS,

IN WHICH

The Sentiments of the best Ancients concerning Philosophy and Liberal Education are fairly represented.

Discite o miseri, & caussas cognoscite rerum,
Quid sumus, & quidnam victuri gignimur; ordo
Quis datus; ———— ———— ————

—Persius[1]

---

1. [Persius, *Satires*, 3.66–68: "Come and learn, O miserable souls, and be instructed in the causes of things: learn what we are, and for what sort of lives we were born; what place was assigned to us. . . ."]

Plutarchus Plasmatias

to

His Friend *Fundanus,*

Concerning Liberal Education, &c.

PART II

It is sufficiently evident, that it will be very difficult for men to attain to wisdom and virtue, if their minds have been depraved by wrong education, or if just conceptions of true happiness and merit have not been early impressed on their breasts, and the habit of self-government fully established there, by right instruction and discipline, timeously begun and steadily pursued. Adversity will be necessary to rouse and correct such, and will hardly be able to accomplish their reformation. All this experience proves by many melancholly examples. But to object against providence on account of our dependance upon the care of others, in what is principal with regard to our happiness, the temper and habitude of our mind, philosophers have shewn to be absurd in many respects. And a brief view of their chief arguments will neither be disagreeable to you, my friend, nor foreign to our subject.

'Tis certainly fit that the mind which is united with a body made to advance gradually to a full grown state, should enter into life in the same infant condition with its mate: They would otherwise be very unfitly paired and yoked. But because an enquiry into the reasons why our bodies are propagated, ripen and decline in the manner they do, would engage us too deeply in the explication of material laws and connexions; let us turn the tables, and confining ourselves to moral laws and their final causes, consider what would be the effect, were we not born into the world with infant minds, standing in need of culture, and to be formed by instruction and example: minds, in one word, totally depending upon the help and care which parents are instigated to bestow upon their children, by affections deeply inlaid into their hearts by nature for this end, and which children are by the same all-forming hand so well prepared to receive from their parents, by affections and dispositions corresponding as exactly to parental tenderness and sollicitude, as any two things in mechanism can tally: This is the case; and let us consider, if it were not so, what would happen? There would be no place for the pleasantest exercises, the sweetest and kindliest offices, the most endearing connexions, and the most tender, warm and affectionate emotions we can form any idea of. How rude and how dislocated (so to speak) would human life be, without the parental and filial ties by which mankind are now so closely knit together? Take away these relations and bonds, the dependance which constitutes them, and the affections so admirably adjusted to them; take these away, and we cut off the most delightful feelings belonging to human nature. Without them, what room would there be for what is in a proper sense denominated humanity? Wherever there is union and society, wherever there is any room for friendship and gratitude, for generosity, or any benevolent office, there must be room for giving and receiving, and consequently there must be reciprocal dependence.[2] Mutual wants are the sole basis upon which society can subsist. For what is social intercourse but reciprocal interchange of services, favours, and kind deeds? And therefore, in every state of rational creatures, there must necessarily be some mutual connexions and dependencies analogous to ours, by which they, like us, are cemented into one body.[3] But by whatever ties and bonds other reasonable agents may be coalited, 'tis matter of experience, that the helplessness of our infant condition, in respect of mind as well as body, and the

2. These affections, ties and duties are often mentioned by Plato and by Cicero. Plutarch has a Treatise upon the natural love of parents to their offspring.

3. The whole intercourse of life consists, as Cicero often says, dando & accipiendo [giving and receiving]. None can question the propriety of ascribing these sentiments to Socrates and other ancients, who is acquainted with them, or with the best modern moralists, who are ever quoting them, or referring to them. See Turnbull's principles of moral philosophy. [George Turnbull, *The Principles of Moral Philosophy*, 2 vols. (London: Noon, 1740).]

common dependance of mankind upon the sollicitude and prudence of their parents, with relation to their nurture and education, are one of the principal links by which we are bound together; and without this connexion, many cares, virtues and duties, which now afford us equally noble and agreeable employment, and without which human life would really be very listless and inactive, could not have place; there would be no foundation or occasion for them.

And hence, by the by, we may observe a fundamental mistake in one of the most knowing and wise of ancient law-givers, Lycurgus. For so far was his scheme of civil government from being adjusted to the original connexions of mankind, arising from the manner of our propagation, and to the affections correspondent to them, that, on the contrary, it was diametrically opposite to nature in this respect, being calculated to extirpate or exclude these primitive ties of humanity. And what was the consequence of thus opposing and counter-working natural principles? Do we not plainly see, from the character of the Spartans, that where the affections, called in a peculiar sense natural, those, viz. belonging to parents and their offspring, as such, are not humoured, or have not full and free scope to exert themselves, there true benevolence cannot grow up into the ruling passion of the heart, but instead of diffusing its benignity thro' the whole soul, thro' every appetite and affection, will be confined within narrow bounds, and allayed with a large mixture of ferocity and haughtiness, as it was in them?[4] There, under pretext that no affection might detract from or weaken the love of their country, but the latter might absorb all other attachments, children were taken early from their fathers and mothers, and educated as the children of the public, that they might know no other parents, and consequently no other obligation or tie but to the public. But the natural sentiments and affections, the workings of which exceedingly humanize the heart, being thus stifled in the very bud, their love of their country, maugre many excellent constitutions designed to prevent that effect, degenerated into a furious lust of conquest, which was not long of

4. This fault or defect Aristotle censures in the Spartan constitution and customs. See Mr. Rollin's observations on the Spartan state in his universal history.

engendering an insatiable desire of riches. They looked upon foreigners as if they had not been men; they treated their slaves or Helots with the utmost barbarity; and they lived with one another, and with their neighbours, in perpetual envy, jealousy and strife. In a word, they were rather fierce and savage, than generous, humane and compassionate: Even their women, laying aside their natural softness and tenderness, were so hardened, that they could behold the wounds and agonies of their expiring offspring, without shedding one affectionate tear, or feeling any degree of pity, any compassionate emotion. Some later philosophers, misled by the same error, have imagined that the unmarried man, who has no children or family to divide his care and concern with the public, will make the firmest and most daring patriot. But if many ties bind faster than one; and if frequent agitations of the mind naturally form a general temper corresponding to them, he who frequently feels tender affections bestirred in his breast, by natural excitements, to father, mother, wife, children, and other relatives, must have a much more sympathizing and benevolent disposition than those who are quite strangers to these generous, kindly exercises of the heart; and being interested in the public welfare by various ties and connexions, unknown to the other, he must be much more strongly and warmly engaged in its interests. More motives concur to animate and support his zeal and courage in defence of the commonweal; and whereas one seldom or never carried beyond private interest, by affections naturally engaging him in the concerns of others, may easily become too narrow, selfish and callous, to be very tenderly affected by the idea of the general good of those, to none of whom he hath any particular attachments; the heart, which is ever and anon called upon by some natural feelings to mind the advantages of others, being thus inured to go out, as it were of itself, is by these generous exercises kept so tender, so sensible to the interests of others, as hardly to stand in need of any impulse from self-interest to rouse it, when dangers to others, as dear to him as himself, demand his kindly helping hand, and brave benign interposal. Besides, what is it that properly deserves to be called public spirit or love of one's country, but rational intrepid zeal for a legal constitution, by which the general good of a whole state is promoted? But how can such zeal be lessened by a hearty concern in the interests of many particulars depending upon this constitution? As well may it be said, that with the more indifference we regard the several constituent parts of a house, or any such whole, the warmer will our attachment to that whole be, as that the natural affections which bind us to many of the members of a state, will weaken our concern for the state itself.

In reality, nature seems to have intended our natural affections to be springs for feeding and extending our benevolence, and for giving it a particular direction or biass, the due influence of which on every member of human society, would render every one truly useful in his sphere; and without which, any benevolent propensity would have been too general and vague. The mind of man is made to expand[5] itself gradually from parts to the whole, or to be warmed by particular affections into an universal love, that at last, in its full effusion, embraces not only all mankind, but the whole system of rational beings, and rises to the supreme Author of existence and happiness himself, whom such a heart naturally represents to itself as infinitely happy in the unerring exercises of boundless goodness directed by infinite wisdom. But the civil policy, which is not conformable in every respect, in this more particularly, to the great lines of nature's drawing, or to the structure of the human mind, and the natural dependencies, bearings and progresses of human affections, is as absurd, and consequently will prove no less abortive, if not pernicious, on account of its repugnancy to the laws of moral mechanism, than it is in any instance whatsoever of mechanism properly so called, to desert or counteract the established laws of nature, according to which alone can human arts operate with success: As such attempts can never answer their end, because the laws of nature are unalterably fixed by its author, and will not bend or yield to human fancy and caprice; so for the same reason, the former can never gain its end, the happiness of mankind, but will either produce

---

5. See the natural progress of the social principle elegantly described by Cicero de finibus, l. 5. c. 23. In omni autem honesto, &c. [Cicero, *De Finibus Bonorum et Malo-rum,* 5.23: "But in the whole moral sphere" (Loeb translation by H. Rackham).] And every one who is acquainted with the doctrine of Plato, knows that he placed the perfection of benevolence in the love of the first cause, who is called in his stile, the first and chief beauty and good.

nothing, or which is worse, bring forth unnatural and monstrous effects. As well may we pretend to abandon or neglect nature in husbandry and gardening, as in moral polity, or in what is principal with regard to it, education. In every thing universally the rule is to take nature's path, or to consult and follow her. But what doth nature more plainly tell us, than that our natural affections are not inlaid into our frame to be effaced or thwarted, but to have proper exercise, and by their natural outgoings so to interest us in the concerns of others, that our minds shall thereby soon become no less sensible to the happiness of our kind, than to our private welfare, and we shall feel our truest bliss to be proportioned to the extent and height of our charity or benevolence? And what therefore is more absurd than the philosophy that teaches us to contract ourselves within ourselves, and to divest our minds of all generous affections, except the politics which pretend to enhance and swell social love by draining or cutting off all its sources; to make the soul more humane, by retrenching all the humanizing affections; or in one word, to unite us more warmly and affectionately to the whole body, by taking off all the attractive forces, all the reciprocal endearments of particular members, by which they are strictly bound and knit together. Did the philosophers who have imagined that all the vast orbs which compose our mundan system, cohere and preserve their order by a common gravitation to a common centre, ever dream that this coherence would be stronger, if the several component parts did not attract one another; or that the general attraction would so much as subsist one moment without the other particular attractions? And yet however that may be, 'tis plain the human mind must rise from individuals to the whole; and such indeed is the virtuous constitution of our soul, that self-love but serves to wake the generous affections.[6] We soon find that the ex-

---

6. This constitution of our mind is very happily described by an excellent poet.

As the small pebble stirs the peaceful lake,
The centre mov'd, a circle strait succeeds
Another still, and still another spreads.
Friend, parent, neighbour, first it will embrace,
His country next, and next all human race;
Wide and more wide, th' o'erflowings of the mind,

ercises of the kindly affections are our best pleasures, and that if we truly love ourselves, we must seek our happiness from that source. All that self-love can do, is to rouse us to seek for gratification to our capacities of enjoyment: And experience soon teaches us, that our best, our most durable, our only satisfying enjoyments are of the social kind; or that there is no valuable gratification that does not some way lean or hearken to our species. What would self-love serve for, had we not particular affections and appetites; for these alone render us capable of enjoyments? But what are these affections and appetites, or what are their objects? Do they not almost all of them chiefly respect some things without ourselves; some things in others; their happiness, their love, their approbation and praise, their vindication or deliverance, and their liking and good-will. But what else is the natural tendency of these affections, but to humanize the mind, and form a generous kindly temper. Self-love may awake our particular affections; but by the out-goings of our particular affections, which are almost all of them of the social kind, the mind will be gradually softened into a generous temperature, and become throughly love and good-will. If self-love should contract the soul, it would, proportionably, as it rendered it less benign, render it less capable of the truest happiness. But every particular social affection hath a sweetening influence on the mind, and tends to establish a liberal disposition and habitude. This is the natural progress of the mind towards perfect universal benevolence; nor can the human soul be improved into the truly virtuous temper, but by giving a right turn to all its particular affections. The health and soundness of the mind consists in the sound or proportionate operation of each part; then is it in perfect order when every affection is in its due tone, and is neither weakened by, nor weakens any other equally natural to the mind, and equally useful in its proper degree and place. Here, as in the natural body, lopping off

Take ev'ry creature in of ev'ry kind.
Earth smiles around, with boundless bounty blest,
And heav'n beholds its image in his breast. Essay on man.

[Alexander Pope, *An Essay on Man*, 4.364–72.]

any thing but excrescences is maiming, and curbing or restraining any member beyond a due pitch is distorting.

But not to insist longer on this topic; to object against the Author of nature, on account of our being born in an infant state of mind, and dependent on education, what else is it, but to demand that knowledge should not be progressive, or that the laws and connexions of nature should be discoverable some other way than by experience in proportion to our situation for taking in ideas or views, and our diligence in comparing effects with effects, and deriving or infering general causes by induction from particular observations, than which nothing can be more preposterous? For if the knowledge of creatures must come from experience and observation, desire of information, docility to the experience of others, and the influence of example and imitation, are absolutely necessary to minds made to acquire knowledge for the regulation of their conduct by culture; and consequently to depend for their advancement in knowledge upon the progress, pains and fidelity of others. And therefore, if we add to this consideration the necessity of habit, or the absolute fitness that repeated acts should beget a propensity and facility of doing what hath been often reiterated, nothing remains for which nature can be blamed with respect to our formation in relation to knowledge or virtue, i.e. moral perfection and happiness. For as to our power or dominion, as it can only enlarge as our knowledge enlarges, so it is found to increase with it in such a manner that knowledge may justly be said to be power, natural knowledge, natural power, and moral knowledge, moral power. These things being duly weighed together with our large stock of natural and generous affections already mentioned, so well adapted to our circumstances, there is nothing for which our frame can be reprehended, unless it is absurdly required that there should be no species of creatures in nature but the very highest that can possibly in the nature of things exist; and we thus quarrel with our Creator for communicating as much goodness, as much perfection and happiness, as infinite power can produce. And indeed all the objections against man, into however many classes they are divided, ultimately terminate in this one, "Why is not man more perfect?" To which the only answer that can be given is, that such a species as man well deserves his place in the rising scale of created life, since he is naturally

furnished with powers, capacities, and affections capable of perpetual improvement, by due culture and diligence. All the objections against man,
or rather against the ways of providence towards man, are reducible into
one, to which this is a sufficient reply.—For whether we object against any
particular part of our furniture for happiness and perfection—or against
the scantiness of our stock—or against the dependence of men upon their
education, and the kind of civil government they chance to be born under—or finally, against the imperfection of distributive justice, with regard
to punishing the vitious, and rewarding the good in this world—all these
objections ultimately result in the same thing, and do not make different
difficulties, but arising from the same root, are not any ground of objection against providence; because that from which they arise is no ground
of objection against it; as will appear by this train of reasoning. "Deficiencies in distributive justice in the course of providence, or which comes to
the same thing, deficiencies or irregularities with respect to public happiness and misery, which are resolvable into the instrumentality of men, i.e.
into our mutual dependence upon one another, in respect of happiness
and misery, can be no objection against the present course of providence,
unless it be a relevant ground of objection against it, that we men are dependent one upon another; we men, who are made to attain to comprehensive views and virtuous habits by observation and exercise, or in one
word, by gradual culture. Distributive justice, or in other words, public
happiness and misery, must depend upon the instrumentality of men, as
far as the mutual dependence of men, one upon another, in respect of happiness and misery reaches. As far therefore as the imperfection of men
reaches, must there be deficiencies or imperfections and irregularities with
regard to happiness and misery, which can only change or amend as men
amend, i.e. as men become wiser and better. And therefore, ultimately all
such deficiencies or irregularities are accountable in the way that the present imperfection of men is accountable: They do not make a separate objection, tho' they be often stated as if they did; but being a necessary consequence from the imperfection of men, they stand or fall with the general
objection taken from it. But when we consider the natural furniture of
mankind for advancement in knowledge and virtue, and the natural rewards attending the suitable exercises of our moral powers, to bring an ob-

jection from the present imperfection of men against the wisdom and goodness of providence, is to impeach providence for having made a species of beings in order to make nature full and coherent, that hath in its power to attain to a very great degree of moral perfection, nay to make perpetual improvements.[7] For to demand more, in order to produce moral happiness and perfection, than having furnished beings with powers and means of improving towards it, is to require something that cannot be specified; because knowledge must be progressive; and virtue is in its nature a gradual acquisition, by perseverance in the right use of moral powers."

All this will be clearer, when we come to review the furniture of the human mind for acquiring knowledge and virtue, and to consider of what improvements it is susceptible in consequence of good education chiefly. Mean time, that we may make this introduction to that enquiry as perfect a vindication as we can, in so narrow a compass, of the ways of God to man, let it just be suggested here, that if false apprehensions which must produce practical errors, the understanding being the guide of the will and affections, if any errors or vices once enter amongst mankind, they will spread in consequence of the influence of information and example, and of the docility and pliableness of young minds; or their readiness to imbibe ideas from others, and to be easily moulded, by education and custom, into any shape, which, however, in consequence of the necessary power of habit, is not without great difficulty undone and effaced. But how can creatures be secured against false ideas, views or judgments, and their effects, otherwise than by furnishing them with the powers and means for taking in just ideas, and forming true judgments? To ask for more is to demand something that hath never been named, and has indeed no name, something absolutely inconceivable in a system governed by general laws, or in which the given powers operate according to settled laws. For frequent preternatural interpositions, to prevent false judgments, or the pernicious influences of false conceptions, upon the affections and will, are

7. Of this furniture we have noble descriptions in Plato and in Cicero, in the first book of his offices, and in his first of laws. Plutarch in his discourse of fortune shews us, that reason is power; all the powers of other beings in one.

absolutely inconsistent with a fixed and general order: But where the laws of powers are not general and uniform, there can be no intelligence, no activity, no power, and consequently no perfection or happiness of the moral kind: And therefore no inconveniences redounding from the fixedness of general laws, can be equal to those that would be the necessary consequences of arbitrary, undeterminable methods of government. In fine, the old apologue,[8] applied with such propriety and success to illustrate the pernicious tendency of dissention between the higher and lower ranks of people in the same civil state, is equally apposite to the objectors or grumblers against providence. For not only are all the common powers and affections of the human mind, with all the laws determining the different effects of their operations in different situations and circumstances, as necessary to the general good of the human mind, as all the members of the body, and all the mechanical laws on which their operations depend, are to its common good: But the various functions for which the several parts of this latter whole are designed and admirably fitted, are not more requisite to its greater perfection and good, than all the various powers and affections, all the different genius's, turns, tempers and capacities of men, are to the greater good of the human system, or of mankind in general. And indeed there can be no whole without variety of parts; and then is a whole good when all its parts are so fitly contrived and assembled as to constitute the best structure for a particular end, worthy of being effected; and then are all the parts of a whole good, when the whole composed of them is good in that sense. If any should say, That if this be the case, then are the worst of characters amongst mankind necessary to the general good or perfection. A little attention to the similitude above used, will shew the absurdity of such an objection. For as it cannot be said, that because all the parts of the human body are requisite to its greater good and perfection, therefore bad eyes, and unsound feet are requisite to the good of the body; so for the same reason, it cannot be said, that because all the powers and affections belonging to mankind are necessary to the greater good of the human system, therefore, corrupted powers and affections, or powers

---

8. This apologue is often used on different occasions by ancient writers.

and affections not in a sound but in a depraved state, are requisite to the greater good of that system. The meaning in both cases equally is, that the organs and faculties belonging to the body, and the powers and affections belonging to the mind, are good with respect to their respective wholes, because the functions they are fitted to perform, while they continue in their sound state, are so. As when we say the human body is a good whole, we do not say whatever happens to the eyes or ears, &c. is good for the whole, but that these organs are well adapted to perform certain very useful and pleasant offices; and are disturbed by no natural cause, the prevalence of which is not exceeding useful with respect to the material world in general; so when we say the human mind is a good whole, we do not say, whatever happens to reason, memory, temper, &c. is good for that whole, but that these powers and faculties are admirably adapted to perform certain functions of the greatest utility, and are disturbed by no natural cause, the prevalence of which is not exceeding useful with respect to the human system in general. And this way of reasoning makes a full solution to all objections against providence, whether in the government of the material, or the rational and moral world, provided this also be kept in view, which is incontestable, namely, that where there is no activity, but a mere succession of impressions and affections, without willing, preferring or choosing, there all is done by some external principle, and nothing is acted, but all is received by, or rather imprinted upon the passive recipient, as is not improbably the case with regard to many species of inferior animals: But where there is a sphere of activity, or the power of willing or choosing, and of effecting things by will, there nothing is imputable to any external principle or cause, but the powers and affections given to such agents by that cause, and the laws regulating the different effects of the various exertions of these original given powers and affections, by will or choice, likewise appointed by that cause. The wills or choices of such agents are solely imputable to themselves. This is likewise to be remembered; for where there is activity, it will not follow that the powers and affections given to agents are not good, because many exertions of them are very bad. But that we ourselves are active, that is, will and nill, and by willing and nilling determine the existence or non-existence of several effects subjected to our will by the laws of our nature, cannot be called into

question without denying experience, and so plunging ourselves into absolute scepticism, and pronouncing all sollicitude, all industry, all praise
and blame absurd.[9] If we are active, then, in order to vindicate providence,
and the Author of nature, no more is necessary but to vindicate our powers, and the laws of our powers, for that only is the Creator's part; the exertions of our powers are our own part. But that we have a sphere of activity, is as certain as that we are, because it is known or certain, by the same
immediate experience which assures us we exist. All I would further suggest upon this head is, that when certain ancients speak of fate, and say all
things are governed by fate, they meant by fate, the words,[10] the laws established by the Creator, according to which all things are produced: The
word signifies a law, or rule of some mind: The fate therefore that governs
the world according to them could be no other than the laws appointed
by its Creator. And the same philosophers distinguished these laws into
laws which constitute the $\tau\alpha$ $\epsilon\phi$ $\eta\mu\iota\nu$ with respect to the various classes of
moral agents, and the $\tau\alpha$ $\delta\eta$ $\epsilon\phi$ $\eta\mu\iota\nu$[11] with respect to them, or the effects
and trains of effects absolutely independent of their wills: And conse-
quently, according to the same philosophers, all was governed by general
laws, and by the general laws of nature each species of moral agents hath
its dominion or sphere of activity allotted to it, which it is their duty and
interest to know, that they may not misplace their sollicitude and industry,
but successfully bestow it on things dependent on their will, and submit
all the rest cheerfully to the disposal of the Governor of the universe, upon
whom they alone depend. If sometimes destiny or fate is said to be superior to the supreme Being himself, the meaning of this was only, that certain relations of things, one to another, are absolutely unalterable, so that
the Creator could not give being to certain things, and properties of
things, and prevent or exclude certain relations and consequences of these
things. Thus the Creator cannot make bodies move in circles, and their

9. The distinction between the $\tau\alpha$ $\epsilon\phi$ $\eta\mu\iota\nu$ [things in our control] and $\pi\alpha$ $o\nu\kappa$ [things
not in our control &c.] the foundation of morality, according to the ancients, is well
known. [See Aristotle, *Nicomachean Ethics*, 1111b30, and also Epictetus, *Enchiridion*,
1.5.4.]
10. See Plutarch of fate, and Arrian upon Epictetus.
11. [See note 9, above.]

orbits not have the properties of circles: Thus the Creator cannot give the capacity of improving in knowledge, and not make this capacity dependent upon care to improve it. To assert fate in this sense, is no more than in other words, to assert the immutability of the natural relations of certain qualities to other qualities.

From this short view of the principles upon which the vindicators of providence and human nature proceed, 'tis evident that the arraigners of providence and human nature take a very partial and incompleat view of things, and do not attend to the beautiful and wise concatination of causes and effects in the moral world, but often blame the effect while they acquit the cause, or *vice versa,* censure the cause while they approve the effect. But the chief stress of the matter lies upon a point, which will be further cleared up by the enquiry into what right education is able to do, which is our present chief scope, and the excellent furniture and constitution of the human mind, in respect of all moral improvements. Neither the necessity and happy effects of good education; nor the admirable capacity of the human mind with regard to advancement in knowledge and virtue, and in happiness proportionable, can be brought into question, when we call to mind the high perfection to which several great personages in ancient and modern times have arrived, and reflect what a large share of their eminence and merit were owing to timeous institution in all the more useful sciences, and which is chief, in the excellence of virtuous conduct, and the turpitude of every vice, joined with suitable discipline and practice.

Lycurgus is said, in order to recommend his laws[12] and institutions to his citizens, and to withdraw them from the corruption and effeminate pleasures in which they were at that time plunged, to have took care to breed up two whelps, the one a grey-hound, the other of a currish breed, in ways opposite to their natures: The former he kept at home, and fed him with good meat, but the last he often carried into the fields to hunting: After having bred them up in these different ways, he brought forth both before the people, and set down good victuals on one side, and let out a hare on the other; upon which the dogs did each pursue his usual

12. Plutarch in Lycurg. and Valerius Maximus.

turn; the greyhound fell greedily on his victuals, the other run after the hare: Then he said to the people, Do you see what a diversity of breeding hath brought about between the two whelps, and what power it hath over them? The remarkable differences between the Lacedemonians and the Sybarites, in consequence of different education, are a strong proof *in specie* of the point we are upon.[13] And indeed we see the power of education, even in smaller things, to be such, that it cannot fail of having a most delightful and valuable success in matters of higher importance. We are told of one Telesias of Thebes, that having been instructed in the true grave ancient music, the only music that anciently made a part of education, from his youth, he afterwards suffered himself to be seduced by the softnesses of the theatrical music, and set himself to the study of those, amongst all the compositions of Philoxenus and Timotheus, that had most the air and character of novelty: But yet when he came to try to compose in the gout of Pindarus, and that of Philoxenus, i.e. both in the ancient and modern taste, he failed intirely in the latter, because the precepts impressed on his mind from his tender age had kept the ascendant. But why should we insist upon these topics? For how much did the greatest men the world ever saw, by their own confession, owe to their happy institution, and how grateful were they to their preceptors on that account? And who dare reproach human nature for incapacity, either of knowledge or virtue, the sublimest knowledge, or the most exalted heroic virtue, if he reflects upon the attainments and lives of many, whose names can never die? They cast us at a distance, and upbraid us because they shew us what we may attain to, and that what we unjustly call natural impotence or weakness, is really no more than contracted indolence, or something worse, for which we have ourselves only to blame? For who ever failed of

13. Plutarch tells us, that the Sybarites brought up their children in the bosom of lazy and idle voluptuousness, whereby they suck'd in various vices, as it were from the breast, and before they could know them. But the Lacedemonians nourished their children with sobriety and without delicacy, inured them to fortitude, temperance, and virtue, &c. The inhabitants of ancient Crete, now Candia, and those of the Islands Baleares, now Majorca, Minorca and Yvica, used to hang up their sons' breakfasts, which, if they had a mind to get, they were to fetch down with arrows, and this made them such famous marksmen.

obtaining knowledge or virtue, who having set his heart upon it as his chief treasure and good, sedulously pursued that glorious mark? Or what more is necessary to be wise and good, nay to conquer the worst habits, and emerge out of the lowest abyss of ignorance and vice, but to dare to make due efforts to rise and to persevere in this brave attempt? 'Tis true, such must first be awaked to perceive their mean and vile state. But what is there about us, that is not continually suggesting to the vitious, their horrible degeneracy from reason, and the dignity of human nature, and often raising remorse in their minds, amidst all their sensual joys, or rather revels? Who is so profligate, so absolutely abandoned by reason, that the beauty of virtue, and his own deformity, never present themselves to his mind? All nature conspires in calling upon us to act like men, i.e. like agents endued with reason, and capable of attaining to the highest perfection; capable of immortal progress in knowledge and virtue, if we be not wanting to ourselves. This is the general voice of the order and good nature pursues in every part of her creation; and with this external voice of nature, our inward conscience, whatever pains may be taken to stifle it, is not unfrequently joining issue, even in the most corrupt breasts, and in times of the most general depravity. Nature must cease to shew her wisdom and virtue in her works, and true goodness to have any lovers and followers among mankind, or the light of a wicked man's understanding must be quite extinguished, before his conscience can cease from reproaching and disquieting him.

But if men may arrive early at a great height of prudence and virtue, by means of right education,—what is right education, or how ought education to proceed? Suffer me to give you an account of a conversation on this subject I had lately the happiness to hear. The persons are well known to you; and it happened on this occasion. Simias is a curious naturalist, and bestows a great share of his time in his garden upon the culture of plants, flowers and trees, especially since he retired from public business, whether out of discontent with the administration, as his friends say, or much against his will, to prevent the disgrace of being discarded, which he saw would not be long of happening, after certain changes at court, as others pretend. He was busy in his garden, when Palemon came to pay him a visit, who, you have heard, is a great admirer of the Socratic doctrine, and hath long given himself up intirely to moral studies, and is indeed an amiable pattern of the strict virtue he lets no occasion slip of praising and recommending, in opposition to a sect from whose professed principles one, as he is wont to say, could not expect to find half the generosity and public spirit their actions often shew: For their system is, that freedom from care and trouble is the chief good attainable in human life. No person is more beloved, even by those against whose doctrine he is ever disputing, tho' they now and then call him an enthusiast.

After a few civilities were interchanged, they fell into conversation about agriculture and gardening, in which Simias shewed uncommon acquaintance with natural history—and Palemon not a little satisfied with the excellent observations his friend had entertained him with, upon the wisdom and goodness that appeared in every vegetable and animal structure in nature, with which we are become intimately acquainted, by the researches of natural philosophers, took at length an opportunity to say, I find, my good friend Simias, that I have been in a mistake about natural enquiries, and have unjustly looked upon them as mere amusements, that had no relation to the main part of philosophy, morals; for I now find, that what you admire, and what gives you most satisfaction in your researches into nature, is the wisdom and goodness you there perceive in every fabric, in every constitution and oeconomy; so that the wisdom and virtue men ought to adore and imitate is never out of your sight.

So far, said Simias, you are right; 'tis indeed the discovery of the wise final causes nature pursues, that makes the most agreeable part of natural philosophy; and here do I choose to turn my eyes, that I may see what delights me; for as to all other things, they lie enwrapped in such thick darkness, that I cannot look towards them without being fretted, if not sour'd.

PAL. Many naturalists appear not to carry their views so far, and to aim at nothing but contenting their curiosity or itch after novelty. But however that may be, what do you mean by saying all the rest is involved in absolute darkness? Sure you cannot mean that moral things are more remote from our investigation, or more difficult to be understood than natural things. For is it not as easy to turn our eyes inward, and contemplate the structure and operations of our mind, as to inspect and anatomize vegetables with the help of microscopes: nothing that passes in our breast can escape our close introspection, if we are attentive, but the naked, unassisted eye can make but little progress in the other research.

SIM. What you say appears very plausible at first sight.—But when we come to the trial, we find the human heart to be a complicated labyrinth, in which we soon lose ourselves; and in order to be convinced how little certainty there is to be expected in this enquiry, which you represent to be so easy, we need only call to mind the various and inconsistent accounts moralists give us of the human mind. They agree in nothing of any moment. And no wonder; for the external eye is not liable to half so many diseases which disqualify it for its functions, as the eye of the mind. Every man, before he can think of this kind of philosophy, hath some ruling passion or other, which gives its own colour to every thing he considers, whether in himself or in other men. So that all moral objects assume just as many various aspects and hues, as those who look to them have different passions and tempers. Nor is it any wonder, that in reality the same moral object should have such different appearances to the same person, since every man's disposition is ever varying; but the present passion, whatever it be, is the glass thro' which every one sees them, and which gives them their present colouring. In short, not to mention many other insuperable difficulties attending moral enquiries, a person must be quite dispassionate to see moral objects in their genuine forms. And where is this person to be found? If moralists are unanimous in any point, it is this, That we must first be able to judge soundly of the temper of our own mind, before we can trust to its judgments about moral things. But where does this rule land us? For in order to judge soundly of our present temper, we must first know the various appearances with which different tempers cloath objects; and to do this, we must have examined all different tempers, and their influences upon the understanding: that is, we must have considered all the tempers, all the passions which may have for ever so short a time the ascendant in the human mind, quite dispassionately, or without any predomining passion, which can never happen while man is man.

PAL. You carry your scepticism about morals very far. But you own that you can discern order, wisdom and goodness in the natural world, don't you?

SIM. Yes, there I see many clear instances of wise and good contrivance, which highly charm me, and putting me in good humour, dispose me fondly to believe that all may be good.—But no sooner do I turn my eye towards the only part of the moral world within our cognizance, than my good humour is changed into disquieting doubts, or rather fears—For how full of villainy and misery is every region in this system? And now that you have revived my suspicions about the constitution and government of things in this chief part of nature, let me tell you, that the most perfect order and beauty in the material system, cannot attone for one blunder or mistake, and much less for any degree of malicious intention in the moral: 'Tis not from the architecture or furniture of his palaces that we infer the moral character of a prince. These may put his intelligence and good taste of architecture, painting and gardening beyond all doubt. But to be satisfied of his wisdom and virtue, we will look carefully into the government of his family and subjects, and form from thence our judgment of his share in the more essential and important qualities of a governor. However all other things may be managed, 'tis only from his sedulous care to promote virtue and reward it, and to make happiness as universal as may be, by a strict and impartial adherence to constitutions and laws, the best upon the whole, that we can pronounce him truly wise, and virtuous or benevolent. Tho' you may tell me that material laws and connexions are only good or evil, in respect of the manners in which perceptive beings are affected by them, and that therefore good laws of matter and motion, are in reality good moral laws, yet surely moral laws and connexions are of the higher and more important class: And therefore it matters but little, comparatively, in how orderly and wise a manner, vegetation, animal growth and sensation may proceed, if the constitutions and laws relating to moral powers, i.e. to our understanding, our will, our affections, or in one word, to virtue and vice, be not likewise the best upon the whole.[14] But here we are quite in the dark, and can hardly affirm any thing positively: Here philosophers split into various factions, each of which hath its favourite sys-

14. The question about moral providence was always reckoned that of the greatest moment in the enquiries into the nature, being, and government of the supreme cause, and is evidently so.

tem, insomuch, that scarcely do they give the same account of any one phenomenon.—Nay, what consistent account can they possibly give of a system so full of disorder and confusion?—Where is true virtue to be found?—Or where it is, how is it rewarded? Vice sprouts up so fast, so naturally in the human mind, that a good man is as rare as a monstrous animal, and no less houted at or ridiculed. How can the soil, the climate, or any thing, be said to be favourable to a plant, which rarely appears, or at least very seldom comes to any perfection in it? or if it does, must force its way thro' a croud of most offensive weeds, which hardly leave it suffi-cient nurture while it lasts, and sooner or later choak, if they do not taint it.—But let us turn away our eyes from this gloomy scene, and forgetting, if we can, the wild confusion that reigns thro' it, solace our minds with a prospect in which all things so exactly obey the best laws, that nothing here is obstructed in its natural progress toward the beauty, perfection and utility of its kind, but by the overpowering force of some law, equally nec-essary to the general perfection of the material system. For here we are able to discern that nature is never deficient, never irregular, but even then op-erates according to the best order, when she seems to less knowing spec-tators most to deviate from her rules, or to fail of her general aim. All the most pernicious effects of air upon vegetative or animal bodies, for in-stance, we know are the consequences of properties belonging to our at-mosphere, without which there could be no such thing as regular vegeta-tion or animal growth.—But you smile.

PAL. It pleases me to think what joy it will give to a mind so enamoured of beauty and harmony as yours, when you come to see all, that you now take to be confusion, to be perfect order and harmony.

SIM. Of that I have told you I despair.

PAL. But sure you are not peremptorily determined not to hear the rea-sons which satisfy a friend that it is so.

SIM. I have heard, my good friend, that you are a very warm defender of moral providence: But I am apt to think your good opinion of the moral world is more owing to your generous turn of mind, than to rational conviction. I have already observed to you, that we never see moral things in their true colours, but in those which they receive from our prevailing passions.

PAL. Were this the case, you would seldom think ill of the moral world. But I am willing to submit the grounds of my belief to your examination. And in order to bring you over to my side, I demand nothing more to be granted to me than you have already done.

SIM. What was it?

PAL. That you can discern wise and good contrivance in numberless vegetables and animals. For by wisdom and goodness doubtless you mean the pursuit of good in the whole frame by the simplest means.

SIM. That is indeed the very thing natural philosophers admire in every animal or vegetable constitution; and they readily confess the wisdom and good order of the sensible world, or that as far as they can carry their enquiries, this maxim is universally true, "That nature does nothing in vain."

PAL. I might then ask you by the by, whether it be a bad thing in our make, or a bad prognostic of the event before we go further in our researches into the human mind, That we find it qualified not only to discern simplicity and wisdom, but to receive high delight from the view of them.—But dropping this consideration for the present, tell me what you want to see with regard to the human mind, but similar wisdom and goodness to that which you acknowledge in the sensible world, i.e. to see it to be framed and furnished in the best manner for a noble end.

SIM. Nothing else indeed.

PAL. Is it not a presumption, that upon enquiry we shall find wisdom and goodness in the fabric or anatomy of the human mind, since we see such proofs of them every where in vegetable and animal structures? For are not human minds principal parts of the same system; and what likelihood is there that the Author of nature has exhausted all his skill and benevolence upon inferior things, or that he either could not, or would not manage the more important parts with equal prudence and benevolence?

SIM. However the presumption may stand, before we look into the moral part, we no sooner cast our eyes thither, than we perceive as clear evidences, either of want of skill, or of malevolence, as we see of order, good taste, wisdom and beneficence in the natural world. I did not expect you would argue with me from the presumption you have mentioned, after I had told you what appeared to me to be the true state of the case. But that you may keep more strictly to the point, I once more tell you, That what confounds me is, that I should see disorder where order is most to be wished and expected, notwithstanding the good order I discern in the less momentous connexions of nature and their effects.

PAL. I did not design to stop where you interrupted me, but was going to add, That what we have reason, when we turn our eyes from the admiration of nature, properly so called, i.e. the sensible world, towards the moral, to presume, we shall find to be the case, is upon enquiry immediately perceived to be the real truth of the matter. For, upon the slightest review of the human mind, it is found to be furnished for a very noble end, being furnished for being happy, by the benevolent exercise of very extensive power. We can have no other notion of perfect happiness, but by conceiving a Being happy in the benevolent exercise of unbounded skill and power. And tho' there may be beings far surpassing man in their dominions or spheres of activity; yet man must certainly be confessed to make a very proper step in the gradation of created beings, if he is indeed invested with a very large dominion, and is at the same time qualified for exercising his power in a benevolent way. For such a state well deserves its place in nature; nature without such a species of beings would not be full or coherent; but such a species of beings would be wanting as is very well furnished for great happiness. Do you consent, my friend, that being made for the benevolent exercise of very high power, is being made for a worthy, a very noble end?

SIM. I do. But I am far from thinking man either hath large power, or that he is made for the benevolent exercise of power. And to prove he is not, what more is necessary than to appeal to the impotence, misery and wickedness of man. In reality, with regard to us, it is hard to say, whether our vices or our wants are most numerous. And therefore this new way of stating the question, for it is new to me I acknowledge, rather augments than diminishes the difficulty, as far as I can yet see.

PAL. It matters not whether the way I state the question be new or not, have you any objection against trying providence in this light, i.e. by considering whether man be not made for the benevolent exercise of very large power.

SIM. Why, indeed, if you can prove this, you will gain your point, I own. But I say, you seem to me to heighten your labour by departing from the more ordinary way of stating the enquiry.

PAL. How is it that?

SIM. Do not you know the question is commonly reduced to this point, viz. whether man be sufficiently furnished for progress in virtue, and our progress in virtue be sufficiently rewarded?

PAL. I thought if I stated the question so, you would have required a definition of virtue, and therefore I began by giving a definition of virtue before I used the word. But so soon as you had agreed to admit the enquiry into moral providence upon the footing I have put it, I was to have asked leave to have called, "being qualified for the benevolent exercise of large power," in one word, "being qualified for virtue;" because I think the best definition that can be given of virtue is the benevolent exercise of power, since, according to this acceptation of the word, agents only can be called virtuous or vitious; and virtue and vice will be applicable to all agents, and denote the sole moral difference which can distinguish exercises of power, namely, malevolent or benevolent intention; for differences of power as to extent, i.e. greater or less, are natural differences.

SIM. I agree; for when words are once fixed to a determinate sense by definitions, why jangle about them? Your business is to shew, 1. That man is made for large exercise of power; and 2. That he is made for benevolent exercise of his large power.

PAL. It is so. And as to the first, pray, let me ask you, if you can tell me the extent of human power or dominion in the natural world?

SIM. Speak more plainly if you can, for I hardly understand you.

PAL. Is there not acquirable by man a vast dominion over material things? Are not all the arts of human invention, by which men are able to render material things subservient to our uses, effects of our power; or do they not give us actual dominion? And are all the invented arts yet at their perfection; or can human invention go no further than it has already done, in rendering natural things subservient to our utility? But as far as human genius can reach in inventing or improving arts, is not man able so far to extend his power?

SIM. I now comprehend you. But alas! my friend, how very lately have arts been brought to any considerable degree of perfection, even the most necessary ones, and how very slow do they proceed?

PAL. Can arts prevent knowledge; or must not the knowledge of nature precede the invention of arts?

SIM. It is plain that arts being rules, by observing which certain effects may be produced which are taken from nature's laws, the knowledge of nature's laws and connexions must be first in order, or come before arts.— But is it not all one, whether I say human knowledge is very scanty and slow, or that human arts are very narrow and slow?

PAL. It is. And therefore, since in the natural world our power keeps pace with our knowledge, if man be very well furnished for great progress in natural knowledge, is he not well made for knowledge?

SIM. To be sure, being well made for an end, and being well furnished for that end, are equivalent phrases. But how can man be said to be well furnished for attaining a large share of that which he has with great difficulty and very slowly been able to attain to but a very pitiful portion of? And this is our case with regard to natural knowledge.

PAL. Tell me, pray, do you think it good reasoning to say, one hath not attained to an end, therefore he is not furnished for it? As for instance, would it be good reasoning to say, a person who has sound limbs and good health is not able to walk, because he never uses his legs, but chooses to loiter in supine indolence? Or would you say one is not fully furnished for doing good to himself and others, who has a large estate, because he neither enjoys it himself, nor makes others the better by it?

SIM. I would not.

PAL. Then by consequence, you will not say man is not sufficiently furnished for acquiring knowledge, because he does not exert his abilities for acquiring it. Again, let me ask you, whether you think it a better and nobler state of being to be furnished for acquiring goods by the skilful application of proper means; or to be directed, or rather impelled to fix upon certain enjoyments by blind instincts, without foresight, choice, contrivance, and actual efforts of power?

SIM. I do not hesitate to pronounce the latter the nobler state of existence. And I must grant the consequence I foresee you are about to draw, viz. That then the only question about man must be, whether we are furnished for acquiring a large share of natural knowledge; not, what we have acquired, but what we are qualified to acquire. And I will therefore yield to you, that man is furnished for acquiring very extensive knowledge and power in the natural world. And I heartily wish men would apply themselves to extend this their dominion on earth, by giving due pains to cultivate natural philosophy, the mother of all the useful or ornamental arts.

PAL. Are we not then come to enquire how we are furnished with respect to moral power?

SIM. We are.

PAL. But here I need not repeat, that knowledge must precede power; nor that the question is not, what we have acquired, but what we may acquire by the furniture nature hath put into our hands, or invested us with.

SIM. What we have already agreed upon with respect to natural knowledge, is equally true in this other case.

PAL. Nor need I tell you, who are so well acquainted with the powers and charms of poetry and oratory, and with the principles of politics, that there are moral arts, i.e. arts drawn from the knowledge of human nature, by which noble effects are gained. Therefore, let me just add one question.

SIM. What is it?

PAL. Will not these arts enlarge or improve with moral knowledge? They cannot precede nor exceed it. But as they must be drawn from the knowledge of nature, of human nature in particular; so must not the experience of various operations and effects of moral causes be antecedent to their deduction?

SIM. I do not perceive what you propose to infer from hence.

PAL. What I would observe from hence, you will quickly perceive to be of very great moment. It is this, men must have been for some time in the world without several arts, because they must have been some time in the world to have had experience of the connexions between effects and causes, from which alone all mechanical arts are deducible. However necessary some perfection in the sciences of agriculture, weaving, building, &c. be, to the comfortable subsistence of mankind, yet experience, supposing whatever degree of attention you please, must have preceded these arts.—In the same manner, not to mention any grounds or causes of greater difficulty in moral sciences, 'tis evident that men must have been for a considerable time without them: that is to say, that however necessary the science of politics, for instance, is to the happiness of mankind, yet long experience of the different effects of moral causes in their various combinations, must have been antecedent to the science of politics.

SIM. I grant it, and own the observation is new and important.

PAL. What remains then, but that I should set an inventory before you of our furniture for acquiring knowledge? Call therefore to mind our senses, our memory, our reason, our imagination, and together with them our sense of harmony and beauty, our delight in comparing effects, and in tracing them to general laws—all which powers are capable of such high improvement, and that very early, by right education, and of giving us, by their improving exercises, such exquisite pleasure and satisfaction. As for our standing in need of culture, and depending upon education, surely you will not object against it. For 1. first of all, how infinitely superior is the pleasure in training and cultivating young minds, to that of training and cultivating plants or flowers! 2. Moral power can be nothing else but power over the understandings, imaginations and affections of moral agents; and as man would be a lower creature, and have much less power, and but very mean employments in comparison of what he now hath, had he no moral power, so did we not come into the world with raw unformed minds, to be open'd, enlarged, and formed by the care of others, man would be deprived of one chief branch of his present moral noble power and business. And which is yet more, 3. We have already observed, that knowledge is in its nature a progressive acquisition, which presupposes experience; but want of immediate experience may, and can only be supplied by the experience and information of others.

SIM. I see very well the necessity that knowledge should be progressive, and consequently a necessity that beings, however well furnished for acquiring knowledge, should stand in need of the experience of those who came before them into the world, and be the better or the worse, according to the neglect or care of those others about them.—And I likewise acknowledge, that teaching and improving the young is a very pleasant work when it is successful. But how rarely it is so, we shall see by and by, when we come to the main part of your assertion, which is, that man is well furnished for the benevolent exercise of power.—Mean time I can't help saying, that men are far from being upon an equal footing with regard to knowledge. On the contrary, however well some may be provided for that acquest, the greater part seem to have no furniture of this kind at all, or at best but a very niggardly provision. And why this partiality?

PAL. I might urge that different degrees of education and of industry, diligence or application, necessarily make such differences amongst mankind, that it cannot be positively said, that there are very great original differences amongst mankind with respect to intellectual furniture.—But setting aside this consideration, which whatever way it be determined, does not much concern the question, let me just suggest to you, That it is manifestly necessary to the general good, that very many men should, either in consequence of certain original differences with respect to their intellectual abilities, or in consequence of circumstances, which by their different influences upon the same original faculty, will produce nearly the same effects as certain original differences would produce, be fitter for execution by bodily labour than for invention: Or in other words, the general good requires, that men should be, as it were, divided by nature into the labouring or executing part, and the consultative or directing part, as we in fact find them to be; tho' we cannot positively say whether it be in consequence of an original partition of abilities, or of such a disposition of the causes and means which excite and bring forth original abilities into exercise, as makes the same variety. This, I say, is necessary to the general good of the human kind. For the comfortable subsistence of mankind requires many hands to execute what a few heads may invent: And in general, without dependency there can be no room for the social exercises, which all consist in giving and receiving. But whereas in the present division of mankind, the executive and inventing or consultative part mutually stand in need of one another, and mutually work for one another, without this division, there could be no mutual dependance amongst mankind, since all mutual dependence must arise from mutual wants, balanced by mutual abilities; and as abilities, so wants can only be either of the bodily or of the mental kind. The human system is indeed, my friend, either by original make, or in consequence of circumstances, producing the same effect, an aristocracy,[15] consisting of the few capable of directing, and of the many more fitted for labour. But were it not so, what would be the effect? There would, in this case, be no place for the agreeable moral exercises of advising, directing and ruling, the natural generous employments of superior wisdom, which carry their own intrinsic rewards along with them; for in order to teach, improve, direct or rule, there must be subjects standing in need of teaching, improvement, direction and rule: Moral, as well as natural power, presupposes subjects or objects about which it may exert itself. Invention, or study and knowledge, by diligent researches into nature, are necessary to guide and direct labour; and the intense thinking requisite to progress in science, is not very compatible with much bodily drudgery: Yet without agents well fitted for labour and toil, knowledge would be of little use; for tho' knowledge be the proper food of the understanding, yet man cannot subsist upon meditation or science; and therefore now, while one part adds to knowledge for the common good, and another acquires by their labour for the common good, both parts are equally useful one to the other, and to the whole; both are mutually dependent; both give and both receive; and for this reason, the division is as equal as may be, consistently with the good of the whole. Further, tho' there be a very great pleasure in giving, yet there is also a pleasure in receiving: The exercises of gratitude are not much inferior in point of satisfaction to those of generosity. But by the natural division of mankind, the former are not wholly on one side, and the latter on the other, since the labouring part do not less need the inventive than they do the other. We might here, my friend, apply the ancient apologue, and say, let not the eye therefore, or the ear and the other different parts of the body, say to the hands or to the feet, I have no need of thee, and so forth.—But to one of your penetration, I need only subjoin to what hath been said, that many political maxims or rules, necessarily ensue from this natural partition of mankind that hath been mentioned, the non-attendance to which hath produced not merely absurd notions, but ridic-

15. This natural inequality of mankind was well-known to Aristotle. See his Ethics and politics.

ulous, nay hurtful attempts in the framing of civil government. Hence, for instance, you will easily see, "That there can be no such thing as a perfect democracy." The attempt, the idea is as repugnant to nature as making the earth a plain, and levelling all the hills and mountains.

SIM. You have crowded many things together here, which are very new to me, I confess; yet I comprehend them, I think, well enough to be able to retain them, till I have leisure to examine the chain of your argument carefully by myself.—Mean time, let us go to the main point, which is, How we are made with respect to benevolence? For I think, at present, the natural aristocracy among mankind would have beautiful and happy effects, were all mankind sufficiently benevolent or virtuous. But sure you cannot say they are.

PAL. I am far from saying they are. But remember what we have already agreed upon, in general, that the question, whether about knowledge or power, or virtue, cannot be, what we are, but what we are fitted and qualified to be?

SIM. That was, and I think must be granted.

PAL. If it must, this question will likewise be soon and easily dispatched; for let me know, pray, what you would reckon sufficient qualification or furniture for benevolent exercise of power, which we have agreed to call virtue, if ours be not? Have not men a sense of the beauty of good actions? Can they contemplate them without approbation? Or can they consider malicious actions without detestation? Have not mankind high pleasure in the exercises of generous affections, as well as on reflecting upon the good actions they produce? And are there not many generous affections belonging to human nature which strongly unite us together? And how difficultly are these affections quite erased out of our minds? How hard a task is it to become quite selfish, and to cast off all regards to others, to parents, to children, to the distressed and suffering, however remote from us; and to feel no resentment against injury or wrong, as such, but when it immediately affects ourselves? In fine, look into your own heart, and tell me what nature hath not done to make you benevolent and good. And then tell me what reason you have to think that every heart is not originally provided with the same stock of benevolent feelings or affections; since we can easily tell how the good affections may be weakened, and how contrary ones may be introduced and become strong; and since we know that man must fly from himself, i.e. shun all correspondence with himself, not to be proportionably miserable, as he is wicked or malicious, tho' placed in the most luxurious circumstances of outward enjoyment.—Methinks I see you consent to all this:—But perhaps you are puzzled by what is commonly called the capital objection against providence.

SIM. I never dispute for disputing sake—and therefore I own I feel the force of what you have said.—But I was just going to state my difficulty to you. Two things have often perplexed me, 1. Why vice sprouts up so naturally in young minds? And, 2. Why vice is suffered to be so prosperous, so triumphant, while virtue generally involves in hardships? Let me hear you upon these two points separately, if you please; for I find you are indeed master of the subject.

PAL. What do you mean by saying vice sprouts up naturally in the human mind?

SIM. Why? do we not see children not only peevish but malicious, before they can utter their ill-nature and tyranical disposition otherwise than by signs?

PAL. I know some have said children are wicked even before they can think. But pray reflect upon the common methods of training up children, even among good parents, and you will not wonder to see passions carefully nursed in children from their first entrance upon life, become early very strong. Because thro' indulgence and flattery, they love power, flattery, dress, being humoured, lording it over others, and have even luxurious palates very early, does it therefore follow, that they are naturally more capable of vitious affections and habits than of generous and virtuous ones? Reflect, that in spite of this corrupt education, and of the bad courses it leads youth into, before they can make serious reflection on the conduct of life; especially, when instead of taking pains to accustom them to reflection, they are rather inured to dissipation, thoughtlesness and wilfulness.—Reflect, I say, how in spite of all this, yet even the worst of our youth, when they come to the years of maturity, cannot totally shun remorse, but reason, of itself, and maugre all neglect to cultivate it, nay all the habits directly repugnant to reflection, often paints their villainy to them in very disgusting colours, and shews them their deformity by holding the glass of their duty to them, in which they clearly see at once the beauty and excellence of the virtue they ought to pursue, and their own vileness in consequence of immoral indulgences. This is universally the case with all men. And what may be concluded from these considerations with regard to our natural furniture for progress in virtue, I leave to yourself to judge: For I do not apprehend that you, who own a beauty in sensible objects, really distinct from deformity, will deny the reality of the moral distinction, i.e. of beauty in virtue, and of deformity in vice. I shall just add therefore, that all the sweet influences of the poetical arts upon us, set it beyond doubt, that our constitution is really benevolent and virtuous. For when or how do these arts charm or please us, but by interesting us in behalf of merit, and exciting tender, compassionate and generous feelings in our minds.

SIM. You are so ripe upon the subject, that I am resolved for the present to give you full scope, that I may learn enough from you of your system, to be able to see at my leisure hours how it hangs together. I will therefore make no opposition to what you have said, that you may go on to answer my second objection.

PAL. You indeed take the proper method of judging of any philosophical system, which is not to object till the whole is laid open: We must here, as in judging of machines, have an idea of the whole before we can form a just notion of single parts.

SIM. This I am convinced of; and therefore you may proceed, if you please, to tell me what you think of the present triumph of vice. You remember the old fable of the dog and the vulture, the moral of which is, that avarice thrives and amasses riches, while modest virtue starves. Is not this the case? In one word, is not the present dispensation of temporal or external goods, as they are called, rather in favour of vice than virtue? Do not tell me they are not real goods because they are so bestowed, and that they are given in this manner by heaven, in order to shew of how little value they are.—This is too *stoical* an answer for me at present.—And far less would I have you to tell me, that this unfair distribution shews there must be another life, in which the distribution of good things will be much wiser and better. For whatever stress may be laid on this argument, it appears to me very preposterous, it being, in reality, to say in other words, That the Governor of the universe now errs, but he will at last correct his error, and become a better dispenser of his bounty.—But contrary to the resolution I had taken, I have interrupted you too long.

PAL. You will own, doubtless, that there are rewards naturally accompanying virtue; or that there is a true peace and joy which virtuous consciousness alone can give. And you are now speaking only of external goods, all which may be reduced to riches, since riches will purchase all external pleasures; wherefore your question comes, in short, to this, "Why do riches ever fall to the share of the vitious, or why are not the virtuous the only persons who enjoy great wealth?" I know I need not caution you, that by riches I mean large property, whether money be in use or not.— Now, in answer to this, let any value be put upon external goods you please, and do you only tell me what purchases them according to the established laws of nature. Is it not industry that acquires or amasses them? Are they not the price of toil, whether the toil be virtuous or vitious? And ought it not to be so? Ought not they to be acquirable by the diligent use of certain means to acquire them; or would you have virtuous industry alone to succeed? Think what this is to demand. For is it not to require, that it should not be in man's power to put out his hand to any purpose, unless his intention be just, generous or benevolent? Is it not further, to require that the sun should only shine, and the rain only fall upon the gardens and fields of the honest? All this, I think, is too plain to need any further illustration. But if the acquisition of external goods be the effect or purchase of industry, according to the laws of nature, as knowledge, virtue, and all internal goods likewise are the fruits of labour and diligence to acquire them.—If this be the case, then are not external goods dispensed arbitrarily in favour of the vitious, but they are purchased according to one general excellent law of nature, the prevalence of which has been confessed in all countries and ages of the world, by some proverb equivalent to this, ωι Θεοι τα᾽ αγαθα τοις πονοις πολουνται, God sells all his gifts to industry. Some persons of less penetration than you, might reply to this, "Do not vast riches drop into the mouths of the sluggard by odd chances?" But you will immediately see, that the succession of a worthless heir or legatee to an estate, or getting one by a lottery, and other such events commonly called casualties, are no objection at all against the truth and reality of the general law of industry. And yet if industry be really the purchaser, insomuch that it is never disappointed but by crosses arising from certain laws of nature, necessary to constitute regular means towards the attainment of ends, without which there can be no science, no industry.—If this be true, as experience plainly shews it to be, then does the best law with regard to acquisitions that can be conceived take place, and all that is said of promiscuous distribution of goods in this world, is false in fact. You desire to hear me out. And to this my first answer I have but one thing more to add, which is, That beings cannot be made for society, without being made to be instrumental in promoting one another's happiness; or which is the same thing, without being dependent one upon another, as to their happiness and misery.—And consequently, the happiness of any district or neighbourhood of men, and of mankind in general, will depend upon their manner of uniting to assist one another.

SIM. What are you to infer from this?

PAL. That the improvement of arts and sciences, and the progress of virtue, the two main articles in human happiness, and the plenty or abundance of external goods, and their proper circulation, will depend necessarily upon the manner in which districts or neighbourhoods of mankind join and unite, in order to promote the common good.—Discord will not produce the good effects of union, nor will one kind and manner of social union produce the same effects as another.—But if the more wisdom, benevolence and industry there is among mankind, the greater always is the common happiness; and if we are sufficiently impelled by several feelings natural to us, to benevolence, and are sufficiently excited by pleasure in the exercise, as well as by the necessity of it, to industry, then are mankind very well constituted, i.e. then is the constitution reproached as much in favour of virtue as it can possibly be; and then are all irregularities, inequalities or deficiencies in respect of happiness not imputable to nature, or to our frame and constitution, and the laws according to which our powers work and produce their effects; but solely to want of industry, or to want of benevolence, i.e. to what we are, and not to what we are made or fitted to be and to do by nature. You are well enough acquainted with nature, my friend, to know that all bodily pains and diseases are the effects of the same excellent general laws of matter and motion which hold the sensible world in the order which is so beautiful to contemplate, and which produces so many external conveniencies, delights and goods.—And you are equally well versed in politics, to know that a right form of civil government, in which the education of persons of all ranks is upon a good footing, would produce a very orderly and happy state.[16]—But if all this be true, we are certainly furnished by nature for a noble end, a very noble acquisition; and being so fitted and placed at present, what ground of fear can there be that well acquired moral powers will be maliciously stop'd short in their progress, and totally demolished, or allowed to subsist, and yet be worse placed hereafter than now? This, my friend, is a short view of my system, as you are pleased to call it. But let me tell you before we part, it is not mine; but has been the system of the best and wisest sages of antiquity. It is as old as any art almost; it is, at least, as old as philosophical enquiries.

SIM. I am pleased to have had this opportunity of hearing you; and will, before we meet again, recollect and carefully examine over and over what you have said. All the recompense I can give you is, that I will not henceforth allow you to be called an enthusiast: For never did I hear any person reason upon his own scheme with so much coolness as you have done; and indeed had the delightful idea fired you, and thrown you into extasy, I should not have been surprized. For whether it be true or not, it is certainly a most comfortable belief to imagine, that all is constituted and governed with the most benevolent intention for the greater good. As for what you have so often hinted concerning education, I have indeed been long disposed to think, that were due care taken about it, human affairs would soon alter their face, and we should consequently have much less reason to find fault with nature; the causes of our present complaints would be exceedingly abated.

PAL. All I desire of you is, to pursue this thought thro' all its consequences, and to remember, that it must be absurd to blame nature for what wrong education produces, or for what might be mended by good

---

16. How much do Plato, Aristotle, Cicero, and all the ancients, insist upon the advantages of a good and the disadvantages of a bad civil constitution?

education, unless we can likewise, with reason, blame nature for making our gardens to depend upon our skill and industry. In truth, as a friend of mine is wont to say on this subject, "The objections against moral providence are no better than demands that nature should have built houses and bridges, and in one word, done all for us, instead of furnishing us with powers and materials, and thus fitting us for having the satisfaction of working for, and acquiring to ourselves and others, the noblest of all enjoyments."—But it is time to part. Plato says well, that were education but once set upon a right footing, virtue and happiness would flow from generation to generation in a perpetual and uninterrupted course. Farewell.

This conversation I have repeated, in order to render justice to the human mind and its Author, by pointing out the noble end for which we are made; or the excellent faculties with which we are endued, that are susceptible of such high improvements by due culture. Nature hath not given us virtue: nay, nature cannot give us virtue, because virtue means an acquisition made by a moral agent himself: But nature hath made us capable of attaining to great virtue, great moral perfection, by adorning us with the capacities requisite to such attainments. And from the same discourse it is easy to collect what ought to be the lesson in liberal education.[17] The doctrine or lesson that ought to be taught is, That the Author of nature is wise and good in all his works, and hath made us capable of attaining to perfection and happiness, by imitating him in wisdom and goodness, or by making the good of our kind the end and rule of all our actions. And how is this lesson to be inculcated, but by shewing youth, instance after instance of wise and good contrivance in the natural world, beginning with the most simple examples, and proceeding gradually to more complex ones; and by leading them from the contemplation of beauty, order, wisdom and goodness, in natural objects, to the consideration of the admirable structure of the human mind, or of its excellent furniture for attaining to the knowledge of nature's wisdom and goodness, and for imitating it; and from thence to the examination of what civil society ought to aim

17. This is Socrates's constant lesson, as we see from Xenophon and Plato.

at, and of the manner in which it ought to be constituted, in order to answer the great purpose of it, which is to promote virtue and public happiness, by producing a regular, orderly and wise society. All the parts of this
lesson hang closely together, and make one very regular pleasant progress.
And as for the science which is necessary as a key to let us into the knowledge of nature's laws in most of her productions, with regard to the motions and appearances of the heavenly bodies in particular, that science being itself a continued train of doctrines concerning the harmonies and
proportions of things, it hath in itself a wonderful influence towards harmonizing the mind, and improving our taste and love of order, proportion
and harmony, and was for this reason called by Plato a purifier of the
mind. And on that account he began very early with geometry, for this is
the science we are now speaking of. When one's mind is well stored with
real knowledge of nature's wisdom and goodness in her works, and well
acquainted, not only with the rules of wisdom and goodness relating to
private conduct, but with those also, which, because they respect societies
of men, are properly called political rules: When one hath attained to great
perfection in this knowledge, then may he be said to have been well instructed or educated, and to have a well cultivated or improved mind; to
have wisdom to be a light to his feet, and a lamp to his paths; wisdom
qualifying him for acting a right part in every circumstance of life, and for
doing great good, and being substantially useful to mankind. To replenish
the mind with this knowledge is the proper business of education. And
how pleasant a work must it be, to have our minds always entertained with
delightful views of wisdom and goodness in nature, and of the happy and
beautiful effects of similar wisdom and goodness in private behaviour, and
in the administration of civil affairs? Whatever be the natural object with
the wise and good structure of which we are charmed, the transition from
hence to the consideration of our duty and dignity, consisting in the emulation of this wisdom and goodness by our actions; or of the happiness,
strength and glory, the equal execution of wise and good orders, constitutions, or laws in society would naturally produce, this transition is always
natural and easy.—We do not in this manner pass from one thing to another, that hath no relation to it, but we make a proper progression from
the moral perfection of the Author of nature, displayed in all his works, to

the moral perfection of mankind, either considered singly or in collective bodies. Some may perhaps say, How then have languages, and the polite arts place, according to this scheme of education? Now, how all the arts, which either prove, embellish, or recommend and enforce any truth, come in or have their place, while the philosophy that hath been briefly delineated is the one lesson, may easily be conceived, by reflecting, that whatever truth youth are led to the knowledge of, they ought, after they are convinced of it by clear and strict reasoning in the didactic way, to be shewn what not only oratory and poetry, but even the pencil hath done or may do to adorn, beautify and inculcate that truth. Before we part with any truth, proper specimens may be brought of what each ornamental art hath done in its province, to set forth that truth in all its lustre and charms, and by this means, to make it touch and sink deep into our heart. For, when the mind hath been often agreeably moved by proper specimens of the power of these arts, then will it be easy to explain to youth the general rules to the observance of which their agreeable influence is owing. And till then, an attempt to explain either the rules common to all the arts, or those peculiar to each art in particular, is preposterous. For the effect, that is, the influence of an art upon the heart, must be known by having been often felt, before we can enquire into the causes which produce this effect. Here, as in other parts of nature, the particular experiences from which general laws can only be inferred, must precede the inference of general laws or rules. It is preposterous, for instance, to speak of the general rules, the observance of which renders a dramatic piece compleat, by making it capable of producing an excellent moral effect upon the mind, before those we speak to are well acquainted with the influences of dramatic pieces upon the human heart: But after one hath been used to and exercised by them, the foundation of the rules to be observed in such compositions will be easily perceived. And it is just so with respect to all the other arts for the same reason. All this, my friend, I conceive, you will find no difficulty in comprehending. But let me add, that teaching philosophy in the manner that hath been briefly hinted, will have but little success, unless it be accompanied with a proper regimen or discipline: unless with teaching be joined care to practice youth in self-government, in acting deliberately and rationally, and in controuling and ruling all their affections.

Practical habits can only be formed by repeated practice. Teaching may enlarge and enrich the imagination and understanding: But if the rules of wisdom are not actually conformed to in practice, we will only be theorists in virtue, and not really virtuous. Youth therefore, at the same time that they are instructed in the proper tone of every affection, and in the place, degree and rank it ought to have in our minds, in order to maintain and uphold that just balance in which the health and beauty of the soul consists—at the same time that they are taught how they ought to rule and govern themselves, they ought to be trained and habituated to right government.

But the truth of this observation, or the necessity of joining discipline with virtuous instruction, will appear more fully by taking a view of the affections belonging to our minds, and considering their uses, or the ends for which they are implanted in us by the Author of nature, and the manner in which they ought to operate. Now all our affections may be divided into two tribes or classes; the family of joy and the family of grief, or the family of love and the family of hatred. But let us go thro' them all as they occur to us; for 'tis no great matter in what order we consider them. Let us begin with curiosity, or our passion for novelty, our delight in regularity, and the admiration with which great objects strike us; for these are the inciters to philosophy, reading or study, and the affections which are chiefly gratified by them, and they are very nearly allied.

Curiosity in children, what else is it, but a natural appetite after knowledge, fitly implanted in our minds to spur us to the search of knowledge: It was fit new objects should please us, that we might thus be excited to be daily adding to our treasure of science. All our knowledge, all our enquiries, are reducible to these two heads. What a thing is? and what it is for? And 'tis remarkable that children, when any thing new comes in their way, by the direction of nature ask first, What is it? whereby they ordinarily mean nothing but the name: And therefore, to tell them how it is called is usually the proper answer to that demand: Their next question usually is, What is it for? And to this it should be answered truly and directly; that is, the use of the thing should be told, and the way explained how it serves to such a purpose, as far as their capacities can comprehend it, and so on with respect to any other circumstances they shall ask about not turning them away till you have given them all the satisfaction they are capable of, and so leading them, by your answers, into other questions. Their enquiries ought not to be slighted, but their curiosity ought to be fostered and encouraged by satisfying it. For we ought to remember, that they are travellers newly arrived in a strange country, and that it is cruel not to give them all the information we can, and much crueller still to deceive and mislead them. And indeed, whatever others may think, a wise man will chearfully embrace every opportunity of attending to the native and untaught suggestions of inquisitive children. For there is really much more to be learned from the unartificial questions of a child, than from the discourses of men who follow the notions they have imbibed from others, and the prepossessions of education. Here there may be affectation or artifice, but there nature guides, and speaks its undisguised inbred sentiments. We ought by no means, to check or discountenance any enquiries a child may make, nor suffer them to be laughed at; but we should rather commend their desire of information, and explain the matters they are curious to know, so as to make them as intelligible to them as suits the capacity of their age. We ought to mark what it is the young mind principally aims at by the question, and not what words he expresses it in. And not to confound his understanding with explications that are above, or with a number of things that are not to his present purpose, but to come down to his capacity, as much as possible, and give him the fullest and plainest answer we can. And when we do so, we shall see how his thoughts will enlarge themselves, and how far beyond what is generally imagined young people can go, if they be led on by fit answers. For knowledge being naturally grateful to the understanding, as light to the eyes, children are pleased and delighted with it exceedingly; especially, if they see that their enquiries are regarded, and that their desire of knowledge is encouraged and commended. And it is more than probable, that the chief reason why many children abandon themselves wholly to silly pastime, and trifle away their hours so insipidly, is because they have found their curiosity baulk'd and rebuted, and their inquisitiveness chided for impertinence or pertness. Whereas, had they been treated with more respect and kindness, and their questions answered, as they should, to their satisfaction, they, in all likelihood, would have taken more pleasure in learning and improving their knowledge, wherein there would be still newness and variety, which is what they are delighted with, than in returning over and over to the same sports and play-things. Letting in knowledge into a dark mind, which is naturally restless in that condition, is no less pleasant to it, than letting in light into an obscure dungeon is to the eye. The mind of man needs but to feel the pleasure of being opened, enlarged and expanded, in order to be enamoured with information and knowledge. And a little success in satisfying their enquiries will soon beget and fix the habit of pursuing science by taking all proper methods of getting instruction and knowledge.

To this serious answering their questions, and informing their understandings in what they desire, should be added some proper ways of commendation. Let others, for this end, whom they esteem, be praised before them, for their knowledge and their application to improve their understandings. We all love praise, and desire of getting honour and esteem by our diligence to acquire useful knowledge, is a passion that ought to be carefully nursed. And in consequence of this natural desire of praise, it is found by experience, that there cannot be a greater spur to the attaining what you would have the eldest to learn and thoroughly understand, than to set him upon teaching it to his younger brothers and sisters. These are the observations of a very great philosopher; who, to what hath been said, adds, That as children's enquiries are not to be slighted, so also great care is to be taken, that they never receive deceitful and eluding answers. They easily perceive when they are slighted or deceived, and quickly learn the tricks of shufling, dissimulation and falshood which they observe others to make use of. We are not therefore to entrench upon truth in any conversation, but least of all with children; since, if we play false with them, we not only deceive their expectation, check their curiosity, and hinder their knowledge, but corrupt their innocence, and teach them the worst of vices.

To these reflections of a very great master of the arts of teaching, we shall subjoin some from another of no less authority.

The two great errors to be avoided with relation to the desire of knowledge are,[18] 1. Precipitancy, or rash assent. And, 2. Misplacing our curiosity

18. Thus Cicero discourses in his first book of offices.

and diligence about obscure, abstruse things, of little use or moment. The first can only be avoided by accustoming young enquirers to the patience of thinking, to mature and full deliberation, and to give assent proportioned to the degree of evidence. They are to be taught not to content themselves with a slight and superficial consideration of things; not to run away too hastily from an object; and not to pronounce judgment rashly. And for this reason, we ought to shew patience and sedateness ourselves in answering their questions, and discover to them by a particular detail, how we came to know what we are explaining to them: How by rashness and precipitancy, one may be misled into mistakes about it: And what care must be had, if we would come to the truth, to attend to every particular circumstance of a thing. The other is avoided, by turning their minds early towards the most useful enquiries, and timeously teaching them to measure the utility of knowledge by the advantages of it to mankind or human society; that is, by giving a right direction to their *admiration,* of which afterwards. All that it is necessary to observe farther on this subject is, that the power of habit serves, in the contexture of our minds, to counterpoise the love of novelty, and by rendering objects more delightful to us, in proportion to our familiarity and acquaintance with them, to prevent our being too desultory and unfixed; as the charms of novelty, on the other hand, serve to counterbalance the force of custom, and to hinder us from contenting ourselves with too small a stock of ideas and knowledge. And therefore, in education, due attention ought to be given to nurse, as it were, these antagonist movers in our mind, so as neither to create satiety, nor a rambling disposition, but to accustom youth to dwell patiently upon the consideration of an object, till they sufficiently understand it, yet so as not to tire and disgust them, by detaining their attention too long, without giving any entertainment to their desire of newness. But how easily may every lesson be sufficiently diversified? For suppose any machine moves their curiosity, when its use and contrivance for that use is explained; the inventor and improvers of it, and the gradual progress of the invention, may be laid before them; and the principle in nature upon which it depends ought not to be forgotten; and from it they may be gradually led to other machines depending on the same natural principle or law—and from thence to the consideration of the wisdom and kindness of the Author of nature in appointing such a law—and from thence to reflect upon

the usefulness of those studies, which by discovering the principles or laws
of nature, enable men from thence to deduce many serviceable adminicles
to mankind.

Our natural delight in symmetry, proportion, and the beauty resulting
from, or always accompanying them, which discovers itself so early in children, by their particular satisfaction in regular figures, is of admirable use,
to spur us on to seek after what is indeed the perfection of every art, simplicity; and to give us high pleasure in observing nature's simplicity.[19] This
affection is therefore to be carefully attended to in education; and will be
perfected, or receive its proper turn, by early leading young minds to give
due attention to the connexion in nature between beauty and utility; by
shewing them that *nature does nothing in vain,* but always avoiding super-
fluity accomplishes its end with the least labour or expence that may be:
that in every structure there is a principal end, to which all the parts conspire, and which is gained in the shortest and simplest manner—That in
the human body, and every animal or vegetable structure, what creates the
chief beauty, in the kind, is the most natural, healthful, or convenient state
of that whole.—And that it is so also in every machine of human invention; in every art, as architecture, painting, statuary, and likewise in every
ingenious composition of the pen. 'Tis easy to one well instructed in all
the arts, and in nature their mistress and guide, to lead young minds gradually from any natural body, to the imitations of it by arts, from thence to
some machine, in which the end is obtained by similar simplicity and frugality—and from thence to what makes the beauty of a description of any
natural or artificial whole, viz. as much brevity as is consistent with perspicuity. Our itch after novelty, may, if not rightly guided, engage us to
pass over the things which every day occur to us, without giving any pains
to understand them, it may hurry us on to remoter and obscure things;
nay, it may degenerate from the liking of rare things for the sake of rarity,
into monster-hunting, or a taste for what is preternatural and deformed.
But because this passion for novelty may take very wrong turns, it does not
surely follow, that the passion itself is not of great use? Creatures made for

19. This likewise is observed by Cicero ibidem.

progress towards perfection of intelligent power, could ill want such an incentive to their proper business. And our natural sense of beauty, together
with our delight in perceiving the final causes, or the utilities of things, is
of excellent use in our frame, to guide our passion for novelty to proper
objects, and to direct it into its best channel. None of the inferior animals
seem to have this sense or faculty; and it by being united with our senses,
prompts and directs us to seek our entertainment from such objects,
chiefly, as at once may gratify our desire of novelty, and our delight in symmetry, beauty and utility.[20] And, as the same author, from whom this observation is taken, sagely remarks, Tho' it be sensible objects that strike us
first and most strongly; yet it is easy for a skilful preceptor to lead young
minds from the contemplation of regularity and beauty in material objects, to the contemplation of regularity and beauty of the moral kind, in
affections, actions and characters; and thus to teach them chiefly to delight
in moral beauty. Very near a-kin to our sense of beauty is our natural sense
of greatness, or the high admiration with which great objects elevate our
minds; and it ought to be early directed and managed in the same manner.
Young minds ought to be early entertained with the beauty, the regularity,
the magnificence of nature, and the greatness which she manifests in her
minutest works.—But from this consideration the contemplator ought to
be immediately led to consider and admire the moral beauty and greatness
of the original Mind, the former of all things, and the source of all beauty
and greatness, as well as of our faculty of perceiving, and of imitating
them, not merely in arts, but in the conduct of life, or in the beauty and
greatness of actions, in which the greatness of the human mind consists.
For, as were there not an original mind, which with perfect wisdom and
goodness unerringly pursues the best, noblest, and greatest end in all his
productions, our capacity of discerning order, beauty and greatness, and
the regularity, harmony and grandeur of created things, would be the work
of blind chance: So, since there is a first Mind, which is consummate
beauty, truth and greatness, the dignity of every created mind must consist
in bearing the nearest resemblance that can be attained, to this fountain of

20. So Cicero observes in his discourse of the nature of the Gods.

all beauty and perfection. Beauty and greatness in effects have so strict a relation to the moral beauty and greatness of their author, that as they cannot be sever'd in nature, so ought they not to be divided or separated in contemplation. And by joining them together, or accustoming the mind to pass from the former to the latter, as its source and cause, moral beauty and greatness will keep the ascendant in the mind, and be the principal object of its esteem and admiration. We cannot turn our eyes inward to consider what passes in our mind, when we are affected either by sensible or moral objects, in an agreeable manner, and are by some greatly elevated above our more ordinary pitch, without being forced to acknowledge the necessary being and prevalency of an imagination, or sense of something beautiful, great, and becoming in things, natural and common to all men, of original growth in the mind, the ground of our admiration, contempt, shame, honour, disdain, and other natural and unavoidable impressions. These affections presuppose this sense, and could not indeed have place without it. All the elegant and polite arts likewise presuppose its existence, and are indeed founded in it. All men court some species of decorum, beauty or grandeur. And therefore is it, that when our sense of beauty and our admiration are not turned towards moral beauty, we pursue and worship some false image of it, some deceitful idol, and make mere outward symmetry and grandeur in dress, equipage, table, and other such external shews, the principal object of our affection. Why indeed are we dazled by pomp and pageantry, ribbons, jewels, and other shining gew-gaws? It is merely because we are strangers to true beauty, real honour, and genuine unfading greatness: It is because we have not been sufficiently accustomed to bring things to the true standard, and to examine appearances strictly, and with due attendance to the source and foundation of true beauty and greatness, viz. large, comprehensive, and generous views, at once engaging and directing a mind to the pursuit of what is best, that is, usefulest. Thus the Author of nature operates, and for this reason the works of nature are beautiful and great: Thus the arts which imitate or rival nature in their highest perfection, work towards their respective ends: And it is being steadily actuated and directed by just and benign views towards the pursuit of public good in all our actions, that constitutes a regular, orderly, beautiful and great mind. From what hath been said of our sense of beauty and greatness, and our delight in novelty, it appears in general, that our loves, desires, hatreds and aversions are not to be left to themselves, but that the great art of education is, to accustom young minds early to the inward work of regulating fancy, and rectifying opinion, on which all depends; to examine the associations that are formed in our minds by the frequent appearances of things; that we may withdraw the fancy or opinion of good or ill, from that to which justly and by necessity it is not joined, and apply it with the strongest resolution to that to which it naturally agrees. This is wisdom, this is freedom, this is strength of mind, this is order and good discipline; this is keeping consort, as near as created agents can, with the Author of nature in all his works, where there is evidently no caprice, no fickleness, no tumult, no disorder, but perfect consonancy, perfect uniformity, consummate order, wisdom and goodness. This strict tutorage of fancy, appetite and affection, is the very reverse of the prevailing easy philosophy of taking that for good which pleases us, or what we merely fancy to be such. Yet 'tis evident; that without perseverance in this discipline, our minds and conduct must be absolute inconsistency and disorder; one cannot be master of himself, but must be a ready prey to every foolish, dangerous imagination and desire. Nor is it less so, that if the fancy and opinion of good be annexed to what is not durable and solid, nor in our power either to acquire or to retain, the more such an opinion prevails, the more we must be exposed to disappointment and vexation. But if there be that to which whenever we apply the opinion of good or great, we find the opinion more consistent, and the good more lasting and solid, and within our power and command, then the more such an opinion prevails in us, the more satisfaction and happiness we will enjoy. For there must be a real measure and standard of good in the nature of things, or comparison and computation are words without a meaning: And the natures and connexions, the properties, effects and consequences of things, will not submit to our fancy or caprice. If there be any such thing as happiness or pain and misery, the idea of good may be misplaced. But how easy is it to make young minds perceive, nay feel, that if the opinion of good be joined to the possessions of the mind, to self-command and mastership of the appetites, to honesty, integrity, friendship, benevolence, honour, and consciousness of inward beauty and worth, resembling in kind to the beauty of that mind which is the Author of all beauty and good.—That this being the fixed opinion and judgment of the mind, if there be likewise resolution enough to adhere to it in our conduct, 'tis impossible we can ever, in this respect, rejoice amiss, or meet with disappointment? How easy is it to satisfy young minds, that it is fancy, merely, which gives the force of good to things of outward dependency, and makes them pass with us as an essential part of our happiness; and that the more we take from imagination in this respect, the more strength we give to the goods of the mind, and consequently to ourselves, on whom the purchase and increase of them depends? If I apply the idea of honour and dignity to the possession of plate, jewels, titles, precedencies, and am thus betrayed to seek them, not as mere conveniencies and helps in life, or means of doing good, but as excellent in themselves, as proper objects of my admiration, and as the causes of my greatest satisfaction and happiness, then will these necessarily be pursued by me preferably to virtue, and consequently integrity will often be sacrificed to them. These false opinions of good may not, at first, be able wholly to subdue our natural sense of moral obligations, but, in proportion as they prevail, they will take from its force, and they will be gradually impairing and diminishing it, as they become stronger by indulgence. But how obvious is it, that the passion raised by such ideas (call it avarice, pride, ambition, vanity or luxury) is indeed incapable of giving any real satisfaction, even in the most successful course of fortune, but is then too attended with perpetual fears of disappointment and loss? How obvious is it, that strict adherence to virtue can alone give true and lasting peace and satisfaction to the mind; and that in this pursuit only, there is no fear of disappointment, nor danger of nauseating or remorse? Whereas, if the conscience be tainted, and a breach be once made upon our integrity, nothing but hurry and confusion, or the perpetual intoxication of debauch can preserve us from the horrors of conscious guilt? In proportion as we are led or rather driven by appetites after external goods, in proportion do we lose our liberty and self-mastership. But the more we are fixed in the esteem of what depends on ourselves, that is, of the riches of the mind, the greater is our liberty and strength of mind; for so much the farther are we removed from depending on others, and the more compleat or sufficient are we in ourselves. In order to understand the force of this reasoning, and know our true self-interest, one needs only to have tasted of liberty and inward strength. And therefore it is the business of education, to give an early notion and taste of inward liberty, and of the value and importance of command over our appetites, and of a confirmed regard to virtue, as our chief good; as that which exalts us to our highest glory, making us like our Creator, and giving us a joy and content able to support us even under the most calamitous outward condition of life. We may know by a little reflexion upon the power of habits, that it is, by indulging any wrong appetite, as malice, revenge, debauch, the opinion of the false good increases; and the appetite, which is a real ill, grows so much the stronger: On the other hand, by restraining this affection, and nourishing a contrary sort in opposition to it, we cannot fail to diminish what is ill, and increase what is properly our good and happiness. The proper method therefore of establishing virtuous affections and habits in the mind, is to teach and inure youth early to make those fancies and appetites themselves the objects of their aversion which justly deserve it, by being the cause of a wrong estimation and measure of good and ill, and consequently exposing to disturbance, vexation, disappointment and unhappiness. And for this reason, the best masters in morals, and the arts of education, have recommended beginning rather by forming our aversion, than by encouraging our admiration, or advised to work rather by weaning our passions from false goods, than by engaging our affections in the warm admiration and pursuit of any good, however true and substantial; that is, to begin by raising their aversion and indignation against the meannesses of opinion and sentiment, which are the causes of corruption and misconduct. Thus the covetous fancy, if considered as the cause of misery, by engaging in pursuits that can never yield solid satisfaction, and betraying into the most shameful vices, and if consequently it be detested as a real ill, must of necessity abate. And the ambitious fancy, if opposed in the same manner with resolution by better thought, must quit the field, and leave the mind free and disincumbered in the pursuit of its better objects. Nor is the case different in the passion of cowardice or fear of pain. For whereas, if we leave this passion to grow upon us, and become our master, it will lead us to the most mean, abject and tormenting state of life; if contrariwise, it be opposed by a juster estimation of real ill, it must diminish of course; and the natural result of such a practice must be the deliverance of the mind from numberless fears and uneasinesses, and the full establishment of freedom and independency of mind, or impregnable virtue. When the mind is made acquainted with the greatest ills it hath to fear, with its worst enemies, its obstructers or seducers from the pursuit of virtue, perceives them to be wholly from itself, and from false opinions, and feels its own power to controul its appetites, and chastise and correct its fancies, then is the principal point in education gained, the resolution and habit of calling appearances of pleasure and good to a severe trial, and of thus giving law and check, instead of loose reins to our affections. And this power, this self-controul, in which the very essence of virtue consists, being once established and confirmed in the mind, then may we adventure to teach youth to admire; because this habit of examination will teach them to admire with reason, and not suffer their admiration to run away with them, or to warm them to such a pitch as to obscure their reason.[21] 'Tis dangerous to give way to admiration by loving and applauding even what is truly great and good, without accustoming ourselves to keep, if we may so speak, so good a bridle-hand, as to be able to stop our fancy, and to make it ply to reason, and give an account of its raptures to it whenever we please. The poet, as well as the rider, must be absolute master of his steed, and be able to let him out and take him in at his will. Do you not see how Bellerophon commands Pegasus, how he keeps him in on our friends ring? And the same command that makes a good poet is necessary to prevent errors in life, which may not improperly be compared with those in writing, to which the high flights of too towering an imagination, not balanced by a cool and accurate judgment, expose. The eye and the ear ought early to be formed to a just relish of true harmony. But we know by experience, that one may become too zealous a lover of painting, architecture or music. The taste of these arts may be just and well-formed, and therefore the admiration may not be foolish, and yet it may be very faulty and blameable. There are other vices belonging to love and admi-

---

21. This is Aristotle's doctrine. It is likewise Arrian's in his commentary upon Epictetus.

ration, besides not knowing why we love and applaud. Intelligent love of
the polite arts may have too large a share of our affections, and enhance
too much of our time and expence: It may warm the mind to a ridiculous
extravagant excess, and take it off from more serious and important pursuits. The same may happen with respect to delight in botany, or any other
science, and to the love of speculation and study in general. One may be
too fond of contemplation, not merely to the prejudice of his health, but
to the hurt of society, as is most evidently the case, when a person of high
birth and fortune, born to serve his country in the higher offices of the
state, contracts an aversion to action and business, and wholly devotes
himself to any branch of speculative philosophy. Nay, religious admiration
itself may be excessive; for persons may be so extasied by rapturous ado-
ration of the supreme Author of all beauty and good, as to forget the un-
wearied activity in doing good, in which he ought chiefly to be imitated
by his active creatures, and their own immediate connexion with mankind, and their first and main business resulting from this natural union
and dependence, namely, laying themselves out to be useful to society to
the utmost of their power. Love of the first beauty may so engross the
imagination, so transport and charm it, that the admirer may be unwilling
to be disturbed in his devotion by the most necessary and momentous duties of social life. And in general, the best, the most reasonable passions, if
frequently indulged, without being called to an account at the bar of cool
and sedate reason, and made to explain their foundation, and thus resolved, as it were, into their first principles, will naturally become too ardent and impetuous to bear controul, occupy too large a share in the
mind, and so justle reason out of its empire, and become absolute masters
within our breasts in the room of reason, which ought to be maintained
sovereign ruler there over every idea, fancy or affection. And hence it is,
that the best grounded affections, thro' over indulgence, and thro' the
want of the discipline that hath been mentioned often, totally unhinge the
mind, and create great disorder in the inward oeconomy. 'Tis not wrong
and ill-founded opinions and passions only, which produce phrenzy: The
best also may become very fatal to the mind, and out it, if we may so
speak. In reality, every affection, tho' never so reasonable in its foundation,
which is become too violent to bear to be stopt in its carreer, and brought

to a deliberate trial, is in this respect extravagant, and consequently a proportionable step towards demency or madness. Now therefore, the only
safeguard against this excess, this ardour and impetuosity of the best affections, is to inure ourselves to call all our affections often to a strict account;
and thus, by frequently exercising our reason in its proper province, to
keep it up in full power, for 'tis its prevalency over them all that makes a
rational state of mind. This prevalency of reason may justly be called presence of reason or mind, because, in consequence of it, the mind is ever
capable of discerning what is best and fittest, and of upholding its authority. But as often as reason exerts itself in catechizing our affections, what
else is the standard by which it ought to measure and try them, but their
tendencies in respect of public utility? This is the sole standard by which
all our affections are to be regulated; for public utility is the most valuable
end, and what is such must be the ultimate rule. And in proportion as one
is acquainted with this measure, is he fitted for the trial and government
of his opinions and passions. But it is not enough to know rules; the actual
application of them is the chief thing. And therefore then is the mind well
instructed and well disciplined, or truly rational, when reason presiding,
steadily and calmly approportionates all the affections in their exercises to
their best use and end, the public good. 'Tis in this sense that reason is
said, even by those philosophers who speak most of cultivating our moral
taste or sense, to be our superior and guiding faculty. For by it ought every
sentiment to be often and profoundly canvassed in the coolest and strictest
manner; and under its government, tho' excellent sentiments may often
warm the mind to a very sublime pitch, yet the general or habitual temper
of the mind is cool and sedate; for which cause, its constant presidence is
properly termed presence of mind, and in other words calmness or equa-
nimity.[22]

But what requires our closest watching is, lest any false ideas of good
should carry off our affections into unprofitable or hurtful pursuits; and
therefore, the principal business of education is to inure youth to take a

22. This doctrine is charmingly inculcated by Arrian, from whom many of the reasonings here against the doctrine of Epicurus are taken.

just view of the goods of human life, and to place their chief happiness not
where fancy may chance to place it, but where nature hath really fixed it,
viz. in a virtuous disposition. The goods which divide human desires and
pursuits, are the riches of the mind and external advantages; and according
to our estimation of them such must our conduct be. For where our treasure is, there will our heart and affections be. Now, what the true value of
external in comparison of internal goods is, these reflections will easily
shew us. First, it is evident from experience, that with regard to the public,
'tis virtuous industry, benevolence, and resignation to providence, that
make a worthy and beneficial member of society. Secondly, with regard to
private happiness, this likewise is the best temper of mind. 'Tis the affections which under the guidance of reason work towards the general good
of our kind, that are the pleasantest exercises of the mind, either in their
immediate exertions, or upon after reflexion. Thirdly, the goods of the
body are unstable and unsatisfactory, while they last, and they must cease
with our mortal part: But the improvements of the mind are not only of a
stable unchanging kind, but everlasting, the soul being immortal; and
consequently they follow us into another state, in which we are strip'd of
our bodily organs, and consequently of all the instruments and means of
mere carnal gratification. From these considerations it clearly follows, that
it is wiser and greater to despise external means of enjoyment than to possess them. And these are the truths which ought to be early insinuated into
and deeply impressed upon young minds. Nor is there indeed any part of
real knowledge from which the mind may not easily and naturally be led
to some, or rather all, of these useful and important reflexions. Every work
of nature shews us in what the dignity, perfection and happiness of the
supreme cause consists, viz. in the most benevolent use of his knowledge
and power. And in what else can the dignity, perfection, and happiness of
any intelligent active creature consist, but in imitating and being like the
supreme Mind, that is, in the best or most benevolent use of all his powers
and faculties; in improving our power for doing good, and exercising it, as
we have opportunity, to the greatest good of our fellow-creatures? All
nature must be reversed before this can cease to be true, "That a well-
improved understanding and benevolent orderly affections, duly submitted to the government of reason, constitute our highest excellence, merit

and happiness." While the Author of the world governs all things by the best laws and in the most excellent manner; while by the constitution of the human mind it continues to be more charmed with the contemplation of order, harmony and good, than of confusion, discord and ill; nay, while reason continues to be reason, or understanding and judgment to be preferable to ignorance and irrationality, it must be an unchangeable truth, "That virtue, or an improved and well-governed mind, is our noblest and best, or most perfect state: And the happiness and the perfection of a being can no more jar or differ, than the essence of a thing can differ from itself." But it is not our business here to confirm this truth. All we have to observe is, that if the power or habit of bringing our fancies and affections to a fair trial, by some accurately considered and improved standard, in consequence of right institution and discipline, be firmly established in the mind, the chief point of education is gained; and there is no danger that our affections go wrong or mislead us. For what hath been said of rational government with respect to admiration, and the other affections which have been mentioned, is equally applicable to all the rest, to love of fame, love of power, compassion, resentment, friendship, and natural affections, properly so called. They are then all of them in their due tones, when they operate under the presidence and direction of reason, towards the greater good of our kind. But that we may leave none of them unconsidered in an enquiry concerning what is principal in education, viz. the right discipline of the passions, instead of explaining further upon the doctrine of the best moralists on this subject, (for I have hitherto been only commenting upon some of their sage precepts) I shall give you the substance of a dialogue concerning the passions between two philosophers of very different sentiments upon this head.[23] The one maintained, that all our affections tending towards interesting us in the concerns of others, ought to be extirpated, and that self-interest was the only thing we had to mind, and therefore self-love was the only legitimate principle in our frame, and all the rest were to be curb'd, or rather lop'd off, as invaders upon its property.

---

23. See Arrian upon Epictetus disser. l. 2. cap. 20. edit. Colon. 201. [Epictetus, *The Discourses*, bk. II, ch. 20, "Against the Epicurians and Academics."]

The other maintained, that every affection originally implanted in us is necessary to our dignity and happiness, and capable of very noble improvement, and that the affections which engage us in the interests of others are so far from being contrary to self-interest, that without them self-love would be robb'd of its best means of giving us enjoyment, or gratifying itself. The former, I think, was called Speusippus, a disciple of Epicurus. The other followed Plato, and his name was Hermogenes.

Speusippus finding Hermogenes indisposed, took occasion to tell him, that it was high time for him, after having impaired his health so much by his continued application to public affairs, and his patriotism, as it is called, to mind himself. For, said he, one's self is one's all, and what can deserve the name of folly, if to waste and consume one's all for others be not? 'Tis demonstration, continued he, that it is the height of wisdom to pursue our true interest. But how can the advantage of others, when it is directly contrary to private quiet, ease and good, be our own interest or happiness?

Hermogenes replied in a pleasant manner, I know, my friend, for a friend, a very good friend you are by your constitution, in spite of your very unfriendly philosophy—I know, my friend, that you so far follow the sage founder of the selfish doctrine you profess, that you have not only avoided all share in public business, all offices or employments in the state, but likewise all family engagements and cares. For I am persuaded, it is not nature but philosophy that has made you obstinately refuse so many sollicitations to change your batchelor state, and become husband, father, and head of a family.

Sp. I am glad to find you so well as to be disposed to rally. I indeed intended very grave and kind advice to you, whose present disorder is intirely owing to your fatigue for the public, which is to you more than wife and children, nay than yourself, through the influence not of nature surely, the first and strongest principle in which is self-preservation, if it be not the only one of her growth, as I am apt to think.—But that I may have the better title to claim a hearing from you in my turn, I am very willing to listen to what you may have to suggest, in concert, no doubt, with my other relations, about changing my condition.

Her. I did not, indeed, my friend, intend to enter upon that subject with you. I meant no more than an encomium upon the sagacious insight into human nature of your great master in philosophy.

Sp. What is it, pray?

Her. Why, I think he well understood the power of nature, and gave an advice to his disciples, without following which they can never attain to the wise self-interestedness he takes to be the perfection of wisdom. 'Twas on this account he sagely exhorted his followers, neither to beget children nor to engage in public affairs. There was no dealing with nature, he foresaw, while these alluring objects stood in the way. Relations, friends, countrymen, laws, politics, constitutions, the beauty and order of government, and the interest of society and mankind were objects which he well understood, would naturally raise a stronger affection than any which was grounded upon the narrow bottom of mere self. His advice, therefore, not to marry, nor engage at all in the public, was wise and suitable to his design. There is no way to be truly a disciple of this philosophy, but to leave family, friends, country and society, to cleave to it. And in good earnest, who would not do it if it were happiness to do so?

Sp. And what can be more evident than that it is so. For where is happiness to be found? Not sure without one's self? Not sure in perplexing cares and toils? Not in sacrificing health and every enjoyment to provide for others? Pray think but a moment upon this one plain question, Is my happiness another's, or is it my own? Can any thing be my interest but my own interest?

Her. I know this is your philosopher's way of reasoning—and no doubt you were just going to tell me, with him, Suffer not yourself to be imposed upon. Beware of the illusion of designing politicians. Take my word for it, there is naturally no such thing as society among mankind. Those who affirm there is, only abuse your credulity. The generous affections, as they are called, are a political engraftment upon nature—Have I not prevented you?

Sp. Is it not really so?

Her. If it be, may I not ask Epicurus, or any of his followers, how this concerns them? Leave us, pray, in quiet possession of our error. What damage will you suffer, if all but you and your followers should be persuaded that there is a natural society among mankind, and that we ought to do all in our power for its support? Why so much concern for us? What can induce you to light your lamp and spend whole nights in your study for our sakes? Why are you at the pains of composing so many books? You will tell us, it is with a view of undeceiving us in these particulars, "That the Gods interest themselves in our affairs, and that happiness consists in something else than in selfishness."—But what is it to you, whether others form a right judgment on these points or not? What tie is there between you and us? Have you any compassion for the sheep because they submit to be shorn, milked and slaughtered? Ought not you to wish that men, lulled to sleep and enchanted by false philosophy or designing politics, would as tamely deliver themselves to the direction of you and your companions?—In short, what was it depriv'd Epicurus of his rest, and engaged him to write all he published? Nature, without doubt, that most powerful principle of human motions, strongly influenced him, and forced his obedience, in spite of all the resistance he could make; such is the invincible force of the social principle in the human mind.—As it is neither possible, my friend, nor conceivable that a vine should shoot like an olive tree, and not according to the impulse of its own nature; so neither is it possible for man to divest himself intirely of human affections. If you castrate a man you cannot extinguish all carnal desires in him. Thus Epicurus, as much as in him lies, has cut off in theory all the relations of husband, father, master of a family, citizen, friend, but the several inclinations of human nature were still intire in him, and had their influence even when he imagined he was opposing them. It was no more in his power to rid himself of those than it was in that of the Pyrrhonists to throw away or put out their senses, tho' no set of men ever took so much pains to do it.[24]

Sp. Sure you do not call this reasoning. But this is the way with those who have once allowed themselves to be worked into an enthusiastic admiration of what they call beauty and order; they like to rant and declaim, giving way to their enchanted imaginations, and will not come to close and cool argumentation.

Her. I am, I assure you, at present, in a very cool mood, and am willing

24. All this is from Arrian, ut supra.

to debate this point with you in the coldest manner you please. Let me therefore, in order to state the case, that we may not wrangle about words, only ask you plainly your opinion, Whether you think kindness of every sort, tenderness, compassion, and in short, all public affection, should be industriously suppressed, and as mere folly and weakness of nature, be resisted and overcome, that by this means there may be nothing remaining in us, which is contrary to a direct self-end; nothing which may stand in opposition to a steady and deliberate pursuit of the most narrowly confined self-interest? Is this your opinion?

Sp. That is neither my opinion nor my master's, as you call him.

Her. What then do you maintain?

Sp. I do not say, that social love, friendship, gratitude, or whatever else by its nature taking place of the self-interesting passions, draws us out of ourselves, and makes us disregardful of our own safety, convenience and good, ought to be suppressed.—For that would be to grant, that they are of nature's growth; but that they are contrary to the only affections of nature's implantation, and ought to be kept out as enemies to private interest, and disturbers of our happiness?

Her. I understand you. But whence then come these affections, if they are not natural to us?

Sp. They are all the offspring of political flattery.

Her. But if they have a father they must likewise have a mother. Upon what stock or principle in human nature are they begot or grafted, call it what you please?

Sp. I did not intend to mislead from the argument by an allegory, when I called them the offspring of political flattery.—But if you would know their mother, it is the pride natural to mankind, upon which they are begot.

Her. So be it. Let us examine a little into the nature of this pride, without which, I think, you have owned, a social principle could not possibly have taken root in any human breast. For to shew you how much I am disposed to avoid rant, and even allegory too, let me tell you, almost in logical form, that if by the pride you have represented as the principle upon which political flattery works, and only can work, in order to excite in us any social regard to others, if, I say, by it you mean any principle in our nature impelling us to affect the regard of others, your argument amounts to this: "There is naturally in the human breast no regard to others but what is grafted by art or flattery, upon a principle in our nature that is in itself regard to others."

SP. I profess I can see no sophistry in saying, that there is no other regard to others natural to us, but desire of esteem, and of power and interest with others by that means; and that all other affections that respect others, which work contrary to self-interest, are political misguidances of our natural appetite after praise and power. But had you asked me to define the pride natural to us, you would have had no occasion for this subtlety, by which, no doubt, you thought to demolish or confound me at once. For I should not have called pride regard to others, but a desire to greaten ourselves in the opinion of others. But to make shorter work with our dispute, or to reduce it into a narrower compass, let me tell you what I assert is, That self-love, or the desire of private good, is the only affection or principle natural to man, and that into however many different pursuits this one principle may be drawn by differing ideas or opinions of good, yet whatever any one pursues, that good is pursued by him under the notion of private good.

HER. Why, truly, if this be all you have to say, our dispute will indeed be very soon over. For I know none who have asserted, that we can be pleased without having pleasure; or pursue as good what we do not conceive to be good. At least, for my own part I am ready to grant to you, that the man who places his good or happiness in serving the public, is as selfish as he who places it in eating and drinking. For had he not supreme pleasure in benevolence; or did he not place his happiness more in it than in any thing else, he would not pursue benevolence, but that something else, whatever it is, which he apprehended to be a greater good. As frivolous as you may think this concession you have now made to me, yet if you stick to it, our dispute is indeed brought to a very narrow point. For it will not be, how many various opinions of good, men may artfully be misled into by flattery, or other methods; nor whether all men are not equally selfish; but merely who is wisest for himself, or who understands his interest and good best. If I do not mistake you, you own that self-love is not what constitutes happiness, but barely the principle that excites to the pursuit of pleasure or gratification. So that the question between us will be, whether nature hath placed the true happiness of mankind in the exercises of social affections and benevolence; or it is ill-grounded fancy which hath misled some men to do so, contrary to the direction and instigation of nature.

Sp. Now you have fairly stated the question.

Her. If I have, then I may expect that you are to prove to me, That in the system of mankind, the interest of the private nature is directly opposite to that of the common one; the interest of the particulars directly opposite to that of the public in general: For if to be well-affected towards the public interest be one's own private interest or good, then must virtue, or benevolence and its exercises, be the advantage, and vice, or disregardlesness of the public, be the injury and disadvantage of every individual. Now, not to mention that such a constitution would be very unlike to what we observe elsewhere in nature; for in no vegetable or animal body, is any part or member ever supposed to be in a good or prosperous state as to itself, when it is under a contrary disposition, and in an unnatural growth or habit as to its whole: Not to mention this consideration, since it only affords a mere presumption, that we may expect to find the same good order and regular constitution in minds.—Let me ask you, whether these affections which draw us out of ourselves, so as to engage us in hazards, toils and hardships, whether they be natural to us, or only raised in us by false opinions of good, must not be exceeding powerful, and therefore exceeding pleasant; for according to the concession I have made, and shall not retract, motives are powerful in proportion to the opinion we have of the goods they set before us.

Sp. What affections do you mean? For, if I grant on the one hand, that when family cares, for instance, make us neglect our own sustinance, and expose ourselves to great sufferings, the affections and the ideas of good, exciting and supporting them must be very strong; it must be owned, on the other, that anger, revenge, and many other passions, which rush us into no less toilsom and hazardous outrages, are likewise very impetuous, and consequently inflamed and maintained by no less strong ideas of good. The fatigues, sufferings or perils, passions drive us upon, will only prove their force, and the power of the fancies which inflame them, it will not prove them to be wise. Men, whatever they do or pursue, whether they scratch themselves or others, if I may be allowed to use so homely a phrase, are pleased with so doing, while the fancy and appetite prevails. But in order to judge of affections, whencesoever they arise, that is, by whatever opinions they are excited, the only rule is, to compare sedately the pleasure with the pain they bring; according to the sage maxim, which indeed contains the whole of wisdom. "Nocet empta dolore voluptas."[25] If there be any such thing as wisdom or prudence this must be its measure; for there can be no other ultimate standard of things but the quantity of real satisfaction they bring; and therefore, unless pleasure be superior to all the pain that succeeds it, the balance lies on the side of pain and not of pleasure. Now, according to this rule, as I must give up revenge, raging lust, furious avarice, and every such passion, which not seeing one inch before them, runs us upon terrible shelves and rocks; so you must, for the same reason give up with patriotism, heroism, magnanimity, and all the so much boasted of public affections, indulgence to which is no less dangerous to safety, ease, quiet, health, and the chief of goods, calm undisturbed repose, miscalled, by reproach, indolence.

HER. Now, I apprehend you have disclosed your whole system. And indeed I am so far from being against your standard, that I think reason, calm reason, ought to preside over and guide all our pursuits. So far therefore we are agreed. But let our enjoyments be as calm and sedate as you please, as remote from all these transports and warmths of fancy, which hinder us from discerning their consequences, and so from making a fair computation of true advantage, pleasure, or interest—yet still enjoyments we must have. Now, I would fain know, whether the public affections, which according to your system are not natural to us, but introduced into our minds by art and opinion, be not such a source of enjoyment to us, that if it were intirely cut off, our provision for happiness would be very narrow and scanty? If they may be so regulated as to be means of enjoyment to us, without involving us in pains superior to the pleasure they afford, whether they proceed from nature or from art and opinion, they

25. [Horace, *Epistles,* 1.2.55: "pleasure bought with pain is harmful" (Loeb translation by H. Rushton Fairclough).]

ought to be preserved as such. Without appetite or affection no one thing can please us more than another, that is, there could be no pleasure, no enjoyment at all. Wherefore, the more appetites and affections we have, the greater capacity we have for happiness. And the conclusion from this, according to your own principle, should, must be, that none of our affections, that we have, or may have the power and means of gratifying, ought to be suppressed or extirpated. That they should be regulated, in consequence of your maxim, from which I do not dissent, so as that they may not create us more pain and uneasiness than pleasure, I own: But that they should be rooted out, I deny, since that would be to diminish or restrict our capacity of enjoyment. Now, for my own part, as I think our affections or appetites after sensible gratifications ought not to be totally erased, but on the contrary, to be indulged within wise and regular bounds, as one part of our capacity for receiving gratifications; so I think the affections which have something in others for their objects, their good, their love and approbation, or whatever it be, ought not to be extirpated, but to be regulated; because, whereas being extirpated, we would be incapable of receiving enjoyment by them, and so our furniture for happiness would be lessened, while they are duly governed, we may have pleasures from them that are not the least considerable ones, in our stock or provision. For in truth I can't help thinking, that were these taken away, so very few capacities of enjoyment would remain to us, that if they be from art, we are more obliged to such art than to nature for our provision.

Sp. Do you then think that the appetites or affections which carry us out of, or beyond ourselves, and have somethings in others for their end, often very incompatible with private good, are as selfish, as those which immediately respect and terminate in our own private and separate advantage?

Her. Pray, my friend, let us avoid all equivocations and quibblings with words, as much as possible. If by selfish, you understand terminating in some private interest, as its ultimate good, then to say the affections which carry us beyond ourselves, to something in others as their end, are as selfish as those which terminate directly and immediately in ourselves, would be to say, those which have not some private good for their immediate end, have private good as much for their immediate end as those

which have it. But if by selfish be meant, either what ever is a part of ourselves, as all our feelings, all our sensations or sentiments, and all the affections and appetites which work in us, and affect us by their motions are—
or whatever may be a mean of pain or pleasure to us, however distant from
our immediate selves that object may be, then are all our sensations, sentiments, feelings, affections, and all the objects and means whereby we
may receive pain or pleasure, equally selfish. But why again have recourse
to mere definitions of the various senses in which self and selfish may be
used, since we have both agreed, that it is only good or pleasure, apprehended as such, that can be desired, or move our affection towards it; and
vice versa, only ill or pain, apprehended as such, that can be hated or move
our aversion. For if we adhere to this simple truth (and nothing can be
simpler, since it is really to say no more than that pleasure is pleasure, and
pain pain) all that remains, all that can remain to be debated is, what pleasures, all things fairly computed, are the most eligible. For he who com-
putes and chooses best, is certainly wisest for himself. And if affections
operating steadily towards the good of our kind, which are called virtuous
affections, be really, upon a fair calculation, the best means of self-
enjoyment, the most eligible pleasures, then is virtue the best choice. In
such reasoning we beg nothing, for it is taking nothing for granted without proof, to give the name of virtuous affections to those which are directed towards the public good by and with conscious free choice, and the
name of vitious to those which with free conscious choice work contrary
to public good, if there really be any difference between public good and
public ill, or the happiness and misery of mankind. In fine, therefore, the
debate between us is, whether social and benevolent affections are not the
best gratifications we know any thing of, in consequence of the frame and
constitution of the human mind? It would be to desert this question to
say, that tho' it were yielded that they are excellent, nay the best pleasures
we know, yet it is art that brings this pleasure about, and not nature. For
that much must be done by art to bring the human mind to its best state,
as well as to bring all flowers and plants to their respective perfections, I
grant; yet this being confessed, it will not follow, that the best state we can
be brought to, by proper culture, is not the intention of nature, with regard to us, in the same sense that the most perfect state plants and flowers

can be cultivated to, by proper care and art, is allowed to be the intention of nature with regard to them, since it is plain, that with regard to minds, as well as to vegetable bodies, the effects of all different sorts of applications must be of nature's settlement or appointment. Vegetables are cultivated by art, yet art does not create, but only brings forth a certain effect, fixed by nature as the effect of certain applications. In like manner, minds open and expand, become capable of relishing knowledge and carrying on curious researches; and they are improved into a social and benevolent disposition, and a capacity of easily, readily and justly discerning the public good, by proper care in the cultivation and exercise of their faculties; but in this case, likewise, art does not create, but only brings forth the moral effects appointed by nature to be the effects of certain means of moral cultivation and exercise. Had not nature so constituted or determined the human mind, that the image of proportion, the image of beauty and order, the image of power, the image of public good, should be pleasing to us, they could never be rendered so by any art.

Sp. Hold there, pray; for granting all that you have said on the subject besides, I would but just know how you can possibly, upon this hypothesis, account for the present state of mankind, among whom we see few acquainted with the charms of proportion, nay, many in love with disproportion and irregularity; very few, indeed, not intoxicated with the love of power, but very few captivated by what you *Platonists* call in your language the *moral species,* and the chief of beauties and goods, public good. Does not this variety, this contrariety, rather, among mankind, prove that nature hath fixed nothing, but that chance or art does all, moulds minds into any forms, gives them any casts, and fashions and refashions, makes and unmakes tempers and affections without any rule, or at least in ways and manners we cannot ascertain.

Her. Would you keep, my friend, to this objection, I think I could easily explain this phenomenon very consistently with what I have affirmed of nature.

Sp. Go on, if you please.

Her. That some men have no notion of proportion, suppose in architecture, will only prove that the mind must be opened or prepared to comprehend and relish proportion: It will not prove, there is not an original

aptitude in the human mind to be cultivated into this taste, in consequence of an original determination of the mind to receive pleasure from
the view of proportion or symmetry. The very thing is daily owned with
respect to proportion of another kind, that harmony, namely, which we
call music. Is there no such thing as music; are there no fixed proportions
respecting sounds of nature's institution, and which cannot be changed,
because the plurality of mankind are unacquainted with these true proportions, and take up with noise very grating to a well-formed ear? To say,
which is fact, that the ear and the eye must be formed by right institution,
in order to have a quick and just relish of the harmonies with which these
senses may be entertained, is no more than to say, that this part of our
happiness is made by nature dependent upon culture or education: For ask
yourself, whether there could be any such arts as architecture or music,
were there not proportions and harmonies settled by nature; and you must
immediately perceive, in general, that there can be no arts but in consequence of laws, connexions and determinations settled by nature. Whatever change is introduced by mechanical arts into a body, is so introduced,
because nature hath fixed the effects of certain operations upon bodies,
and whatever is produced or introduced into minds, to the better or to the
worse, is brought about because nature hath settled all the effects of all the
different mental applications and operations, as well as of bodily ones.
When I say certain good modifications of the mind, which make it a better
disposed member of the general community of mankind, are natural, I
neither say that they can be produced without art, nor do I say the contrary modifications are not natural, or that they may not be brought about
by corruptive applications and excesses. All I say is, that in consequence of
the constitution of the human mind, and of the settled connexions relating to it, there is an art of improving, as well as a method of depraving the
human mind: And that as we would think it unreasonable to say, That
because plants and flowers may be neglected, and so never arrive to their
most beautiful and perfect state, therefore their most beautiful and perfect
state to which they may be brought by proper culture, is not the state nature intended; so it must be equally unreasonable, by parity of argument,
to say, that because there are various ways of corrupting human minds,
therefore the beautiful state to which they may be improved and trained

by care, early begun and steadily pursued, is not the state nature intended them for. Let me just add, that nothing could be more absurd, than to assert in direct terms, that there is a perfection and imperfection with regard to every vegetable, and that mental powers or qualities are the only ones in nature to which neither perfection nor imperfection can be attributed. But if this be so, then 'twere to be wished men would enquire into the perfection attainable by the human mind, and into the arts of bringing the human mind early to such perfection. Indeed we see, confess and admire every day, in many instances, ancient and modern, the perfection attainable by the human mind. And this is none other but a benevolent disposition united with the capacity of discerning and pursuing the good of mankind. It is this we admire as the beauty, the strength, the glory of an Epaminondas, a Scipio, and every great character in history. And if we cannot help admiring this perfection, and considering it as yielding greater happiness, even in adversity, than the most luxuriant prosperity can afford to one of the reverse temper and character, let us own the human mind is made to approve and to pursue virtue, and that virtue, and virtue alone, is true honour and happiness—and forsaking all other meaner cares and studies, let us think first, how we may improve daily in virtue ourselves, and next, how we may form our youth early to the love of virtue, and to the capacity of quickly and readily discerning what the love of it, i.e. the love of public justice, liberty and happiness requires in every condition, circumstance, and incident of human life. For human life is so diversified and chequered as it is, merely, that it may be a school for training, and a theatre for exercising and displaying various virtues—and after formation and trial, cometh in its due place, the time and scene of rewards.

Sp. You are, as to your sect generally happens, immediately warmed by the very name of virtue. However, I can't but own, that some definitions and principles you have cooly enough laid down in the beginning of this discourse, begin to stagger me a little, and to create a suspicion in my mind, that some of the maxims which I have hitherto been accustomed to take on trust in my reasonings about virtue, and the obligations to it, may be at bottom but quibbles. I am far from being weary of the discourse; but would, before I venture further, have some time to recollect what hath passed, and to examine accurately with my self, "What we of our sect mean by selfish, and what by disinterested, what by natural, and what by artificial." You, I find, are willing to take these words in any sense we please, if we will keep to it. And I own, that when one of a lively warm genius comes to paint out to me virtuous characters, men capable of serving the public, and solely delighting in so employing themselves, I can't help loving, admiring, and ambitioning the character, whether this be nature or the effect of education.

HER. Well do I know, my friend, that your heart and your philosophy are at variance; and so it was with your grand master. You are none of those who have taken up Epicurus's doctrine to be a screen to them against the natural upbraidings of their consciences for the dissoluteness of their manners. On the contrary, the honesty of your heart and practice, I know, often makes bold struggles within you, against a system of opinions, the general prevalence of which, you cannot but see and own, must destroy all that is great or glorious in human life. For did they once spread and become universal, who would labour for society, who would contend for liberty, who would toil for the improvement of the arts of peace, or who would risk their lives in war for public good?—Have you considered, that according to the philosophy you now and then maintain, all the great legislators and patriots in ancient and modern times, which are the glory of mankind, are fools?[26]

SP. Away with the mean, ungrateful thought.—Any doctrines which result in such a base, ungenerous, ignominious conclusion, must be false. But you have now warmed me too much to be able to judge.

HER. Let us not, however part till I have added, That if those great men in history, to whose labours human society have owed their happiness, their useful arts, their excellent laws and policies, their liberty, be truly great, a real honour to mankind, and were truly happy, whatever fate they had, thro' whatever opposition and persecution they passed,—then to cherish the benevolent disposition, and to educate in the knowledge of the interests of mankind, is the way to train youth to true happiness and great-

---

26. Thus Cicero, de finibus, charges and reasons against Epicurus.

ness; and therefore the true education, and the most useful study and employment of the experienced. But I have done, being unwilling to tire you.

In these recitals, my friend, of conversations, every thing, almost, relating to ancient education, hath been handled, two things only excepted: Their care to accustom youth to read prose and verse with intelligent graceful voice and gesture; for this, you know, was the chief part of what they called music amongst the Greeks: And their care to unite, with their studies, such exercises as tended to give health, vigour and grace of body; and at the same time, to form betimes a manly intrepidity and presence of mind in danger. But as your question chiefly regarded the instructive or didactic part of education, I think it hath been sufficiently answered. We find they preferred to private or public education a middle way between the two, in which there would be place for exciting emulation, and yet sufficient care could be taken of the morals of youth, and due regard be had to variety of genius's.—We have observed how necessary they thought it was, to join good discipline and right practice with instruction, in order to form good habits. And we have found that the chief end of all their instructions being to fit and qualify youth for the various duties of life, in its different stations, conditions and relations, they took care to render all the arts subservient to this lesson, by which means the lesson was agreeably sweetened and diversified, and, at the same time, a just taste was also formed of beauty in writing, and in every other ingenious art. In these conversations it hath also been enquired, why nature hath left so much to education or art; or why the happiness of every particular is so dependent upon the examples, the manners, and the instructions of others. This momentuous question hath been fully treated of, and in discussing it, we have had full occasion to shew the sentiments of the ancients concerning the rich furniture of the human mind, and the perfection to which it might be brought by proper culture, and likewise to delineate the chief parts or branches of that culture, which would soon establish virtuous habits, right self-government, and the capacity of judging concerning good and evil, fit and unfit, with relation to private or public happiness in the most complicated cases. That I may not tire instead of satisfying you, I shall add no more upon this most important subject, but one admirable conversation between Socrates and Demodocus, who came to the former with his son Theages, to consult with him about his education.[27]

DEM. I have something, Socrates, that I would gladly communicate to you if you are at leisure; nay, if your business be not of very great consequence, I could wish you would take leisure for my sake to hear me.

SOC. I am quite at leisure, especially if I can be of any use to you. Therefore, pray, tell me what you have to say.

DEM. Shall we then retire a little into the portico of Jupiter the Saver, which is here just by.

SOC. So be it, if you choose it.

DEM. Let us go then, Socrates. There is a great affinity, methinks, between the condition of plants, and all the fruits of the earth, nay, and that of all animals too, and the condition of mankind. We who apply ourselves to agriculture, find it easy enough to do all the preparatory work for planting; and even the planting business itself is soon dispatched: But after what we have planted hath taken root, and begins to live, then the plant requires no small care and culture. That after-work, of cherishing and cultivating plants to their perfection is very difficult. And so it appears to me to be with regard to men. For I judge of other men's experience by my own. The planting or generation, call it which you will, of this son of mine was an easy matter: But rearing him up and educating him hath cost me many an anxious thought, much trouble and sollicitude. I have many things to say on this subject, such are my concerns and fears.—But a desire which hath lately seized him greatly disquiets me; not that it is a mean or an ignoble one, but because it is attended with great danger.—For, you must know, Socrates, that he hath taken a strong fancy to be what we call a wise man, or philosopher; some of his equals, as I imagine, who have frequented the city, by repeating some discourses they had heard there, having excited his emulation. They have in truth so edged him, that he has been for some time past incessantly importuning me to take more care of his instruction, and lay out some of my money upon some sophist, capable to render him

---

27. The greater part of this dialogue is to be found in Plato under the title of Theages: The latter part is only taken from other parts of Plato's works. Nothing is put into Socrates's mouth, which either Plato or Xenophon does not make him say in effect.

a wise man or a philosopher. I don't much value money. But I apprehend no small danger to him from this his new flame, which makes him so impatient. I have therefore endeavoured to moderate this his zeal, by words, as much as I could, in order to elude and divert, if not extinguish it: But since I find this won't do any longer, I have thought it wiser to yield to him, lest company he may fall into, when I am not with him, should corrupt him. This, in fine, is my business here at present, to find out some one of your most celebrated sophists, to whose discipline I may commit him. Wherefore, if you can give me any advice about this matter, I desire and expect it from you.

SOC. 'Tis a true proverb, Demodocus, that advice is a sacred thing. And if the saying hold true in any case, it must be chiefly so in respect to the affair you now propose. For there is nothing about which one ought to deliberate and consult with more seriousness and solemnity, than one's own right conduct, and the proper institution of his children. Let us therefore, in order to come to the best resolution about this affair, first settle and agree about the thing in question, lest having had from the beginning different ideas of the matter, we should lose much time and many words in debating and consulting, and then at last find out, to our mutual shame, that we had been long conferring together, without understanding what we were about.

DEM. You are much in the right, Socrates. So certainly ought we to do.

SOC. To be sure we should, but yet not quite in the way I first thought of. I have changed my mind a little as to that. It has just come into my head, that the youth may not be desiring precisely what we imagine, but something else. And if this should happen to be the case, we would still act an absurder part both of us, by consulting gravely about yielding or not yielding to what he had not at all in his head. The best way, therefore, in my opinion, is to begin with him, and to endeavour to learn from himself what he desires.

DEM. What you propose is indeed the best course.

SOC. What is your son's name, Demodocus, that I may know how to accost him.

DEM. His name is Theages.

Soc. You have given him a very august one. Come here, pray, Theages, and tell me, Do you desire to be a wise man, and do you, in earnest ask your father to endeavour to find some person by whose conversation and instruction you may be rendered such?

Theag. That truly is my most earnest request.

Soc. Whom then do you call wise, those who are skilled in somethings or not?

Theag. Those who are skilled and learned, no doubt.

Soc. Why? hath not your father taken care to have you instructed in those things in which young gentlemen generally are instructed, as reading, music, and the genteel exercises?

Theag. He has.

Soc. Do you think there is still some science wanting to compleat your education, which your father ought not to neglect?

Theag. I do.

Soc. What is it, pray? Tell us that we may take care to have it done.

Theag. My father knows very well what it is, for I have often told him. But he hath put you upon this art with me, by pretending not to understand what I had desired of him. For by this and other shifts hath he often endeavoured to elude my sollicitations, and he will not put me under the care of any master.

Soc. But there were no witnesses to what formerly passed between you. Now, therefore, take me for a witness to your request, and speak out plainly before me, what that wisdom is in which you desire to be instructed.—Let us hear; for if, e.g. it was the art of navigation you had a mind to learn, and I should ask what science you desired to know, would you not immediately call it by its name, and tell me you meant the skill or art of navigation?

Theag. I would.

Soc. Or if it was the art of driving chariots, would not you tell me it was so, and name it directly.

Theag. Most certainly.

Soc. Well then, the science or art you now desire to learn has it a name or not?

THEAG. Yes surely, it has a fixed name.

SOC. Do you then know the art but not know its appellation; or do you know both?

THEAG. I know very well how it is called.

SOC. Tell me then what it is?

THEAG. Who gives it any other name but that of wisdom?

SOC. What do you think of the art we were just now speaking of, the art of charioteership, is it knowledge or is it ignorance in your opinion.

THEAG. I don't think it ignorance.

SOC. It is therefore knowledge or wisdom.

THEAG. It is so.

SOC. You call it so, don't you, because it is the art of yoking horses and directing courses?

THEAG. Just so.

SOC. In like manner, you allow navigation to be an art, because it is the science or art of directing ships, don't you?

THEAG. I do.

SOC. Well then, Is there any thing which we learn to govern, rule or manage, by the art you are desirous of being instructed in?

THEAG. Yes, I take it to be the art of ruling or managing men.

SOC. Do you mean sick men?

THEAG. No truly.

SOC. Right, because that is the business of the medicinal art.

THEAG. Just so.

SOC. Is it the art of directing singers in the choirs?

THEAG. No.

SOC. For that you'll say is music.

THEAG. It is.

SOC. Is it then the skill of presiding and directing in the schools or theatres of the exercises.

THEAG. Nor that neither.

SOC. For that you call the gymnastic art.

THEAG. Yes.

SOC. Tell me in the manner I have explained to you, the subjects of these other arts, what men and in what affairs your art governs, or teaches to direct?

THEAG. I take it to be conversant about ruling of those who are united together in communities or cities.

Soc. I understand now what art you mean: you do not mean the art that directs plowers and planters; for that is agriculture: Nor that which directs smiths and joiners, and other artisans; for that is skill in the mechanical arts.

THEAG. It is neither.

Soc. It is then the art of governing all men and women, whatever their different employments and conditions may be, as men and citizens? Is it not?

THEAG. Yes, this is the wisdom I have long desired to be instructed in.

Soc. Then you can tell me whether Aegisthus, he, to wit, who killed Agamemnon at Argos, had this skill of governing all sorts of classes and conditions of men.

THEAG. Not at all.

Soc. What then do you think of Peleus the son of Aeacus in Pthia? Or of Periander at Corinth?—Or to name no more, Archilaus, the son of Perdiccas, who lately ruled over Macedonia? Did not they know the art you desire to learn?

THEAG. They did.

Soc. And Hippias too, the son of Pisistratus, who lately ruled over this city, did not he too know how to rule over men?

THEAG. Sure.

Soc. Tell me then, if you please, by what name you think Bacis and Sibylla, and our own Amphilytus ought to be distinguished?

THEAG. By what other, pray, but that of prophets?

Soc. Very right; and therefore tell me by what name Periander and Hippias ought to be called on account of their way and manner of ruling?

THEAG. What else but tyrants?

Soc. Does not then every one who desires to rule over men as they did, desire to be a tyrant?

THEAG. So it would seem.

Soc. Is then the science you are desirous of, the art of tyranny?

Theag. It appears to follow from what I have said.

Soc. And since you, little rogue, have been desiring to rule over us tyranically, are you angry with your father for not sending you to be instructed in the arts of tyranny. But let us go on now we know your desire. And what if we should here call in the authority of Euripides. For he says somewhere,

$$\Sigma o\phi\acuteo\iota \ \tau\upsilon\rho\rho\alpha\nu\nu o\iota \ \tau\acute\omega\nu \ \sigma o\phi\omega\nu \ \sigma\upsilon\nu o\iota\sigma\iota\acute\alpha.^{28}$$

If therefore any one should have asked Euripides how tyrants may attain to their art; the answer he would have given would have been to the same effect as if he had said, Husbandmen learn their skill by commerce with the skilled in that art; cooks theirs, in the same manner, by conversation with those who are skilled in theirs, and so must rulers and tyrants learn their science.

Theag. You now trifle with me when I thought we were just come to the point.

Soc. Why so? Did not you say it was the art of empire over citizens you desired to understand?

Theag. Yes, I am not ashamed to speak it out. I could wish to have the universal empire of the world; and if that can't be, the larger the empire the better. And I believe you and all men desire power and empire; some perhaps to be God: But that I have not said I desire.

Soc. However, what you desire is to rule over subjects or citizens?

Theag. Yes indeed, but not violently as tyrants, but over voluntary free men, as other illustrious magistrates in our city.

Soc. You mean as Themistocles, and Pericles, and Cimon, and all the others who excelled in the administration of our republic.

Theag. Just so indeed.

Soc. Well, if you would be instructed in the art of horsemanship,

---

28. ["Tyrants are made wise by the company of the wise." The authorship of this line is disputed. The scholia on Aristophanes assigned the fragment to Sophocles (Fragment 14). Aelius Aristides referred to it as "Euripides' line" in *Pros Platon Huper Ton Tettaron* (Jebb's edition, p. 288, line 4).]

would you not have recourse to one skilled and experienced in the practice of that art.

THEAG. I would.

Soc. Well then, in the present case, ought you not to have recourse to persons experienced and practised in the arts of government?

THEAG. I have heard of discourses ascribed to you, in which you said that the sons of persons experienced in magistracy and rule, were generally no wiser than the sons of ordinary artisans. And I take it to be very true, as far as I have been able to observe, or am capable of judging. And would it not be very foolish in me to expect instruction from those who take no care of the institution of their own sons?

Soc. Well, if it be so, what would you think, suppose you were a father, and your son desired to be bred a painter, if he should be angry with you for not giving him the proper institution in that art, when in the mean time he refused to go to the painters to be instructed—What, I say, would you think of your son in this case? Would you not think him very unreasonable?

THEAG. I should have reason.

Soc. But is not this the case between you and your father? You are angry because he does not send you where you may learn the arts of civil government; and yet you yourself do not expect to find this instruction where alone surely it can be expected?

THEAG. Come, Socrates, would you take me under your care I should be happy. I desire no other master.

DEM. My son judges well. That would be a happiness indeed. Let me therefore intreat you by all the sacred bonds of friendship, and by your love of the public, and of virtue.

Soc. You are right, my friend, to be deeply concerned about the education of your son: But what vain things have I said or done that could make you imagine I could think myself fitter for undertaking that task than yourself, who are more aged and experienced in all parts of life than I, and have honourably discharged several high public trusts, with none of which I ever intermedled? If your son desires to be instructed, and yet does not expect instruction from persons who have been conversant in public affairs, but is looking about for one who professes the art of educating

youth, there is Prodicus the Cean, Gorgias Leontinus, and Polus of Agri-
gentum, who are followed wherever they go, by bands of our noblest and
richest youth, who leave the inspection and tutorage of their fathers and
illustrious relations, to be instructed by them, and do not grudge very large
sums to these preceptors. I know none of those arts which they boast of.
All I pretend to is the skill of insinuating into young minds the love of
virtue. I know the secret of gaining their esteem and confidence; and I
have made it the chief business of my life to warn them against the snares
and dangers of the world, and to enamour them of virtue, as the chief
beauty and good in human life. These teachers vaunt of deep erudition, of
profound insight into the mysteries of nature, and of the art of giving an
appearance of probability to any side of any question: They teach their
scholars to define and divide, to subtilize, perplex and dispute, and these
talents make indeed a dazling shew: But all I pretend to is, to instil into
young minds the love of justice, of truth, of mankind, and to raise their
abhorrence and aversion against every vice. I shew them the beauty of virtuous actions in real characters, and paint out to them the strength of
mind, and the quiet, the self-satisfaction, and undisturbable happiness
which virtue and virtue only can give. And I show them the absurdity and
ridiculousness of some vices, and the fatal consequences of others; their
pernicious effects within the breast of the guilty person himself, as well as
to society. I take pleasure in pointing[29] out to them, in the final causes of
nature's operations, as far as we can trace them, the wisdom and goodness
of the first Cause, by which all things were brought into being, subsist and
operate, in order to lead them to the admiration and love of this first universal mind, union with whom, by the love and imitation of that goodness
which is his happiness and excellency, is the supreme felicity of a rational
being: The only one that can abide: The only one that can support under
adversity: And indeed the chief joy of prosperity; for what is the greatest
pleasure it affords, is it not the power of doing good, and banishing or
alleviating misery. I go with them to the portico's and temples adorned

29. None can doubt, who are acquainted with Plato and Xenophon, that Socrates's
doctrine and manner of teaching is here fairly represented.

with pictures and sculptures, and by pointing out to them the beauties of
such works, lead them to attend to the measures, the proportions, which
make at once natural beauty and utility, in whatever class of objects these
arts imitate or take their rules from. I thus lead them from nature to art,
and reciprocally from the arts which emulate nature to nature herself, and
inure them to entertain themselves with the admiration of nature's wisdom and goodness, and to inculcate upon their minds from that consideration, their own proper business, in imitation of, and in concert with the
great Author of nature; to fit themselves for doing all the good they can,
by cultivating in their hearts a benevolent principle, and by giving all diligence to replenish their minds with the knowledge of what is best in every
circumstance. And believe me, after the mind is well disposed, and capable
to judge of fit and unfit, in the more ordinary circumstances of human life,
it will not be difficult to judge well of more abstruse and complex cases,
which require keeping in mind many circumstances, such as civil constitutions, laws and policies. For inuring youth to keep but one maxim in
their view, as the standard to try these by, will, after the habit of thinking
is well established, make that much easier work than is imagined. The
maxim is, "That policies, constitutions and laws are good or evil, in proportion to their tendency to encourage or discourage the benevolent industry which is the cement of societies, and indeed the mother of all the
blessings in human life." I have not time now to explain upon this maxim,
and shew how, in consequence of it, honours ought to lie open in states to
all ingenious and good men, or to point out many other such conclusions
of great moment, which result with equal clearness from this principle.
But the maxim itself is evident, and it is the standard by which we are to
try and judge of all civil establishments. And in order to lead to it, and
inculcate it deeply on the minds of youth, I am ever telling them proper
parts of our own history in particular, and unfolding the characters of the
persons who were chiefly concerned in these transactions, the different
parts they acted, and the different motives and views they were actuated
by in their behaviours. This is all I can pretend to. I take all opportunities
of doing this; and the oftner I see Theages the welcomer he shall be to me.
For thus shall I be assured, that he loves true virtue, and desires the best
knowledge, the science of human duties. He who loves virtue will soon

understand what it requires in any circumstance of life, and what are the properest ways of expressing, i.e. of enforcing and endearing its precepts, in which last consists the excellency of writing.

The End of Part II.

An Essay on Liberal Education

IN WHICH

The properest methods of instructing youth in the Belles-lettres, the polite arts, philosophy, and which is chief, in virtue, are fully considered:

Doctrina sed vim promovet insitam
Rectique cultus pectora roborant.

—HOR.[1]

---

1. [Horace, *Odes,* 4.4.33–34: "Yet training increases inborn worth, and righteous ways make strong the heart" (Loeb translation by C. E. Bennett). This is also Locke's motto for *Some Thoughts Concerning Education.*]

An Essay on Liberal Education, &c.

Instruction in the science or art of right living is the chief lesson in education, to which all others ought to be rendered subservient, and what this science is, and what may justly be called false learning.

If there be any such thing as duty, or any such thing as happiness; if there be any difference between right and wrong conduct; any distinction between virtue and vice, or wisdom and folly: In fine, if there be any such thing as perfection or imperfection belonging to the rational powers which constitute moral agents; or if enjoyments and pursuits admit of comparison; good education must of necessity be acknowledged to mean proper care to instruct early in the science of happiness and duty, or in the art of judging and acting aright in life. Whatever else one may have learned, if he comes into the world from his schooling and masters a mere stranger to the world, quite unacquainted with the nature, rank, and condition of mankind, and the duties of human life (in its more ordinary circumstances at least) he hath lost his time; he is not educated; he is not prepared for the world; he is not qualified for society; he is not fitted for discharging the proper business of man.

The way therefore to judge whether education be upon a right footing or not, is to compare it with this end; or to consider what it does in order to accomplish youth for choosing and behaving well in the various conditions, relations, and incidents of life. If education be calculated and adapted to furnish young minds betimes with proper knowledge for their guidance and direction in the chief affairs of the world, and in the principal vicissitudes to which human concerns are subject, then is it indeed proper or right education. But if such instruction be not the principal scope to which all other lessons are rendered subservient in what is called the institution of youth, either the art of living and acting well is not man's most important business, or what ought to be the chief end of education is neglected, and sacrificed to something of far inferior moment.

The enquiries which are the most suitable employments of man, because none other so nearly concern him, are beautifully described to us by an excellent moralist.

> *Discite, o miseri, & caussas cognoscite rerum,*
> *Quid sumus, & quidnam victuri gignimur; ordo*
> *Quis datus; aut metae quam mollis flexus, & unde:*
> *Quis modus argento: quid fas optare: quid asper*
> *Utile nummus habet: patriae, charisque propinquis*
> *Quantum elargire deceat: quem te Deus esse*
> *Jussit, & humana qua parte locatus es in re.*
> *Disce: nec invideas, quod multa fidilia putet.*
> *In locuplete penu, &c.*
>
> PERS. Sat. 3.[2]

And these therefore are the researches into which youth ought first to be led. Accordingly we find the same poet in another satire describing with the warmest gratitude the care his tutor had taken to direct and assist him in this true philosophy.

> *Cumque iter ambiguum est, & vitae nescius error*
> *Deducit trepidas ramosa in compita mentes,*

---

2. [Persius, *Satires*, 3.66–74: "Come and learn, O miserable souls, and be instructed in the causes of things: learn what we are, and for what sort of lives we were born; what place was assigned to us at the start; how to round the turning-post gently, and from what point to begin the turn; what limit should be placed on wealth; what prayers may be rightfully offered; what good there is in fresh-minted coin; how much should be spent on country and on your dear kin; what part God has ordered you to play, and at what point of the human commonwealth you have been stationed. Learn, I say, and do not grudge the trouble because your neighbour has many a jar going bad" (Loeb translation by G. G. Ramsay).]

Me tibi supposui: teneros tu suscipis annos
Socratico, Cornute, sinu. Tunc fallere solers
Apposita intortos extendit regula mores;
Et premitur ratione animus! vincique laborat,
Artificemque tuo ducit sub pollice vultum.
Tecum etenim longos memini consumere soles,
Et tecum, &c.

PERS. Sat. 5.[3]

Where are we? Under what roof? On board what vessel? Whither bound? On what business? Under whose pilotship, government or protection? What are we? Whence did we arise? Or whence had we our being, and to what end are we designed? To what course of action are we destined by our natural frame and constitution? What have we to do? How are we to steer? What to pursue, and what to avoid? What goal are we to aim at; and how are we to direct and turn the chariot? These are the great and important questions with regard to which till one is able to satisfy himself, he is an absolute stranger to himself, to his nature, origin, end, interest and duty. And it is surprizing indeed to consider, that a man should have been long come into the world, and carried his reason and sense about with him, and yet have never seriously ask'd himself this single question, Where am I? or what? But, on the contrary, should proceed regularly to every other study and enquiry, postponing this alone as the least considerable. How early may the mind of man, which nature hath framed so curious, so inquisitive, so fond of knowledge, and with such a strong desire of happiness, be awakened to this research, and deeply interested in it by a lively feeling of its importance! For what questions are more natural, more obvious, and at the same time, more touching and rousing than these? Indeed no man could long think or look about him, without being led to

---

3. [Persius, *Satires*, 5.34–42: "at an age when the path of life is doubtful, and wanderings, ignorant of life, parted my trembling soul into the branching crossways—I placed myself into your hands, Cornutus; you took up my tender years in your Socratic bosom. Your rule, applied with unseen skill, straightened out the crooked morals; my soul, struggling to be mastered, was moulded by your reason, and took on features under your plastic thumb. With you, I remember, did I pass long days, with you."]

these enquiries, or having been once pointed to the search, easily quit it, till he had come to some determination with relation to these momentuous points, were he not misled by education into other pursuits; were not his natural curiosity turned by his guides towards other objects, and his imagination taught to amuse itself with investigations that carry him far away from the researches which most concern him. The melancholly phenomenon is not otherwise to be accounted for. And this we know, that whatever first catches and charms our fancy by its specious appearance, will so warmly engage our affection, and so wholly engross our mind, as to leave no room for other ideas to enter; or give such a turn to our pursuits, that it will be very difficult to take us off from them, however trifling, or however hurtful they may be. As the clay may be moulded either into a toy, or a serviceable utensil, so may the young mind either be dissipated, and rendered quite airy, volatile, and absolutely averse to thinking; made fond of the most idle and insignificant exercises, by bad, or turned towards the most serious and useful enquiries by good education. We are indeed in the hands of persons about us in our infancy, as the clay in those of the potter: From these we take our first and most lasting ideas and impressions; by them are we shaped and fashioned into a form of mind almost as indelible as natural complexion. Can the Aethiopian change his colour or the leopard his spots? No more can he, who hath been accustomed from his childhood to do evil, learn to do well. But train up a child in the way wherein he ought to walk, and he will never forsake the paths of truth and virtue. Direct him to the researches best befitting and most interesting him, and inure him, by proper discipline, to right practices, and he will adhere to them, and bless his instructors and formers for ever.

The power of habit shall be fully considered in another place. And sure we need not stay any longer to prove, that man is the properest study of man: And therefore that it ought to be the chief scope of education to teach man what he is, or rather what he is intended to be and may become, by proper application and culture; or what is his chief business, duty and good. Let us therefore, in this chapter, consider what this knowledge means and comprehends: And what the false learning is, by which youth are misled from this truly useful science.

Youth may easily be led to observe, that there is a perfection to which plants and flowers may be improved; or that there is a perfection to which horses and other animals may be formed. And hence they may very naturally be led to enquire what is the perfection to which man may be cultivated, and what is the culture and what the means for accomplishing this noble end. And to know the stock, the furniture, with which nature hath favoured man, the best use of this provision, the end for which it is bestowed upon us, the dignity to which we may arrive by the proper cultivation and employment of it; and what is this due culture and best employment of the powers conferred upon us, that make our stock for use and enjoyment.—This is to know man; to know his rank in nature, the end of his creation, and his relation to the universe, and to its supreme Maker and Lord. And thus alone can one know what he was designed for, or what he ought to aim at and intend; what is his best employment and truest good, the noblest and wisest course he can pursue. Now it will not be difficult to make one early understand what a clear, strong and well furnished understanding means; or that the mind is in a state of darkness with regard to all that most immediately concerns it, till it is able to discern what it is and whence it came, what powers it is possessed of, and what is the best use of them.—Nor will it be found difficult to make youth soon perceive, that self-command and mastership over our affections, is power and dominion, is liberty, is greatness of soul, and absolutely necessary in order to right judging and choosing: They may easily be taught how dangerous blindness or precipitancy are; and that the perfection, the dignity of a being endowed with the power of comparing, computing, judging and choosing, called reason, consists in reason's holding the reins of government with a steady hand, and letting out or taking in the affections, and directing all their courses according to its best views, upon duly weighing and ballancing the consequences of pursuits and actions. And when these two lessons are understood, a hearty disposition to promote the greater good of mankind, and a large capacity for usefulness in society, will quickly be perceived to be man's glory, perfection and happiness: the surest way to true honour, and the securest means of self-enjoyment. How soon may very young minds be instructed in just notions of honour and happiness, by painting out to them, in their proper colours, different actions and characters; the character of the deliberate judicious man, in opposition to that of the rash, headstrong one, who suffers himself to be hurried away by every fancy, passion or appetite.—The character of the man who knows himself, and what is the best part he can act in every incident or relation of life, and sees deeply into the secrets of nature, in opposition to him who knows nothing about himself or his duties, or about any of the objects of nature that surround him.—The character of the benevolent man, who is capable of discovering readily what the interests of society require at his hands, and steadily pursues the public good, and is therefore not flattered with mere lip-praise, but sincerely and cordially loved and honoured, in opposition to him who, contracted within himself, thinks of no other end but the gratification of some one or other of his own sensual, selfish appetites, and who may therefore be crowded with flatterers and parasites, but is really despised, nay hated.—Young minds, by describing, by pointing out characters to them in history, life, or fictitious portraits of men and manners, may very soon be taught to know man's furniture, duty, honour, and true felicity: They will soon be able to discern all the beauty and excellence of that admirable picture Horace draws of Lollius; and to perceive that they and their tutors ought to have it, and such like characters of truly great and good men ever before them as the mark, the glorious mark to be aimed at, and attained to by their education and studies.

> ———— ———— *Non ego te meis*
> *Chartis inornatum sileri,*
> *Totve tuos patiar labores*
> *Impune, Lolli, carpere lividas*
> *Obliviones. Est animus tibi*
> *Rerumque prudens, & secundis*
> *Temporibus dubiisque rectus;*
> *Vindex avarae fraudis, & abstinens*
> *Ducentis ad se cuncta pecuniae;*
> *Consulque non unius anni,*
> *Sed quoties bonus atque fidus*
> *Judex honestum praetulit utili, &*
> *Rejecit alto dona nocentium*

Vultu, & per obstantes catervas
Explicuit sua victor arma.
Non possidentem multa vocaveris
Recte beatum: rectius occupat
Nomen beati, qui Deorum
Muneribus sapienter uti,
Duramque callet pauperiem pati.
Pejusque letho flagitium timet:
Non ille pro caris amicis
Aut patria timidus perire.

HOR. l. 4. od. 9.[4]

The knowledge which this admirable poet tells us, is absolutely requisite to a fine writer, is yet more so to make a good and amiable man; a man of worth and merit in society, one truly happy in himself, and really beloved by mankind.

Qui didicit patriae quid debeat, & quid amicis,
Quo sit amore parens, quo frater amandus, & hospes,
Quod sit conscripti, quod judicis officium, quae
Partes in bellum missi ducis.

HOR. Art. Poet. l. 312.[5]

---

4. [Horace, *Odes*, 4.9.30–52: "Not thee, O Lollius, will I leave unsung, unhonoured by my verse; nor will I suffer envious forgetfulness to prey undisturbed upon thy many exploits. A mind thou hast, experienced in affairs, well-poised in weal or woe, punishing greed, fraud, holding aloof from money that draws all things to itself, thou a consul not of a single year, but so oft as, a judge righteous and true, thou preferrest honour to expediency, rejectest with high disdain the bribes of guilty men, and bearest thine arms victorious through opposing hosts. Not him who possesses much, would one rightly call the happy man; he more fitly gains that name who knows how to use with wisdom the blessings of the gods, to endure hard poverty, and who fears dishonour worse than death, not afraid to die for cherished friends or fatherland."]

5. [Horace, *Ars Poetica*, 312–15: "He who has learned what he owes his country and his friends, what love is due a parent, a brother, and a guest, what is imposed on senator and judge, what is the function of a general sent to war" (Loeb translation by H. Rushton Fairclough).]

And accordingly he often recommends this same philosophy, as what ought to be the study of every man who would live honourably and happily in the world, and the main business of education. Now, how youth may be best formed into this knowledge, taste and character, the same author likewise tells us, by setting before us the methods his own father took of instructing him in virtue, and warning him against folly and vice.

————— *Insuevit pater optimus hoc me,*
Ut fugerem exemplis vitiorum quaeque notando.
Cum me hortaretur, parcè, frugaliter, atque
Viverem uti contentus eo quod mi ipse parasset:
Nonne vides, Albi ut male vivat filius? utque
Barrus inops? magnum documentum, ne patriam rem
Perdere quis velit. A turpi meretricis amore
Cum deterreret: Scetani dissimilis sis.
&c.

HOR. Sat. lib. 1. Sat. 4. l. 105.[6]

What the natural consequence of such wise care was, he describes in the same satyr thus,

————— ————— *Neque enim, cum lectulus, aut me*
Porticus excepit, desum mihi: Rectius hoc est:
Hoc faciens vivam melius: sic dulcis amicis
Occurram: &c.

ibid. l. 133.[7]

6. [Horace, *Satires*, 1.4.105–12: "'Tis a habit the best of fathers taught me, for, to enable me to steer clear of follies, he would brand them, one by one, by his examples. Whenever he would encourage me to live thriftily, frugally, and content with what he had saved for me, 'Do you not see,' he would say, 'how badly fares young Albius, and how poor is Baius? A striking lesson not to waste one's patrimony!' When he would deter me from a vulgar amour, 'Don't be like Scetanus'" (Loeb translation by H. Rushton Fairclough).]

7. [Horace, *Satires*, 1.4.133–36: "for when my couch welcomes me or I stroll in the colonnade, I do not fail myself: 'This is the better course: if I do that, I shall fare more happily: thus I shall delight the friends I meet.'"]

His father's method of instructing him in virtue by examples, naturally led him to the practice, and formed in him the habit of self-conversation or self-examination, and of often reflecting with himself upon his conduct, and upon what is fair and laudable in conduct, and what the reverse, without which one cannot make progress in virtue, or even maintain acquaintance with himself. The nature and excellent effects of this home-discipline are delightfully exhibited to us by a noble example of the practice in the meditations or self-communing of one of the best of princes, M. Antoninus Philosophus, whose amiable virtues cannot be too often set before young minds, in order to shew them the transcendent beauty of virtue, and excite their emulation to be equally wise and good.

Teachers of youth ought therefore to select characters for their young pupils, contrasting the virtues with the opposite vices, as the most effectual way of shewing them to what perfection and dignity men may attain, and how corrupt and abominable they may become through the deceitfulness of vice, if they are not upon their guard against every immoral indulgence. For 'tis by examples that good and bad conduct, with their various effects and consequences, the strength and grace to which men, by proper diligence, may arrive, and the baseness and misery into which vice plunges, most strongly appear: Characters not only point out the virtue that ought to be loved, the wise part that ought to be acted, and what on the other hand is equally vile and dangerous, much more clearly and vividly than precepts, as a picture gives a much more lively idea of any sensible object than the best description: But they actually bring forth good affections into exercise, and by so doing establish right approbations and right aversions in our minds, and thus work into habit and temper that divine ambition of excelling in virtue; which, when it is firmly rooted in the heart, is a living, permanent principle, ever abounding in the great and good deeds to which all the happiness in the world is solely owing, and without which outward affluence is a nusance, a pest. For every vice naturally carries along with it something hurtful to society. And 'tis by wisdom and virtue alone that any good can be extracted out of its native venom, or that its genuine tendency to empoison and corrupt, is alloyed or tempered, as every more shining character in history shews us, by representing to us the struggles to reform, oppose, check, or defeat vice, which constitute its beauty and excellence. This, indeed, is the moral lesson every more exalted example in the records of human affairs presents to us in the most striking light, and which cannot be too early or too forcibly inculcated from fact and experience, "That for a while, prudence and virtue may stem or abate the ravages, the pestiferous influences of abounding wickedness and dissolution of manners: But when vice is become too rampant and impetuous even for much virtue to correct it, then public ruin is unavoidable: Vice is the disease, virtue the medicine, and when the distemper overpowers the remedy, the body politic, like the natural body, is irrecoverably lost, perdition must ensue." The characters of the more considerable personages in moral history, will afford, to a judicious instructor, excellent opportunities of enforcing, of deeply riveting this important lesson upon young minds. And when they have well digested it, then are they duly prepared and seasoned for entering into the world: But without a thorough understanding and feeling of this truth, one is not sufficiently qualified for directing his own conduct, even in any of the more ordinary spheres of life, but still wants a tutor or guide.

Characters well drawn are (as we have said) lively pictures of the virtues to which men may arise by due application and culture, shewing at once in what we are defective, and to what perfection we may arrive. They set to our view the strength, the force, the comprehensiveness into which our judgment and other intellectual faculties may be improved, and most affecting instances of what is yet a higher qualification than the finest imagination, the most tenacious memory, or the best replenished understanding, that absolute command of our passions, and that godlike benignity of soul, which by spreading happiness all around, as far and as largely as duly improved power can reach, is attended with a sense of inward greatness, and of true merit, with all wise and good beings, which is indeed the highest, and the only lasting, because the most rational fecility: In one word, they exhibit to us in the most touching manner, all the perfections attainable by men: They not only demonstrate the possibility of attaining to them; but powerfully upbraid our indolence, and so rouse our emulation.—Accordingly, teaching by well chosen characters hath been warmly recommended by all the ancient sages. 'Twas thus we are told that Cato the elder, who would not entrust the education of his son to any other, formed his judgment and ambition. He composed for his use characters of the principal persons in ancient times, the most distinguished in his own state, particularly, with a short history of the greatest actions of each, that his son might by this means be early acquainted with patterns the most worthy of his imitation, and model himself by them. And indeed there have been many instances of very young persons, even in modern times, who have been perfectly acquainted with examples of every excellence, every accomplishment, every virtue in human life; and which is yet more, could give a concise, distinct account of the rise and fall of the more remarkable ancient states and empires, in a manner that sufficiently proved they understood and felt what they were able to relate, and that at an age when the greater part of youth are quite rude and ignorant. And what progress in languages, or in any other art, is to be compared with this knowledge? For what do they profit or avail without it? This, we are assured, was the science that was most carefully and early instilled into the minds of all the great examples of public spirit and true fortitude and wisdom amongst the Greeks and Romans, which their history shews. To this principally was it owing, that so many in ancient times were capable of giving counsel about the most important public affairs, and serving their country in various capacities, at an age when with us, according to the more prevailing methods of education, we still excuse ignorance and childishness, and expect nothing manly: Nor could they otherwise have so early attained to such a pitch, not only of virtue, but of civil and political wisdom.

But it is proper to consider yet a little more particularly, that knowledge of human nature, and of the duties of rational and civil life, which is best taught by examples or characters.

Such is our innate desire of knowledge, that children, so soon as they can speak, express their eager inquisitiveness into the nature and use of every new object that falls within their observation. They naturally ask *what* it is, and *for what* it serves? Now this native curiosity ought to be indulged, nay cherished and improved into an equal sollicitude to know what they themselves are, and for what end they are made, and may easily be so; and after satisfying, as much as is possible, their curiosity about other things, whether animate or inanimate, ask them but what they themselves are, whence they come, and for what they are designed, and you will quickly see the question rouse all their attention, and kindle a very keen desire to know what and for what they are. And the properest first answer to this question is, to tell them that they are made and designed by the one Author of all things, who made every thing for a good end, and hath abundantly qualified every thing for its end, to improve and grow by diligent culture into the perfection which renders such or such persons so serviceable to mankind, and procures them such universal love and honour. Let the first examples be taken from amongst those whom they have seen, and have naturally, or by acquaintance, some love or regard for: But go on with them, drawing the characters to them, one after another, of such persons as have really been a glory, an eternal honour to mankind, till they have fully conceived, that doing good to mankind is true glory and happiness, and the great end for which man is sent into the world, and formed and furnished as he is, with understanding, memory, reason and various active powers; and till you have raised an ambition in them to imitate these characters, and anxiety to know by what steps, by what methods they may arrive at such perfection.

Take hold of their curiosity to understand the nature and use of every thing; commend it, and let them know that one of the chief excellencies of man, and one of the main ends for which he is framed an intelligent creature, is to improve his understanding, and enrich his mind with knowledge, by satisfying this curiosity, and enquiring diligently with them into the reasons and uses of things: Give them an account of the progress many curious searchers into nature have made in this knowledge; and tell them, that if they will converse with men and with books, and preserve their curiosity, attention and docility, they shall soon know the natures and uses, not only of many things near them, but even of very distant objects, the sun, the moon and the stars. Shew them early, by fit examples, the proper method of searching into and finding out the properties of things and their uses. Above all, let them early be led to observe that knowledge of nature is not only in itself pleasant, exceeding pleasant, and the proper perfection of the intellectual faculties, with which kind nature hath furnished and adorned us; but that knowledge is power, and that the Author of nature hath made a large dominion to be acquirable by mankind, by their understanding and reason: shew them how air, water, and all the ele-

ments, and almost all bodies, have been rendered subservient to the advantage or conveniency of human society, by the knowledge of their qualities. They will thus be early led at once to perceive the beauty, and taste
the pleasure of natural knowledge, and to remark, that the proper business
of mankind on earth, is to obtain a large dominion, command, or lordship
there, by subduing, as it were, every element, every object to their use, and
that by extending their insight into natural causes, i.e. the natural properties of things, and the laws according to which they produce effects: For
thus, and thus alone, is man's property, power or dominion augmentable:
And by thus adding to human knowledge and power is human life sweetened, adorned, greatened. We can only here hint the heads or chief articles
of that knowledge, to the desire of which youth ought early to be incited:
As for the proper methods of accomplishing this end by conversation,
these may be learned from several of Socrates's discourses recorded by
Xenophon: And of them and the Socratic method in general, we shall afterwards have occasion to treat at some length. Till by satisfying the natural curiosity of youth about the natures and uses of several things, they
have got an idea of knowledge in general, and know what it is, how it
ought to be carried on, and what good ends it serves, besides the immediate satisfaction it gives to the mind, they cannot understand what makes
the perfection of the understanding faculty. But by instruction in the natures and uses of several objects, they will soon acquire a notion of intellectual perfection, or understand what a well-furnished mind means, and
wherein its excellency and usefulness consists; and be wonderfully fired by
the characters of those to whose researches into nature we are indebted for
all the knowledge of, and all the dominion over, or in nature we enjoy. Let
them see how all the arts by which we subsist with any degree of comfort,
spring from the knowledge of nature, acquired by attention to the properties of things and their laws. And they will thus see why knowledge
ought to be sought, and how it ought to be pursued, and of what use to
mankind they are, who increase our knowledge of nature, and thereby improve advantageous arts, or invent new ones of any considerable utility.
And by the same observations they will easily be led to observe the wisdom
and goodness of the Maker of all things, in giving things their respective
qualities and powers, and so fitting them for certain ends; and in giving to

man the capacity of applying such an infinite variety of things to the uses
of human society by his reason, which is therefore, as it were, all the powers scattered through inferior beings, animate or inanimate, in one. From
which reflection there arises a very natural and obvious consequence that
ought never to be omitted, whatever particular nature or frame be the object of the lesson, viz. "That to aim at and pursue the good of our kind by
our actions, is to imitate the Author of nature, and to act in concert with
him, and therefore the sure way of approving ourselves to him, and gaining his favour." Let the subject be often changed, but still let the lesson
upon the qualities of whatsoever object and its uses, end in these reflections, till having been, by frequent examples, all conspiring to confirm and
illustrate them, deeply rivetted in the mind, they will naturally recur to it
on every occasion: For thus knowledge will be made an incitement and
spur, not only to application in the speculative way, but to action properly
so called, that is, activity in rendering knowledge subservient to the advantage, conveniency, ornament or grandeur of human life. Thus will public
good become habitually present to their minds, and their predomining
motive and passion; the sole measure to them of worth and merit, as indeed it ought to be.

As much as early incitement to the love of natural knowledge is neglected in education; yet, as they must not have observed the natural dispositions of children, who have not remarked that nature points, directs
and prompts them to it very strongly, and thus shews what ought to be
our first care about them; so, they must not know what natural knowledge
means, or to what we owe all the advantages of life, and to what alone we
can owe the exercise of our power and dominion in our habitation, earth,
who do not consider it as the study that hath the nearest connexion with
our interest and dignity, and which ought therefore to be principally encouraged by society, and made the chief scope of education. To give an
early turn towards the right method of advancing this knowledge, for the
sake of promoting human power and conveniency, is to give the most useful disposition to youth: because, without extending our knowledge, we
cannot enlarge our power and dominion; but, by increasing it, we really
augment and extend the lordship in this lower world, which the Author of
nature hath plainly designed we should acquire, and in proportion to

which will our happiness or eminence, as men, always be. To increase the happiness of mankind by industry, by arts, by commerce, is evidently the properest, because the usefulest employment of our active powers. And it is knowledge of nature that alone can enlighten or direct our activity and industry. Promoting public good is the noblest, the best End, the worthiest occupation. But what is promoting public good? Wherein does it consist, but in extending that knowledge of nature, which by every discovery it makes of the properties of things, shews us, that the Author of nature steadily intends, and unerringly pursues the universal good; and enables us to render the life of mankind more convenient, more comfortable, more beautiful and great, by qualifying us to subject natural things to our use and advantage? In proportion to the harmonious consociations of mankind in promoting these ends, must human ease and grandeur be.—And in proportion as the pursuit of these ends is hindered, disturbed, discouraged, or neglected, in proportion do men, or combinations and societies of men, fall short of the felicity and perfection nature hath put in their power to acquire.

So soon as youth are led by proper teaching to observe whence all the arts arise, and what advantages redound from the encouragement and improvement of them, it will be very easy to lead them to take notice of what ought to be the end of these coalitions of mankind called civil societies, and wherein their beauty, order, dignity and strength must consist. For, if the happiness and grandeur of human life must be owing to well employed industry, and industry must owe its guidance to the knowledge of nature, that model or constitution of society must be the best which best protects and encourages well-employed industry: And those to whom we owe good models of civil government, and all the political knowledge necessary to found and preserve well-regulated societies; or to teach us how to prevent and how to remedy the diseases to which they are incident, by laying open to us their causes, their symptoms, their prognostics, and their antidotes—Those are the great souls to whom mankind are under the highest obligations.—Those are the true heroes to whom eternal glory is due. Those truly great men having studied human nature and human affairs, knew human happiness must be the effect of human industry skilfully and benevolently employed, and how the spirit of such industry must be supported and promoted; what causes tend to abate or corrupt it, and by what methods these ought to be removed or checked; they were able to discern whence obstacles to, or perversions of public spirit arise, and how it can only be preserved alive, or revived when languishing and decaying.—And to them therefore, and to the study by which they procured such useful prudence, do we owe an insight into human nature, and the springs of human actions, and moral events good and bad, the utility of which is glaringly manifest. It will be easy, I say, after youth understand that the happiness of mankind must be owing to the industry of man skilfully employed for promoting public good, to make them conceive, that the art of supporting and reviving this spirit of benevolent industry, is a most useful science, and that which must direct in founding or reforming societies, governments and laws, and to inflame their minds with a desire of this knowledg. And when they know what natural knowledge, and what this last kind of science, which is properly called politics, mean; and have had some eminent characters of both classes pointed out to them, they will then understand what is the proper study of man, what knowledge in general, and what the perfection and culture of human understanding towards its perfection, signify and comprehend. Many have told me, and I have myself experimented it, that many young lads, who had for a long time been inured to look upon syntax and prosody as the principal part of learning, and had no notion, no tincture of any other science, have in a few months time, by proper conversations, been made acquainted not only with the properties and final causes of many natural objects, but with the rise and use of several arts, the nature of human happiness, and the way of promoting it, viz. by benevolent industry, directed by the knowledge of nature to the pursuit of things useful to society; but likewise have, by an easy transition from thence, to the end of civil government, been informed with a just notion of public liberty, and thereby inflamed with a warm affection towards it, and an earnest desire for instruction in the true politics above described, and in the history of those to whom mankind have been chiefly indebted for founding good governments, and cultivating and improving that science. However difficult this kind of instruction may be thought by any, 'tis certain that till one hath made some advances in it, and conceived a hearty liking for it, whatever else he may have learned, his mind is not replenished with science of things, or turned towards the best and usefullest study: nay, he cannot so much as understand what real science means, or what are its objects and ends; nor, consequently, have any idea of the improvement or perfection of the understanding. But that it is not so difficult to guide young minds very early into the right path of finding out even what orderly and well-regulated society means, any one will soon be convinced who will try the experiment, and making a proper use of the natural curiosity of the human mind, lead it gradually to observe how much we are obliged for the conveniencies of life to agriculture, manufactures of various sorts, shipping, and so forth; and to take notice whence we have these arts, that is, from what study or knowledge; and to infer from the advantages redounding from the industrious cultivation of those arts, that it must be the chief end of society to defend and encourage industry and ingenuity, by securing to the ingenious and industrious the acquests of their labour against all fraud and violence. Let but the various benefits of ingenious, skilful, benevolent industry be recounted to them, and give them but a view of the insight into nature's connexions and laws, that must enlighten and guide industry, and they will soon perceive how much it is the interest of every district of mankind to unite under common laws and guidance, for the common defence and encouragement of the benevolent industry, which is the source of so many great goods; and be inspired with ardent desire to understand what are the best, the strongest or firmest barriers against oppression or tyranny, and the stablest security for property, or for every one's enjoying with undisturbance, the free possession, use and disposal of all he can purchase by his honest art and toil. Give them an account of the inventers and improvers of arts, and of the manifold advantages we reap from such discoveries, and shew them the glory due to them, and cheerfully rendered to them by history, and they will at once see what is the proper employment of human understanding, or wherein its riches and greatness lies, and perceive the application and order of study requisite to attain to equal glory on the account of like usefulness in society, and be fired with zeal to improve their intellectual powers in the same manner; with an antipathy against idleness on the one hand, and fraud or violence on the other, and with love of public order, liberty and justice, and of the constitutions that tend, by preserving them, to encourage and uphold the industrious benevolent spirit, without which nothing that is good or great, beneficial or beautiful in human life can subsist. And are not the beginnings of this taste and temper the proper first elements or beginnings of education, in the knowledge and duties of man? Is not this a good foundation? Or what else ought to be the foundation laid in human minds, whether we consider private or public happiness? What have we done to qualify youth for rational or social life till this be done? And when this point is gained, how quickly will youth be reared up into men equally capable and disposed to promote the general happiness of mankind? I may perhaps, be thought to have insisted too long already upon this point. But however obvious it may be, (and nothing indeed can be more plain or certain, to any one who thinks, than that the knowledge we have described is that alone which can be called knowledge of things, and that alone by which the interests of human society can profit; and that one cannot so much as understand what intelligent faculties, and their improvements and perfections mean, but by the education or instruction that hath been delineated); yet the neglect of this knowledge in education till it is too late, is a sufficient reason for having dwelt so much upon it.

The next lesson, or that which is most a-kin to what hath now been mentioned, and hath the closest connexion with it, is of the highest importance. 'Tis to give youth a just notion of the extent of human power or industry, or of the distinction made by nature between things within and things without our power; things subject to us, and things nowise dependent upon us. Nothing can be more manifest than that till this difference be well understood, men may, will, misplace their labour. And a few instances will soon lead youth, formed and inured to attention, into a true general idea of the things which are submitted to us by nature, or within our dominion. It will not be difficult to make such apprehend, that the general and specific qualities of all bodies, together with the laws of motion according to which their effects are produced, are fixed unalterably by the Author of nature; and therefore that human power cannot change these, but that in order to render bodies subservient to our uses, we must know their properties and powers, and the laws of these powers, and work upon them or apply them to our use, according to these properties and their laws. They may be easily led to observe, that we cannot alter the gravity and springiness of the air, nor the law of gravity in water, but we can render both air and water, in many instances, serviceable to us, in consequence of these immutable properties: They may easily perceive, that the specific gravities of bodies are immutable, and that the same quantity of the same matter hath always the same weight, and yet we may make a lighter body move a heavier out of its place, by adding to the velocity of the lighter, in proportion to what it wants in weight: Experiments to prove these, and many other such physical truths, are easily performed, and as easily understood: And when a few such truths have been explained and confirmed by proper experiments, youth will learn from such lessons what is meant by properties of bodies, and by general fixed laws of motion, and what human art may do, how it must go to work, and what it is absurd for art to attempt. But this being understood, the distinction between the proper objects of human art, sollicitude and industry, and those things which are not subject to us, but are really divine things, i.e. things solely dependent upon the Author of nature, and therefore, with regard us, objects of resignation and submission to the divine disposal, will readily be comprehended, together with one excellent final cause of this difference, viz. the necessity that general unalterable laws should be uniformly observed by nature in its operations, in order to our being capable of knowing or imitating nature, or rendering material things subservient to any useful end with respect to ourselves, since otherwise we could neither know nature, nor have any power or dominion in nature, any natural sphere of activity.

From this observation which results from, and therefore ought to be inculcated from every experiment about whatever corporeal object, it will be a very natural transition to pass to the consideration of our moral power, and of what moral effects are not within our power. Any one may be easily led to perceive, that we cannot add to the number of our senses, or receive any outward sensations or ideas but from experience, but that we can separate, mix and compound our ideas taken in by experience in various manners: And in like manner, that we cannot add to our intellectual faculties, or form any idea of any power of that class, of which we are not partakers in some degree by nature, but yet we can cultivate and improve all these powers of understanding, comparing, judging, reasoning,

imagining, and so forth, to a perfection, which without culture they cannot attain to, but must sink and decline: And in the same way that there
are original determinations in our minds, to be so and so affected by certain moral objects, as well as by corporeal ones, such as actions and characters, which we cannot alter, and that frequent associations of ideas, and
repetitions of affections and actions must of necessity produce habits; but
yet we have it in our power to examine our opinions, and to chastise and
correct our fancies, and by this discipline to take off our affections from
improper objects, and to place them aright, or according to the true esti-
mations of pleasures and pains. A few instances of this kind, exemplified
by characters of men who had the full command and mastership of themselves, i.e. of their passions, by means of home-discipline, or of frequently
calling their appetites and affections to the tribunal of reason, to be examined and directed or corrected, will soon give youth a notion of our
moral power, of inward liberty, and the rule of reason; and shew them, that
the chief business of man is to govern himself aright; and for that reason,
not only to have just ideas of objects and pursuits, but likewise to inure
himself to examine and catechize, so to speak, his affections; and will inflame them with the love of this moral dominion or self-command, without which it may soon be made to appear, that one cannot be great or
happy, but must, on the contrary, live in a most tumultuous, irregular
manner, and be a prey to every specious fancy that may be presented to his
sense or imagination.

It will not be unpleasant to observe to them the analogy between our
power over natural things and our moral power: That neither extends to
the making of properties or laws, but that both consist in producing effects
in consequence of fixed properties and laws; and both of them chiefly lie
in separating and mixing or compounding. But it is yet of greater importance, that they should attend to this difference between them, That tho',
with regard to natural effects, skilful industry be generally successful, yet
whereas external industry may be obstructed and mar'd by several causes
which we can neither foresee nor prevent, inward industry, or application
to the improvement of our moral faculties, never fails of attaining its end:
And thus the culture of our minds is much more dependent upon us than
that of our gardens and fields. So true is this, that steady resolution to con-

quer the most inveterate bad habits is sure of victory. A physiognomist pronounced Socrates choleric and amorous by his natural temperament. Those who knew his mildness and love of virtue, laughed at the mistake. But he who knew himself better owned that he had been so, and that it had cost him very hard labour to conquer these passions the physiognomist attributed to him. And from thence he took occasion to discourse of man's power to subdue his appetites and passions, to recover himself from vitious habits, and ascend by brave perseverance to the greatest height of virtue. Youth may be easily led to perceive, that our appetites are governed by our opinions of objects: And therefore, that in order to direct them we must have just apprehensions of things, and inure ourselves to deliberate and compute, before we yield or give way to the sollicitations of any affection. Freedom and strength of mind consist in this command of reason over our appetites and passions, which can only be gained by steadily accustoming ourselves to think and compare maturely and fully before we choose, and not suffering every fancy that may assail our minds, instantly to kindle an ardent impetuous desire. And wisdom consists in having just ideas of pleasures and pains, true notions of the moments and consequences of different actions and pursuits, whereby we may be able to measure, direct or controul our desires or aversions. One able to oppose desires, and to call his opinions to account, and furnished with the knowledge of the effects and consequences of actions requisite to shew him how he ought to behave in every case, is qualified for life. But without the latter, one cannot judge, but is in darkness. And knowledge, without the former, can only serve to create remorse for not taking or not following its counsels. Let them therefore early see the necessity, in order to happiness, in order to have power and liberty, of establishing judgment or reason as the ruler in their minds; and of having their understandings replenished with true and just ideas of all the objects and pursuits in human life, in order to be able to regulate their conduct aright. For what can be more obvious, than that this is the proper business of all who would be timeously prepared for steering wisely through the various rocks and shelves of life, for avoiding dangers and attaining to true happiness? In truth, when the deliberative habit, the patience of thinking before we choose, and the power of resisting fancy till we have brought it to the test of reason and truth, is firmly established in the mind, there will be little hazard of mistaking or erring. For right and wrong, in most circumstances of life, are easily distinguished. We need but ask our own hearts what it becomes us to do, and we will soon perceive, or rather feel what is duty and what not. The foolish choices and pursuits of men, are not so much owing to false judgments, as to the habit of acting precipitantly, and without examining our fancies and appetites. Ask the youngest infant, how he ought to be affected towards the Author of his being, and of all things, who hateth nothing that he hath made, but extends his benevolent care to all his creatures, and he will immediately reply, that he ought to love him, and endeavour to approve himself to him, by imitating his goodness. Ask him what he owes to his parents, what to his brothers and sisters, what to his friends, what to his country, what to all men, and you will find that his own heart will prompt and direct him to just answers; and that a strong sense of the obligations to piety, filial reverence and love, justice, veracity, gratitude, benevolence, immediately exerts itself upon the first proper call, so natural is it to the mind: That is, so right do our affections stand with regard to moral objects, when they are duly tried by them.

The proper study of mankind is man, and for this reason, one who hath the instruction of youth at heart will early direct them to observe all the natural determinations of the mind, such as our determination to distinguish between involuntary and free actions, and to regard ourselves and others as the authors of, and accountable for the latter, and them only: A determination of which we can by no means divest ourselves: a difference which we are necessarily determined to make, and without which we could have no ideas of justice or injustice, blame or merit, because mere accident and designed hurt would affect us in the same manner, did we not make this distinction: And consequently, a determination to be differently affected by the actions of agents, as they are apprehended to be done with or without choice, upon which the whole order of human society, and of all civil intercourse, absolutely depends. Those who delight in puzzling and perplexing clear truths, may argue as subtily as their wit, or rather sophistry can, to prove that men are accountable for none of their actions. But of a necessary determination in our nature to distinguish violence and compulsion from voluntary and free acting, we are as sure as we are of our existence. And the reality of the distinction is certain beyond all dispute, from the double necessity we are under to make it physical and moral. By the former, I mean the insuperable determination of our minds to make a difference, e.g. between the falling of a tile and the voluntary throwing of it: By the latter, the multiplied inconveniencies and absurdities that would follow upon any one's divesting himself, were it possible, of this determination, and acting as if there was no foundation for it. Another determination in our nature is, to approve free actions that are good or beneficial, and to disapprove such as are ill or hurtful. This determination supposes or includes the former. We do not praise or blame, where we apprehend there was not free choice; but if actions are apprehended to have been done with understanding and election, we are necessarily determined to approve such, if they be kind and contributive to the public weal, and to condemn them if they be unkind and detrimental. The meaning of this, in other words is, That the Author of nature hath designed that good or virtuous actions should immediately, upon a fair view of them, excite our liking and approbation, and vitious ones our dislike and abhorrence; and accordingly, we are necessarily so affected by these moral ideas, as often as they are fully presented to our minds. 'Tis absurd to suppose us not indifferent to them, unless we grant that the Author of nature intended that we should be differently affected by them: For it is to suppose an effect not designed, but taking place without any cause, any foresight and will that it should be. And that originally our affections stand right with regard to good and wrong, however afterwards they may be corrupted or perverted, will be evident from every trial of young minds in this moral way. Paint actions and characters to them of opposite kinds, and you will soon see that their approbation and disapprobation are always quickly and rightly moved, i.e. moved as the public or common good of mankind requires they should. And after these trials, they may easily be led to reflect upon this determination of our minds, to approve and disapprove, and its excellent final cause.

Very near a-kin to this is our determination to receive pleasure from uniformity amidst variety, or in other words, from order, proportion and harmony in sensible objects; which sense, when well improved, is so rich a source of entertainment, being the mother of all the harmonious arts, as

they may justly be called, since symmetry, order or harmony is their object
and end, architecture, statuary, painting, music, and to a considerable degree, poetry and oratory. It is this determination or sense that qualifies us
for admiring and enjoying the beauty and order of nature, and for relishing beauty and order wherever we find it, in art, in writing, in painting, in
building, &c. That it originally stands right, that is, towards the beauty
which is the effect of regularity and simplicity, will be found by making
proper experiments upon young minds; and to what pitch of perfection it
may be improved, let the many ingenious, noble productions of the imitative arts witness. And that young minds, after proper trials in this way,
may easily be directed to take notice of the excellent final cause of this determination, is too obvious to need any proof, since by it we are disposed
to the love of simplicity, neither nature nor art being beautiful, but in consequence of observing this rule, *nil frustra,* or avoiding superfluous labour,
operating in the shortest way, and adding strength to what is principal in
every structure or whole. Nor is the connexion between this latter and the
moral sense just mentioned, and their mutual tendency to strengthen each
other, less manifest, seeing the pursuit of virtue is nothing else but the pursuit of order in the government of the affections, and of order in the frame
and government of society.

By a few reflections on these determinations of the human mind, illustrated and confirmed to them by well-chosen examples, they will soon perceive, that man is made for virtue and good order, or to receive his highest
and only uncloying gratifications, from outward and inward order and
harmony; and that it is the steady pursuit of order and harmony in every
particular structure and oeconomy, and in the whole of nature, that is the
delightful employment of the eternal all-perfect Mind, from whom all perfections, all beauties, all ideas, senses, determinations, powers and faculties
proceed. But in order to make men acquainted with themselves, true philosophy will also lay open to her pupils, all the affections and passions of
the human mind, and shew their various manners of operation, and what
virtues and vices belong to each of them, and their final ends or causes;
why, or for what uses they are implanted in us. Some writers on human
nature have much obscured the doctrine of the passions by ways of speaking about them, liable to all the absurdities of supposing ideas in the mind

antecedent to experience; and another yet greater, that passions or propensities to objects may precede the ideas of these objects; not to mention a third, viz. that there can be a strong propensity towards an object before one has had repeated views of it, and the imagination hath by these been warmed into a vehement delight in the contemplation of it, and is thereby inflamed with a habitual impatient itching after it. But, in reality, passion means propension, or a strong attachment towards an object, for every passion is a strong inclination or disposition towards an object, engendered and supported by the frequent recoiling of a very strong and warm picture or idea of that object. By the natural constitution or determination of the mind, the idea of fame, e.g. is agreeable to the mind, and exalts our desire. But the image of fame must have been very often repeated, so that the idea of all its sweets and charms is become very lively, and very apt to return into the mind upon every occasion or hint, before the mind can be possessed of a strong propensity to it, able to overcome every other idea. It is the same with regard to power, or with regard to virtue or public good. Power or public good must have often been contemplated by the mind; the images of them must have been deeply engraved upon it by frequent repetition: The mind must have been much warmed by a lively view of their charms, and have by their often recoiling upon it with all their force, contracted a close union, as it were, with them, and a keen tendency towards the pursuit of them. The case is the same with regard to all the other passions of the pleasing or joyful kind; and what hath been said of them may easily be applied to those of the opposite family or class, grief, fear, hatred, &c. called very properly the family of pain.

But this I have mentioned, not that I would have youth perplexed with subtleties, but to shew teachers the necessity of leading youth early to observe, that the aptitude of our minds to be agreeably affected by the images of power, fame, and in general, by all the objects that attract our minds, and the aptitude of our mind to be disagreeably moved by all the objects that are naturally painful to us, and so raise our aversion—That these aptitudes or determinations are of great use, as is likewise the force of association and repetition: But that it is by association and repetition of ideas that desires or aversions are kindled into propensities or passions. That being thus apprized of the manner in which passions are generated, they may learn to be upon their guard against wrong or false associations of ideas, and accustom themselves strictly to examine all their fancies, and the desires raised by them: They may take care that their judgments be just and true, and their desires proportioned to the real natures and values of objects. For thus alone can the growth of sensual passions be prevented; thus alone can true ideas, and true associations of ideas, and true judgments be firmly established in the mind, and passions conformable to them be formed and strengthened. If virtue, and the honour of acting steadily the best, the worthiest part, be the solidest good, then surely ought the passion for virtue, and the glory of adhering to virtue, to be cherished, till it becomes the ruling passion in the mind. But the way to do this, is to impress deeply upon the soul such a full notion of the excellency of virtue, as being habitually present to the mind, shall be able to hold it fast to it, and to bear head against all the allurements of vice, or all the dangers with which virtue may at any time be threatened. Draw the character to him, suppose of an Epaminondas, a Scipio, or a Titus, in whom the love of the public held the ascendent over all other desires so firmly, that nothing was able to shake or corrupt them, and let them know by what close attention to their mind they preserved such a full conviction of the preferableness of integrity to all pomp and pageantry. But let them see likewise, that even where the love of virtue is firmly established, false pleasure of one or other species may, if the guard is relaxed, gradually gain ground, and at last quite efface that glorious passion, and establish into its room the lust of wealth, or any other passion of the basest kind. Shew them how virtuous inclinations grow and strengthen: But shew them likewise how they are weakened, and how the vitious ones get foot and spread, and gradually supplanting their rivals, at last so totally deprave the mind, that the vices which formerly appeared so hideous and abominable that they could not be seen or thought of without horror and detestation, assume at last, if not a smooth and fair, yet a much less frightful appearance. Let youth see all the various turns the same passions take in different circumstances: Let none of the vices that may grow out of any of them, or into which any of them may be perverted, be hid from youth: And far less let the counterfeits of the virtues be concealed from them: But let them early be taught to distinguish generous from base and cruel ambition, true from false courage, and so on with regard to all the other virtues: For the most dangerous enemy to every virtue is that vice which hath the nearest resemblance to it, or can best assume its likeness. Thus only can they be prepared for judging of actions, and the persons concerned in them, when they come to read history. And thus alone can they be seasoned or fortified against the corruptions, snares and dangers of the world. In these lessons, to characters it will be of great use to add proper fables, of which ancient method of teaching we shall afterwards have occasion to treat.

If any one should say, that such philosophical reflections are above the compass of young minds; tho' we must return again to this subject, and shall then shew, that it is far from being so difficult as is generally imagined, to convey the true philosophy into young minds, besides which there can be no other guide for the right conduct of life; yet let it be just suggested here in the first place, that till we begin to employ them in observing the final causes always aimed at and unerringly attained by nature in all her productions, and from thence to infer the wisdom and goodness of divine providence, in the formation and government of all things, and our obligation to imitate this character; and in observing the final causes of all the senses, powers, faculties and affections belonging to the human mind, together with their perfections and imperfections, or virtues and vices, and in drawing the same conclusion from thence with regard to providence and our duty.—Till we employ youth in such observations, nothing is done to furnish them with real knowledge, and we leave them absolutely in the dark with respect to the science of the greatest importance, and into which therefore they cannot be too early initiated. Till we thus exercise them, nothing is done to give them the best disposition, a propensity towards the most useful enquiry, or a taste and relish of the noblest as well as pleasantest study: And yet while due pains are not taken to form a good and useful temper, 'tis well known that the mind of course will either be contracting wrong habits, by improper exercise, or losing its natural docility, pliableness to instruction and quickness of apprehension. If the mind be not from the beginning well employed, it must take a pernicious turn, or become idle and averse to thought or serious exercise. For the human mind is ever either growing and improving, or shrinking and declining. If it be not advancing towards perfection, and becoming better, it is in this sense, at least, continually becoming worse, that it is daily waxing less capable of improvement. In the second place, I would ask, if they who are so apt to pronounce such institution too deep, or at least too grave and serious for young minds, have made any experiments with respect to the capacity of youth for relishing and entering into moral truths? Tis well known that the parables, fables and allegories with which ancient instructors began in the education of youth, were intended to convey moral maxims into the mind in an agreeable insinuating way. And they must be strangers to them, who think that moral truths are not capable of being rendered very pleasing, of being instilled into and impressed upon the youngest mind, in the most taking and engaging manner. But if this be the knowledge with which they ought early to be tinctured, or towards the love of which their minds ought timeously to be bended, then let teachers of youth use all their invention, and employ all their art to sweeten moral lessons, and make them as entertaining as they must be profitable. Let all the youth read be of this kind. And let not preceptors imagine that there is no way of teaching but in the formal manner of giving a lesson. This is a great mistake in education. By familiar conversation, children's curiosity may be roused much more effectually, and by it they may be taught a great deal more in a little time, than can possibly be done in the austere magisterial way of calling them to a lecture. I have known boys, before they were seven years of age, acquainted with the figure of our earth, its revolutions round its axis and round the sun, and the more remarkable phenomena arising from these causes, well acquainted with geography, and some part of astronomy, and impatient to understand the science which enables to measure the magnitudes, densities and distances of the planets. And I never found any difficulty in raising their curiosity to know, or in making them understand, for instance, the properties of air and water, upon which sailing depends, and by this means the use of air and winds, and of fresh and salt water—or even in ripping up, as it were, to them the bowels of the earth, and shewing them the various minerals and metals with which they are stored, and the uses of them—in explaining vegetation—or in going on gradually with them through the whole of natural philosophy till they had a pretty good notion of the final causes of most things, and were very desirous of instruction in the science, which is the Key by which men have been enabled to open nature's mysteries, and discover the laws according to which she works, and according to which human arts produce, and can only produce all their useful effects.—It will not be found difficult to make them conceive, that acquaintance with the properties of streight or curve lines, and with figures of all sorts, must be of great use in unraveling nature, in order to determine the methods in which effects are to be attempted by art, since they may easily be led to understand that all motion is in some line of direction. And desire being once incited to be instructed in this science, as a key to nature, a little practice in it will wonderfully open and enlarge their minds.—But from the final causes of physical appearances, is not the transition to the final causes of moral phenomena, i.e. to the consideration of the human mind, and its powers and affections, and their improvements, very natural? Nothing certainly can be more so. And therefore no lesson or conversation upon any final cause in the natural world ought to be let pass without taking occasion from thence to lead the young scholar to the consideration of the Author of nature, and our duty to him, i.e. our obligation to imitate him, by assiduous endeavours to enlarge our capacity of doing good, and by employing all the powers we have already acquired to the best purpose.

The unity of natural and moral philosophy will appear more fully afterwards. But I must again repeat it, that the great secret of education lies in finding out proper means of making young minds fall in love with useful researches, the enquiries that best become man, because they are of the highest importance to him, viz. researches into the order of the universe, and the good order of the human mind. For besides this one science, there is no true, no solid, no useful knowledge. Many other arts may serve or minister to it: But if this science be neglected, or if one is left an utter stranger to it, however specious his enquiries or occupations may appear to be to himself or others, they are but misleaders from the main and only profitable one. And therefore Cebes, in his allegorical picture of human life, agreeably to the doctrine of his master Socrates, the greatest of mere mortal philosophers, pronounces all other sciences, when separated from the moral science, false learning, and seducers from true wisdom. Need one stay long to convince any reasonable person that the knowledge of words, abstracted from that of things, can be of no value; and that a turn towards merely verbal criticism is one of the most pernicious youth can take. The solidity of mathematics, and its advantage to mankind, is prov'd by many effects of those beneficial arts and sciences which depend on it. But will this knowledge alone qualify for the government of the passions? Or can it, by itself, teach men how to regulate their appetites and conduct their actions? And what availeth the study of outward proportions and harmonies, if these never lead their admirer to serious reflections upon moral order and harmony, the harmony of the divine Mind, and of all his works; and the harmony of affections, which resembles created minds to their Author, and is therefore their glory and happiness. These two studies have naturally a very near connexion and affinity, and may therefore be both pursued at once very consistently. But if one's whole time be so occupied, even by such geometrical researches as bid fairest for adding to human power, that the knowledge of man himself, and his duties, is entirely neglected, that person, with all his knowledge, must be in profound ignorance with regard to what most concerns him, his inward liberty and happiness; and what is indeed the chief beauty, the supreme harmony, a well-ordered heart and life. Even enquiries into nature herself, if the student rests in the mere physical explications, and is not taught and inured to search for final causes, not only stop short of what ought to be principally attended to; but they, by so doing, mislead from the true philosophy, as we find Socrates[8] once and again observing. But of all the pretended sciences, none is more dangerous than that which seemeth to have the divine and human mind for its object; and yet, instead of leading to the knowledge of virtue and duty, habituates the student to take up with subtleties that have never produced, and can indeed never produce any other fruit but contentious jangling about empty puzling paradoxes. Let us hear an excellent author[9] upon this subject, whose censures have a far better

8. Plato's Phaedon.

9. [Anthony, Third Earl of Shaftesbury, *Characteristicks of Men, Manners, Opinions, Times,* foreword by Douglas Den Uyl (Indianapolis: Liberty Fund, 2001), 1:177–87.

claim to be hearkened to than mine. "If in the literate world, saith he, there be any chocking weed, any thing purely thorn or thistle, 'tis in all likelihood that very kind of plant which stands for philosophy in some famous schools. There can be nothing more ridiculous than to expect *manners* or *understanding* should sprout from such a stock. It pretends, indeed, some relation to *manners,* as being definitive of the natures, essences, and properties of spirits; and some relation to *reason,* as describing the shapes and forms of certain instruments employed in the reasoning art. But had the craftiest of men for many ages together been employed to find out a method to confound *reason,* and degrade the *understanding* of mankind, they could not perhaps have succeeded better than by the establishment of such a *mock-science.*—The philosopher who pretends to be wholly taken up in considering his higher faculties, and examining the powers and principles of his understanding; if, in reality his philosophy be foreign to the matter profess'd; if it goes besides the mark, and reaches nothing we can truly call our interest or concern, it must be somewhat worse than mere ignorance or idiotism. The most ingenious way of becoming foolish *is by a system.* And the surest method to prevent good sense is to set up something in the room of it. The liker any thing is to wisdom, if it be not plainly *the thing itself,* the more directly it becomes its opposite.—If a passenger should turn by chance into a watch-maker's shop, and thinking to inform himself concerning watches, should enquire of what metal, or what matter each part was composed? what gave the colours, or what made the sounds? without examining what the real use was of such an instrument, or by what movements its end was best attained, and its perfection acquired: 'Tis plain that such an examiner as this would come short of any understanding in the real nature of the instrument. Should a philosopher, after the same manner, employing himself in the study of human nature, discover only what effects each passion wrought upon the body; what change of aspect or features they produced, and what different manner they affected the limbs and muscles; this might possibly qualify him to give advice to an anatomist or a limner, but not to *mankind* or *himself:* Since, according to this survey, he considered not the real operation or energy of his subject, nor contemplated the man as *real man,* and as a human agent; but as a *watch or common machine.* The passion of fear (as a modern philosopher informs me) determines the spirits to the muscles of the knees, which are instantly ready to perform their motion, by taking up the legs with incomparable celerity, in order to remove the body out of harm's way.—Excellent mechanism! But whether the knocking together of the knees be any more the cowardly symptom of flight, than the chattering of the teeth is the stout symptom of resistance, I shall not take upon me to determine. In this whole subject of enquiry, I shall find nothing of the least self-concernment. And I may depend upon it, that by the most refined speculation of this kind, I shall neither learn to diminish my fears or raise my courage. This, however, I may be assured of, that 'tis the nature of fear, as well as of other passions, to have its increase and decrease as it is fed by *opinion,* and influenced by custom and practice.

"These passions, according as they have the ascendency in me, and differ in proportion with one another, affect my character, and make me different with respect to myself and others. I must therefore, of necessity, find redress and improvement in this case, by reflecting justly on the manner of my own *motion,* as guided by *affections,* which depend so much upon apprehension and conceit. By examining the various turns, inflexions, declensions, and inward revolutions of *the passions,* I must undoubtedly come the better to understand a human breast, and judge the better both of others and myself. 'Tis impossible to make the least advancement in such a study, without acquiring some advantage from the regulation and government of those passions on which the conduct of life depends. For instance, if *superstition* be the sort of fear which most oppresses, 'tis not very material to enquire, on these occasions, to what parts or districts the blood or spirits are immediately detach'd, or where they are made to rendezvous. For this no more imports me to understand, than it depends on me to regulate or change. But when the grounds of this superstitious fear are considered to be from *opinion,* and the subjects of it come to be thoroughly searched and examined; the passion itself must necessarily diminish, as I discover more and more the imposture which belongs to it. In the same manner, if *vanity* be from *opinion,* and I consider how *vanity* is conceived, from what imaginary advantages, and inconsiderable grounds, if I view it in its excessive height, as well as in its contrary depression, 'tis impossible I should not, in some measure, be relieved of this distemper.

Laudis amore tumes? sunt certa piacula—
Sunt verba & voces, quibus hunc lenire dolorem
Possis, & magnam morbi deponere partem.
HOR. lib. 1. ep. 1.[10]

"The same must happen in respect of *anger, ambition, love, desire,* and the other passions, from whence I frame the different notions I have of interest: For as these passions veer, my interest veers, my steerage varies, and I make alternately now this, now that, to be my course and harbour. The man in anger has a different happiness from the man in love; and the man lately become covetous has a different notion of satisfaction from what he had before when he was liberal. Even the man in humour has another thought of *interest* and advantage than the man out of humour, or in the least disturb'd. The examination therefore of my humours, and the enquiry after my passions, must necessarily draw along with it the search and scrutiny of my opinions, and the sincere consideration of my *scope and end.* And because the study of *human affections* cannot fail of leading me towards the knowledge of *human nature* and of *myself,* this is the philosophy which by nature has the pre-eminence above all other science or knowledge. Nor can this, surely, be of the sort call'd *vain or deceitful,* since it is the only means by which I can discover *vanity and deceit.* This is not of that kind which depends on *genealogies* or *traditions,* and ministers *questions* and vain janglings. It has not its name, as other philosophies, from the mere subtlety and nicety of the speculation, but by way of excellence, from its being superior to all other speculations, from its presiding over all other sciences and occupations, teaching the measure of each, and assigning the just value of every thing in life.—This gives to every inferior science its just rank; leaves some to measure sounds, others to scan syllables, others to weigh vacuums and define spaces and extensions, but reserves to herself her due authority and majesty, keeps her state and ancient title of, *Vitae Dux, virtutis indagatrix,*[11] and the rest of those just appellations

10. [Horace, *Epistles,* 1.1.34–36: "Are you swelling with ambition? There are fixed charms. . . . There are spells and sayings whereby you may soothe the pain and cast much of the malady aside." (Turnbull has altered the order of the lines. His version runs line 36, line 34, line 35.)]

11. [Cicero, *Tusculan Disputations,* 5.2.5: "O vitae philosophia dux, o virtutis inda-

which of old belong'd to her, when she merited to be apostrophiz'd as she was by the orator, 'Tu inventrix legum, tu magistra morum & disciplinarum.—Est autem unus dies bene & ex praeceptis tuis actus peccanti immortalitati anteponendus.'[12] Excellent mistress! But easy to be mistaken! whilst so many hundreds wear as illustrious apparel, and some are made to outshine her in dress and ornament.

"In reality, how specious a study, how solemn an amusement is raised from what we call *philosophical speculations?* The formation of ideas, their compositions, comparisons, agreements and disagreements!—What can have a better appearance, or bid fairer for genuine and true philosophy?— But if by all this I cannot learn how to ascertain my ideas, and keep my opinion, liking and esteem of things the same—where, philosopher! are thy ideas? where is truth, and certainty, and evidence so much talk'd of? 'Tis here, surely, they are to be maintain'd, if any where. 'Tis here I am to preserve some just distinctions and adequate ideas, which, if I cannot do a jot the more by what such philosophy can teach me, the philosophy is in this respect imposing and delusive. For whatever its other virtues are, it relates not to *me myself,* it concerns not *the man,* nor any other ways affects *the mind,* than by the conceit of knowledge, and the false assurance rais'd from a suppos'd improvement.—Philosopher, let me hear concerning what is of some moment to me. Let me hear concerning life, what the right notion is, and what I am to stand to upon occasion; that I may not, when life seems retiring, or has wore itself to the very dregs, cry *vanity!* Condemn the world, and at the same time complain, that *life is short and passing!* For why so *short,* if not found *sweet?* Why do I complain both ways? Is vanity, *mere vanity,* a happiness? Or can misery pass away too soon? This is of moment to me to examine. This is worth my while. If, on the other side, I cannot find the agreement or disagreement of my ideas in this place, if I can come to nothing certain here, what is all the rest to me? What

---

gatrix expultrixque vitiorum!" "O philosophy, thou guide of life, o thou explorer of virtue and expeller of vice!" (Loeb translation by J. E. King).]

12. [Cicero, *Tusculan Disputations,* 5.2.5: "thou hast discovered law, thou hast been the teachers of morality and order. . . . Moreover one day well spent and in accordance with thy lessons is to be preferred to an eternity of error."]

signifies it how I come by *my ideas,* or how *compound them,* which are *simple,* and which *complex?* If I have a right idea of life now, when perhaps I think lightly of it, and resolve with myself, 'That it may easily be laid down on any honourable occasion of service to my friends, or country, teach me how I may preserve this idea; or at least, how I may get safely rid of it, that it may trouble me no more, nor lead me into ill adventures.' Teach me how I came by such an opinion of worth and virtue; what it is, that at one time raises it so high, and at another reduces it to nothing; how these disturbances and fluctuations happen? By what innovation, what composition, what intervention of other ideas? If this be the subject of the philosophical art, I readily apply to it, and embrace the study. If there be nothing of this in the case, I have no occasion for this sort of learning, and am no more desirous of knowing how I form or compound those ideas which are marked by words, than I am of knowing how, and by what motions of my tongue or palate I form those *articulate sounds,* which I can full as well pronounce, without any such science or speculation."

∞ CHAPTER II ∞

Concerning the formation of good habits in young minds; the proper methods of cultivating virtuous dispositions; and the practices by which the vices are early engendered and strengthened, and of the best means for correcting and reforming them.

What we have hitherto been recommending is not instruction in any particular notional system of opinions or tenets, but in facts relating to the frame and government of the natural world, and to the constitution of the human mind of the greatest importance, ascertainable by experience only, and to be deduced and confirmed from thence; and which, tho' of different kinds, are so closely connected, that the transition from observations of either kind to the other is exceeding easy and natural. And we have not yet finished this article, but must return to it again, and treat more fully of the true philosophy, and the best methods of instructing youth in it. However, before we go further, because a great deal may be done towards the right formation of youth, of the last consequence to their happiness, before they can understand maxims or rules; nay, because, unless the mind be prepared for wholesome instruction by previous culture, instruction will fare like good seed cast into foul, weedy or stony ground, we shall therefore here treat a little of what ought to be the first and most early care in education, the formation of a right temper, by carefully nursing and cherishing good dispositions in young minds. Socrates, and other ancients, seem to have had particular pleasure in running a parallel between agriculture and the improvement of the mind: But in no respect does the comparison or likeness hold more exactly than in this, that as the ground must be properly prepared for the reception and nourishment of good seed, so the mind must by apposite care be moulded into a fit temperament or disposition for embracing and cherishing the seeds of good doctrine. In both cases, the first or previous care is of the greatest moment. Instruction will be but thrown away, it cannot sink into the mind, or take firm root there, so as to fructify, if the mind be not pure and clean, pliable, or docile and open to truth and knowledge, but will quickly be chocked by the opposite illiberal temperature. The human mind cannot continue long quite a *tabula rasa;* some images must of course be gaining upon its affections, and consequently, forming some propensities or habits. And we may leave it to any thinking person, who is acquainted with the world, and has but reflected, that reason must be artfully invited and drawn forth into action, and requires much culture in order to ripen and strengthen it, whereas our senses, from the first dawn of life, are continually assailed by outward objects, and speedily rush up to their maturity.—We may leave to such to judge what chance there is for the virtues getting the start of all vitious appetites and habits in young minds, if particular care be not taken, from their first entrance into the world, of adhibiting proper culture and discipline, and of steadily watching and directing all their ideas, desires and movements. Some philosophers, indeed, have represented vice as co-genial with the mind, not considering how absurd it is to suppose a work to come depraved and vitiated from the hands of the all-perfect Creator, were it conceivable, as it is not, that habits or passions of any kind could precede ideas, or be engendered otherwise than by association of ideas and repetition of acts. But, on the contrary, it is virtue, not vice, that is natural to the mind, in any sense that any habit can be said to be so, since origi-nally the affections in the human mind stand right with regard to moral objects; since long before we are able to reason or draw inferences, from the first moment that good actions and characters are set before or per-ceived by us, virtue is a fair and lovely species, and immediately begets our esteem and approbation, whereas vice is an ugly form, and creates our aversion and abhorrence. There is no necessity of supposing the mind nat-urally biassed towards vice, in order to account for the ill humours, the crossness and peevishness, or the sensuality and interestedness and lust of power which so early discover themselves in children. If we but consider not only to whom the care of the nursery is generally committed, and with whom children are most habitually conversant, but even the common methods of conduct in very wise and good parents themselves towards their infants, our wonder at the general early corruption of young minds will cease, and we will find that tutors and preceptors have ground to complain, that their task is weeding work; and that children are given into their hands not to be educated, but to be cleansed and purged from bad habits, which, till they are effaced and rooted out, shut the door against all sound instruction, or disappoint the effects of the best teaching. For in what vice are not children generally trained up? or what evil affection is not fostered and cherished in their minds? I have elsewhere[13] treated of this subject at some length; and therefore I shall here only transcribe a few observations upon it from an excellent author,[14] well worth the most attentive perusal of parents, and all who are employed in the important business of forming youth. And is it not indeed very strange, that the power of habit or custom should be so universally known and confessed, and yet that so little attention should be paid to this very powerful principle in the institution of youth?

"The great mistake, says he, I have observed in people's breeding their children, is that care hath not been taken, in its due season, to render their minds obedient to discipline and pliant to reason, when at first they were most tender and easy to be bowed. Parents being wisely ordained by nature to love their children, are very apt, if reason watch not that natural affection very warily, to let it run into fondness. They love their little ones, and it is their duty: But they often with them cherish their faults too. They must not be crossed, forsooth, they must be permitted to have their wills in all things; and they being in their infancy not capable of great vices, their parents think they may safely enough indulge their little irregularities, and make themselves sport with that pretty perverseness which they think well enough becomes that innocent age. But to a fond parent, that would not have his child corrected for a perverse trick, but excused it, saying, it was a small matter, Solon very well replied, 'Ay, but custom is a great one.' The fondling must be taught to strike, and call names, must have what he cries for, and do what he pleases. Thus parents, by humour-

---

13. In the discourses intitled, *Plutarchus Plasmatias,* &c.
14. [John Locke, *Some Thoughts Concerning Education,* §§34–37.]

ing and cockering them when little, corrupt the principles of nature in their children, and wonder afterwards to taste the bitter waters when they themselves have poisoned the fountain. For when their children are grown up, and these ill habits with them, when they are now too big to be dandled, and their parents can no longer make use of them as play-things, then they complain that the brats are untoward and perverse; then they are offended to see them wilful, and are troubled with those ill humours which they themselves infused and fomented in them; and then, perhaps too late, would be glad to get out those weeds which their own hands have planted, and which now have taken too deep root to be easily extirpated. For he that has been used to have his will in every thing, as long as he was in coats, why should we think it strange, that he should desire it, and contend for it still when he is in breeches? Indeed, as he grows more towards a man, age shews his faults the more, so that there be few parents then so blind as not to see them; few so insensible as not to feel the ill effects of their own indulgence. He had the will of his mind before he could speak or go; he had the mastery of his parents ever since he could prattle; and why, now he is grown up, and is stronger and wiser than he was then, why now of a sudden must he be restrained and curbed? Why must he at seven, fourteen, or twenty years old, lose the privilege which the parents indulgence till then so largely allowed him? Try it in a dog, or a horse, or any other creature, and see whether the ill and resty tricks they have learned when young, are easily to be mended when they are knit; and yet none of those creatures are half so wilful and proud, or half so desirous to be masters of themselves and others, as man. We are generally wise enough to begin with them when they are very young, and discipline betimes those other creatures we would make useful and good for somewhat. They are only our own offspring that we neglect in this point; and having made them ill children, we foolishly expect they should be good men. For if the child must have grapes and sugar-plumbs, when he has a-mind to them, rather than make the poor baby cry, or be out of humour; when he is grown up, must he not be satisfied too, if his desires carry him to wine and women? They are objects as suitable to the longing of one of more years, as what he cried for, when little, was to the inclinations of a child. The having desires accommodated to the apprehensions and relish of these several ages, is not the fault, but the not having them subject to the rules and restraints of reason: The difference lies not in the having or not having appetites, but in the power to govern or deny ourselves in them. He that is not used to submit his will to the reason of others, when he is young, will scarce hearken or submit to his own reason, when he is of an age to make use of it. And what a kind of man such a one is like to prove, is easy to foresee.

"These are oversights usually committed by those who seem to take the greatest care of their children's education. But if we look into the common management of children, we shall have reason to wonder, in the great dissoluteness of manners which the world complains of, that there are any footsteps at all left of virtue. I desire to know what vice can be named, which parents, and those about children do not reason them into, and drop into them the seeds of, as soon as they are capable to receive them.

"Our author observes how they are taught, and encouraged in cruelty and violence; how their vanity and love of dress is fostered; and then he adds: Those of the meaner sort are hindered by the straitness of their fortunes from encouraging intemperance in their children, by the temptation of their diet, or invitations to eat and drink more than enough. But their own ill examples, whenever plenty comes in their way, shew that 'tis not the dislike of drunkenness and gluttony that keeps them from excess, but want of materials. But if we look into the houses of those who are a little warmer in their fortunes, their eating and drinking are made so much the business and happiness of life, that children are thought neglected if they have not their share of it. Sauces and ragousts, and food disguised by all the arts of cookery, must tempt their palates, when their bellies are full: And then, for fear the stomach should be overcharged, a pretence is found for t'other glass of wine to help digestion, tho' it only serves to increase the surfeit. Is my young master a little out of order, the first question is, what will my dear eat? What shall I get for thee? Eating and drinking are instantly pressed: And every body's invention is set on work to find out something luscious and delicate enough to prevail over the want of appetite, which nature has wisely ordered in the beginning of distempers, as a defence against their increase, that being freed from the ordinary labour of digesting any new load in the stomach, she may be at leisure to correct and master the peccant humours. And where children are so happy in the case of their parents, as by their prudence to be kept from the excess of their tables, to the sobriety of a plain and simple diet; yet there too, they are scarce to be preserved from the contagion that poisons the mind; tho' by a discreet management, while they are under their tuition, their healths may perhaps be pretty well secured, yet their desires must needs yield to the lessons which every where will be read to them upon this part of epicurism. The commendation that eating well has every where, cannot fail to be a successful incentive to natural appetite, and bring them quickly to the liking and expence of a fashionable table. This shall have from every one, even the reprovers of vice, the title of living well. And what shall sullen reason dare to say against the public testimony? Or can it hope to be heard, if it should call that luxury which is so much owned, and universally practiced by those of the best quality? This is now so grown a vice, and has so great supports, that I know not whether it does not put in for the name of virtue, and whether it will not be thought folly, or want of knowledge of the world, to open one's mouth against it. And truly I should suspect, that what I have here said of it might be censured as a little satire out of my way, did I not mention it with this view, that it might awaken the care and watchfulness of parents in the education of their children: when they see how they are beset on every side, not only with temptations but instructors to vice, and that perhaps in those they thought places of security. I shall not dwell any longer on this subject, much less run over all the particulars, that would shew what pains are used to corrupt children, and instil principles of vice into them. But I desire parents soberly to consider what irregularity or vice there is, which children are not visibly taught, and whether it be not their duty and wisdom to provide them other instructors."

This author after these remarks, which will lead every thinking person to many others of the same kind, goes on to consider how good habits may be formed in young minds.[15] "It seems plain to me, says he, that the principle of all virtue and excellency lies in the power of denying ourselves the

15. [Locke, *Education*, §§38–44.]

satisfaction of our own desires, where reason does not authorize them. This power is to be got and improved by custom, and made easy and familiar by an early practice. If therefore I might be heard, I would advise, that contrary to the ordinary way, children should be used to submit their desires, and go without their longings, even from their very cradles. The very first thing they should learn to know should be, that they were not to have any thing, because it pleased them, but because it was thought fit for them. If things suitable to their wants were supplied to them, so that they were never suffered to have what they once cried for, they would learn to be content without it; would never with bawling and peevishness contend for mastery; nor be half so uneasy to themselves and others as they are, because from the beginning they are not thus handled. I say not this, as if children were not to be indulged in any thing, or that I expected they should in hanging-sleeves, have the reason and conduct of counsellors. I consider them as children who must be tenderly used, who must play and have play-things. That which I mean is, that whenever they craved what was not fit for them to have or do, they should not be permitted it, because they were little and desired it. Nay, whatever they were importunate for, they should be sure, for that very reason, to be denied. The younger they are, the less, I think, are their unruly and disorderly appetites to be complied with; and the less reason they have of their own, the more are they to be under the absolute power of those in whose hands they are. From which, I confess it will follow, that none but discreet people should be about them. If the world commonly does otherwise, I cannot help that. I am saying what I think should be, which if it were already in fashion, I should not need to trouble the world with a discourse on this subject. But yet I doubt not, but when it is considered, there will be others of opinion with me, that the sooner this way is begun with children, the easier it will be for them and their governors too. And that this ought to be observed as an inviolable maxim, That whatever once is denied them, they are certainly not to attain it by crying or importunity, unless one has a mind to teach them to be impatient and troublesome, by rewarding them for it when they are so. Those, therefore, that intend ever to govern their children should begin it whilst they are very little, and look that they perfectly comply with the will of their parents. Would you have your son obedient to you when past a child? Be sure then to establish the authority of a father, as soon as he is capable of submission, and can understand in whose power he is. If you would have him to stand in awe of you, imprint it in his infancy; and as he approaches more to a man, admit him nearer to your familiarity: So shall you have him your obedient subject, as is fit, whilst he is a child, and your affectionate friend when he is a man. For methinks they mightily misplace the treatment due to their children, who are indulgent and familiar when they are little, but severe to them, and keep them at a distance when they are grown up. For liberty and indulgence can do no good to children: Their want of judgment makes them stand in need of restraint and discipline. And, on the contrary, imperiousness and severity is but an ill way of treating men, who have reason of their own to guide them, unless you have a mind to make your children, when grown up, weary of you, and secretly wish your death.—If a strict hand be kept over children from the beginning, they will in that age be tractable, and quietly submit to it, as never having known any other: And if, as they grow up to use of reason, the rigour of government, be, as they deserve it, greatly relaxed, the father's brow more smoothed to them, and the distance by degrees abated, his former restraints will increase their love, when they find it was only a kindness to them, and a care to make them capable to deserve the favour of their parents, and the esteem of every body else. Thus much for the settling your authority over your children in general. Fear and awe ought to give you the first power over their minds, love and friendship in riper years to hold it: For the time must come when they will be past the rod and correction; and then, if the love of you make them not obedient and dutiful, if the love of virtue and reputation keep them not in laudable courses, I ask what hold will you have upon them to turn them to it? Indeed, fear of having a scanty portion if they displease you, may make them slaves to your estate, but they will be never the less ill and wicked in private; and that restraint will not last always. Every man must some time or other be trusted to himself and his own conduct; and to be a good, a virtuous and able man, one must be made so within. And therefore, what he is to receive from education, what is to sway and influence his life, must be something put into him betimes: Habits woven into the very principles of his nature, and not a counterfeit carriage and dissembled outside, put on by fear, only to avoid the present anger of a father, who may perhaps disinherit him. This being laid down in general, as the course that ought to be taken, 'tis fit we now come to consider the parts of the discipline to be used. I have spoken so much of carrying a strict hand over children, that perhaps, I shall be suspected of not considering enough, what is due to their tender age and constitutions. But that opinion will vanish when you have heard me a little farther. For I am very apt to think, that great severity of punishment does but very little good, nay great harm in education: And I believe it will be found, that *caeteris paribus,* those children who have been most chastised, seldom make the best men. All that I have hitherto contended for is, That whatsoever rigour is necessary, it is more to be used the younger children are, and having by a due application wrought its effect, it is to be relaxed and changed into a milder sort of government. A compliance and suppleness of their wills being, by a steady hand, introduced by parents, before children have memories to retain the beginnings of it, will seem natural to them, and work afterwards in them, as if it were so, preventing all occasions of struggling or repining. The only care is, that it be begun early, and inflexibly kept to, till awe and respect be grown familiar, and there appears not the least reluctancy in the submission and ready obedience of their minds. When this reverence is once thus established (which it must be early, or else it will cost pains and blows to recover it, the longer it is deferred) 'tis by it, mixed still with as much indulgence as they made not an ill use of, and not by beating, chiding, or servile punishments, they are for the future to be governed, as they grow up to more understanding." Our author, after bringing several arguments to prove that corporal punishment contributes not at all to the mastery of our natural propensity to indulge present pleasure, and to avoid pain at any rate, but rather encourages it, and thereby strengthens that in us which is the root from whence spring all vitious actions and all the irregularities of life. That this sort of correction naturally breeds an aversion to that which 'tis the tutor's business to create a liking to.—And if it does prevail, and works a cure upon the present unruly distemper, it is often bringing in the room of it a worse and more dangerous disease, by breaking the mind, or producing a slavish temper and dissimulation—he proceeds to observe:[16] "On the other side, to flatter children, by rewards of things that are pleasant to them, is as carefully to be avoided. For this but authorizes the child's love of pleasure, and cockers up that dangerous propensity which we ought by all means to subdue and stifle in him. You can never hope to teach him to master it, whilst you compound for the check you give his inclination in one place, by the satisfaction you propose to it in another. To make a good, a wise, or a virtuous man, 'tis fit he should learn to cross his appetite, and deny his inclination to riches, finery, or pleasing his palate, &c. But when you draw him to do any thing that is fit, by the offer of money, or reward the pains of learning his book by the pleasure of a luscious morsel, when you promise him a lace-cravat, or a fine new suit, upon the performance of some of his little tasks, what do you, by proposing these rewards, but allow them to be good things he should aim at, and thereby encourage his longing for them, and accustom him to place his happiness in them.—I say not this, that I would have children kept from the conveniencies or pleasures of life, that are not injurious to their health or virtue. On the contrary, I would have their lives made as pleasant and as agreeable to them as may be, by a plentiful enjoyment of whatsoever might innocently delight them, provided it be with this caution, that they have those enjoyments, only as the consequences of the state of esteem and acceptation they are in with the parents and governors; but they should never be offered or bestowed on them as the rewards of this or that particular performance, that they shew an aversion to, or to which they would not have applied themselves without that temptation.—Rewards, I grant, and punishments must be proposed to children, if we intend to work upon them. The mistake, I imagine is, that those that are generally made use of, are ill-chosen. The pains and pleasures of the body, are, I think, of ill consequence, when made the rewards and punishments whereby men would prevail on their children. For, as I said before, they serve but to increase and strengthen those inclinations, which it is our business to subdue and master. What principle of virtue do you lay in a child, if you will remedy

16. [Locke, *Education*, §§52–62.]

his desire of one pleasure by the proposal of another? This is but to enlarge his appetite and instruct it to wander. By this way of proceeding, you foment and cherish in him that which is the spring from whence all the evil flows, which will be sure on the next occasion to break out again with more violence, give him stronger longings, and you more trouble. The rewards and punishments then, whereby we should keep children in order, are quite of another kind, and of that force, that when we can get them once to work, the business, I think, is done, and the difficulty is over. Esteem and disgrace are of all others the most powerful incentives to the mind, when once it is brought to relish them. If you can once get into children a love of credit, and an apprehension of shame and disgrace, you have put into them the true principle, which will constantly work and incline them to the right.—Children, earlier perhaps than we think, are very sensible of praise and commendation. They find pleasure in being esteemed and valued, especially by their parents, and those whom they depend on. If therefore the father caress and commend them when they do well, shew a cold and neglectful countenance when they do ill, and this accompanied by a like carriage of the mother, and all others that are about them, will in a little time make them sensible of the difference; and this, if constantly observed, I doubt not but will of itself work more than threats and blows, which lose their force when once grown common, and are of no use when shame does not attend them. But to make the sense of esteem or disgrace sink the deeper and be of more weight, other agreeable or disagreeable things should constantly accompany these different states, not as particular rewards and punishments of this or that particular action, but as necessarily belonging to, and constantly attending one, who by his carriage has brought himself into a state of disgrace or commendation. By this way of treating them, children will, as much as possible, be brought to conceive, that those that are commended, and in esteem for doing well, are necessarily beloved and cherished by every body, and have all other good things as a consequence of it, and on the other side, that when any one by miscarriage falls into disesteem, and cares not to preserve his credit, he will unavoidably fall under neglect and contempt; and in that state, the want of whatever might satisfy or delight him will follow. In this way, the objects of their desires are made assisting to virtue; when a settled experience from the beginning teaches children, that the things they delight in, belong to, and are to be enjoyed by those only who are in a state of reputation. If by these means you come once to shame them out of their faults (for besides that I would willingly have no punishment) and make them in love with the pleasure of being well thought on, you may turn them as you please, and they will be in love with all the ways of virtue. Concerning reputation, I shall only remark this one thing more, That tho' it be not the true principle and measure of virtue (for that is the knowledge of a man's duty, and the satisfaction it is to obey his Maker in following the dictates of that light God has given him, with the hopes of acceptation and reward) yet it is that which comes nearest to it; and being the testimony and applause that other people's reason, as it were by a common consent, gives to virtuous well-ordered actions, it is the proper guide and encouragement of children, till they grow able to judge for themselves, and to find what is right by their own reason. This consideration may direct parents how to manage themselves in reproving and commending their children. The rebukes and chidings which their faults will sometimes make hardly to be avoided, should not only be in grave, sober, and compassionate words, but also alone and in private. But the commendations children deserve, they should receive before others. This doubles the reward by spreading their praise: The backwardness shewn in divulging their faults will make them set a greater value on their credit themselves, and teach them to be more careful to preserve the good opinion of others, whilst they think they have it. But when being exposed to shame, by publishing their miscarriages, they give it up for lost, that check upon them is taken off; and they will be the less earnest to preserve others good thoughts of them, the more that they suspect their reputation with them is already blemished."

Thus we see education must begin, in order to gain its ends, much more early than is commonly imagined, otherwise the nursery will so spoil and corrupt children, that it will hardly be possible ever to reclaim or reform them. 'Tis in vain to heap rules on children; 'tis impossible for poor little ones to remember a tenth part of them, much less to observe them. But would you have them speak, read, pronounce, and behave gracefully, let them be formed by good example and practice, to intelligent graceful speaking and reading, and genteel behaviour. "Pray remember," says Mr.

Locke,[17] for it is from his treatise on education I have been all this while copying, "children are not to be taught by rules which will be always slipping out of their memories. What you think fit for them to do, settle in them by an indispensible practice, as often as the occasion returns, and if it be possible, make occasions. This will beget habits in them, which, being once established, operate of themselves easily and naturally, without the assistance of the memory. But here let me give two cautions. 1. The one is that you keep them to the practice of what you would have grow into a habit in them by kind words and gentle admonitions, rather as minding them of what they forget, than by harsh rebukes and chiding, as if they were wilfully guilty. 2. Another thing you are to take care of is, not to endeavour to settle too many habits at once, lest by variety you confound them, and so perfect none. When constant custom has made any one thing easy and natural to them, and they practice it without reflection, you may then go on to another. By this method of treating children, by a repeated practice, we shall see whether what is required of a child be adapted to his capacity, and any way suited to the child's natural genius and constitution. For that too must be considered in a right education. We must not hope wholly to change their original tempers, nor make the gay pensive and grave, nor the melancholly sportive without spoiling them. God has stamp'd certain characters upon men's minds, which, like their shapes, may, perhaps, be a little mended, but can hardly be totally altered and transformed into the contrary. He therefore, that is about children, should well study their natures and aptitudes, and see by often trials what turn they easily take, and what becomes them; observe what their native stock is, how it may be improved, and what it is fit for: He should consider what they want, whether they be capable of having it wrought into them by industry, and incorporated there by practice, and whether it be worth while to endeavour it. For in many cases, all that we can do, or should aim at, is to make the best of what nature has given, to prevent the vices and faults to which such a constitution is most inclined, and give it all the advantage it is capable of. Every one's natural genius should be carried as far

17. [Locke, *Education*, §66.]

as it can, but to attempt the putting another upon him will be but labour in vain. And what is so plaister'd on, will at last sit but untowardly, and have always hanging to it the ungracefulness of restraint and affectation. Affectation is not, I confess, an early fault of childhood, or the product of untaught nature: It is of that sort of weeds which grow not in the wild uncultivated waste, but in garden-plots under the negligent hand, or unskilful care of a gardener. Management and instruction, and some sense of the necessity of breeding, are requisite to make any one capable of affectation, which endeavours to correct natural defects, and has always the laudable aim of pleasing, tho' it always misses it, and the more it labours to put on gracefulness, the farther it is from it. For this reason, it is the more carefully to be watched, because it is the proper fault of education, a perverted education indeed, but such as young people often fall into, either by their own mistake, or the ill conduct of those about them. He that will examine wherein that gracefulness lies which always pleases, will find it arises from that natural coherence which appears between the thing done and such a temper of mind as cannot but be approved of as suitable to the occasion. We cannot but be pleased with an humane, friendly, civil temper, wherever we meet with it. A mind free, and master of itself and all its actions, not low and narrow, not haughty and insolent, not blemished with any great defect, is what every one is taken with. The actions which naturally flow from such a well-formed mind, please us also, as the genuine marks of it; and being, as it were, natural emanations from the spirit within, cannot but be easy and unconstrained. This seems to me to be that beauty which shines through some men's actions, sets off all they do, and takes with all they come near, when, by a constant practice they have fashioned their carriage, and made all those little expressions of civility and respect which nature or custom has established in conversation so easy to themselves, that they seem not artificial or studied, but naturally to flow from a sweetness of mind, and a well-turned disposition. Affectation, on the other side, is an awkward and forced imitation of what should be genuine and easy, wanting the beauty that accompanies what is natural, because there is always a disagreement between the outward action and the mind within, one of these two ways; either, when a man would outwardly put on a disposition of mind, which then he really has not, but endeavours by a forced carriage to make a shew of, yet so, that the constraint he is under discovers itself: And thus men affect sometimes to appear sad, merry, or kind, when in truth they are not so. The other is, when they do not endeavour to make shew of dispositions which they have not, but to express those they have by a carriage not suited to them: And such in conversation are all constrained motions, actions, words or looks, which, tho' designed to shew their respect or civility to the company, or their satisfaction and easiness in it, are not yet natural nor genuine marks of the one or the other, but rather of some defect or mistake within. Imitation of others, without discerning what is graceful in them, or what is peculiar to their characters, often makes a great part of this. But affectation of all kinds, whencesoever it proceeds, is always offensive; because we naturally hate whatever is counterfeit, and condemn those who have nothing better to recommend themselves by. Plain rough nature left to itself, is much better than an artificial ungracefulness, and such studied ways of being ill-fashioned. The want of an accomplishment, or some defect in our behaviour, coming short of the utmost gracefulness, often escapes observation and censure. But affectation, in any part of our carriage, is lighting up a candle to our defects, and never fails to make us be taken notice of, as either wanting sense, or wanting sincerity. This governors ought the more diligently to look after; because, as I have above observed, it is an acquired ugliness, owing to mistaken education, few being guilty of it, but those who pretend to breeding, and would not be thought ignorant of what is fashionable and becoming in conversation. And if I mistake not, it has often taken its rise from the lazy admonitions of those who give rules, and propose examples without joining practice with their instructions, and making their pupils repeat the action in their sight, that they may correct what is indecent or constrained in it, till it be perfected into an habitual and becoming easiness."

Our author goes on in the same manner, shewing how civility, deference, liberality, fortitude, and every virtue may early be formed in young minds. What I have quoted from him will send those who are in earnest about the education of their children to his excellent work itself, and lead the thinking into a very useful train of reflections on this important subject. And his observations upon this more essential part of education are compleat; nothing can be added to them.

A skilful tutor, who understands the anatomy, so to speak, of the human mind, the several natures, and the mutual bearings and dependencies of our affections, and that sound balance of them, in which the health, the vigour, the beauty and grace of the mind consist, will take, or rather make occasions for drawing them all forth, after their proper objects and in their proper tones; he will teach his pupil to admire, and to love, to compassionate, and even to be angry in due measures and on fit occasions. He will carefully nourish love of truth, desire of knowledge, aversion to falshood and cruelty, a manly intrepidity, and a sweet yet not servile complaisance and docility. And these qualities make a proper soil for receiving instructions: In such minds, the seeds of wisdom will find a warm and friendly reception, take firm root, and soon bring forth the most excellent fruits. But till such a temper as hath been described is become habitual, natural, for custom is a second nature, the mind is hard and impenetrable, light and sandy, or rank with poisonous weeds; and therefore instructions will either make no impressions, be quickly dissipated, or chocked and corrupted. Our Saviour's parable of the sower[18] is an excellent similitude or allegory for the illustration and confirmation of this important truth. When the precepts of virtue, for these are the good seed he came to sow, are heard carelessly and without regard, so that the first idle fancy or wanton appetite quickly drives them out of the mind, they are as seed that falls upon the beaten road, and never entering at all into the ground is picked up by the birds.—If they meet with a genius that snatches them up through the love of novelty, but hath not constancy or firmness enough to weigh and ponder them, and so deeply enforce and rivet them upon the heart, they are as seed that falls upon ground, where the earth being very shallow, it springs up indeed very quickly, but having no depth of root, as soon as the sun shines hot, it withers away: in this case the smallest amusement carries off the mind, and the good seed abideth not.—But if the

18. [Matthew 13:3–9.]

mind be over-run with carnal desires, instruction is then like seed that falls among weeds and thorns, which springing up with it, overgrow and kill it.—Finally, a well-disposed mind, not disturbed by irregular passions, but deeply impregnated with the love of truth, knowledge and virtue, firmly and warmly embraces good precepts and institutions; and there the seed dies not but is fruitful, and like corn that falls into a good, well manured, clean soil, bringeth forth a plentiful, a beautiful, an useful harvest. By proper care the temper may be formed before children are capable of understanding rules or reasonings. And indeed, if it is not, it is as absurd to expect much from lessons, as for the husbandman to hope for a good crop from the good grain he sows, if he hath been at no previous pains to dress and prepare his fields. This is an essential part in both husbandries. But yet in education who thinks of it? Who dreams of extending their concern about children even to their birth, by proper care about the first objects and ideas that are presented to their minds, and the exercise, discipline, or training of their appetites and passions? Who considers it as the essential part of education, to convey proper ideas early into young minds, or by fit means of trial and exercise to teach due affections to sprout, pullulate and strengthen? This, however, is the principal art: Nor will it be found a difficult one, by any who is conversant in the structure of the human mind, and the manners in which associations of ideas are formed, and passions are called forth into exercise. Right practice is the chief thing, as our Author observes. Let them have good example continually before their eyes, and let them be encouraged to imitate it, and to reiterate good actions by rendering them praise, and all marks of love and esteem when they do well, and by gentle tender admonitions when they mistake or slip.—Let them hear often other children commended for their docility, their reasonableness, their manliness, their goodness, sweetness and grace.—Let them be kept from all infectious company; but yet let them be inured to treat even their servants with kindness and gentleness.—Let them, in fine, be habituated to see nothing, or hear nothing but what is good, graceful, liberal and praise-worthy—And let their minds be early inflamed with the desire of the love, esteem, approbation and praise of the wise and experienced; and by such care and practice we shall quickly see every virtue begin to bud, and be surprized to find how soon reason itself will dawn, call for information, relish instruction, and lovingly embrace every opportunity of expanding and satisfying itself. Such a mind will love light: There is nothing in it that light can discover but what will yield it thorough satisfaction. For the first moral reasonings that are presented to one of such a disposition, will shew to his mind the reasonableness and beauty of the train and temperature it is in, and fill it with gratitude to its formers for their care to make him, before his own reason could do it, what they knew his reason must approve, so soon as it should be awaked and cleared up, to discern the comeliness of well-disciplin'd affections, and a rightly disposed heart. We are the shorter upon this head, because Mr. Locke has treated so fully of it. To what he says of the example of parents, and of the choice of a tutor, let me but add the sentiments of one of the best men, as well as the politest writers in the later ages, at least, of the Roman state.

Pliny the younger to Corellia Hispulla on choosing a tutor for her son.[19]

"Since I paid so great a respect to your father (who was a person of uncommon virtue and merit) that I can't say whether my admiration or love of him was superior; and since I carry on that affection to you in his memory and honour, I can't help desiring and endeavouring, as far as I can, to make your son resemble his grandfather. I prefer indeed him by the mother's side, tho' he by the father's was a man well approved and reputed; and his father himself and his uncle are distinguished by a particular fame. His growth will be equal to them, if he be trained up in a liberal education; and the hand that is to form him is of the first importance to it. As yet his tender age has confined him to your eye and domestic tutors, where there is little or no room to go astray. But now his studies are to be carried beyond the threshold, you must look about for a Latin master of rhetoric, whose school maintains a due severity, and a chaste regular management. For our youth is possess'd, among other gifts of nature and fortune, of a great personal beauty, that requires, in this slippery state of life, not only an instructor, but a guardian and a governor. I think I can warrant *Julius*

---

19. [Pliny, *Letters*, 3.3.]

Genitor to you. I love the man, yet my esteem for him, which is founded upon judgment, is no prejudice to that judgment. He is a man of correct life and prudent, indeed somewhat too austere and hard for this libertine age. You may plentifully find his mastery in eloquence; for an open and plain faculty of speaking is presently discerned. Human life has a variety of depths and caverns in it; in all which, take my word for *Genitor.* Your son will hear nothing from him that will not be useful, and learn nothing which it were not better to know. He will be admonished by him as frequently as by you and myself, what images of his ancestors he is to honour, what celebrated names he must answer. And therefore, by the favour of heaven, commit him to a master, who will first give a frame to his manners, and then to his eloquence, which is ill learned without them."

The character of a proper person for the formation of youth in their earliest years, as well as when they are qualified by a right temper of mind for institution in the liberal sciences, is yet more fully drawn by the same excellent hand, in another letter, wherein he describes the many excellent qualities of Euphrates, and recommends him to Atrius Clemens.

To Atrius Clemens.[20]

"Whatever figure this city of ours may have formerly made in the belles-lettres, she seems in this age to exceed herself; for which I could produce you abundance of shining instances, but shall at present content myself with one, and I mean the learned *Euphrates.*

"'Twas my good fortune to be thoroughly and intimately acquainted with him in Syria, when I was but a young and raw soldier, at my studies in those parts, who finding me resolv'd on sparing no pains to court his friendship, soon saved me that trouble, by his unreserved openness and compleat practice of that humanity which he makes it his business to teach.

"And now I feelingly wish I had ever been able to accomplish those hopes, which he was then pleased to conceive of me, in any proportion to that augmentation, which he himself has since added to the stock of his

---

20. [Pliny, *Letters,* 1.10.]

own merits: Or perhaps I may at this day admire them the more, because I understand them somewhat better; tho' even still I am far from pretending that I sufficiently do so. For as in painting, sculpture, or statuary, the very parallel case is in literature, none but a master can adequately judge of him that is so. And yet, if I be not mightily mistaken, there are more than a few talents so exalted, and so bright in Euphrates, as cannot well miss catching and delighting the eye, even of the tender-sighted.

"His disputations are acute, weighty and elegant; frequently not short of the stretch and loftiness of Plato himself. As to his manner of speaking, 'tis fluent, with a perpetual variety, charming and sweet to the last degree, and equally effectual for leading or driving an opponent.

"What I shall mention next is, That his stature is tall and his face comely, with a long head of hair, and a large white beard; which tho' but accidental, and generally insignificant circumstances, yet in him are peculiarly venerable. There is nothing shocking in his aspect; no melancholly, yet a great gravity. Should you happen to meet him, you'd instantly reverence him, without being the least dash'd at the sight of him.

" 'Tis a question, whether the strict probity of his life, or the affable ease of his behaviour be most remarkable? His method is ever to rebuke the vice, not the man, and to mend faults rather than rub hard upon them. He could scarce give you a piece of advice, but you would be apt to run after him and hang upon him for more. There is such a pleasure in being convinced by him, one would almost beg him to go back and argue it over again.

"And now, except it be to vex myself the more, why do I dwell on the thoughts of a man whom I am debarr'd from enjoying? Ty'd, as I am, to a state-office of no less slavery than grandeur; my fate is to be attending at a treasury-board, signing petitions, auditing accompts, scribling whole packets of letters, and between you and me, no very wise ones neither.

"Nor indeed can I sometimes, as opportunity offers, forbear making this very complaint to *Euphrates* himself; but he truly spurs me on, and encourages me, insisting upon it, that the dispatch of public business, the hearing of causes, the passing decrees, the research and distribution of justice, and lastly, the putting into practice the theory of the schools, are not barely parts, but the most glorious branches of human understanding.

"This, however, is the only point in which he and I shall be likely to differ, it being next to impossible to allow any of these matters equivalent with the hearing from morning to night, and improving by his own inimitable lectures.

"I therefore take the liberty of advising you, who are a happy master of your own time, directly to submit yourself to this filing and polishing, as soon as you come next to town, and, if I was you I should not be long of coming.

"To conclude, I am none of those who too often are inclinable to envy and grudge others all advantages unenjoyed by themselves; but can, on the contrary, be sensible of no little pleasure from seeing any of my friends overflow and abound in what, perhaps, it is my own misfortune to want even a competency of."

What care the ancient Greeks and Romans took of choosing proper persons to place about their children from their earliest years, and of the whole of their formation, we learn from Plutarch in his treatise on education. And a passage in an excellent writer[21] relating to the education of Cicero well deserves our attention.

"His father Marcius also was a wise and learned man, whose merit recommended him to the familiarity of the principal magistrates of the republic, especially Cato, L. Crassus, and L. Caesar; but being of an infirm and tender constitution, he spent his life chiefly at Arpinum, in an elegant retreat, and the study of polite letters.

"But his chief employment, from the time of his having sons, was to give them the best education which Rome could afford, in hopes to excite in them an ambition of breaking through the indolence of the family, and aspiring to the honours of the state. They were bred up with their cousins, the younger Aculeo's, in a method approved and directed by L. Crassus, a man of the first dignity, as well as the first eloquence in Rome, and by those very masters whom Crassus himself made use of. The Romans were, of all people, the most careful and exact in the education of their children:

---

21. [Conyers Middleton, *The History of the Life of Marcus Tullius Cicero,* 3rd ed., 3 vols. (London: W. Innys, R. Manby, 1742), 1:8–11.]

Their attention to it began from the moment of their birth; when they committed them to the care of some prudent matron of reputable character and condition, whose business it was to form their first habits of acting and speaking; to watch their growing passions, and direct them to their proper objects; to superintend their sports, and suffer nothing immodest or indecent to enter into them; that the mind preserved in its innocence, nor depraved by a taste of false pleasure, might be at liberty to pursue whatever was laudable, and apply its whole strength to that profession in which it desired to excel. It was the opinion of some of the old masters, that children should not be instructed in letters till they were seven years old; but the best judges advised, that no time of culture should be lost, and their literary instruction should keep pace with their moral; that three years only should be allowed to the nurses, and when they first began to speak, that they should also begin to learn. It was reckoned a matter of great importance what kind of language they were first accustomed to hear at home, and in what manner not only their nurses but their fathers spoke;[22] since their first habits were then necessarily formed, either of a pure or corrupt elocution: Thus the two Gracchi were thought to owe that elegance of speaking for which they were famous, to the institution of their mother Cornelia, a woman of great politeness, whose epistles were read and admired long after her death for the purity of her language. This probably was part of that domestic discipline in which Cicero was trained, and of which he often speaks: But as soon as he was capable of a more enlarged and liberal institution, his father brought him to Rome, where he had a house of his own, and placed him in a public school, under an eminent Greek master, which was thought the best way of educating one, who was designed to appear on the public stage, and, as Quintilian observes, ought to be so bred as not to fear the sight of men, since that can never be rightly learned in solitude, which is to be produced before crowds. Here he gave the first specimen of those shining abilities which rendered him afterwards

22. That this was the general practice and care in the best times of that republic, we learn from Cicero in his Brutus, and elsewhere, from Quintilian, and the author of the dialogue de causis corruptae eloq. attributed by some to Tacitus, and many other ancient writers.

so illustrious; and his school-fellows carried home such stories of his extraordinary parts and quickness in learning, that their parents were often
induced to visit the school for the sake of seeing a youth of such surprizing
talents." The subsequent parts of this great man's education shall be described afterwards, from the same admirable writer of his life. Mean time,
we see how much, in the opinion of all wise men, depends upon the first
dressing or culture of minds, their earliest habits and lessons. 'Tis owing
to the neglect of this most essential part of institution, that education is
now, generally speaking, mere weeding or cleansing work. Youth are now
sent to masters with minds full sown with prejudices and passions, fond
of every thing but instruction, quite heedless and dissipated, if not obstinate and perverse. And in such a corrupt soil must not the best seed be
lost, be quickly choaked! But since this is commonly the case, we must not
leave this most difficult part of our subject quite untouched. Plutarch, in
his lives of the ten orators tells us, that one Antiphon, who had long professed philosophy and education, at last not only wrote upon the method
of curing all distempers of the mind, but set up a shop at Corinth with a
sign-piece, promising to heal all intellectual diseases by certain words, if
the patients would tell their cases honestly, and follow his prescriptions.
Perhaps Horace may have had this mental physician and his placade in
view, when he says,[23]

> *Sunt verba & voces, quibus hunc lenire dolorem*
> *Possis*, &c.[24]

But this spiritual-doctor, either for want of business or of success soon quit
this trade. The task is indeed very unpleasant and very difficult: It is not
however desperate. There is no disorder of the mind, no inward ail or per-
turbation which may not be considerably mitigated, if the distempered
person can but once be brought to feel his disease, desire cure, and to listen
to advice and follow discipline, as Horace beautifully tells us in the lines
immediately following that just mentioned.

---

23. This is the more probable that he manifestly sneers at a prevailing superstitious
regard to the number three in the following lines.
24. [See note 10 in Part III, above.]

Invidus, iracundus, iners, vinosus, amator;
Nemo adeo ferus est, qui non mitescere possit,
Si modo culturae patientem commodet aurem.

HOR. ep. 1. l. 1.[25]

Hard indeed would it be for mankind were not this true, considering how exposed we lie from our infancy to manifold perversions and seducements! And however corrupt the world is, we have had at all times examples, glorious examples of the power of the human soul to subdue and master the worst and most inveterate habits, the most tumultuous and irregular passions. And the bold efforts of reason to conquer vice and establish and maintain the authority over our affections and appetites due to it as a rational and governing principle, are accompanied with such a self-approving sense of true fortitude as sufficiently rewards them. No triumphs are equal to the triumphings of the mind in its inward conquests. But what is the method of cure? The first step to freedom from captivity to any evil passion or habit, is willingness to receive advice, and conviction of the unreasonableness, deformity, and pernicious consequences of such a slavery: For these will soon be followed with courage and resolution to rescue ourselves from it. Indeed when docility and tractability, and the patience of thinking and hearing reason are once gained, victory is at hand; the hardest part of the warfare is accomplished. Mr. Locke, in the same treatise we have already praised, hath several excellent remarks upon some very dangerous diseases of the mind, and the proper methods of curing them. We may learn from him how cowardice is introduced into young minds, and how it may be extirpated, and true fortitude established.[26] "Fear is a passion, saith he, that, if rightly governed, has its use. And tho' self-love seldom fails to keep it watchful and high enough in us, yet there may be an excess on the daring side: Fool-hardiness and insensibility of danger, being as little reasonable, as trembling and shrinking at the approach of every little evil. Fear was given us as a monitor to quicken our industry and keep

25. [Horace, *Epistles*, 1.1.38–40: "The slave to envy, anger, sloth, wine, lewdness—no one is so savage that he cannot be tamed, if only he lend to treatment a patient ear."]
26. [Locke, *Education*, §115.]

us upon our guard against the approaching of evil: And therefore, to have
no apprehension of mischief at hand, not to make a just estimate of the
danger, but to run heedlesly into it, be the hazard what it will, without
considering of what use or consequence it may be, is not the resolution
of a rational nature, but brutish fury. Those who have children of this
temper have nothing to do, but a little to awaken their reason, which self-
preservation will quickly dispose them to hearken to, unless, which is usually the case, some other passion hurries them on headlong without sense
and without consideration. A dislike of evil is so natural to mankind, that
no body, I think, can be without the fear of it: Fear being nothing but an
uneasiness under an apprehension of that coming upon us which we dislike. And therefore, whenever any one runs into danger, we may say, it is
under the conduct of ignorance, or the command of some more imperious
passion, no body being so much an enemy to himself, as to come within
the reach of evil out of free choice, and court danger for danger's sake. If
it be therefore pride, or vain-glory, or rage that silences a child's fear, or
makes him not hearken to its advice, those are by fit means to be abated;
that a little consideration may allay his heat, and make him bethink himself whether this attempt be worth the venture. But this being a fault that
children are not so often guilty of, I shall not be more particular in its cure:
Weakness of spirit is the more common defect, and therefore will require
the greater care.

"Fortitude is the guard and support of the other virtues, and without
courage a man will scarce keep steadily to his duty, and fill up the character
of a truly worthy man. Courage, that makes us bear up against dangers
that we fear, and evils that we feel, is of great use; an estate, as ours is in
this life, exposed to assaults on all hands: And therefore, it is very advisable
to get children into this armour as early as we can. Natural temper does
here, I confess, a great deal. But even where that is defective, and the heart
is in itself weak and timorous, it may, by a right management, be brought
to a better resolution. What is to be done to prevent breaking children's
spirits by frightful apprehensions instilled into them, when young, or be-
moaning them under any little suffering, I have already taken notice. How
to harden their tempers, and raise their courage, if we find them too much

subject to fear, is farther to be considered. True fortitude, I take, to be the quiet possession of a man's self, and an undisturb'd doing his duty, whatever evil beset, or danger lies in his way. This there are so few men attain to, that we are not to expect it from children. But yet something may be done; and a wise conduct, by insensible degrees, may carry them farther than one expects. The neglect of this great care of them, whilst they are young, is the reason, perhaps, why there are so few that have this virtue in its full latitude when they are men. I should not say this in a nation so naturally brave as ours is, did I think that true fortitude required nothing but courage in the field, and a contempt of life in the face of an enemy. This, I confess, is not the least part of it, nor can be denied the lawrels and honours always justly due to the valour of those who ventured their lives for their country. But yet this is not all. Dangers attack us in other places besides the field of battle; and tho' death be the king of terrors, yet pain, disgrace, and poverty have frightful looks, able to discompose most men whom they seem ready to seize on: And there are those who contemn some of these, and yet are heartily frightened with the other. True fortitude is prepared for dangers of all kinds, and unmoved whatsoever evil it be that threatens. I do not mean unmoved with any fear at all. Where danger shews itself, apprehension cannot without stupidity be wanting. Where danger is, sense of danger should be; and so much fear as should keep us awake, and excite our attention, industry and vigour, but not disturb the calm use of our reason, nor hinder the execution of what that dictates.

"The first step to get this noble and manly steadiness is, what I have above mentioned, carefully to keep children from frights of all kinds, when they are young. Let not any fearful apprehensions be talked into them, nor terrible objects surprize them. This often so shatters and discomposes the spirit, that they never recover it again, but during their whole life, upon the first suggestion, or appearance of any terrifying idea, are scattered and confounded; the body is enervated, and the mind disturbed, and the man scarce himself, or capable of any composed or rational action. Whether this be from an habitual motion of the animal spirits, introduced by the first strong impression, or from the alteration of the constitution by some more unaccountable way, this is certain, that so it is.

Instances of such, who in a weak and timorous mind, have born all their whole lives through, the effects of a fright when they were young, are every where to be seen, and therefore, as much as may be, to be prevented.

"The next thing, is by gentle degrees to accustom children to those things of which they are too much afraid. But here caution is to be used that you do not make too much haste, nor attempt this cure too early, for fear lest you increase the mischief, instead of remedying it. Little ones in arms may be easily kept out of the way of terrifying objects, and till they can talk and understand what is said to them, are scarce capable of that reasoning and discourse, which should be used to let them know there is no harm in those frightful objects which we would make them familiar with, and do, to that purpose, bring nearer and nearer to them. And therefore, 'tis seldom there is need of any application to them of this kind, till after they can run about and talk. But yet, if it should happen, that infants should have taken offence at any thing, which cannot be easily kept out of their way; and that they shew marks of terror as often as it comes in sight, all the allays of fright, by diverting their thoughts, or mixing pleasant and agreeable appearances with it, must be used, till it be grown familiar and inoffensive to them.

"The only thing we are naturally afraid of is pain or loss of pleasure. And because these are not annexed to any shape, colour or size of visible objects, we are frighted with none of them, till either we have felt pain from them, or have notions put into us that they will do us harm. The pleasant brightness and lustre of flame and fire so delights children, that at first they are always desirous to be handling of it: But when constant experience has convinced them, by the exquisite pain it has put them to, how cruel and unmerciful it is, they are afraid to touch it and carefully avoid it. This being the ground of fear, 'tis not hard to find whence it arises, and how it is to be cured in all mistaken objects of terror. And when the mind is confirmed against them, and has got a mastery over itself and its usual fears on lighter occasions, it is in good preparation to meet more real dangers. Your child shrinks and runs away at the sight of a frog; let another catch it, and lay it down at a good distance from him: At first accustom him to look upon it; when he can do that, then to come nearer to it, and see it leap without emotion; then to touch it lightly when it is held fast in another's hand, and so on till he can come to handle it as confidently as a butterfly or a sparrow. By the same way any other vain terrors may be removed, if care be taken that you go not too fast, and push not the child on to a new degree of assurance, till he be thoroughly confirmed in the former. And thus the young soldier is to be trained on to the warfare of life, wherein care is to be taken that more things be not represented as dangerous than really are so; and then, that whatever you observe him to be more frightened at than he should, you be sure to lead him on to by insensible degrees, till he at last quitting his fears, masters the difficulty, and comes off with applause. Successes of this kind, often repeated, will make him find that evils are not always so certain or so great as our fears represent them; and that the way to avoid them, is not to run away or be discomposed, dejected, or deterred by fear, where either our credit or our duty requires us to go on.

"But since the great foundation of fear in children is pain, the way to harden and fortify children against fear and danger, is to accustom them to suffer pain.—Not to bemoan them, or permit them to bemoan themselves on every little pain they suffer, is the first step to be made. The next thing, is sometimes designedly to put them in pain: But care must be taken that this be done when the child is in good humour, and satisfied of the good will and kindness of him that hurts him, at the same time that he does it. There must no marks of anger or displeasure on the one side, nor compassion or repenting on the other go along with it: And it must be sure to be no more than the child can bear without repining or taking it amiss, or for a punishment. Managed by these degrees, and with such circumstances, I have seen a child run away laughing with good smart blows of a wand on his back, who would have cried for an unkind word, and have been very sensible of the chastisement of a cold look from the same person. Satisfy a child by a constant course of your care and kindness that you perfectly love him, and he may, by degrees, be accustomed to bear very painful and rough usage from you, without flinching or complaining. The softer you find your child, the more you are to seek occasions, at fit times, to harden him. How much education may reconcile young people to pain and sufferance, the examples of Sparta sufficiently shew: And they who have once brought themselves not to think bodily pain the greatest of evils, or that which they ought most to stand in fear of, have made no small advances towards virtue. I am not so foolish as to propose the Lacedemonian discipline in our age or constitution. But yet I do say, that inuring children gently to suffer some degrees of pain without shrinking, is a way to gain firmness to their minds, and to lay a foundation for courage and resolution in the future part of their lives."

Our author, after other observations upon fortitude and timorousness to the same purpose, goes on to consider how children usually become cruel, and how that temper may be remedied. But I shall only take notice of a few things he says concerning one of the most incurable of all the diseases young minds are incident to.[27] "Contrary to the busy inquisitive temper there is sometimes observable in children a *listless carelesness,* a want of regard to any thing, and a sort of trifling even at their business. This sauntering humour I look on as one of the worst qualities can appear in a child, as well as one of the hardest to be cured, where it is natural. But it being liable to be mistaken in some cases, care must be taken to make a right judgment concerning that trifling at their books or business, which may sometimes be complained of in a child. Upon the first suspicion a father has, that his son is of a sauntering temper, he must carefully observe him, whether he be listless and indifferent in all his actions, or whether in some things alone he be sluggish or slow, but in others vigorous and eager. For tho' he finds that he does loiter at his book, and let a good deal of the time he spends in his chamber or study run idly away, he must not presently conclude that this is from a sauntering humour in his temper. It may be childishness, and a prefering something to his study which his thoughts run on: And he dislikes his book, as is natural, because it is forced upon him as a task. To know this perfectly, you must watch him at play, when he is out of his place and time of study, following his own inclinations; and see there whether he be stirring and active; whether he designs any thing, and with labour and eagerness pursues it, till he has accomplished what he aimed at, or whether he lazily and listlesly dreams away his time. If this sloth be only when he is about his toil, I think it may be easily cured.

27. [Locke, *Education,* §§123–27.]

If it be in his temper, it will require more pains and attention to remedy it. If you are satisfied by his earnestness at play or any thing else he sets his mind on, in the intervals between his hours of business, that he is not of himself inclined to laziness, but that only want of relish of his book makes him negligent and sluggish in his application to it; the first step is, to try by talking with him kindly of the folly and impertinence of it, whereby he loses a good part of his time, which he might have for his diversion: But be sure to talk calmly and kindly, and not much at first, but only those plain reasons in short. If this prevails, you have gained the point in the most desirable way, which is that of reason and kindness. If this softer application prevails not, try to shame him out of it, by laughing at him for it, asking every day when he comes to table, if there be no strangers there, how long he was that day about his business? And if he has not done it in the time he might well be supposed to have dispatched it, expose him and turn him into ridicule for it, but mix not chiding; only put on a pretty cold look towards him, and keep it till he reform, and let his mother and tutor, and all about him do so too. If this work not the effect you desire, then tell him he shall be no longer troubled with a tutor to take care of his education; you will not be at the charge to have him spend his time idly with him; but since he prefers this or that (whatever play he delights in) to his book, that only he shall do; and so in earnest set him to work on his beloved play, till he be fully surfeited, and would at any rate change it for some hours at his book again. But when you thus set him his task of play, you must be sure to look after him yourself, or set somebody else to do it, that may constantly see him employed in it, and that he be not permitted to be idle at that too. This is what I propose, if it be idleness, not from his general temper, but a peculiar or acquired aversion to learning, which you must carefully distinguish. To be clear in this point, the observation must be made when you are out of the way, and he not so much under the restraint of a suspicion that any body has an eye upon him. In those seasons of perfect freedom, let some body you can trust mark how he spends his time, whether he unactively loiters it away, when without any check he is left to his own inclination. Thus, by his employing of such times of liberty, you will easily discern whether it be listlesness in his temper, or aversion to his book that makes him saunter away his time of study. If some defect in his constitution has cast a damp on his mind, and he be naturally listless and dreaming, this unpromising disposition is none of the easiest to be dealt with, because generally carrying with it an unconcernedness for the future, it wants the two great springs of action, foresight and desire, which how to plant and increase, when nature has given a cold and contrary temper will be the question. As soon as you are satisfied that this is the case, you must carefully enquire whether there be nothing he delights in: Inform yourself what it is he is most pleased with; and if you can find any particular tendency his mind hath, increase it all you can, and make use of that to set him on work, and to excite his industry. If he loves praise or play, or fine cloaths, &c. or on the other hand dreads pain, disgrace, or your displeasure, &c. whatever it be he loves most, except it be sloth, (for that will never set him on work) let that be made use of to quicken him, and make him bestir himself. For in this listless temper you are not to fear an excess of appetite (as in all other cases) by cherishing it. 'Tis that which you want, and therefore must labour to raise and increase; for where there is no desire, there will be no industry. If you have not hold enough of him in this way to stir up vigour and activity in him, you must employ him in some constant bodily labour, whereby he may get the habit of doing something. The keeping him hard to some study were the better way to get him an habit of exercising and applying his mind. But because this is an invisible attention, and no body can tell when he is, or is not idle at it, you must find bodily employments for him, which he must be constantly busied in, and kept to; and if they have some little hardship and shame in them, it may not be the worse, that they may the sooner weary him, and make him desire to return to his book. But be sure, when you exchange his book for his other labour, set him such a task to be done, in such a time, as may allow him no opportunity to be idle. Only, after you have by this way brought him to be attentive and industrious at his book, you may, upon his dispatching his study within the time set him, give him as a reward some respite from his other labour, which you may diminish, as you find him grow more and more steady in his application, and at last, wholly take off, when his sauntering at his book is cured."

From these few examples, we learn how every distemper of the mind ought to be treated, or what are the proper, the most likely methods of reclaiming from bad habits. Gentle admonitions, mild reasoning, a fair and tender representation of the dangers into which a bad habit may plunge, confirmed by examples, and pleasant polite raillery mixed with these, are the first remedies that ought to be tried. And if all sense of shame, and all sense of danger be not totally erazed out of young minds, these methods will gradually have their due effect. Let the fatal consequences of the particular vitious propensity that is to be cured, be set before the young man's eyes; shew him in proper characters the beauty of the opposite virtue, and by other examples, the pernicious tendency of his vice, and if he can be alarmed or piqued, if he be sensible to disgrace or to peril, he will listen, provided the admonitions are given with all the marks of love and affection. I have known fables, or feigned stories artfully told to, or thrown in the way of youth, of very strong passions, and in great danger from them, have admirable success. Some tutors, with pupils grown up to an age, in which, if the mind be not very well disposed, it is generally very impetuous and obstinate, have been of great use to them, by applying this remedy in a discreet, well-bred, polite manner, and have thus prevented their running into very great extravagancies, nay reclaimed them when they were on the very brink of ruin. Generally speaking, reproof or advice is best administered by a tale: Few out of their hanging-sleeves can bear a direct attack: And fables and stories may be suited to every age, as well as to every vice. But if the habits be such, as if not corrected, must expose to very great mischiefs, to vices that must be punished in all well-governed states, surely it is necessary to leave no methods of curing them untried. Corporal punishment for any thing but downright vice, such as lying, injustice, cruelty, ingratitude, or indocility and obstinacy, ought never to be used. In the schools abroad, whipping or beating is never employed but to correct vices by punishment, which all magistrates must punish, and that with almost the same forms civil chastisements are ordered and inflicted, that is, with a form of trial and judgment resembling the methods in civil courts. And there are instances in our own country, even of numerous schools which have produced excellent scholars, in which whipping into learning was never practised. Mr. Locke hath, by unanswerable arguments, shewn the bad consequences of corporal punishments, except for the correction of very bad habits, of obstinacy in particular: And indeed, if youth are quite deaf to reason, and absolutely irreclaimable by its soft methods, unless we would suffer them to run headlong into infamy and ruin, not to try all ways of making them feel by disgrace and suffering the danger they run, is cruel. But let them know the dangers and punishments in society, their vices, if not reformed, must expose them to, and that it is to prevent these greater ones, that the more tolerable are now employed. And to add to the disgrace, in imitation of the method generally practised in civil governments, let the punishment be executed by some of the lowest servants. He that spareth the rod, saith the wise man, hateth the child, i.e. he does not take the necessary methods of preventing his otherwise unavoidable ruin. This, we have reason to presume is Solomon's meaning; for he hath often most emphatically recommended all the softer and milder methods of reasoning or shaming young men out of their follies, and of gaining them to hearken to wise counsel, and to love knowledge and understanding. He therefore is to be understood as commanding corporal chastisement, when all other gentler means have proved fruitless, and vices that must render one very hurtful to society, and can hardly escape punishment in society, cannot otherwise be reformed. Let parents carefully distinguish between childishness and levity almost natural to that age, since it is only reason, thinking and experience, that can cure them, and direct vice, such as disregard to truth, for instance, and they will quickly see a necessity of making a distinction likewise in punishment between the one and the other. I do not say that the domestic discipline may not extend to several vices, such as ingratitude, for example, which most civil governments have found inconvenient to punish: But let it be vice alone to which punishments are applied in the discipline or correction of youth, that they may perceive and feel themselves the difference between vices and other lighter follies. In fine, all the reasons for punishing vices in society hold so much the more strongly for the discipline in education we have been pleading for; because it may happily prevent bad habits from going to a height, that must force society to exert its coercive or vindictive authority. For good order, and the general welfare of mankind will require, that examples of terror be made to the rest of the citizens, by severely animadverting upon the crimes of those, who not having been properly corrected in their youth for vices, so soon as they shewed themselves to be too obstinate to yield to admonition and reproof, are become insufferable pests. But all these matters are so fully handled by Mr. Locke, that we need not insist longer upon them; especially, since we shall have occasion to take up this subject afresh in the following chapter.

∞ CHAPTER III ∞

Of teaching languages, and of the exercises and their uses; together with the observations of the ancients upon punishments and reproofs confirmed by examples.

Mr. Locke's sentiments about the proper methods of teaching the Latin language, or rather talking it into children, are well known, and they are supported by incontestible arguments: He had known several examples of good success in that way: And the advantageousness of the practice hath been since confirmed by many experiments. I shall only copy a few paragraphs from him on this head, and then go on.[28] "If grammar ought to be taught at any time, it must be to one that can speak the language already, how else can he be taught the grammar of it? This, at least, is evident from the practice of the wise and learned nations amongst the ancients. They made it a part of education to cultivate their own, not foreign tongues. The Greeks counted all other nations barbarous, and had a contempt for other languages. And tho' the Greek learning grew into repute amongst the Romans towards the end of their common-wealth, yet it was the Roman tongue that was the study of their youth: Their own language they were to make use of, and therefore it was their own language they were instructed and exercised in. But more particularly, to determine the proper season for grammar; I do not see how it can reasonably be made any one's study but as an introduction to rhetoric; when it is thought time to put any one upon the care of polishing his tongue, and of speaking better than the illiterate, then is the time for him to be instructed in the rules of grammar, and not before. For grammar being to teach men not to speak, but

28. [Locke, *Education*, §168, §167.]

to speak correctly, and according to the exact rules of the tongue, which is one part of elegancy, there is little need of the one to him that has no need of the other; where rhetoric is not necessary grammar may be spared. I know not why any one who should waste his time, and beat his head about the Latin grammar, who does not intend to be a critic, or make speeches and write dispatches in it. When any one finds in himself a necessity or disposition to study any foreign language to the bottom, and to be nicely exact in the knowledge of it, it will be time enough to take a grammatical survey of it. If his use be only to understand some books wrote in it, without a critical knowledge of the tongue itself, reading alone will attain this end, without charging the mind with the multiplied rules and intricacies of grammar. We ought to distinguish three cases. 1. Men learn languages for the ordinary intercourse of society and communication of thoughts in common life, without any further design in their use of them. And for this purpose the original way of learning a language by conversation, not only serves well enough, but is to be preferred as the most expedite, proper and natural. Therefore, to this use of language, one may answer, that grammar is not necessary. This so many of my readers must be forced to allow, as understand what I here say, and who, conversing with others, understand them without ever having been taught the grammar of the English tongue, which I suppose is incomparably the greatest part of Englishmen, of whom I have never yet known any one who learned his mother-tongue by rules. 2. Others there are, the greatest part of whose business in the world is to be done with their tongues and with their pens; and to those it is convenient, if not necessary, that they should speak properly and correctly, whereby they may let their thoughts into other men's minds the more easily and with the greater impression. Upon this account it is, that any sort of speaking, so as will make him to be understood, is not thought enough for a gentleman. He ought to study grammar amongst the other helps of speaking well, but it must be the grammar of his own tongue, of the language he uses, that he may understand his own country['s] speech nicely, and speak it properly without shocking the ears of those it is addressed to, with solecisms and offensive irregularities, and to this purpose grammar is necessary. But it is the grammar only of their own tongues, and to those only who would take pains in cultivating their language, and in perfecting their stiles. Whether all gentlemen should not do this, I leave to be considered, since the want of propriety and grammatical exactness is thought very misbecoming one of that rank, and usually draws on one guilty of such faults the censure of having had a lower breeding and worse company than suits with his quality. If this be so (as I suppose it is) it will be matter of wonder why young gentlemen are forced to learn the grammars of foreign and dead languages, and are never once told of the grammar of their own tongues: They do not so much as know there is any such thing, much less is it made their business to be instructed in it. Nor is their own language ever proposed to them as worthy of their care and cultivating, tho' they have daily use of it, and are not seldom, in the future course of their lives, judged of by their handsome or awkward way of expressing themselves in it. Whereas the languages whose grammars they have been so much employed in, are such as probably they shall scarce ever speak or write. Would not a Chinese who took notice of this kind of breeding, be apt to imagine, that all our young gentlemen were designed to be teachers and professors of the dead languages, and not to be men of business in their own. 3. There is a third sort of men who apply themselves to two or three foreign, dead, and, which amongst us are called the learned languages, make them their study, and pique themselves upon their skill in them. No doubt those who propose to themselves the learning of any language with this view, and would be critically exact in it, ought carefully to study the grammar of it. I would not be mistaken here, as if this were to undervalue Greek and Latin. I grant these are languages of great use and excellency, and a man can have no place amongst the learned in this part of the world, who is a stranger to them. But the knowledge a gentleman would ordinarily draw for his use out of the Roman and Greek writers, I think he may attain without studying the grammars of those tongues, and by bare reading, may come to understand them sufficiently for all his purposes. How much further he shall at any time be concerned to look into the grammar and critical niceties of either of these tongues, he himself will be able to determine, when he comes to propose to himself the study of any thing that shall require it.—The formation of the verbs first, and afterwards the declension of the nouns and pronouns perfectly learned by heart, may facilitate the acquaintance with the genius and manner of the

Latin tongue, which varies the signification of verbs and nouns, not as the modern languages do, by particles prefix'd, but by changing the last syllables. More than this of grammar I think he needs not have till he can read himself Sanctii Minerva, with Scioppius and Perizonius's notes."

These are the sentiments of a very great man, drawn, as he tells us, from experience; and they have been confirmed since by repeated trials. Suffer me only to say, that the prevailing method of teaching Latin may be pursued, without making that or any other language, as is generally done, the sole employment of youth, in their most retentive, as well as docile years. He who looks upon Latin and Greek, or any part of what is commonly called literature, as the main part of education, must be very improper, very unqualified for the great and important business of instructing and fitting youth timeously for the duties and business of life. And how much is it to be regretted, that instruction in the useful sciences is so long delayed, seeing they must be confessed to be of much superior utility to the deepest skill in languages; but more especially, since there is indeed time enough for both? How many young lads have made great proficiency at home, under proper tuition and care, in geography, history and morals, as well as in French, Greek and Latin, at an age when boys come from our greater schools with Latin syntax and prosody, perhaps by rote, but without any taste of solid science, and for that reason absolute strangers to the spirit and sense of the ancient authors they can mechanically construe? Why may not two or three hours a day suffice for any one learned language? And how much might be done in the rest of the day, by taking proper methods? The design of education is to light up gradually the understanding; or to use another similitude, it is to teach young ideas and judgments to shoot and bud. But whether bestowing all the time in cramming the memories of children with mere words, be doing any thing to beget the love of true knowledge, or to reform and strengthen their understandings, we may form some notion from the confessed difference between a man of taste in classical learning, and the mere pedant or verbal critic, in comparison to which tall, full-grown tree, the young construer and etymologist, with his grammar and rhetoric at his finger-ends, is but the budding slip. Why is the best of their time thrown away upon erudition, perfection in which, if it be not united with other knowledge, makes, in the opinion of all good judges, one of the lowest characters even in the republic of letters? 'Tis a turn of mind which none who know the world would wish his son to take: And why then is he wholly employed in a way that can give him no other bent? For what can we expect, at best, if words be all the business, but mere verbalism? Can any one hesitate which to choose, whether that his son should early be acquainted with men, manners and things, or that he should early be a profound linguist, without any tincture of the substantial sciences, supposing it impossible to mix instruction in them with languages? But it is far from being impracticable: Progress in the one needs not exclude due pains about the other, as hath been found in many instances, whatever the ordinary methods in the schools may be. Need I dwell long on this subject? What man of sense, if he thinks of the matter seriously, and balances impartially the values of things in his mind, would not rather have his son at fourteen tolerably skilled in geography and history, acquainted with the true method of unraveling nature, and discovering her laws and final ends, and with the duties which justice, public love, and generosity and fortitude require at his hands, and able to express truths of these classes with propriety and taste, in his own language, tho' he should yet have made but small proficiency in any learned or foreign language, rather than utterly ignorant of all these sciences, but quite master of the Greek and Latin grammars, which is all that can be learned, where nothing else is taught? Let instruction in real knowledge be the chief care from the first dawn of reason, if verbal knowledge be not of greater excellence and utility. And let us not imagine that the understanding opens otherwise than in proportion to the pains taken to let in light into it, and to brighten and strengthen it by instruction and proper exercise. As candle lighteth candle, so doth instruction light up the understanding. And the longer fit methods of drawing forth reason to seek information, and of informing the mind are delayed, the more difficult instructing work becomes. 'Tis the same here as with regard to the body: The fibres of the latter do not become more stiff and inflexible, for want of early use, than the intellectual faculties become, if they are not exercised, dull or restive, and unsusceptible of their proper movements. And if any one can think information in natural or moral history more unentertaining or insipid to youth than grammatical lessons, and the *rationale* of the latter more easy and comprehensible to them, let him but try the difference, and he will quickly find the former highly agreeable to the youngest scholar, and that he will make with delight very speedy progress in science; whereas grammar is exceeding irksome to him, and is not at all understood by youth, even after their memories can rote it away most fluently. Every one who will allow himself to think, must immediately perceive that the use and design of grammar and all its rules, cannot be understood till the mind is pretty well stored with the knowledge of things, seeing the foundation of the chief grammatical rules in every language can be none other but either perspicuity, propriety, force or elegance, and harmony of expression. But if this be true, it requires no proof, that tho' the books that are put into children's hands, in whatever language they are taught, should not only be correct but elegant, and they should be used to pronounce gracefully, and speak or write accurately, yet they ought not to be much plagued with rules, till they are able to trace the more essential ones to some good reasons for them, founded in one or other of the designs of discourse just mentioned. As one may not only have a very good ear for music, but even be able to play very well upon some musical instrument, tho' he does not understand the principles and foundations of combination in music; so is it with respect to grammar and languages in a great measure. In teaching music, care is taken first to form the ear, and then, and not till then, is it thought expedient to teach the scholar the maxims or rules of composition. And for the same reasons, the like method ought to be pursued in teaching grammar and rhetoric, that the feelings of the ear may, by these arts, be enabled to justify themselves to the understanding, as far as philosophy or reason can have place with relation to the structure and idiom of a language; for here, no doubt, much must be resolved into mere custom. But grammar, rightly taught, will teach to distinguish what rules are really founded on this reason, e.g. to prevent ambiguity, or some such other equivalent one, and what are founded on harmony and rhythm, and what merely on chance and subsequent use. When it is proper to read grammar in a critical, or rather philosophical manner with youth, 'tis certainly the grammar of their own native tongue for which they are to have most use in life, that they ought most carefully and accurately to be instructed in. The Greeks, perhaps, made more early advances in the most useful sciences than any youth have done since, chiefly on this account, that they studied no other language but their own: This, no doubt, saved them very much time: But they applied themselves carefully to the study of their own language, and were early able to speak and write it in the greatest perfection. 'Twas from the Greeks that the Romans derived all their philosophy and learning; and therefore the Roman youth were timeously taught the Greek tongue: But they did not neglect their own, but studied it more carefully than we now do Greek and Latin, without minding or giving ourselves any trouble about our own tongue. This, not to tire the reader with many proofs of it, we may learn from the compliment Horace pays to Maecenas;

Docte sermones utriusque linguae.
Od. 8. carm. l. 3.[29]

And the passages from ancient authors, which are commonly quoted by Horace's commentators in their notes on that place; one in particular, in the beginning of Cicero's book of offices, wrote for the use of his son. "Ut ipse ad meam utilitatem semper cum Graecis Latina conjunxi, neque id in philosophia tantum, sed etiam in dicendi exercitatione feci, idem tibi censeo faciendum, ut par sis in utriusque orationis facultate."[30] And from the account Quintilian gives us of his method of teaching grammar and rhetoric, thinking preceptors may glean excellent rules and helps for teaching the grammar of any language.

All I now contend for is, that there is time enough for teaching many dead and foreign languages, without being forced to neglect more substantial and important parts of education. Let French and Italian be early talked into youth, as is usually done with excellent success. And as for Latin, let conjugations and declensions, and some more general rules of

---

29. [Horace, *Odes,* 3.8.5: "you versed in the lore of either tongue!"]

30. [Cicero, *De Officiis,* 1.1: "just as I for my own improvement have always combined Greek and Latin studies—and I have done this not only in the study of philosophy but also in the practice of oratory—so I recommend that you should do the same, so that you may have equal command of both languages" (Loeb translation by Walter Miller).]

construction be taught regularly: But let the more difficult and abstruse parts of grammar be delayed till their understandings being enriched with useful knowledge, and their ears having been accustomed to clear, strong and elegant expression, they are qualified for examining, with the assistance of masters, the received principles of rhetoric, of which grammar is the first, and yet the most difficult part. Let due pains be taken to make Latin as easy to them as possible, by ranging the words to them in their natural order, and explaining the author, they read, to them in English, as near to the Latin as the idioms of these two languages permit. Let no helps be denied them, that will either save them time or harsh labour; none especially which will remove all the difficulty that may arise to very young scholars, merely from want of acquaintance with their own tongue. But let care be taken the translations or other helps that are allowed them in this view, be just and good in every respect, i.e. be good English, as well as true explications of the author's meaning. It will be soon enough to begin Greek with youth when they have got a sufficient stock of Latin words to be able to interpret Greek into Latin; and then they will be improving in the latter every step they advance in the former. But whatever language they are learning, one chief thing is to trace with them metaphorical words, which are by far the greatest number in every language, to their roots and primitive significations, and to point out to them the analogies or resemblances in nature, which lay the foundations for similitudes or comparisons, and metaphors which are similitudes expressed in single words, without the formality of telling us that a comparison is designed. This is necessary, in order to one's being able to comprehend quickly and relish fully the propriety and force of metaphors: And exercises of this kind must not only enrich and improve the fancy, but exceedingly ripen and extend the judgment: For there is not a more useful or more entertaining branch of knowledge, than to be gathering from nature just conceptions, and large views of the likenesses and correspondences which obtain throughout all her works, even those which at the first sight seem most heterogeneous or desperate, and consequently to have the least relation or affinity. And I need not tell those who have any notion of poetry, painting and sculpture, commonly called, with great justice, because of their close dependence, the sister arts, that were there not such an extensive analogy

between the moral world and the natural, that almost every moral sentiment may be figured or pictured to us under some material semblance,
these arts would be utterly unknown to us: There would be no foundation
for them in the frame and contexture of things. To give a just taste of metaphorical language, is to teach to judge what is or what is not a proper image for conveying a clear and warm idea of a subject intended to be illustrated by a lively and true picture of it to the imagination. And so far
teaching of languages coincides with philosophy, or is at least an essential
step towards forming good taste, and quickening, embellishing and refin-
ing the fancy. The perfection of wit and taste consists in finding out readily
proper material images for exhibiting moral sentiments in an agreeable
garb or dress. And therefore, without overlooking the likenesses and resemblances in nature, which make a most entertaining branch of knowledge, and are the basis of all the ingenious imitative arts, and without neglecting the culture of the imagination, this part of teaching cannot be
omitted.

Much depends upon a fit choice of books for young scholars. Quintilian did not think it expedient to read all Horace with his disciples. And
Plutarch lays down many excellent cautions about reading the poets with
youth, in order to put them into the way of drawing solid advantages from
them, and to prevent the bad influence the magic of fiction and numbers
must have, if they be not wholesomely employed. If we would form good
taste, let them not touch or taste any thing that is not truly chaste and
elegant: And if we would preserve their hearts pure and uncorrupted,
which is still of greater consequence, let all evil or infectious communication be far removed from them; let them have no fellowship with what
must pollute their minds or inflame hurtful passions. Let fables, allegories,
and characters, which tend to insinuate in an agreeable manner moral
truths or precepts into their minds; which display the folly, absurdity, and
deformity of the vices, or the beauty and excellence of the virtues be early
read to them and by them. This was the ancient practice, as we are assured
by many authors: And our Saviour himself hath, by his frequent use of
parables, given a particular recommendation, or rather sanction to this
method of instruction. A treatise strongly recommended to preceptors by
Mr. Rollin, as one of the best they can put into the hands of young Latin

scholars, intitled, *Historiae selectae e profanis scriptoribus*, &c. were more poetry, i.e. more descriptions and recommendations of the several virtues, and more dehortations from their opposite vices taken from the poets, and some fables added to it under proper heads, would make a perfect book for the use of schools, it being nothing else but excerpts from the Latin writers in their own language, containing moral maxims and precepts, confirmed by characters and histories. I have often wished that there were, for the use of young Latin students, a collection made from Cicero, whose works would furnish a great deal, and other Roman authors, of observations upon final causes in nature, or the wisdom and goodness of God's works of creation and providence: And one who is very well qualified for it, hath given me encouragement to expect such a work very soon from his hands. And when youth are by such reading prepared for considering the nature of composition, I know not why any other author should be preferred to Cicero himself, i.e. to proper select parts from him, on the beauty of writing. For there all the rules of oratory are fully explained? Nay, there all the different species of true and false wit are more perfectly described and illustrated than in any of our modern systems of rhetoric.

But let me, upon a subject where I would willingly avoid all appearance of dictating to more experienced teachers, just add, That what the very ingenious and worthy Mr. Rollin has said upon teaching languages, deserves the most careful perusal from every one who is engaged in the instruction of youth, because his rules are drawn from his own experience, or such as he could equally found upon. That I may not, however, swell this book too much, I shall only give the substance of what he has collected from the ancients, upon an article which all good men will acknowledge to be by far the most momentuous branch of education.[31]

"The education of youth hath ever been regarded by the best philosophers and the wisest legislators as the most certain source of happiness, not only to families, but to states or kingdoms. In effect, what is a republic or kingdom but a vast body, whose vigour and health depends upon that of

---

31. [Charles Rollin, *De la manière d'énseigner et d'étudier les belles-lettres, Par raport à l'esprit & au coeur*, 2 tomes (Paris: Estienne, 1740), 2:520–73.]

the families, which are, as it were, its parts and members, none of which can fail in its functions without detriment to the whole? But is it not good education which puts all the citizens, the great and noble, more especially, into a condition of executing with dignity their respective offices? Is it not evident that the youth of a state are the nursery by which it is preserved and renewed? From it come fathers of families, magistrates, ministers, in one word, all persons of authority and power? And may we not be assured, that faults in education will shew their bad effects, in the behaviour of those who are placed in these stations? Laws, in truth, are the foundation of states; and by maintaining regularity and good order in them, support public peace and tranquillity. But whence do the laws derive their force and vigour, if not from good education, accustoming the minds of subjects to approve and submit to them? Without this precaution, they are but a very feeble barrier against the passions of mankind.

Quid leges sine moribus vanae proficiunt.
HOR. od. 25. lib, 3.[32]

"Plutarch makes a very judicious observation upon this subject, that deserves to be weighed with attention. It is in his remarks upon Lycurgus. That wise lawgiver, says he, did not think it sufficient to commit his constitutions and orders to writing, being persuaded that the most effectual way of rendering states happy, and any people virtuous, is by practising them in, and inuring them to virtue, till its habits are become natural. For the principles and dispositions which are engraved upon the heart by education, remain firm and unshakeable, as being founded on inward conviction, and the bent and inclination of the will, which is a much stronger and more lasting bond than constraint, and therefore becomes a law to youth, and holds in their minds the quality of a legislator. Here, methinks, is the truest idea that can be given of the difference between laws and education. The laws, by themselves, are a severe imperious mistress, a kind of necessity which fetters man, in what he naturally loves most, and is most jealous of, I mean his liberty. They fret and grieve him, they oppose and

32. [Horace, *Odes*, 3.24.35–36: "Of what avail are empty laws, if we lack principle?"]

contradict him, they are deaf to all his remonstrances and desires; they are inflexible, and speak to him always in a menacing tone, and exhibit nothing to his view but punishments. And therefore it is not surprizing that he should willingly shake off this yoke, when he can do it with impunity, and give himself up to those natural inclinations which the laws had only restrained, not changed or destroyed. 'Tis not so with respect to education. It is a sweet and insinuating mistress, an enemy to all violence and constraint, that delights to act only in the way of persuasion, and endeavours to make its instructions liked by speaking always truth and reason, and aims at making virtue easier by rendering it more amiable. These lessons commencing with infancy, grow up and strengthen with the child, and spreading their roots by degrees, soon pass from the memory and the understanding into the heart, and by practice and habitude become a second nature, which it is almost impossible to efface or alter. 'Tis not then to be wondered at, that the ancient sages should have so earnestly recommended particular concern about education, and considered it as the securest way of rendering a state truly stable and flourishing. Their capital maxim was, that children belonged more to the republic than to their parents, and therefore, that their institution ought not to be left to the caprice of the latter, but be the care of the public. 'Tis true, every species of government hath its particular genius. The spirit and character of a common-wealth is one thing, and that of a monarchical state is another. But 'tis by education that the spirit and character of a people is formed. It is in consequence of the principles we have now laid down that Lycurgus, Aristotle, Plato, and in one word, all those ancients who have left us instructions concerning civil government, declare with one voice, that it is the principal, the most essential duty of a magistrate, a minister, a legislator, a prince, to give attention to the education, in the first place of their own children, who often succeed to their dignities, and in the next place to that of the subjects in general, which constitute the public body; and they have observed that all the disorders of states chiefly spring from neglect of this double duty. Plato quotes an illustrious example of it in the person of one of the most accomplished princes in ancient history, the famous Cyrus. He wanted none of the qualities necessary to make a truly great man, but this one we are now to mention. Being entirely occupied by his conquests, he abandoned to his women the education of his children. So that these young princes were not brought up according to the hard and austere discipline of the Persians, which had such excellent success with regard to Cyrus himself, but in the manner of the Medes, that is to say, in luxury, softness and voluptuousness. Their ears were open to nothing but praise and flattery: All who came near them bended the knee, and laid themselves at their feet; and they thought it essential to their grandeur to keep at an immense distance from all the rest of mankind, whom they looked upon as of a different species. An education from which all controul, all checks were banished, had, says Plato, the effect one must naturally expect from it. The two princes, immediately after the decease of their father, armed the one against the other, neither being able to bear a superior or equal; and Cambyses becoming, by the death of his brother, absolute master, threw himself, like one who had lost his senses, and was quite infatuated, into excesses of all kinds, and brought the Persian empire to the very brink of ruin. Cyrus had left him a vast extent of provinces, immense revenues, an army of incredible numbers; but all this contributed to his ruin, through want of another good, infinitely more valuable, which he neglected to leave him, I mean a good education.

"Philip King of Macedon behaved in another manner. So soon as he was a father (and it was in the middle of his conquests, and in the time of his greatest exploits) he wrote the following letter to Aristotle. 'I acquaint you that a son is born to me. I do not thank the Gods so much for his birth, as for his happiness in being born while there is an Aristotle in the world. For I hope that, being educated under your care, he will become worthy of the glory of his father, and of the empire I shall leave him.' This was speaking and thinking like a great prince, who well knew the importance of good education. Alexander had the same sentiments. An historian tells us, that he loved Aristotle as his father, because, said he, to the one I owe my life, to the other the art of living well.

"If it be a great fault in a prince not to give due attention to the education of his own children, it is not a less one to neglect that of his subjects in general. Plutarch, in his parallel between Lycurgus and Numa, remarks very judiciously, that it was this neglect that rendered all the good designs

and noble establishments of the latter ineffective. The passage is remarkable. All the care of Numa, says he, being solely aimed at maintaining
Rome in peace and quiet, evanished with him: For immediately after his
death, the double-gated temple, that really during his time kept in the De-
mon of war, as if he had been chained by him, burst open, and Italy was
forthwith filled with blood and slaughter. And thus his best orders proved
abortive, and did not long subsist, because the only support that could
preserve and uphold them was wanting, good education of the youth. It
was a quite opposite conduct which supported for so long a time the laws
of Lycurgus in their full power. For as the same Plutarch observes, the oath
which he exacted from the Lacedemonians would have been but a very
weak resource after his death, if he had not taken care by his regulations
about education to imprint his laws upon their manners, and to make
them suck in with their first milk the love of his polity. Accordingly we
find, that his chief ordinances preserved themselves more than five hundred years, as a good and strong tincture that had penetrated to the very
bottom of the soul. It is astonishing to think how far back the best persons
of antiquity carried their attention and vigilance in this matter. They recommended taking the greatest precaution from the very birth of infants,
with relation to the persons put about them. We know that Quintilian had
taken from Plato and Aristotle what he says with relation to nurses. He
advises, like these sages, that in the choice of them regard ought to be had
to their language and accent, but yet more especially to their temper, character and manners. And the reasons he gives are admirable. What is
learned in infancy gently slides into the mind, and quickly taking deep
root there is not easily erazed. Young minds are like fresh vessels, which
preserve a long time the flavour of the first liquor that is poured into them;
or as wool which never recovers its first whiteness after it has been dyed.
And the misfortune is, that bad habits last longer than good ones. It was
for the same reasons, that these philosophers looked upon it to be one of
the chief duties of those charged with the education of children, to remove
far from them the slaves and domestics, who by their discourse, and yet
more by their example, might be hurtful to them. They added to this care
another, the neglect of which will be the condemnation of many christian

parents and masters. They kept carefully from infants not only all books, but all paintings, sculptures, or tapistry that could raise any dangerous image in their minds. All such corruptive pieces of art were strictly forbidden; and it was thought incumbent upon the magistrates to take care that these might be prohibitions were carefully observed. They were persuaded, that from objects so proper to kindle and flatter bad passions and appetites, there proceeded a most pestilential and contagious air. These sages earnestly desired that care might be taken that every thing should teach and inspire virtue, inscriptions, pictures, statues, spectacles, conversations; that every thing, in fine, that presents itself to the senses, and strikes the eyes or ears, should breath a salutary air, which might imperceptibly insinuate itself into young minds, and being aided and supported by the instructions of masters, might, from their tenderest years blow up and cherish in them the love of virtue, and a relish for honest things. There is in the original Greek of Plato, a delicacy of expression of which no other language is susceptive. And tho' the passage be long, I thought it not amiss to quote a great part of it, to give some idea of his stile. I return to my subject, and I shall conclude this article, by entreating the reader to consider how paganism itself always regarded it as the principal duty of fathers, mothers, magistrates and princes, to watch over the education of children, as an affair of the last moment to private and public happiness. In fact, whilst the mind is yet tender and flexible, it may be moulded and formed just as we please, whereas age and long habit render faults almost incorrigible. 'Frangas enim citius, quam corrigas quae in pravum induruerunt.'[33]

"In order to succeed well in the education of youth, the first step, methinks, one ought to take, is to settle well the scope to be proposed, to enquire which is the road to it, and to choose an able and experimented guide, qualified for conducting to it. Tho' it be in general a very wise and judicious rule, to avoid all singularity, and to follow the established customs; yet I know not, if with regard to the affair in question, this maxim does not admit of some exception, and there be not reason to fear the dan-

---

33. [Quintilian, *Institutio Oratoria*, 1.3.12: "For once a bad habit has become engrained, it is easier to break than bend."]

gers and inconveniencies of a sort of servitude, that makes us follow blindly the steps of those who went before us, and consult custom more than reason, and regulate ourselves by what has been, rather than by what ought to be done: From whence it not unfrequently happens, that an error once established, goes from hand to hand, and from age to age, and so becomes almost a law that can't be prescribed. But are mankind so happy, that the greater number always approves what is best? Doth not the very contrary happen much the oftenest? If we think with any degree of seriousness upon the matter, it will easily be granted, that the design of masters is not merely to teach their scholars Greek and Latin, or to instruct them in making themes, verses, amplifications; to load their memories with historical dates and aeras; to teach them to rear up syllogisms in mood and figure, or to draw lines and figures upon paper. These arts are, I deny not, useful and estimable, but as means, and not as the end; when they lead us to something else, and not when they are rested in as the principal part of instruction; when they serve as preparatives and instruments for better things, the ignorance of which renders every thing else useless. Youth would be to be pitied indeed, if they were condemned to pass eight or ten of their best years in learning, at great expence, and with incredible labour, one or two languages, and other such things, for which they may perhaps have very rarely any occasion. The great use of masters, in the long carrier of studies, is to accustom their disciples to thinking and serious application, and to make them love and esteem the sciences, to excite a hunger and thirst in them after solid knowledge, which will spur them to seek after it, when they leave the schools and colleges; to direct them into the true road to it, and to imprint upon their minds a deep sense of its value and price, and by this means, to qualify them for the different employments to which divine providence may call them. Nay, the scope of masters ought to be something more yet, which is to form their hearts and inclinations; to inspire into them good principles, the principles of honour and probity, and to train up in their minds good habits; to correct and amend in them by soft and sweet methods, any bad dispositions they may have discovered, such as pride, insolence, self-conceit, selfishness, and a spirit of railery, that delights in irritating and insulting, or a habit of laziness and indolence, which would render the best accomplishments profitless. Education,

properly speaking, is the art of fashioning the heart and mind. It is of all
the sciences the most difficult and the rarest: It is the most important, but
it is not studied enough. To judge of the matter by common experience,
one would say, that man is the most untractable of all animals. This is the
judicious reflection with which Xenophon begins his institution of Cyrus.
After having remarked that herds of sheep or cattle never rebel against
their leaders, whereas amongst mankind nothing is more common. It
seems, says he, as if we ought to conclude from hence, that it is more difficult to command men than beasts. But upon casting his eyes towards Cyrus, who was able to govern so many provinces, and keep them in peace,
and to make himself equally beloved by conquered nations and his own
natural subjects, he infers, that the fault is not owing to the refractoriness
of those who ought to obey, but to superiors who know not how to rule.
We may say the same of those who are charged with the education of children. It must be owned that the spirit of man, even in the tenderest age, is
impatient of the yoke, and inclines to what is forbidden. But what ought
we to conclude from this, but that the art of managing youth requires great
prudence and address; and that youth yield more readily to mild methods
than to violence? We often see a horse skittish, and spurn and fret at the
bit, when it is the fault of his rider, who curbs and checks him unskilfully:
Mount another on the same horse, better versed in horsemanship, and he
will manage him very easily. To gain this end, the master's first care ought
to be to find out the genius and character of his trust: For accordingly
ought he to regulate his management. Some children are retained by fear,
and others are dispirited and discouraged by it. Some are hardly to be diverted or drawn from study and application: Others only study by fits and
starts. To attempt to bring all upon the same level, or to subject all to one
rule and discipline, is to force nature. The prudence of a master lies chiefly
in keeping the middle between two extremes: For here the good borders
so near upon the bad, that it is easy to mistake the one for the other, and
this it is that renders the government of young folks so difficult. Too much
liberty begets licentiousness, and too much restraint, on the other hand
breaks the spirit. Praise awakes and rouses, but it also inspires vanity and
presumption. We must therefore study to keep a just mean, that may
balance or avoid these two inconveniencies, and imitate the conduct of

Isocrates,[34] with regard to Ephorus and Theopompus his scholars, who were of very different characters. This great master, who had no less success in teaching than in writing, as his disciples and writings proved, employed the bridle to keep in the vivacity of the one, and the spur to awake and push forward the other; and did not dream of treating them both in the same manner. His aim in reducing the one and goading the other, was to bring each to the particular perfection of which his nature was capable. Here is the model that ought to be followed in education. Infants carry in their minds the principles, and, as it were, the seeds of all the virtues and vices. Great sagacity is requisite to distinguish their several genius's and characters; to find out their humours, their talents, their propensities, and, above all, their predomining passions, not with the view or hope of changing entirely their temperament, as for instance, to render one gay who is naturally grave and morose, or him serious who is naturally sprightly and lively. There are certain characters which like bodily deformity may be mended a little, but cannot be wholly changed. Now, the way to know children is to give them liberty from their earliest years to discover their inclinations, and to exert their natural humours; to bear with their little infirmities, that they may not be afraid to let them appear, to observe them narrowly, especially when they are at play, and do not hide or disguise themselves. For young people are naturally open and simple: But when they imagine they are observed, they are fettered, and this puts them upon their guard.

"It is also of great moment to distinguish the nature of the faults to which children are incident. In general, there is a probability that those in which their childhood, bad education, ignorance, misleading, and bad example have any share, are not remediless: And there is ground on the contrary to fear, that the faults which are rooted on the natural character of the mind, and the corruption of the heart, will be found very difficult to be cured, such as insincerity, dissimulation, flattery, a propensity to talebearing, in order to sow division, to envy and evil-speaking; a taunting mocking spirit, especially if it exert itself against advice, or things revered

---

34. Quintilian l. 2. c. 8. Cicero l. 3. de orator. n. 36.

as sacred, a spirit of contradiction and obstinacy, and which is the ordinary consequence of it, a willingness and readiness to pervert and misconstruct.

"To get authority over children early is of principal consequence to masters during the whole course of education. I mean by authority a certain air and manner, which imprints respect and gains obedience. And 'tis neither age nor stature, nor the tone of the voice, nor menaces, which give this authority; but a moderate, agreeable, firm character of mind, which is always master of itself, and is always guided by reason, and never acts by caprice or in passion. 'Tis this excellent quality which preserves all in order, maintains an exact discipline, makes rules to be observed, saves from the trouble of reprimanding, and almost totally prevents the necessity of any other punishments. But it is from the very beginning that parents and masters must get this ascendency. If they do not seize the favourable minute, and put themselves from the first in possession of this authority, they will ever after find insurmountable difficulties in obtaining it, and the child will be master. There is in the heart of man a love of independency, which develops and shews itself in the tenderest years, and from the cradle. Now this is the season for breaking hardness and obstinacy, by accustoming children from their cradles to overcome their appetites, and to have no will of their own, but to yield and obey willingly. If what they cried for was never given them, they would quickly learn to give over fretting and peevishness, and by consequence, would not be so troublesome to themselves and others as they are generally rendered during their whole lives by ill-judged indulgence to their humours in their infancy. When I say this, I do not mean, that we should have no indulgence for children: I am far from such a disposition. I only say that nothing ought to be yielded to their crossness and peevishness: On the contrary, if they redouble their importunity they ought to be made to feel, that for this very reason they are not to have what they call for. And this we should lay down for a certain maxim, that after we have once refused them, we must resolve not to succumb to their obstinacy, unless we have a mind to teach them to be impatient and chagrined by so gratifying them. Don't we see several well-bred children, who at table, whatever be before them, desire nothing, but take chearfully whatever is given them? Whereas, in other families children call tumultuously for whatever they like, and must be served first. Now whence comes this difference but from difference of discipline and education? The younger infants are, the less ought we to indulge their disorderly desires. The less reason they have, there is the more necessity of their absolute subjection to the will of their governors. And when they have once contracted this habit of pliableness, the trouble is over, and obedience will ever after be very easy to them.

Adeo in teneris consuescere multum est.
VIRG. Geo. l. 2. v. 272.[35]

What I have said of younger infants may be applied to those of riper years. A scholar who is put under a new master, makes it his first business to study and sound him. He will leave no artifice untried to find him out, and get the ascendent over him. But when he finds all his ruses and arts to no purpose, and that his master, with tranquillity and steadiness pursues his method, and will be obeyed, then the young man surrenders himself with good grace, and this kind of little war, or rather short skirmish which served to try forces on both sides, terminates happily in a peace and good understanding, which render all the after-time they have to be together very sweet and pleasant.

"The respect upon which the authority I have been speaking of is founded includes two things, fear and love, which mutually support and assist one another, and are the two chief handles or springs of government in general, in the management of youth in particular. Being of an age, in which reason is not yet very strong, and far from being able to rule, fear must sometimes come to its assistance, and take its place. But if fear be alone, and not followed very close with something to soften it and give delight, it will not long be listened to, its lessons will have but a very slight and transitory effect, which the hope of impunity will quickly dissipate. Wherefore, in education the great skill and ability of a master consists in mingling force to retain children, without dispiriting them, with love to gain them without softening them. On the one side mildness takes off

---

35. [Virgil, *Georgics,* 2.272: "So strong is habit in tender years" (Loeb translation by H. Rushton Fairclough, revised by G. P. Goold). Quoted in Quintilian, *Institutio Oratoria,* 1.3.13.]

what is harsh and austere in commanding; it blunts the sting of empire: On the other, prudent severity fixes the volatility and unsteadiness of an age not yet capable of deep reflection, or of governing itself. 'Tis then this happy mixture of sweetness and severity, fear and love, which procures authority to a master, is the soul of government, and inspires into pupils that respect which is the firmest bond of submission and obedience, in such a proportion, however, that it is mildness that ought to predomine and have the ascendant. But it may be said, that this mild way of governing youth, and of making one's self beloved by his pupils, is much easier to be pursued by a private tutor than by masters of public schools. I own it is very difficult to preserve, in the management of a numerous school, that wholesome temperament between severity and excessive sweetness, of which we have been speaking. But it is not impossible; for we have seen it put in practice by some rare persons, who had hit on the secret of making themselves at once feared and loved. The whole depends upon the character of the masters. Quintilian tells us what the qualities of such a master must be, and how he must conduct himself in order to gain the affection of his disciples.[36]

"1. Because it is a general maxim that love cannot be bought but by love, 'Si vis amari ama,' the first thing Quintilian demands is, that a master should put on the sentiments and feelings, the bowels of a parent for his charge, and consider himself as holding the rank of those who have committed their children to him. 2. Next, That he should indulge no vices in himself, and suffer none in others. But that his austerity should have nothing rude in it, and his facility, on the other hand, no mixture of the too soft, lest he be either despised or hated. 3. That he be not choleric or passionate; but that on the other side, he do not shut his eyes against faults that deserve his animadversion. 4. That his manner of teaching be simple, calm, patient, and correct; and that he count more upon his own application and distinctness than upon the assiduity of his scholars: That he take pleasure in answering their questions: Nay, that he often prevent

36. [Quintilian, *Institutio Oratoria*, 2.2.1–8.]

them, and raise their curiosity by asking them proper questions if they do not come to him with any. 5. That he do not grudge them the praise they have merited in due place and time, but that he be not too lavish of it; for the one discourages, and the other occasions a dangerous self-confidence and security. 6. When he is obliged to reprove, let it be done without bitterness or irritation. For many have contracted an aversion to study, because their master's reprimands to them were as surly as if he had conceived a hatred against them. 7. That he speak often to them of virtue, and always with high relish, delight and commendation: That he always set it forth to them in the most engaging, captivating colours, as the most excellent and precious of all treasures, the most worthy possession of a reasonable agent; that which gains one the greatest honour, as a quality absolutely necessary to procure universal esteem and love, and as the only means of true happiness. The more pains he takes in informing them of their duties, the less will he be necessitated to chastise. Let him every day teach them himself something which they will take pleasure to carry with them, and by which they will profit. Tho' reading may furnish with good examples, yet what a master says of himself *viva voce,* has quite another force, and produces quite a different effect, especially if it come from a master whom the scholars love and honour. For we much more willingly hearken to and imitate those for whom we have preconceived a liking and esteem.

"Those are the qualities which Quintilian requires in a master of rhetoric; (and they are equally requisite to every one who is entrusted with the care of youth) to the end, saith he, that where there are great numbers of students, the prudence of the master may preserve the younger from infection, and his gravity may check the licentiousness of those who are of an age more difficult to govern. For it is not enough that he be a man of virtue, if he be not also able to keep his disciples in order by exact discipline. Let us not doubt but a preceptor of this character will make himself both feared and loved. But the greater part seem to think, that they take a much surer way, namely that of reproof and punishment. It must be acknowledged, that this method appears easier, and that it costs less to the master than the insinuating mild manner, but it is as true, that it succeeds

much worse. For by punishments one never arrives at the great end of education, which is to persuade, and to inspire the sincere love of virtue.

"The common compendious way for correcting children is the rod, the
only one many of those entrusted with education seem to know. But this
remedy often produces a worse disease than those it is employed to redress;
especially, if it be employed out of season and measure. For besides that
the whip and the rod have something indecent, low and servile in them,
they are not in themselves proper remedies for faults, and there is no likelihood that correction will be of any use to a child, if the shame of suffering
for having done amiss make not a greater impression upon his mind than
the pain of being beat or lashed. Besides, these punishments give him an
incurable aversion against the very things one ought to take all pains to
make him like. They do not change the temper, but only restrain it for a
while, and so only serve to make the passions break forth with more violence, when the curb is removed, and they feel themselves at liberty. They
often stupify the mind, and oftener still harden in the vice we would reform: For an infant, who has so little sense of honour as not to be sensible
to a reprimand, accustoms himself to stripes like a slave, and is at length
very little affected by very severe punishments. Ought we to infer from
this, that chastisements should never be applied? I am far from being of
that opinion. I know what the wise man says against parents who spare the
rod. But it is plain from the general tenor of his writings, that he only en-
joins corporal punishment in case of obstinacy and insensibility to honour
and reproof. Punishments may therefore be employed, but for faults of
great importance, even as violent cures are never used but in extreme danger. Every person who is set over others, in order to correct those under
his tuition, ought first to use gentle remonstrances, try the persuasive way,
and endeavour to make honour, truth and justice relished; and to inspire
esteem for virtue and abhorrence against vice. If this method won't do, he
may then have recourse to more violent and more piquing reproaches. But
let him not proceed to corporal punishment till he hath tried all other
milder means in vain, and that by degrees, leaving still some hopes of pardon, and thus reserving greater severities for the most desperate cases.
When we compare a person of this prudence and moderation with a brutish, passionate, violent master, such as Orbilius, to whom Horace, who

had been his scholar, gives the character of *Plagosus*,[37] who does not perceive the difference of the effects that may be expected from their very opposite methods? Which of the two preceptors would we prefer, says Seneca, him who by his sage advices and counsels, and by motives of honour applies himself to amend his scholars, or him who tears their hides into pieces with his rod for a grammatical blunder, or some such like fault? If we should take this way to manage a horse, would we not quite spoil him? A skilful horseman never goes so rudely to work: And why must men be treated more roughly than brutes? The truth of the matter is, what makes it necessary to have at any age recourse to severe punishments, is chiefly the indulgence by which children are spoil'd in their tender years. Would we inure them betimes to obey reason, a reasonable habit would soon be fixed in their minds, that would save us the trouble and pain of punishing them in their more advanced years. But it is of the greatest importance to distinguish faults that demerit punishment from pardonable ones. I scruple not to place in the latter class all those which are done through inadvertency or ignorance, and which cannot be attributed to malice or bad intention, there being none that render culpable but those of the will. Of this kind are many levities and childish frailties which experience and age will infallibly correct. Nor do I think the whip or rod ought to be employed for any slips a child may commit in reading, writing, dancing, in learning any language, as Latin, Greek, &c. except in certain cases, of which I shall speak afterwards. There ought to be other punishments for faults in which there appears no bad disposition of the heart, nor no desire to shake off the yoke of authority. It is likewise the duty of parents and masters to contrive different sorts and degrees of punishments for different faults. It depends upon them to attach shame or ignominy to a thousand things which are indifferent in themselves, and that only become punishments in consequence of the ideas attached to them.—The only vice, in my opinion, that deserves severe treatment, is obstinacy in evil: A determined evident obstinacy. For we must not give this name to faults of levity and inconstancy, into which children, naturally heedless and unfixed, may

37. [Horace, *Epistles,* 2.1.70–71.]

frequently relapse without having bad dispositions. Suppose a child has told a lie; if it was violent fear drove him to it, the fault is much less on that score, and requires no more than a gentle reprimand. But if it be deliberate and voluntary, and pertly persisted in, it is a real fault that certainly merits punishment. Yet I think even for such a fault the rod ought not to be used the first time; for beyond this what can we do with children? It is the last remedy with relation to them. Does a father, says Seneca, disinherit his son for the first fault, however gross it may be? No. He tries all methods of reclaiming him, and making him return to himself; and it is only when he has lost all hopes of his amendment that he carries matters to such an extremity. A master ought in his sphere to observe the same rule. I say just the same of indocility and disobedience, when they are accompanied with obstinacy, or an air of arrogance, contempt and rebellion. But there is a particular kind of obstinacy with respect to study, and which we may call obstinate idleness, which commonly creates a great deal of trouble to masters, and that is, when children will learn nothing unless they be forced to it. I own nothing is more embarrassing, or more difficult to manage than this character, especially, if insensibility and indifference be joined with indolence, as is not uncommon. 'Tis in such a case, particularly, that a master stands in need of all his prudence, and of all his art, to render study, if not agreeable, at least not nauseous to his disciple, by mixing severity with mildness, threats with promises, punishments with rewards. When nothing else will succeed, one may have recourse to chastisement, but not daily and customarily; for such a remedy is worse than the disease. When punishment is necessary, there are proper times or seasons, and there is a proper manner of inflicting it. No less address and dexterity is requisite in treating the distempers of the mind than in managing those of the body. Nothing is more dangerous to the former than a cure unseasonably applied. A wise physician watches the favourable moment for applying his remedy: He waits till the patient is in a condition to bear it: The first rule therefore, with regard to the chastisement of children, is not to punish them in the very instant they are found in a fault, lest they be irritated and pushed by such severity to extremity: But time ought to be given them to come to themselves, and perceive their fault, and the necessity or justice of punishing them for it, that they may thus be in a condition for profiting by chastisement. The master ought never to punish in passion or anger, more especially, if the fault committed anywise regard his own person in particular. He ought to bear in mind that fine saying of Seneca to a slave, with whom he had reason to be angry, 'I would punish you as you have deserved, were I not in passion.' 'Twere to be wished that all persons invested with authority over others were in this respect like the laws, which punish without any commotion or disquiet, and that purely for the sake of justice and public good. The scholar soon perceives the least appearance of wrath in his master's face or tone of voice, and then he is apt to conclude, that it is not so much his regard to his duty, as the ardor of his passion that instigates him: And there needs no more to render punishment quite fruitless; because the youngest children are sensible that it is reason alone that hath a right to correct. As punishment ought very rarely to be inflicted, so all fit means ought to be used to make it answer its end. Shew, for instance, a child all you have done to avoid coming to this extremity. Let him see that you are really grieved to be forced to it. Speak often in his hearing to other persons of the unhappiness of those who have so little regard to honour and reason, that there is a necessity for using severities with them. Retrench the ordinary marks of your love, till you find that he begins to want consolation. Let the punishment be private or public, as you shall find it necessary for the child's good, to shew him your tenderness, or to bring him to greater shame. Let public shame be reserved for your last resource. Make use sometimes of some reasonable person to take proper pains with him to bring him to himself, to whom he is likely to open his mind with more freedom than he dare to you. But, above all, let it be evident that you desire no other submissions of him but what are reasonable. Endeavour to convince him, so that he may condemn himself, and so nothing may remain for you to do but to mitigate his punishment. These general rules ought to be applied according to particular circumstances. But if the youth is insensible to honour or shame, care ought to be taken that the first punishment be such as will work its end in place of a more noble motive. I need not say that blows on the head or face are absolutely forbidden to masters by universal consent. They ought not to punish but to correct, and passion cannot correct. Let a master but ask himself if it is in cold blood, and without any emotion he gives a blow to a child? Anger, which is itself a vice, can it be a proper remedy for curing the vices of others?

"No less precaution and prudence are necessary in giving reprimands than in inflicting corporal chastisements; because there is more frequent occasion for the former, and the consequences of them may be equally pernicious. To render them of use, there are three things principally to be observed, the cause, the time, and the manner of giving them. 'Tis not an uncommon error to have recourse to reproof for very slight faults, hardly avoidable by children: And this takes off all their force, and renders them fruitless when they are proper. I have not forgot the observation I have already quoted from Quintilian, that the way to punish rarely is to admonish often. 'Quo saepius monuerit hoc rarius castigabit.'[38] But there is a distinction between admonitions and reprimands. The former savour more of the friend than of the master. They are always accompanied with an air and tone of sweetness, which makes them agreeably received, and therefore they may often be used. But because reproofs always provoke self-love, and not unfrequently borrow a severe mien and tone, they ought to be reserved for the more considerable defaults, and consequently be seldomer employed. The prudence of a master chiefly shews itself, by taking the proper moments when the mind of the young offender is best disposed to profit by correction. These moments Virgil elegantly calls, 'Molles aditus, mollissima fandi tempora'; and in discerning these he places the address of a negotiator, 'Quibus rebus dexter modus.'[39] Never reprove a child, says Mr. de Fenelon,[40] neither in his nor your first emotion. If you do it in yours, he may perceive that you act precipitantly and in anger, and are not moved by reason or love; and thus you will irrecoverably lose your authority: If, while he is in heat, his mind cannot be free or calm enough to avow his fault, overcome his passion, and perceive the utility and rea-

---

38. [See note 36 in Part III, above.]

39. [Virgil, *The Aeneid,* 4.293–94: "temtaturam aditus et, quae mollissima fandi tempora, quis rebus dexter modus" ("will essay an approach and seek the happiest season for speech, the plan auspicious for his purpose") (Loeb translation by H. Rushton Fairclough, revised by G. P. Goold).]

40. [François de Fénelon, *De l'Education des Filles,* ch. 5.]

sonableness of your advice: Let him always see that you are absolute master of yourself; and nothing can better evidence that than your patience and calmness. Watch him every moment for several days, if it be necessary, till you catch a proper time for correcting him. 'Tis indeed a very difficult matter to give correction and reproof in a profitable manner. The reason is, because the affair we undertake is, to make men perceive what they do not like to perceive: It is attacking self-love in its tenderest and most sensible part, and where it never yields without violent resistance and struggling. One loves himself whatever he be, and will needs find out reasons for justifying his self-conceit: Hence it is, that various deceitful colours are studied for varnishing over our defects or faults. And therefore it is not to be wondered at, if men take it amiss to be contradicted or condemned, because thus an attack is made at one and the same time upon a mistaken understanding and a corrupted heart. This it is that renders correction and reprimand so delicate a matter to manage. We must let nothing appear to a youth that may mar the end of reproof. We must therefore avoid provoking his anger by harsh words, or his pride by marks of contempt. Let not matters be exaggerated; and it would be right even never to tell a child of a fault without shewing him how he may surmount or remedy it. Parents and masters, says Cicero, are sometimes obliged to use a high tone of voice and strong words in their corrections, but that ought rarely to be done, as physicians only have recourse to certain medicines in extremity. And reprimands, however strong it may be necessary that they should be, ought to have nothing harsh or incensing in them; for if anger mixes in any degree with punishment, it entirely spoils it of its effect. Let the child see that if we use strong terms, it is with regret, and purely for his good. We may reckon upon it, that reproofs have had their full success when they bring the youth to acknowledge his fault, and to desire to have his failures pointed out to him, and to receive the advices given him with docility. When we have gained so much, we have made great progress. For the child who desires to improve, has already made considerable proficiency. 'Tis a sure mark of a solid judgment, and a good mind, when one becomes sensible of faults to which his eyes had hitherto been shut, as it is a good sign when the patient begins to feel his sores. Some children are naturally of such a happy disposition that it is enough to shew them their

duty: They do not need long lectures from masters, but immediately discern the fair and fit, and yield themselves to truth and reason. Seneca calls
such, *Rapacia virtutis ingenia*.[41] There are, we may say, such sparks of all
the virtues in these minds, as require but very gentle blowing to be kindled
into a bright flame: But such characters are rarer, and want but little guidance. There are others who have indeed a very good natural foundation,
but their minds seem to be block'd up against instruction, either because
they have not had early instruction to open their minds, or because, being
brought up in a soft manner, and in total ignorance of their duty, they have
contracted many bad habits, which are a kind of rust that it is very difficult
to remove. Such stand most in need of masters; yet masters seldom fail of
correcting and reforming their faults, when they employ much mildness
and patience for that effect. These methods may be called, in one word,
using reason with children, acting always without choler, and always
giving a reason for your conduct towards them. We ought, says Mr. de
Fenelon, to try all means of making those things which we exact of young
people agreeable to them. If you have any thing laborious or troublesome
to propose to them, give them to understand, that the pleasure that is to
ensue to them from it, will abundantly recompense their pain: Never fail
to let them see the advantage of whatever you teach them; the use of it in
life and civil commerce. Tell them it is to qualify them for doing what they
must one day do: It is in order to ripen their judgments; it is to accustom
them to reason solidly and judiciously about the affairs of life. 'Tis proper
always to point out to them a useful or agreeable end of their labour, that
may support them in it: And they ought never to be put upon any thing
by mere force or absolute authority. When they deserve, whether punishment or rebuke, they themselves should be led to perceive the necessity of
correcting them, and be asked whether they think it possible to treat them
in any other manner. I have been astonished, says Mr. Rollin, to see, when
the reasonable but provoking necessity of chastisement, or a public rebuke, might have chagrined scholars, and tempted them to rebellion, what

41. [Seneca, *Epistulae Morales,* 95.36: "minds which seize quickly upon virtue" (Loeb
translation by Richard M. Gummere).]

impression the account I gave them of my conduct made upon them, and how they condemned themselves, and consented that I could not deal otherwise with them. For I owe this justice to all who have ever been under my tuition, to acknowledge here, that I have almost always found them very reasonable, tho' they were not exempt from all faults. Children are much sooner capable of understanding reason than we are apt to imagine, and they naturally love to be treated as reasonable creatures from their tenderest years. And this good disposition ought carefully to be cherished in them: We ought to make good use of this sentiment of honour, and employ it as a very proper handle to turn them towards virtue. They are likewise very sensible to praise, and masters ought to take hold of this disposition, and endeavour to make a virtue of it. It would discourage them never to commend them when they do well. And tho' praise is a little dangerous, on account of its tendency to intoxicate with vain conceit; yet it may be employed to animate youth without puffing them up. For of all the motives proper to affect a reasonable soul, there are none which have more force than a sense of honour and shame: Indeed, when we have formed in youth a delicate sense of these, all is gained. They feel a sincere pleasure in being applauded by their parents, and those on whom they depend, more especially. If they therefore caress them and give them praise when they behave well, and if they look down upon them and slight them when they do wrong, and if they make it a rule to themselves to treat their children uniformly and steadily in this manner, this management will make much deeper impression upon them than menaces or even corporal punishments. But to render this usage truly beneficial, two things are to be observed. First of all, when parents or masters are cold or indifferent to children, all others who are about them ought to behave in the same manner towards them, that they may find no consolation for the just anger of their parents or preceptors, in the caresses of governesses or servants. For then they are necessitated to reflect on their faults, and they can't choose but conceive an aversion against what brings such a general contempt upon them. In the second place, when parents or masters have once assumed a sour or cold look, they must take care not, as it often happens, to lay it very soon aside, and put on their former tenderness and cheerfulness. For if they manage children in this way, it will soon be perceived that their reprimands are but a storm that quickly passes away. Children ought therefore not to be restored to favour, till their care to reform their faults has sufficiently evinced the sincerity of their professed repentance for them. Recompences ought to be employed in education; for tho' these, no more than praise, ought to be the principal motive that actuates them, yet both may be rendered subservient to the promotion of virtuous dispositions in them, both may be employed to animate and spur them on in their studies. Is it not fit and advantageous that they should know, that they can never suffer, but must always gain by good behaviour, and therefore that their interest, as well as their duty, should engage them to perform carefully and diligently what is required of them, whether with relation to study or conduct? But recompences ought to be wisely chosen, as well as judiciously applied. One certain rule with regard to this matter, to which, however, for ordinary, very little attention is paid, is, that dress, finery, or delicacy, or other things of these kinds, ought never to be presented to their minds under the idea of rewards. The reason is obvious. 'Tis by promising such things to them under the notion of recompences, that a taste, liking, and propensity towards them is engendered and raised in their minds: 'Tis thus they are inspired with esteem for what they ought to despise. The same rule holds with respect to money, the passion for which is so much the more dangerous that it is so general, and that it must grow up with age. They ought to be inured to consider money in no other view but as the means of doing good to others. I have known several scholars, who of their own proper motion and accord divided any money that was given them into three parts, one of which was destined to charitable uses, another to purchase books, and the remainder to their innocent diversions. Children may be recompensed by allowing them innocent amusements, which require a little activity and industry; by taking them out to walk, at which time conversation may be used to great advantage; and by little presents of books, pictures, prints, or by carrying them to see curiosities or rarities of nature or art, as the art of printing, for instance, or any ingenious manufacture. The wisdom of parents and masters lies in contriving proper rewards, and in diversifying them, inciting a liking to them or desire of them; in keeping a certain fit order in the distribution of them, by beginning always with the more simple, and making these last as long as possible. But above all, let promises to them be punctually performed: Let this be an indispensible rule in the government of youth. For one of the vices we ought to take the greatest care to correct, or rather to prevent, is lying: Against this, too great an aversion or abhorrence cannot be raised. We must always speak of it to them as something base, unworthy, cowardly, that absolutely dishonours a person, and that is not to be born with even in slaves. Dissimulation, equivocation, and feigned excuses, approach very near to this vice, or at least never fail to draw into it. And therefore children ought early to know, that twenty faults will much sooner be pardoned than one simple disguisement of the truth to cover other faults. For which reason, when the child candidly confesses his fault, let his ingenuity be applauded, and his transgression be forgiven, without ever upbraiding him for it, or even so much as mentioning it to him afterwards, unless it becomes a mere ruse in him to escape correction; for then it is incompatible with candour and sincerity. All that youth hear from their masters or parents, ought to conspire to inflame their minds with the love of virtue and truth, and to excite their abhorrence of doubleness or falshood. And therefore we ought never to use any blind to please them, or prevail with them to do what we would have them to do: Never to make any promises or threats which they know are not to be executed. For this way of treating them would but teach and confirm them in the cunning to which they commonly have very early but too strong a propension. Accustom them to tell freely and ingenuously what gives them pleasure or pain: And let them understand that cunning always bewrays a bad heart; because one only has recourse to it to hide what he really is, or to give himself an appearance of being what he is not: lead them to remark the ridicule of certain artifices others may have used; the bad success such arts commonly have, and the contempt they generally bring upon those who use them. Make them ashamed when you catch them dissembling; and sometimes deprive them of what they like, because they shewed a disposition to get it by little cunning arts; and assure them they shall have what they ask honestly and without disguise. 'Tis on this point, chiefly, that we ought to pique their sense of honour. Shew them the difference between a child who is sincere and loves truth, in whom every body places entire confidence, because he is looked upon as incapable of lying or dissembling, and another of whom one is always suspicious and diffident, and to whose words none gives any credit, even when he tells truth. Be sure to put them often in mind of what Cornelius Nepos (and Plutarch gives the same encomium to Aristotle) observes of Epaminondas, that he was such a lover of veracity that he never would lie, not so much as in jest.[42] What I have been saying proves it to be the indispensible duty of parents and masters, to be very strict to truth in all their dealings with those under their care; the indispensible duty of masters, in particular: For in truth, according to the common course of the world, it is their business to defend their pupils against the bad influence of the conversation and example even of parents, as well as against the false prejudices and wicked principles that are authorised by too general practice. They ought to be to their scholars their faithful guardians and monitors, which, as Seneca speaks, are to take care to preserve and deliver them from popular errors, and to inspire into them principles founded on and conformable to reason. They themselves ought therefore to be so deeply impregnated with the sincere love of reason and truth, as never to think or speak but with prudence and veracity. For nothing can be done or said before children which has not some effect upon them: 'Tis upon what they hear and see that they model themselves. 'Tis from the discourses and practices of those about them they imbibe their first and most lasting notions and passions. For this reason it is, that Quintilian, as we have already observed, so frequently exhorts masters to speak frequently to their pupils of honesty and candour. And Seneca tells us what excellent impressions his master's discourses of this kind made upon him. The passage is exceeding beautiful:[43] 'Scarcely can one imagine what force good discourse has upon youth, or how strongly it influences the young mind. For the flexible tender hearts of children are easily turned towards virtue. Being docile, and not yet infected by any corruptive contagion, truth very easily finds admittance into their minds, provided it but meets with an intelligent advocate to plead its cause, and display its merit to them. For my own part, when I heard

42. [Cornelius Nepos, 15.3.2.]
43. [Seneca, *Epistulae Morales,* 108.12–14.]

Attalus inveigh against any vice, any disorderly practice, or any irregularity in life, I pitied mankind, and thought nothing estimable but a man capable of such sentiments. When he set himself to describe the advantages of poverty, and to prove that all above a moderate competency ought to be regarded as a useless, a troublesome burden, he made me in love with poverty. If he decried vitious pleasures and praised chastity, frugality, sobriety, and purity of soul, I found myself heartily disposed to renounce all pleasures, even the most innocent and legitimate. But there is a shorter and surer way yet of conducting the young to the love of virtue, and that is by good example. For the language of actions is much stronger and more persuasive than that of words. "Longum iter est per praecepta, breve & efficax per exempla."[44] 'Tis a great happiness when youth meet with masters whose whole lives are one continued lesson: Masters whose actions never belie their instructions, but who do what they advise, and avoid what they blame, and who are yet more admired for their conduct than for their learning or eloquence.'

"Now, is there any thing wanting in what hath been said concerning the duties of parents and preceptors? I think not. And yet let me tell Christians, that all hitherto is taken from pagan writers: 'Tis from Lycurgus, Plato, Cicero, Seneca, Quintilian, I have borrowed all these instructions I have been giving, conformity to which would render education an unfailing source of virtue, and therefore of public and private happiness. 'Tis plain, from what hath been said, that it is vice only that ought to be punished, and not unattentiveness or heedlessness, or any other faults in learning languages, or even sciences. Here all that can be done is to render study as agreeable as possible. But as this is the most important, so it is the most difficult art in the institution of youth. For among the vast number of masters who do not want merit in other regards, how few are there that are capable of succeeding in this point? Good success in it depends much upon the first impressions that are made upon young minds, and consequently, upon the great attentiveness of those masters who are employed in teaching the first elements to children, to prevent their conceiving any

44. [Seneca, *Epistulae Morales*, 6.5.]

aversion to reading and study, which at first they cannot like, lest the dis-
agreeableness of it should be remembered, and follow them to a more advanced age. In order to this, says Quintilian,[45] study should be made a play
or amusement to children: Let a sprouting genius be flattered and encouraged to shew itself, by asking him little simple questions, and be animated
by praise and commendation, that the infant may have ground to be content with himself, and pleased with his having learned something. Sometimes it may be proper to teach another what one refuses to learn or attend
to, in order to provoke his jealousy and emulation. Enter also into little
disputations sometimes with children, and let them have a seeming victory
over you: Endeavour likewise to bait or engage them to study, by recompenses suited to their age. But the great secret, says Quintilian, for rendering study agreeable to young minds, is the master's knowing how to make
himself beloved by them. When this is the case, they willingly hearken to
him, they chearfully yield to his teaching, they are desirous to gain and
keep his favour, and thus they take a pleasure and pride in receiving his
lessons; nay, they even receive his admonitions and corrections with submission: being very sensible to his applause, they exert themselves to merit
his friendship, by acquitting themselves well, and doing their duty with
complacency and good grace. There is in the minds of children, as well as
of men, a natural fund of curiosity, that is, a desire to understand, know
and learn, of which great advantages may be made, in order to render
learning pleasant and delightsome. All they see being new to them they
naturally ask questions, and demand the names and uses of every thing
that presents itself to them. We ought therefore to answer their interroga-
tories without shewing any chagrin or uneasiness, any marks of dissatisfac-
tion with their curiosity; we ought rather to applaud it, and endeavour to
content it, by the clearest and exactest answers to their questions we can
devise: We ought never to rebuke them, or to trifle with them: But above
all, we ought never to put them off with blinds, or to prevaricate with
them, and endeavour to deceive or impose upon them. For this they will

---

45. [Quintilian, *Institutio Oratoria,* 1.3.9–10.]

soon discover, and the discovery will have a very bad effect upon their minds, as hath been already observed in this treatise. In every art and science, the beginnings, the first rudiments are dry and insipid, and consequently forbidding. And for this reason, it is of moment to abridge and facilitate the toil of learning them as much as can be done, or to take off as much as may be from their harshness, by mixing as much sweetness with the draught as possible. 'Tis on this account I think the way of beginning by reading and explaining authors to young folks preferable to that of making them compose themes; because the latter is more irksome and difficult, and exposes them more to reprimands and chastisements. In private education, a skilful, well-qualified master does all he can to make study palatable and of easy digestion, so to speak. He waits for proper opportunities of teaching, studies the taste, temper, and genius of his pupil; he mixes play and amusement with labour and study; he seems to leave matters to their own choice; he avoids formality in giving his lessons; he keeps up and quickens their appetite by means of little interruptions; in one word, he turns himself into a thousand shapes, and invents a thousand arts for accomplishing his end. In colleges or large schools many of these arts are not practicable. In a numerous class, preservation of order and discipline demands a certain regularity and uniformity which all must exactly observe, and which is therefore an embarassment upon masters, that renders their accommodating themselves to different tempers and genius's almost impossible. It requires great prudence, great address, to govern with steady reins a great number of youth of differing characters; some lively to impetuosity, others phlegmatic and slow; some whom it is necessary to keep in with bit and bridle; others to whom you must give head; others who want a goad or spurring.—It is extremely difficult, I say, to manage at the same time so great a diversity of minds, so as to bring all, notwithstanding all differences of humour, ability and character, to the same goal, in the same path or tract. It must be acknowledged, that it is this that makes the principal difficulty with respect to public education; it is this that renders it a work of so much prudence and patience. But in instructing youth, this essential principle is ever to be kept in view, 'That study depends upon the will, and admits not of violence or constraint.'

'Studium discendi, voluntate quae cogi non potest, constat.'[46] You may confine a youth within the school, double his labour by way of punishment, force him to fulfil his appointed task, or deprive him of play and recreation if he don't. But to labour thus like a galley-slave under the rod, is that to study? Or what can be the fruit of this drudgery, and the austerity forcing to it, but hatred to books, and study, science, instruction and teachers, for their whole after-life? 'Tis the heart, the will that must be gained, and they can only be gained by mildness, by friendship, good-will, persuasion, and by the allures of pleasure, exciting a desire in youth to be instructed and become knowing: And let lessons be as much diversified as possible: Keep them not long at a time about mere words: Nay, let them feel that they are never learning mere vocables or phrases, but are always gaining some real knowledge that will be useful to them, that fits them at least for conversation, and gains them approbation and esteem. Teaching philosophy, or the knowledge of nature and mankind, admits of great diversification without breaking its unity; and so likewise do lessons upon any language. Hardly can we read any author with young people suited to their age, in which maps, medals, prints of statues, bas-reliefs, &c. have not naturally place as the best helps; and they are adminicles that wonderfully entertain, please and enlarge the mind. For a reward to a little application in getting words, let them be instructed in some part of science, amused with some useful experiment, with the description and anatomy of some plant or of some animal, or with the history of some great man's actions or sayings, or some other such moral lesson. Travel with them, by way of recompence to some dry labour, over some part of the globe, and give them an account of its soil, climate, product, government, manners and customs, great men and principal revolutions. Take these and such-like methods of rewarding their more insipid tasks, and at the same time, facilitate what is really drudgery as much as possible, and you will find young minds grow in curiosity, and wonderfully expand and strengthen by such care, if the master be withal of a gentle and gracious temper and carriage, and knows how to mingle, in due proportions, familiarity and

46. [Quintilian, *Institutio Oratoria*, 1.3.8.]

facetiousness with gravity and seriousness." The greater part of these observations and advices are delivered to us by Plato, Cicero, Quintilian, and other ancient observers of human nature, from their experience. And we have laid them together almost in the order Mr. Rollin has given them to us in his excellent treatise upon teaching the belles-lettres and sciences, because so ranged they make a system; and they thus come to us with the additional confirmation of his own experience, together with that of Mr. de Fenelon and Mr. Nicol, and others of the best men, as well as best writers of that country: And upon comparison, they will be found perfectly agreeable to the sentiments of two of our own greatest men upon the important subject of education, Mr. Locke, whom we have already so often quoted, and Mr. Milton, whose incomparable piece on education deserves the most serious perusal of all concerned in the formation of youth. What we have said in the former part of this chapter concerning grammar, is exactly conformable to Mr. Milton's[47] opinion about this matter, as well as Mr. Locke's.[48] He justly considers rhetoric as making a part of logic. And beginning with logic in teaching philosophy, he, agreeably to the doctrine of Plato concerning this matter, represents as very absurd. For, if the business of logic be to teach the art of communicating or imparting knowledge to others, in an orderly, perspicuous and agreeable manner, does it not presuppose a mind already well freighted with substantial knowledge? Or if its business be to range ideas into categories, classes, or tribes, and observe their relations and dependencies, or differences, does not such work suppose a mind well stored with various ideas, previously collected by various observation and reading? If the end and intention of logic be to compare various sorts of reasoning amongst themselves, and hence to draw general rules for improving knowledge, searching into nature, making experiments, inferring conclusions from particular observations, and avoiding error, can any one be fit for this nicely critical work without being acquainted by use with all the variety of certain and probable evidence, without having been practised in reasoning and concluding in very

47. [John Milton, *Of Education,* in *Complete Prose Works of John Milton* (New Haven: Yale University Press, 1959), 2:402–3.]
   48. [Locke, *Education,* §§188–89.]

different manners about a great diversity of objects? Or if the end of logic and rhetoric be to lead youth to make reflections upon the imperfections and abuses of words; the puzling obscurities in which the plainest matters may be involved by words, the various arts of moving the passions, and the sources and rules of all the different species of elegant composition, is this proper work for raw, unfurnished, empty, unexperienced minds? Do we take, says Plato, an inventory of an empty house? Or would we employ one in furnishing a house, and ranging and inventarying its furniture and utensils, who is an utter stranger to houshold arts, and the implements these require, and their respective uses? Do we send one to count without arithmetick, or to measure without a standard?

All that has hitherto been said, will, we think, receive no small confirmation from the account left us by Plato and Xenophon, concerning the education of the Persian princes and nobles. The manner of educating the future master of the empire in Persia, is admired by Plato, and recommended to the Greeks as a perfect model for a prince's education. He was never wholly committed to the care of the nurse, who however generally was a woman of mean and low condition; but from among the chief officers of the houshold, some of the most approved merit and probity were chosen to take care of the young prince's person and health till he was seven years of age, and to begin to form his manners and behaviour. He was then taken from them and put into the hands of other masters, who were to continue the care of his education, to teach him to ride as soon as his strength would permit, and to exercise him in hunting. At fourteen years of age, when the mind begins to open and attain to some maturity, four of the wisest and most virtuous men of the state were appointed to be his governors or preceptors. The first taught him magic, that is in their language, the worship of the Gods, according to their ancient maxims, and the laws of Zoroaster the son of Oromasus; he also instructed him in the principles of government. The second was to accustom him to speak truth and to administer justice. The third was to teach him not to be overcome by pleasures, that he might be truly a king, and always free, and master of himself and his desires. The fourth was to fortify his courage against fear, which would have made him a slave, and to inspire him with a noble and prudent assurance, so necessary for those that are born to command. Each of these governors excell'd in his way, and was eminent in that part of education assigned to him. One was particularly distinguished for his knowledge in religion and the art of governing. Another for his love of truth and justice: This for his moderation and abstinence from pleasures: That for a superior strength of mind and uncommon intrepidity. I do not know, says a very ingenious writer, whether such a diversity of masters, who, without doubt were of different tempers, and had perhaps different interests in view, was proper to answer the end proposed; or whether it was possible that four men should agree together in the same principles, and harmoniously pursue the same end. Probably the reason of having so many was, that they apprehended it impossible to find any one person possessed of all the qualities they judged necessary for giving a right education to the presumptive heir of the crown; so great an idea had they of the importance of a prince's education. Be this as it will, it is well worth our notice, that all this care, as Plato himself remarks in the same place, was frustrated by the luxury, pomp and magnificence with which the young prince was surrounded; by the numerous train of attendants that served him with a servile submission; by all the appurtenances and equipage of a voluptuous, effeminate life of pleasure: the invention of new diversions seemed to engross all his attention: Dangers which the most excellent disposition could never surmount: The corrupt manners of the nation therefore quickly debauched the prince, and drew him into the reigning pleasures, against which the best education is hardly a sufficient defence. The education here spoken of by Plato can only relate to the children of Artaxerxes surnamed Longimanus, the son and successor of Xerxes, in whose time lived Alcibiades, who is introduced in the dialogue whence this observation is taken. For Plato elsewhere informs us, that neither Cyrus nor Darius ever thought of giving the princes their sons a good education: And what we find in history concerning Artaxerxes Longimanus, gives us reason to believe, that he was more careful than his predecessors in the point of educating his children, but was not much imitated, in that respect by his successors. It was strange, indeed, that Cyrus, who was so good a prince, and knew so well, by his own experience, the happy effects of good education, should have been so negligent about that of his sons. For he had been brought up according to the laws and customs of the Persians, which were, according to Xenophon's account of them, in his Cyropoedeia, excellent in those days with respect to education. The public good, the common benefit of the nation, was the only principle and end of all their laws. The education of children was looked upon as the most important duty, and the most essential part of government. It was not totally left to the care of fathers and mothers, whose blind affection and fondness often render them incapable of that office; but the state took it upon themselves. Boys were all brought up in common, after one uniform manner, where every thing was regulated, the place and length of their exercises, the times of eating, the quality of their meat and drink, and their different kinds of punishment. The only food allowed either the children or the young men was bread, cresses and water; for their design was to accustom them early to temperance and sobriety: Besides, they considered that so frugal and plain a diet, without any mixture of sauces or ragouts, would enable them to undergo the hardships and fatigues of war to a good old age. Here boys went to school to learn justice and virtue, as they do in other places, to learn arts and sciences; and the crime most severely punished was ingratitude. The design of the Persians in all these wise regulations, was to prevent vice, being convinced how much better it is to prevent faults than to punish them: And whereas, in other states, the legislators are satisfied with establishing punishments for criminals, the Persians endeavoured so to order it as to have no criminals amongst them. Till sixteen or seventeen years of age the boys remained in the class of children; and here it was they learn'd to draw the bow, and to fling the dart or javelin; after which they were received into the class of young men. In this they were more narrowly watched and kept under than before, because that age requires the narrowest inspection, and has the greatest need of restraint. Here they remained ten years, during which time they passed all their nights in keeping guards, as well for the safety of the city, as to inure them to fatigue. In the day time they waited upon their governors to receive their orders, attended the king when he went a hunting, or improved in their exercises. The third class consisted of men grown up and formed; and in this they remained five and twenty years. Out of them all the officers that were to command in the troops, and all such as were to fill the different posts and commands or employments in the state, were chosen. When they were turned of fifty, they were not obliged to carry arms out of their own country. Besides these there was a fourth class, from whence men of the greatest wisdom and experience were chosen for forming the public council, and presiding in the courts of judicature. By this means, every citizen might aspire at the chief posts in the government, but not one could arrive at them till he had passed through all these several classes, and made himself capable of them by all these exercises. The classes were open to all; but generally such only, as were rich enough to maintain their children without working sent them thither.

I do not quote this extraordinary care of a state about education as a model that can or ought to be exactly followed in every form of civil government, but as one from which excellent maxims of government, and for the regulation of the most essential part in it, viz. education, may be gathered, abundantly confirming the more material observations that have been already mentioned, with relation to the chief end to be proposed and pursued in the institution and formation of youth, of those in particular whose birth and fortune call upon them to qualify themselves early for high and important offices in their country's service. The sentiments of the best sages of Greece, in her more glorious days, have been fairly represented and fully discoursed upon in the former part of this work. Here we shall only take notice, that in after-times, even when the affairs and manners of Greece were sadly declined, we are assured that in the schools at Apollonia, whither Julius Caesar sent Octavius to be educated, in order to be qualified for succeeding him in the empire, care was taken to instruct youth in the arts of speaking and writing, but principal care was taken first of all to improve their reason and replenish their understandings with the most useful science, the knowledge of human obligations, which did not stop short at the more general and obvious duties of life, but went higher, and comprehended the arts and maxims of government, and all the laws of nature and nations relative to political affairs, the rights of war and peace, treaties, alliances, commerce, and in one word, all external or internal businesses of states and public magistrates; and to this teaching they joined such exercises as fitted for military command. To this school was *Maecenas* also sent, and there did he lay the foundation of his friendship with Augustus, which was of so great use to that prince afterwards. For

Maecenas it was that gave this emperor a turn towards the muses; and to him chiefly was it owing that the government of an absolute prince, who in the first part of his conduct gave terrible proofs of a cruel temper, became afterwards so sufferable, which is the best that can be said of his or any arbitrary reign, however artfully it may be softened and sweetened. Chains are still chains, how much soever they are gilded or adorned.

We have already given some account of the first or most early part of Cicero's education from an excellent writer of his life, and we shall here add what the same author hath collected to us from Cicero himself chiefly, concerning the subsequent and finishing parts of the same great man's studies and exercises, by which he became so early capable of rendering the most eminent services to his friends and to his country in very difficult times.[49]

"After finishing the course of his puerile studies, before described, it was the custom to change the habit of the boy for that of the man, and take what they called the manly gown, or the ordinary robe of the citizens. This was an occasion of great joy to the young man, who by this change passed into a state of greater liberty and enlargement from the power of their tutors. They were introduced at the same time into the *Forum,* or the great square of the city, where the assemblies of the people were held, and the magistrates used to harangue them from the *Rostra,* and where all the public pleadings and judicial proceedings were usually transacted: This therefore was the grand school of business and eloquence; the scene on which all the affairs of the empire were determined, and where the foundation of their hopes and fortunes were to be laid: So that they were introduced into it with much solemnity, attended by all the friends and dependents of the family; and after divine rites performed in the capitol, were committed to the special protection of some eminent senator, distinguished for his eloquence or knowledge of the laws, to be instructed by his advice in the management of civil affairs, and to form themselves, by his example, for useful members and magistrates of the republic. Writers are divided about the precise time of changing the puerile for the manly gown: What seems

49. [Conyers Middleton, *Life of Cicero,* 1:12–19, 21, 27–29, 36–37, 43–44, 46–49.]

the most probable is, that in the old republic it was never done till the end of the seventeenth year: But when the ancient discipline began to relax, parents out of indulgence to their children, advanced this aera of joy one year earlier, and gave them the gown at sixteen, which was the custom in Cicero's time. Under the Emperors it was granted at pleasure, and at any age, to the great, or their own relations, for Nero received it from Claudius, when he just entered into his fourteenth year, which, as Tacitus says, was given before the regular season. Cicero being thus introduced into the *Forum,* was placed under the care of Q. Minucius Scaevola the augur, the principal lawyer as well as Statesman of that age; who had passed thro' all the offices of the republic with a singular reputation of integrity, and was now extremely old: Cicero never stirred from his side, but carefully treasured up in his memory all the remarkable sayings which dropt from him, as so many lessons of prudence for his future conduct; and after his death applied himself to another of the same family, Scaevola the High-Priest, a person of equal character for probity and skill in the law; who, tho' he did not profess to teach, yet freely gave his advice to all the young students who consulted him. Under these masters he acquired a complete knowledge of the laws of his country; a foundation useful to all who design to enter into public affairs, and thought to be of such consequence at Rome, that it was the common exercise of boys at school, to learn the laws of the twelve tables by heart, as they did their poets and classic authors. Cicero particularly took such pains in this study, and was so well acquainted with the most intricate parts of it, as to be able to sustain a dispute on any question with the greatest lawyers of his age; so that in pleading once against his friend S. Sulpicius, he declared by way of raillery, what he could have made good likewise in fact, that if he provoked him, he would profess himself a lawyer in three days time.

"The profession of the law, next to that of arms and eloquence, was a sure recommendation to the first honours of the republic, and for that reason was preserved, as it were hereditary, in some of the noblest families of Rome; who, by giving their advice gratis to all who wanted it, engaged the favour and observance of their fellow-citizens, and acquired great authority in all the affairs of state. It was the custom of those old senators, eminent for their wisdom and experience, to walk every morning up and down the *Forum,* as a signal of their offering themselves freely to all who had occasion to consult them, not only in cases of law, but in their private and domestic affairs. But in later times, they chose to sit at home with their doors open, on a kind of throne or raised seat, like the confessors in foreign churches, giving access and audience to all people. This was the case of the two Scaevola's, especially the augur, whose house was called the *oracle of the city,* and who in the Marsic war, when worn out with age and infirmities, gave a free admission every day to all the citizens, as soon as it was light, nor was ever seen by any in his bed during that whole war. But this was not the point that Cicero aimed at, to guard the estates only of the citizens: His views were much larger; and the knowledge of the law was but one ingredient of many, in the character which he aspired to of an universal patron, not only of the fortunes, but of the lives and liberties of his countrymen: For that was the proper notion of an orator or pleader of causes, whose profession it was, *To speak aptly, elegantly, and copiously on every subject which could be offered to him, and whose art therefore included in it all arts of the liberal kind, and could not be acquired to any perfection, without a competent knowledge of whatever was great and laudable in the universe.*

"This was his own idea of what he had undertaken; and his present business therefore was, to lay a foundation fit to sustain the weight of this great character: So that while he was studying the law under the Scaevola's, he spent a large share of his time in attending the pleadings at the bar, and the public speeches of the magistrates, and never passed one day without writing and reading something at home, constantly taking notes, and making comments on what he read. He was fond, when very young, of an exercise which had been recommended by some of the great orators before him, of reading over a number of verses of some esteemed poet, or a part of an oration, so carefully as to retain the substance of them in his memory, and then deliver the same sentiments in different words, the most elegant that occurred to him. But he soon grew weary of this, upon reflecting, that his authors had already employed the best words which belonged to their subject; so that if he used the same it would do him no good, and if different would even hurt him, by a habit of using worse. He applied himself therefore to another task of more certain benefit, to translate into Latin the select speeches of the best Greek orators, which gave him an opportunity of observing and employing all the most elegant words of his own language, and of enriching it at the same time with new ones, borrowed or imitated from the Greek. Nor did he yet neglect his poetical studies; for he now translated Aratus on the phaenomena of the heavens into Latin verse, of which many fragments are still extant; and published also an original poem of the heroic kind, in honour of his Countryman C. Marius. This was much admired, and often read by Atticus; and old Scaevola was so well pleased with it, that in an Epigram which he seems to have made upon it, he declares, that it would live as long as the Roman name and learning subsisted. There remains still a little specimen of it, describing a memorable omen given to Marius from the oak of Arpinum, which, from the spirit and elegance of the description, shews, that his poetical genius was scarce inferior to his oratorial, if it had been cultivated with the same diligence. He published another poem also called Limon, of which Donatus has preserved four lines in the life of Terence, in praise of the elegance and purity of that poet's stile. But while he was employing himself in these juvenile exercises for the improvement of his invention, he applied himself with no less industry to philosophy, for the enlargement of his mind and understanding; and among his other masters, was very fond, at this age, of Phaedrus the Epicurean: But as soon as he had gained a little more experience and judgment of things, he wholly deserted and constantly disclaimed the principles of that sect; yet always retained a particular esteem for the man, on account of his learning, humanity and politeness. The peace of Rome was now disturbed by a domestic war, which writers call the Italic, Social, or Marsic, during the hurry of which, the business of the Forum was intermitted; the greatest part of the magistrates, as well as the pleaders, being personally concerned in it: Hortensius, the most flourishing young orator at the bar, was a volunteer in it the first year, and commanded a regiment the second. Cicero likewise took the opportunity to make a campaign, along with the Consul Cn. Pompeius Strabo, the father of Pompey the great. This was a constant part of the education of the young nobility; to learn the art of war by personal service under some general of name and experience; for in an empire raised and supported wholly by arms, a reputation of martial virtue was the shortest and surest way of rising to its highest honours; and the constitution of the government was such, that as their generals could not make a figure, even in camps, without some institution in the politer arts, especially that of speaking gracefully; so those who applied themselves to the peaceful studies, and the management of civil affairs, were obliged to acquire a competent share of military skill, for the sake of governing provinces and commanding armies, to which they all succeeded of course, from the administration of the great offices of state. Cicero, we find, was not less diligent in the army than he was in the Forum, to observe every thing that passed; and contrived always to be near the person of the general, that no action of moment might escape his notice. The transactions of the Forum were greatly interrupted by civil dissentions; in which some of the best orators were killed, others banished. Cicero however attended the harangues of the magistrates, who possessed the *Rostra* in their turns; and being now about the age of twenty one, drew up probably those rhetorical pieces, which were published by him, as he tells us, when very young, and are supposed to be the same that still remain on the subject of invention: But he condemned and retracted them afterwards in his advanced age, as unworthy of his maturer judgment, and the work only of a boy, attempting to digest into order the precepts which he had brought away from the school. In the mean while Philo, a philosopher of the first name *in the Academy,* with many of the principal Athenians, fled to Rome from the fury of Mithridates, who had made himself master of Athens, and all the neighbouring parts of Greece. Cicero immediately became his scholar, and was exceedingly taken with his philosophy, and by the help of such a professor gave himself up to that study with the greater inclination, as there was cause to apprehend, that the laws and judicial proceedings which he had designed for the ground of his fame and fortunes, would be wholly overturned by the continuance of the public disorders. But Cinna's party having quelled all opposition at home, while Sylla was engaged abroad in the Mithridatic war, there was a cessation of arms within the city for about three years, so that the course of public business began to flow again in its usual channel; and Molo the Rhodian, one of the principal orators of that age, and the most celebrated teachers of eloquence, happening to come to Rome at the same time, Cicero presently took the benefit of his lectures,

and resumed his oratorical studies with the same ardor. But the greatest
spur to his industry was the fame and splendor of Hortensius, who made
the first figure at the bar, and whose praises fired him with such an ambition of acquiring the same glory, that he scarce allowed himself any rest
from his studies either day or night: He had in the house with him
Diodatus the stoic, as his preceptor in various parts of learning, but more
particularly in logic; which, Zeno, as he tells us, used to call a close and
contracted eloquence, as he called eloquence an enlarged and dilated logic;
comparing the one to the fist, or hand doubled, the other to the palm
opened. Yet with all his attention to logic, he never suffered a day to pass,
without some exercise in oratory, chiefly that of declaiming; which he generally performed with his fellow-students, M. Piso and Q. Pompeius, two
young noblemen a little older than himself, with whom he had contracted
an intimate friendship. They declaimed sometimes in Latin, but much oftener in Greek; because the Greek furnished a greater variety of elegant
expressions, and an opportunity of imitating and introducing them into
the Latin; and because the Greek masters, who were far the best, could not
correct and improve them, unless they declaimed in that language. Cicero,
in fine, runs through all that course of discipline which he lays down as
necessary to form the complete orator: For in his treatise on that subject,
he gives us his own sentiments in the person of Crassus, on the institution
requisite to that character, declaring, *That no man ought to pretend to it,
without being previously acquainted with every thing worth knowing in art
or nature; that this is implied in the very name of an orator, whose profession
it is to speak upon every subject which can be proposed to him; and whose eloquence, without the knowledge of what he speaks, would be the prattle only
and impertinence of children.* He had learned the rudiments of grammar
and languages from the ablest teachers; gone through the studies of humanity and the politer letters with the poet Archias; been instructed in
philosophy by the principal professors of each sect, Phaedrus the Epicurean, Philo the Academic, Diodotus the Stoic; acquired a perfect knowledge of the law from the greatest lawyers, as well as the greatest statesmen
of Rome, the two Scaevola's; all which accomplishments were but minis-
terial and subservient to that, on which his hopes and ambition were singly placed, the reputation of an orator: To qualify himself therefore par-

ticularly for this, he attended the pleadings of all the speakers of his time; heard the daily lectures of the most eminent orators of Greece, and was perpetually composing somewhat at home, and declaiming under their correction: And that he might neglect nothing, which could help in any degree to improve and polish his stile, he spent the intervals of his leisure in the company of the ladies; especially of those who were remarkable for a politeness of language, and whose fathers had been distinguished by a fame and reputation of eloquence. While he studied the law therefore under Scaevola the augur, he frequently conversed with his wife Laelia, whose discourse, he says, was tinctured with all the elegance of her father Laelius, the politest speaker of his age: He was acquainted likewise with her daughter Mucia, who married the great orator L. Crassus, and with her granddaughters, the two Liciniae, one of them the wife of L. Scipio, the other of young Marius, who all excelled in that delicacy of the Latin tongue, which was peculiar to their families, and valued themselves on preserving and propagating it to their posterity.

"Thus adorned and accomplished, he offered himself to the bar about the age of twenty-six, not as others generally did, raw and ignorant of their business, and wanting to be formed to it by use and experience, but finished and qualified at once to sustain any cause which should be committed to him. Two years after he went abroad: And we have a clear account from himself of the real motive of his journey: 'My body, says he, at this time was exceedingly weak and emaciated, my neck long and small, which is a habit thought liable to great risk of life, if engaged in any fatigue or labour of the lungs; and it gave the greater alarm to those who had a regard for me, that I used to speak without any remission or variation, with the utmost stretch of my voice and great agitation of my body: When my friends therefore and physicians advised me to meddle no more with causes, I resolved to run any hazard, rather than quit the hopes of glory, which I proposed to myself from pleading: But when I considered, that by managing my voice, and changing my way of speaking, I might avoid all danger, and speak with more ease, I took a resolution of travelling into Asia, merely for an opportunity of correcting my manner of speaking: So that after I had been two years at the bar, and acquired a reputation in the Forum, I left Rome, &c.' He was twenty-eight years old, when he set forward upon his travels to Greece and Asia, the fashionable tour of all those who travelled either for curiosity or improvement: His first visit was to Athens, the capital seat of arts and sciences; where some writers tell us that he spent three years, tho' in truth it was but six months: He took up his quarters with Antiochus, the principal philosopher of the old academy: And under this excellent master renewed, he says himself, those studies which he had been fond of from his earliest youth. Here he met with his school-fellow T. Pomponius, who, from his love to Athens, and his spending a great part of his days in it, obtained the sirname of Atticus; and here they revived and confirmed that memorable friendship, which subsisted between them through life with so celebrated a constancy and affection. Atticus being an Epicurean, was often drawing Cicero from his host Antiochus to the conversations of Phaedrus and old Zeno, the chief professors of that sect, in hopes of making him a convert, on which subject they used to have many disputes between themselves: But Cicero's views in these visits was but to convince himself more effectually of the weakness of that doctrine, by observing how easily it might be confuted, when explained even by the ablest teachers. Yet he did not give himself up so intirely to philosophy as to neglect his rhetorical exercises, which he performed still every day diligently with Demetrius the Syrian, an experienced master of the art of speaking. It was in this journey to Athens that he was initiated, most probably, into the Eleusinian mysteries. The reverence with which he always speaks of these mysteries, and the hints he has dropt of their use and end, seem to confirm what a very learned and ingenious writer has delivered of them, that they were contrived to inculcate the unity of God, and the immortality of the soul. From Athens he passed into Asia, where he gathered about him all the principal orators of the country, who kept him company through the rest of his voyage, and with whom he constantly exercised himself in every place where he made any stay.

"The chief of them, says he, was Menippus of Stratonica, the most eloquent of all the Asiatics; and, if to be neither tedious nor impertinent be the characteristic of an Attic orator, he may be justly ranked in that class. Dionysius also of Magnesia, Aeschylus of Cnidos, and Xenocles of Adramyttus were continually with me, who were reckoned the first rhetoricians of Asia: Nor yet content with these, I went to Rhodes, and applied myself

again to Molo, whom I had heard before at Rome, who was both an experienced pleader and a fine writer, and particularly expert in observing
the faults of his scholars, as well as in his method of teaching and improving them: His greatest trouble with me was to restrain the exuberance of a
juvenile imagination, always ready to overflow its banks, within its due
and proper channel. But as at Athens, where he employed himself chiefly
in philosophy, he did not intermit his oratorial studies, so at Rhodes,
where the chief study was oratory, he gave some share of his time also to
philosophy, with Possidonius, the most esteemed and learned stoic of that
age; whom he often speaks of with honour, not only as his master but as
his friend. It was his constant care that the progress of his knowledge
should keep pace with the improvement of his eloquence; he considered
the one as the foundation of the other, and thought it in vain to acquire
ornaments before he had provided necessary furniture: He declaimed here
in Greek, because Molo did not understand Latin; and upon ending his
declamation, while the rest of the company were lavish of their praises,
Molo, instead of paying any compliment, sat silent a considerable time,
till observing Cicero somewhat disturbed at it, he said, as for you, Cicero,
I praise and admire you, but pity the fortune of Greece, to see arts and
eloquence, the only ornaments that were left to her, transplanted by you
to Rome. Having thus finished the circuit of his travels, he came back
again to Italy, after an excursion of two years, extremely improved and
changed, as it were, into a new man: The vehemence of his voice and action was moderated; the redundancy of his stile and fancy corrected; his
lungs strengthened, and his whole constitution confirmed. This voyage of
Cicero seems to be the only scheme and pattern of travelling from which
any real benefit is to be expected: He did not stir abroad till he had compleated his education; for nothing can be more pernicious to a nation than
the necessity of a foreign one; and after he had acquired in his own country
whatever was proper to form a worthy citizen and magistrate of Rome, he
went, confirmed by a maturity of age and reason, against the impressions
of vice, not so much to learn, as to polish what he had learned, by visiting
those places where arts and sciences flourished in their greatest perfection.
In a tour the most delightful of the world, he saw every thing that could
entertain a curious traveller, yet staid nowhere longer than his benefit, not

his pleasure detained him. By his previous knowledge of the laws of Rome, he was able to compare them with those of other cities, and to bring back with him whatever he found useful, either to his country or to himself. He was lodged, wherever he came, in the houses of the great and eminent, not so much for their birth and wealth, as for their virtue, knowledge and learning; men honoured and reverenced in their several cities, as the principal patriots, orators, and philosophers of the age: These he made the constant companions of his travels; that he might not lose the opportunity, even on the road, of profiting by their advice and experience: And from such a voyage, it is no wonder that he brought back every accomplishment which could improve and adorn a man of sense."

I could not choose but give this account of Cicero's education at full length, because such an example sets forth to our view the proper methods of education and study with more force, and therefore will make a stronger impression than the best expressed maxims or precepts. Let me just subjoin to what hath been said, an admirable letter of Pliny the younger to his friend Fuscus about his studies, from which admirable hints may be taken for the direction of the studies and exercises of young gentlemen, after they are got above the first elements of instruction.

Pliny to Fuscus.[50]

"You ask me in what method you ought to study at your country house, where you have been a long time. The most useful rule, and what many have prescribed, is to translate Greek into Latin, or the contrary. By this exercise, the propriety and beauty of expression, the richness of figures, the facility of explication, and the talents of invention are acquired by an imitation of the best patterns. Besides, what might have escaped you in reading, cannot slip you in translating. It increases your understanding and judgment. You may likewise, after reading a thing, only to know the subject of it, handle it yourself, with a resolution not to fall short of your author. Then compare your writings with his, and carefully examine the odds of perfection. Your pleasure will be great, if you sometimes find you

---

50. [Pliny, *Letters,* 7.9.]

surpass him; and your spirit of emulation will be proportionable if he exceeds you in every thing. You may sometimes cull out the choicest passages, and vie with them. This struggle is private, and therefore not rash, tho' daring. Tho' we know many that have gone through this sort of contention with great applause, and have outgone those they were contented to follow, because they did not despair of it. When you have forgot your writing, you may take it up again; retain some parts, retrench others, make additions and alterations. I own this is laborious and fatiguing, but the trouble is attended with advantage; to recover your spirits afresh, and revive a force that has been broken and laid aside; and in short, join new limbs, in a manner, to a body that was framed before, without any disorder to the last structure. I know your present study is the eloquence of the bar, but I would not always persuade you to use that controversy and warlike stile. For as the earth is revived with a variety of different seeds; so our frailties are relieved now with this and now with that way of thinking. I would have you sometimes employ yourself upon some passage of history, or write an epistle with a particular care, or a copy of verses. For even in pleadings we are often obliged to use an historical and poetical manner of description; and a close and pure vein of language is drawn from epistles. It is likewise proper to amuse yourself with writing verses; I do not mean with long continued poems, (for that cannot be effected without the freest leisure) but by smaller pieces of pleasantry, of a concise turn, very proper to distinguish any serious cares and employments. These are called the sportings of poetry: But these sportings often procure a fame equal to the most solid performances. And so, for why should not I give a taste for verse by verses?

> As wax obedient to the forming powers,
> Displays a varying shape, a diff'rent kind;
> As sacred fountains quicken num'rous flowers,
> So various arts do cultivate the mind.

And hence it is that the greatest orators, and the most excellent men, have thus employed or diverted themselves, rather, have done both by poetry: For it is wonderful, how the mind is relaxed and bent again by these studies; for they take in love and hatred, anger, pity, politeness, every thing that belongs to life, or conversant in the business of the bar. There is likewise the same use in these as in other poems; that as they tie up to the rules of verse, they give us a greater relish for the prose, and that which we find easier on the comparison we write with more alacrity. Perhaps I have told you more than you required, yet I have omitted one thing, that is the choice of your authors and subjects in reading, tho' this is implied in the former rules for writing. Remember to single out the best books in their kind; for it is a common observation, that much is to be read, but not many authors. Who these are is a point so commonly known and appealed to by all, that it wants no demonstration. Besides, I have stretched my letter to so extravagant a length, that while I give you directions for study, I have encroached upon your time for it. Why do not you therefore resume your Writing-tables, and either begin some of these works that I have pointed out to you, or pursue what you have begun already? Farewell."[51]

Hitherto we have treated of teaching and study: But the minds even of grown and highly improved men cannot bear to be continually bent upon grave and deep meditation: They must often be refreshed by proper unbending and well-chosen relaxations: much more is this true with regard to the young. Uninterrupted application to study would soon wear out the whole force of their tender minds: And it is because of the necessity of corporal exercise to invigorate the soul as well as the body, that nature hath made children so fond of motion, so restless and lively: Let one be kept closely to reading, without allowing him any respite from thinking, or any exercise to his body, and were it possible to preserve long, by such a method, his liking to study and knowledge, or his health and vigour, yet we would soon find such an one become no less soft in his mind than in his outward man: Both mind and body would thus become gradually too relaxed, too much unbraced for the fatigues and duties of active life: Were it possible for such to improve, or so much as to preserve the natural force of their understanding, which it is not, yet their active powers would daily be losing of their strength and springiness, so to speak, and such a mind

---

51. I copy this letter from the English translation of Pliny's letters by several hands.

would soon become very unmanly, very timid and sluggish. Such, in fine, is the union between body and soul, that the same exercises which are conducive, when rightly managed, to consolidate or strengthen the former, are likewise equally necessary and fit to produce courage, firmness, and manly vigour in the latter. All this is well known, and therefore requires no proof: And what indeed doth knowledge avail, if the mind be not fit for action, but averse to it; or if every danger, every gloomy incident, every slight difficulty in life, intimidates and unhinges the mind, or makes it quake, tremble, and dissolve with fear? The disease is not uncommon amongst mere scholars, in whose education the liberal manly exercises have had no share. And what is the obvious conclusion from all this? But that certain exercises, tending at once to give health and vigour to the body, and strength and intrepidity to the mind, ought to be united in the institution of youth, with philosophy, rhetoric, and the sciences, and not severed the one from the other, as they too generally are, as if mind and body had no dependance, or as if, where there was knowledge of duty, due courage and hardiness of mind could be taken up at any time. I might here entertain my readers, not disagreeably, with some account of the ancient gymnastic exercises, in which the youth amongst the Greeks and Romans were daily practised, and that without much trouble to myself, by translating from several admirable dissertations upon all of them, in the memoires of the French academy of belles-lettres. But it is enough to our purpose to observe, that in these ancient nations, hunting, wrestling, and other such vigorous exercises, which required presence of mind, and caution without fear, were thought absolutely requisite to the formation of the souls, as well as of the bodies of their youth: And the fitness of some such exercises to all youth is strongly recommended by our own *Milton,* and all our best writers on education, on the same account; for reasons, which the least experience or reflection will immediately suggest, namely, for mutually and equally fortifying body and mind. Plato[52] makes an excellent observation upon the natural tendency of the gentle or soft studies and exercises on the one hand, and that of rougher and hardier ones on the other, from

52. De Repub. l. 3. [Plato, *The Republic,* book 3.]

which he infers the fitness of mixing them together, in due proportions, in the education of youth, whom we would form into a just temperature of body and mind, whether with respect to their own private happiness, or with respect to public service and utility. According to this admirable philosopher, speculations even about those duties of life, which require undaunted presence of mind, or fearless circumspection, are not sufficient, by themselves, without proper inurance to hardships, difficulties and dangers, to produce true fortitude of mind: And far less can other meditations or enquiries harden or invigorate the mind, and produce manly intrepidity: And far less still can music, and the other soft sciences do it, the genuine pleasures of which, however, cannot be supposed to be forbidden man by the Author of his frame, without imagining the supreme Being to act inconsistently with himself, since he hath framed man not only with eyes and ears, but also with a natural sense of harmony and proportion, improveable to a very great degree of perfection: The frequent repetition of certain exercises, in which dangers are to be foreseen, avoided and warded off, or bravely encountered and surmounted, are the only proper means of forming and improving this useful, this indispensibly necessary good temper of mind, by often calling it forth into action, and putting it to trials. But yet, on the other side, constant practice in the rough, austere, bold exercises, were no methods used to prevent the effect, would render the minds of men too savage and ferocious, and their manners quite rude, harsh and disagreeable, as we find from the character of the Spartans, in whose education the polite arts and sciences had no place, being quite excluded by their legislator. The middle between these two extremes, is the happy, the desirable temper: Gentleness that danger will quickly rouse to thought and courage, and foresight and fortitude, that will act with equal mildness, gentleness and firmness. And in order to produce or form such a disposition, exercises requiring vigour, both of body and mind, must be skilfully blended with more mollifying arts and studies, which have a natural aptitude to humanize the mind, and preserve it from degenerating into ferocity, as the other to strengthen and invigorate it, against all the too softening passions.

These are the reasons for which certain hardy exercises were reckoned by the ancients so essential a part in the formation of a liberal character:

Such exercises, in particular, as qualified for just war in the defence of one's country against hostile invasions. And no doubt, the better adapted the exercises of youth are to this end, the better will they serve the general purpose of exercises, with the additional advantage of fitting youth for the arts and toils of warfare in the public service. For which cause, could it be done, it would not be amiss, that in numerous schools young men were, according to ancient methods already taken notice of, not only initiated in warlike discipline, and trained to arms, but likewise accustomed to watch and keep guard. But not to dwell upon what mere gown men having very little notion of, will be very apt to stumble at, let it just be observed, that sedentary diversions are by no means the proper relaxations of students, neither in relation to health, nor the higher purpose that hath been just mentioned. And yet because certain times and places do not admit of any other, and some amusements to recreate their minds, must be allowed to students, it will not be wrong in bad weather, or the evenings, now and then, to practise them in such games as require some degree of thought, and they will find to be the fashionable diversions of the world, when they enter into it, provided care be taken to accustom them to play, not only without avarice and fairly, but with complaisance, ease and gracefulness. Montagne, I think, tells us, that his father used to play now and then at cards with his children, to inure them to temper, patience and candour in game, and thus secured them against the bad effects plays established in the world might otherwise have had upon them, so soon as they came into the world, and saw amusements that they had been kept strangers to. Let not children be restrained from any recreations that are innocent, but on the contrary, let them be taught to join in them with a genteel complaisance, when good company proposes it, and be accustomed to look with detestation upon unfairness, passion or avarice, and the other evil passions to which too great an itch for such diversions exposes. For till we can banish all play from among those, who being reckoned the fashionable part of the world, have the power of establishing modes, they will but be so much the fonder of what they were restrained from, so soon as they get loose from tutorage. 'Tis indeed no unnecessary part of genteel education, as the world now goes, to fix in young minds betimes proper and true sentiments concerning such amusements; an abhorrence of the vices they too often lead into, and the becoming disposition with which one ought to engage in them. But no sedentary recreations can be made the more common or frequent diversions of youth without detriment to their health; and which is of more consequence, without overlooking what is essential to the character of one fit to serve his country: A mind capable to forego pleasures and suffer hardships, when duty to his friends or country requires it; a mind not insensible to danger, or rashly desirous of it, but yet able to look danger in the face without confusion or disorder; a mind whose force peril unforeseen only serves to awake and call forth into brave behaviour, and which fully possessing itself, can then best discover prudent expedients, when there is most use for such sagacity. The fitter bodily exercises are for gaining this useful end, so much the properer are they, both in respect of body and mind, with relation equally to particulars themselves and society in general. Wherefore riding, fencing, wrestling, handling arms, and other such manly exercises, ought to have their place in the schools where youth are taught the languages and sciences. There ought to be fixed times for them, and daily practice in them too, and not in books only, ought to be made a task. Both being necessary, they ought to be judiciously intermingled, so that the one may serve as a relief from the other. But tho' youth ought to be obliged to perform their parts both in exercise and study, because both are requisite to complete a truly liberal and manly temper and character; and that study alone may not be looked upon as work and labour; yet it must likewise be permitted to young people, in their youngest years more especially, sometimes not only to divert themselves, but to do it after their own fashion, provided it be innocently, and without prejudice to their health; for there can be no recreation without delight, which depends not always upon reason, but oftner on fancy. Through the whole course of education, from infancy itself, care should be taken, that what is of real advantage to them, they should always do with pleasure, and before they are wearied with one, they should be timely diverted to some other useful employment. But if they are not yet brought to that degree of perfection, that one way of improvement can be made to them a recreation from another, they must be let loose to the play they fancy, and be weaned from excessive fondness for it by a surfeit of it. But from studies or exercises of real use, they ought always to be sent away with appetite, at least be dismissed before they are quite weary and sick of them, that so they may return to them again with delight, as to something they have real pleasure in. For we must never think them rightly formed, till they can find satisfaction in the application to laudable things; and the profitable exercises of the body and mind taking their proper turns, make their time and improvement pass on very agreeably, as it were in one continued train of recreations, whereby the fatigued or wearied part is constantly refreshed and recruited. That this may be done in most children, if a right course be taken to raise in them the desire of esteem, credit, and reputation, there are examples enough to leave us no room to doubt. And such management never fails to make them in love with the hand that directs them, as well as with the virtuous and commendable course they are directed into. It is an essential duty in masters, to take care to appear not enemies, but friends to the pleasures and satisfactions of their pupils. And this great advantage, besides, may be gained, by allowing free liberty to children in their diversions, that this freedom will discover their natural tempers, inclinations and aptitudes, and be thereby a proper means of directing wise parents in the choice of the business and employment of life they shall design them for; and of suggesting fit remedies to them in the mean time, for redressing any wrong bent of nature whatsoever they may observe their children to be in most danger from. Above all things, inspectors of children ought to take care that children play or divert themselves together without fraud or chicane on the one hand, or violence, roughness and imperiousness on the other. They should be taught to have all the deference, complaisance and civility one for the other imaginable. And in this way will they quickly find more pleasure than in the other, when they see it procures them respect, love and honour, and that far from losing any superiority by it, it makes them beloved by their play-fellows, and esteemed by their parents and masters, and all who know and observe them. In order to this, it must be a constant rule with parents and preceptors not to receive or hearken too readily or favourably to the querulous accusations of children, one against another. For these are frequently but the clamours of anger, envy, or revenge, desiring aid. It weakens and effeminates children's minds to indulge them in complaining: And on the contrary, if they suffer sometimes crossing and pain from others, without being allowed to bemoan themselves and make complaints, this will teach and inure them to sufferance, and harden them early. But tho' we ought not to countenance and encourage the complaints of those who are apt to accuse, on every slight occasion, yet on the other side, care ought to be taken to curb the violence and insolence of the injurious. When you yourself happen to observe any such thing, let the offender be reproved before the injured party: But if the complaint be really worth your notice and prevention another time, then reprove the faulty child by himself alone, out of sight of him that complained, and make him go and ask pardon and make reparation for the injury he has done. This, when it appears to come as it were from himself, will be the more cheerfully performed and more kindly received; love will be confirmed and strengthened between them, and a habit of civility will thus grow familiar among children; a habit which every one of experience will acknowledge to be of the greatest utility in life, in civil commerce, and which for that reason cannot be too early or too carefully formed and cherished. To compleat this character, and make them not only courteous, civil and obliging, but liberal, teach them to part with what they have easily and freely, and with becoming grace to their friends; and let them find by experience, that the most liberal has always most plenty, with esteem, praise and love into the bargain, and they will quickly learn to practise it. Special care ought to be had, that children do never trifle with the rules of justice: But education should aim at something higher, and endeavour betimes to inspire a generous temper into children, and for that reason, take occasions to incite them to be kind and liberal, and to make them feel the pleasure of doing affectionate offices, and of being beloved for their goodness. Practice in accustoming children to share with one another, and to impart what they get one to another with joy and complacency, will make them kinder and civiler to one another, and consequently to others, than all the rules about good manners with which children are ordinarily incumbered and plagued. Indeed covetousness of having in our possession, and under our power more than we have need of, being the root of all evil, should be early and carefully weeded out, and the contrary quality ought to be diligently implanted and cultivated. This social sense, or benign disposition, should be encouraged by great commendation and credit, and strict care that the child lose nothing by his bounty. Let all the instances he gives of tenderness, humanity and generosity, be always repaid and with interest; and let him thus sensibly perceive, that the goodness he shews to others is no ill-husbandry for himself; but that it brings a return for kindness both from those who receive it, and those who look on. Make it a generous contention or emulation among children who shall outdo one another in this way; and by this means, by a constant practice, children having made it easy to themselves to part with what they have, benevolence may be settled in them into an habit, and they will soon come to take a most sincere pleasure, and a noble pride in being civil, kind and bountiful to others.

Upon this excellent disposition, it will be easy to build that amiable quality commonly called good breeding, and upon no other foundation can it be raised. For whence else can it spring but from a general good-will and regard for all people, deeply rooted in the heart, which makes any one that has it careful not to shew in his carriage, any contempt, disrespect, or neglect of them, but to express a value and respect for them, according to their rank and condition, suitably to the fashion and way of their country? 'Tis a disposition to make all we converse with easy and well-pleased. Good-breeding we may see from this short account of its only firm foundation in goodness of heart, consists in two things. First, a disposition of the mind not to offend others, or make them uneasy. Secondly, the habit of expressing that disposition in the most acceptable and agreeable way. From the former of these one is called civil or humane; from the other well-fashioned, or well-bred: And when these two meet, that is, when the agreeable manner of shewing civility is become natural, then is a man called thoroughly polite. And in truth, it is this lovely quality which gives true beauty to all other accomplishments, or renders them useful to their possessor, in procuring him the esteem and good-will of all that he comes near. Without this charming perfection, his other qualities, however good in themselves, make him but pass for proud, conceited, vain, or foolish. "Courage, says an excellent writer,[53] in an ill-bred man, has the air, and escapes not the opinion of brutality; learning becomes pedantry; wit, buffoonery; plainness, rusticity; good-nature, fawning: And there cannot be a

---

53. [Locke, *Education*, §93.]

good quality in him which want of breeding will not warp and disfigure to his disadvantage. Nay virtue and parts, tho' they are allowed their due commendation, yet are not enough to procure a man a good reception, and make him welcome wherever he comes. No body contents himself with rough diamonds, and wears them so, who would appear with advantage. When they are polished and set, then they give a lustre. Good qualities are the substantial riches of the mind, but 'tis good breeding sets them off. And he that will be acceptable must give beauty as well as strength to his actions. Solidity, or even usefulness, is not enough: A graceful way and fashion in every thing is that which gives ornament and liking. And in most cases, the manner of doing is of more consequence than the thing done. For upon that depends the satisfaction or disgust wherewith it is received. This, therefore, says the same author, which lies not in pulling off the hat, nor making of compliments, but in a due and free composure of language, looks, motions, posture, place, &c. suited to persons and occasions, and can be learned only by habit and use, tho' it be above the capacity of children, and little ones should not be perplexed with rules about it, yet it ought to be begun, and in a good measure learned by a young gentleman whilst he is under a tutor, before he comes into the world upon his own legs: For then usually it is too late to reform several habitual indecencies which lie in little things. For the carriage is not as it should be, till it is become natural in every part, falling, as a musician's fingers do, into harmonious order without care and without thought. If in conversation a man's mind be taken up with a sollicitous watchfulness about any part of his behaviour, instead of being mended by it, it will be constrained, uneasy and ungraceful." 'Tis therefore by accustoming children to decency and gracefulness in reading, speaking, in the whole of their behaviour, even in their first diversions with one another; but above all, by cherishing and strengthening in them a generous and humane temper, that they alone can become thoroughly well-bred and civil. The opposites therefore to this delightful temper and manner, are carefully to be corrected and amended, the chief of which are,[54] 1. a natural roughness which makes a man con-

---

54. [Turnbull is paraphrasing Locke, *Education*, §143.]

sult his own humour and inclinations only, and very uncomplaisant to others, so as to have no regard to their tempers or conditions. Every one agrees, that not to mind what pleases or displeases those we are with, is downright clownishness: Yet we may often find one in a very fashionable dress give an uncontrouled swing to his own humour in company, with absolute indifferency how others take it. It is however a brutality that is incompatible with the least tincture of good-breeding. For the very business and scope of good manners is to bend men's tempers to compliance and accommodation with those we have to do with. 2. Contempt or want of due respect, bewrayed either by looks, word or gesture. This always creates uneasiness from whomsoever it comes: For self-love and pride naturally revolt against it. No body can bear being slighted. 3. Nothing is more repugnant to civility than a censorious temper, or an itch to find fault with others, and expose their weaknesses. Raillery is the most refined way of touching upon the faults of others. And because censuring, to deserve that name, must be managed with wit, pleasantry, and good language; and when it is such it usually gives entertainment to the politest company, people are apt to mistake concerning it, and think there is no incivility in it when it keeps within fair bounds. Hence it is, that this conversation obtains so much, and is so well received amongst people of the better rank. But let it be considered how contrary it is to humanity, to entertain the rest of a company at the cost of one, who being set to shew in burlesque colours, cannot be without uneasiness, unless the subject for which he is rallied be really matter of conversation. For then the pleasant images which make the raillery, carrying praise as well as sport with them, the rallied party finds his account and takes part in the diversion. But raillery being so delicate a matter, that the smallest mistake or wrong turn may spoil all, none ought to meddle with it who has not a very dextrous hand at it. And young people, more especially, should not venture upon it with their elders in particular. Complaisance may degenerate, it often does, into what we call an every man's man, a softness that yields to the humour of every company, howsoever unreasonable. Now strict regard to truth and virtue is the only remedy against this excess of pliableness: And it ought to be often represented to youth as what it really is, cowardice. But tho' complaisance does not require that we should assent to all the opinions or reasonings, or relations that the company we are in may be entertained with, nor that we should silently pass over all that is vented in our hearing, much less, that we should comply with every riot or foolery that may be proposed, yet there is in some people what is very properly called a spirit of contradiction, a disposition resolutely, and without regard to right or wrong, to oppose some one, or perhaps every one of the company, whatever they say or do, which surely must be diametrically repugnant to civility; since humanity requires, that all marks of regard and good-will should always accompany even reasonable contradiction to, or dissention from any person. And in truth, he who opposes in any other way, may gain the argument, but he will lose what every good man will far prefer to such a victory, the esteem and love of those who hear him. We may lay it down as a rule, founded on human nature, that he recommends himself very ill to another as aiming at his happiness, who in the services he does him, gives him pain, and makes him uneasy in the manner of doing them. He that understands how to make those he converses with easy, without degrading himself to low flattery or servile complaisance, has hit on the secret charm of living agreably in the world, and of being both useful and acceptable wherever he goes. Civility, therefore, is what in the first place should with great care and attention be rendered habitual to children and young people. And we may see, from the characteristics of it, how well it consists with the true courage and manly intrepidity which the exercises above mentioned are the proper means of producing, and strengthening betimes in young minds. But it is not sufficient to intitle one to the character of well-bred, that he has even the best heart, the most benign, social and generous disposition; one must likewise be acquainted with the proper language by which this excellent temper should shew and express itself, and have it at command, so as not to have it to seek from rules laid up in his head or memory on every emergency, but so ready at his hand, as that he naturally falls into the decency and gracefulness of looks, voice, words, motions, gestures, and the whole of outward demeanour, which takes in company, and makes those whom we converse with easy and well-pleased. For this is properly the outward language whereby the internal civility of the temper is expressed. And hence it evidently follows, that this, like all other languages, must very much depend upon the fashion and custom of every country, and in the rules and practice of it can therefore only be learned from observation, and by frequenting the society of those who are allowed to be exactly well-bred. But nothing is more proper to give children a becoming confidence and easy behaviour, and so to raise them to the conversation of those above their age, than dancing. For though its effect consist chiefly in outward gracefulness of motion, yet I know not how, it gives children manly thoughts, or at least manly carriage more than any thing. There is what we justly call a false modesty, or a sheepish bashfulness, a clownish shamefacedness before strangers, or those above, one which confounds the thoughts, words and looks, and makes a person lose himself to such a degree, as not to be able to do any thing, or at least not to do it with that ease and gracefulness which pleases. Now dancing is a proper remedy for this, and together with it the frequenting of good company will soon introduce the contrary habit; not forwardness, pertness, or impudence, but genuine, winning, unabashed modesty. Dancing therefore, being that which gives graceful motions all the life, and above all things, manliness and a becoming assurance to young children, it cannot be learned too early, after they are once of an age and strength capable of it. But you must be sure to have a good master, that knows and can teach what is graceful and becoming, and what gives a freedom and easiness to all the motions of the body. One that teaches not this is worse than none at all, natural rusticity being more tolerable than an affected mien. What hath been said of dancing extends that exercise no further than so far as it tends to perfect a genteel, graceful carriage. And it hath never gained its effect, till it hath the influence upon outward behaviour which Quintilian thus describes. "Neque enim gestum componi ad similitudinem saltationis volo, sed subesse aliquid, in hac exercitatione puerili, unde nos non id agentes, *furtim decor ille discentibus traditus prosequatur.*"[55] "I would not have one carry his body as if he were dancing, but I would have something of the puerile exercise to remain, so that without thinking of it, we may do every thing naturally, and with the grace it is principally designed to render habitual to us." Quintilian here seems to have had in view these elegant

---

55. [Quintilian, *Institutio Oratoria*, 1.11.19.]

lines of Tibullus, which contain an inimitably beautiful description of outward grace, and its charming effects upon all who see it.

> *Illam quicquid agit, quoquo vestigia flectit,*
> *Componit furtim subsequiturque decor;*
> *Seu solvit crines, fusis decet esse capillis;*
> *Seu compsit comptis est veneranda comis.*
> *Urit seu Tyria voluit procedere pulla;*
> *Urit seu Nivea candida veste venit.*
> *Talis in aeterno felix vertumnus Olympo*
> *Mille habet ornatus, mille decenter habet.*
>
>   TIBUL. l. 4. el. 2.[56]

After all, example is the chief thing, in order to form a genteel well-bred
youth. And therefore it is necessary that the tutor under whose formation
youth are put, be well-bred, and understand all the maxims of civility and
good manners, in all the variety of persons, times and places. They are
greatly mistaken, who think the whole of good-breeding consists in a certain way of pulling off the hat or making a leg: And they are much more
so, who imagine it is enough if a preceptor be a sober man and a scholar.
Good-breeding is the accomplishment that is most necessary to be formed
by the example and care of a governor. And this is an art not to be learned
or taught by books. Nothing can give it but good example and observation
joined together. It is fit that an habitual gracefulness and politeness in all
his carriage should be settled in a pupil before he goes out of his tutor's
hands, that he may not need advice in this point when he has neither time
nor disposition to receive it, nor has any body left to give it him. A tutor
ought therefore, in the first place, to be well-bred. And a young gentleman
who gets this one quality from his governor, sets out into the world with

---

56. [Tibullus, 3.8.7–14: "Whatsoever she does, whithersoever she turns her steps,
Grace follows her unseen to order all aright. Hath she loosed her hair? Then flowing
locks become her. Hath she dressed it? With dressed hair she is divine. She fires the
heart if she chooses to appear in gown of Tyrian hue; she fires it if she comes in the
sheen of snowy robes. Like her, on everlasting Olympus, bounteous Vertumnus wears a
thousand garbs, and wears with grace the thousand" (Loeb translation by J. P. Post-
gate).]

great advantage, and will find, that this one accomplishment will more open his way to him, and get him more friends, and carry him farther in the world than all the learning he could have imbibed from him, tho' that, as we have already shewn, should not be neglected. Indeed, besides being compleatly well-bred, the tutor should know the world throughly, the vices, the humours, the follies, the cheats and artifices of the age he is fallen into, and particularly of the country he lives in, that he may be able to shew them to his pupils as he finds him capable, and so teach him skill in men and manners.

But having elsewhere touched on this subject, I shall conclude this chapter, which is already swelled to a very great size, on account of the various particulars it was requisite to consider in it with some exactness, nay minuteness, by observing what a stress the Romans laid upon politeness, or urbanity, as they called it. It appears from an elegant discourse of Monsieur Simon upon this subject, in the memoirs of the academy of belles-lettres at Paris, that what they so called, comprehended purity of language and graceful pronunciation, and for this reason, they took special care of the language and accent, even of the nurses they put about young children: It comprehended likewise graceful demeanor of the body, or easy and genteel outward carriage: It comprehended civility, complaisance, and study to please company, and make them cheerful and happy. But it particularly meant a certain pleasantry or facetiousness of conversation, which promoted gaiety and good humour, without putting any one to pain or uneasiness. And to produce or form all these good qualities in children gradually, were the Romans at due pains. Mr. Simon having observed this, adds this remark. "May I here, says he, make a reflexion upon the education we commonly give our children? It is very remote from the precepts I have mentioned. We take a vulgar woman for a nurse, and it is from her the child learns to speak: To the nurse succeeds a governante, who speaks not a bit better; and out of her hands the child passes into those of a preceptor to whose capacity so little attention is paid, that it is not thought necessary he should have any. Hath the child arrived to six or seven years of age, he mixes with a herd of equally ill-bred boys at college, where under the pretext of teaching him Latin, no regard is had to his mother-tongue.

And what happens? What we see every day. A young gentleman of eighteen, who has had this education, cannot read. For to articulate the words, and join them together, I don't call reading, unless one can pronounce well, observe all the proper stops, vary the voice, express the sentiments, and read with a delicate intelligence. Nor can he speak a jot better. A proof of this is, that he cannot write ten lines without committing gross faults; and because he did not learn his own language well in his early years, he will never know it well. I except a few, who being afterwards engaged by their profession, or their natural taste, cultivate their minds by study. And yet even they, if they attempt to write, will find by the labour composition costs them, what a loss it is not to have learned their language in the proper season. Education amongst the Romans was upon quite a different footing: The Greek was their learned language; it was taught in public schools; they gave application to understand it; but they were no less sollicitous to learn the grammar of their own. Masters taught them early the principles, the difficulties, the subtleties, the depths of it. Masters of rhetoric instructed them in all its riches and beauty. When they went from these schools they were perfect masters of their own language, they never were at a loss for proper expressions; and I am much deceived if it was not owing to this that they produced such excellent works with so marvellous facility. When we consider the writings Cato the Censor, Cicero, Varro, and many others left behind them, men who had so much other business to employ them, men who had such a share in all the affairs of their times, we can't comprehend how they could be equal to all they really did: And nothing can account for it but the reason we have given. It is not astonishing therefore, if the urbanity, which consists primarily in the purity of language, was so common among the Romans, and is so rare amongst us.— Urbanity came afterwards to signify that character of politeness which reigns in the air and manners of a person. But urbanity taken in this sense is the fruit of good education. Accordingly the great men I have mentioned, whom we may consider as the legislators of education, have recommended every thing that can contribute to polish youth. They would have music, dancing, and the genteel exercises, and even the theatre itself, all the arts, in one word, concur to give them the graces which render knowledge and virtue amiable. 'Dandum etiam aliquid Comoedo,'[57] says Quintilian. "Youth ought to take lessons even from players"; not barely to learn a correct and just pronunciation, but to form their countenance and gesture. With regard to music, he makes it to be an art absolutely necessary to all who would pass for persons of liberal education. And it is because music, according to Aristoxenus, comprehends two kinds of numbers or measures; one for regulating the voice, and the other for regulating those motions of the body whence results good grace in the outward carriage. As to the exercises, 'tis well known what stress the ancients laid upon them, and what share they had in the formation of their youth. Tilt and tournament came in the room of the ancient exercises, and were for some time in great vogue amongst us; and at present to the gymnastic exercises of the ancients, which a learned member of this academy hath so accurately described in his dissertations upon them, have succeeded those exercises which our youth learn at our academies, of which, however, they are now become less fond than they were formerly: Cicero would rather have a young man to form himself upon the model of soldiers, who have, to say the truth, generally a much easier and freer air than most others. These were the methods the Romans took to acquire the urbanity for which they are so celebrated: Methods so much the more easy, that a very little practice in them suffices for giving an agreeable exterior to more solid and more essential virtues. It must be acknowledged, however, that these methods of polite education are now very much neglected. Some go so far as to affirm, that they are not necessary to all conditions of persons. Thus do many of our people of the gown think. And hence it is, that the urbanity I have been discoursing of, and which would so well befit them, is not very common among them. For why may not one speak here what he really thinks, when he hath no other view but the public-good? The austere and rigid education which they for the greater part receive, and by natural consequence give to their children, degenerates into a sort of gravity which Mr. le Duc de la Rochefaucault defines to be a mysterious exterior, invented to hide the defects of the mind; I should rather chuse to say the

---

57. [Quintilian, *Institutio Oratoria*, I.II.I.]

defects of education. They do not reflect, that very often the want of urbanity suffices to make the greatest talents, and the greatest virtues, hated or contemned. The Romans had in this respect great advantage above us. Amongst them professions were not distinguished or confined within narrow bounds, as they are amongst us. Here one of the robe is merely one of the robe; a magistrate is solely a magistrate; a scholar a mere scholar; a soldier nothing but a soldier; a churchman has his particular functions, and he meddles with little else. It was not so in ancient Rome: The same person had many different talents; he was a scholar, barrister, soldier, priest, augur, at one and the same time. I can easily imagine, that a person who was sufficiently qualified for so many different professions, derived graces from each of them, which mutually diffused themselves through all the rest. And hence I understand that Roman urbanity was not an empty name. In fact all the Romans, during some time, at least, went to war. The first of their employments were equally military and civil; I mean that of quaestor, which we may compare to that of our pay-master to, or intendant of the army. Was there ever a mere barrister, or one who attended the bar more closely than Cicero? Yet he commanded an army, he had the title of general, and kept it a considerable time. Horace, tho' he does not boast of his courage, had however served under Brutus. But the same persons knew how to distinguish themselves in time of peace as well as of war. A general of the army, after having extended the Roman dominion by his conquests, after having gained victories, and had the honour of a triumph, returning to Rome, and becoming a simple citizen, found, in the diversity of his talents, new employment for his ambition. He became a protector of the laws, a defender of oppressed innocence; and at the bar or in the senate disputed the prize of eloquence with the most distinguished orators. It is no wonder that such a person pleaded or harangued with the same courage he fought, as is said of Caesar; nor that he mingled with the exercises of the bar the military graces he had imbibed by commerce with the gentlemen of the sword; nor that by consequence, he should have surpassed us so far in what I call urbanity. Add to this, that all persons of birth at Rome travelled into Greece, and went to improve their taste of the polite arts in the very bosom of politeness; not to mention their having Greeks at home, very well qualified to instil early that taste into them, or to cultivate it. All these are advantages we want, and many of them are not agreeable to our manners, our customs, our form of government. But for this reason, the culture I am now speaking of is so much the more necessary: And it consists, as hath been said, in a good education, and proper after-care. I will give you a strong example of what these may do with regard to urbanity. It is in Horace, as far as I am able to judge, that the character of urbanity shines more than in any other of the Latin poets. Now we need only call to mind a passage, in which this poet having very modestly praised himself, rather for the vices from which he was free, than for any virtues he possessed, attributes all the honour of his merit to the education his father had given him.

> *Causa fuit pater his, qui macro pauper agello*
> *Noluit in Flavî ludum me mittere———*
>
> ——— ——— ——— ———
>
> *Sed puerum est ausus Romam portare docendum*
> *Artes, quas doceat quivis eques atque senator*
> *Semet prognatos: ——— ——— ———*
>
> ——— ——— ——— ——— ———
>
> *Ipse mihi custos incorruptissimus omnes*
> *Circùm doctores aderat.*
>
> Lib. 1. sat. 6.[58]

See here a model of education worthy of being imitated. But what did Horace himself add to this care? Not satisfied with the masters he had at Rome, he went to seek others at Athens: So he himself informs us.

> *Adjecere bonae paulo plus artis Athenae.*
>
> Ep. l. 2. Ep. 2.[59]

---

58. [Horace, *Satires,* 1.6.71–82: "I owe this to my father, who, though poor with a starveling farm, would not send me to the school of Flavius . . . nay, he boldly took his boy off to Rome, to be taught those studies that any knight or senator would have his own offspring taught. . . . He himself, a guardian true and tried, went with me among all my teachers."]

59. [Horace, *Epistles,* 2.2.43: "Kindly Athens added somewhat more training."]

Tho' he was not very brave, yet he would needs make some campaigns, probably to learn the military art, the properest and most improving to young men. But neither the licentiousness which commonly attends that profession, nor the amusements and dissipation into which youth is so apt to run, ever diminished his taste for study and polite literature: He loved them so much as to think books as necessary to life as the things which support it.

> *Sit bona librorum & provisae frugis in annum*
> *Copia.* ——— ——— ———
>
> Ep. l. 1. Ep. 18.[60]

Born a poet, he composed verses rather like a gentleman than a poet by profession, despising the approbation of the vulgar, and sollicitous only to please a small number of select readers.

> ——— *Neque te ut miretur turba, labores,*
> *Contentus paucis lectoribus.*
>
> Sat. l. 1. Sat. 10.[61]

Accordingly in reading Homer, with whom he was so charmed, he studied him as a philosopher more than as a poet: He thought he was reading Chrysippus or Crantor, and referred every thing he read in him to life and manners!

> *Qui, quid sit pulchrum, quid turpe, quid utile, quid non,*
> *Plenius ac melius Chrysyppo & Crantore dicit.*
>
> Ep. l. 1. Ep. 2.[62]

His distance by birth from the great did not dispirit him, but encouraged by his happy endowments, he frequented the most noble, and knew

---

60. [Horace, *Epistles,* 1.18.109–10: "May I have a good supply of books and of food to last the year."]

61. [Horace, *Satires,* 1.10.73–74: "and you must not strive to catch the wonder of the crowd, but be content with the few as your readers."]

62. [Horace, *Epistles,* 1.2.3–4: "who tells us what is fair, what is foul, what is helpful, what not, more plainly and better than Chrysippus or Crantor."]

how to please them. Admitted on one side into the familiarity of a Pollio, of Messala, of Lollius, of Maecenas, of Augustus; and on the other side, being in strict friendship with Virgil, with Varus; with Tibullus, with Plotius, &c. in one word, with all the best men of Rome; I am not surprized that he, by commerce with these great men, acquired that politeness, that delicate refined taste, which his writings make us feel. This is what I call continued culture, and such as is requisite to accomplish the character of urbanity. In reality, however good one's education may have been, if one ceases to improve and cultivate his mind and manners by reflexion, and by conversation with well-accomplished persons, and above all, with persons bred at courts, to whom politeness is as it were natural, he cannot avoid falling into something very opposite to politeness and urbanity. Accordingly it is reported of Cicero, that he could not let the smallest fault in speaking pass unreproved in his son; and of Caesar, that as much as he was taken up with his grand projects, he studied purity of language in his tents, amidst the noise and hurry of arms. Some may perhaps look upon these things as trifles; but to such let me make the answer Quintilian gives on a very like occasion. 'These accomplishments do not hurt those who use them as steps by which they may rise to others, but those only who stop there, and confine themselves to them alone.'

"As for that part of urbanity which belongs to raillery, it hardly admits of precepts. Here at least my guides fail me, for both affirm it cannot be taught. Cicero says there is no art of wit or pleasant raillery; and in one of his dialogues, one of the personages expresly tells us, that having seen some Greek book intitled, the art of raillery, he expected at first to have learned something from it, but that in fact he found nothing in it but some examples of pleasant and witty sayings; for says he, the Sicilians, the Rhodians, but above all, the Athenians excelled in this way. Hence he concludes, that it is not a thing that can be taught by rules; and he gives a very good reason why. It is a talent that must be born with one, or for which one must be formed by nature herself. However Quintilian, who is more particular in treating things than Cicero, thinks young people may be turned or improved in this way by proper methods. Yet after all, these great masters only prescribe a certain temperament or moderation that ought to be preserved in raillery, that it may have that air of urbanity which is so adorning to a man of worth. What they principally recommend to us is, first of all, not to affect to make persons laugh; and they observe, that raillery better becomes one in defending than in attacking, because there it cannot be suspected of being studied or premeditated. Besides, it is natural for one to defend himself with such arms as he is attacked with. In the second place, they advise always to spare persons to whom we owe respect, or with whom we are in friendship. A maxim which it seems easy to observe, but which, however, it is almost impossible for those to observe who have naturally a turn for raillery. This made Ennius say, that it is easier for a wit to hold burning coals in his mouth, than to keep in a smart thing that presses to get out. Accordingly among the Romans, Crassus is the only person who is brought as an example of one who had a singular talent for raillery, but could keep within the rules of decency; and who could as easily forbear being witty as give way to his pleasantry. Quintilian gives us excellent precepts upon this head, precepts worthy of the Christian morality. 'Let our wit and pleasantry, says he, always be innocent, and let us not prefer a smart saying to a friend. A humane, well-bred man will be facetious and witty with decency. It is putting too high a value upon wit and pleasantry, to give scope to it at the expence of probity.' And hence we may learn with what care we ought to avoid all raillery that is gross and low; and how attentive we ought to be, lest through affectation of wit we become scoffers or buffoons, a character very unbefitting a person of dignity and merit. True pleasantry does not excite noisy laughter, it only gently tickles the soul. Plautus was not relished by Horace: It was because Plautus so often sinks into the low comic, and was fitter to divert the vulgar than people of education and good taste. With these precautions, raillery will have no more salt than is necessary to give life to conversation; refined from every thing that is bitter and offensive, it will be humane and polite, which proves what I said in the first part of this discourse, that urbanity in its strict sense, is a moral virtue, which renders society amiable and pleasant; and therefore I shall end this article with what Quintilian says, after giving a definition of manners. 'Urbanity, besides the perfections I have already mentioned, requires a stock of benevolence, a liberal cast of mind, which is rarely to be found but in persons of birth.'

"That I may omit nothing that may be said about the means of acquiring it, I shall take notice of two defaults which are its opposites. The first is a certain timidity which gives one an embarassed air, and degenerates into false modesty. The remedy proposed for this by the author I have so often cited, is an honest assurance, or rather the intrepidity of a good conscience, to which must be added knowledge of the world, and great practice in it, without which an able man, with all his learning and wit, will make but a very awkward figure. The other is too great a desire to appear polite; whence proceeds I know not what affectation and formality, that spoils all. For if this character be not natural, as it were, to us, I would rather prefer rusticity, which, at least, has the merit of simplicity. In fact, whatever is not easy, but studied, instead of being graceful, gives pain to every spectator; and where grace is wanting, there true urbanity or politeness is not. Whatever is over-done, says Quintilian, is unbecoming; and for this reason, even what is in itself agreeable loses all its beauty, if it exceeds certain limits, and is not prudently moderated. But it is much easier to feel all this than to explain it. The perception of it depends more upon taste than upon precepts. And yet it is by adding politeness to knowledge and virtue that liberal education is finished and rendered complete."

The true philosophy, and the proper methods of teaching it more
fully described; where the Socratic method of teaching; and in-
struction by fables, parables or allegories are considered.

It was impracticable to get through the subject of the former chapter, so as
to render this treatise on education as full and compleat as it ought to be,
without entering into a particular detail that may perhaps be tedious to
those who are much conversant with it. But now we return to a matter
which is in itself more entertaining, and where we can have but small assistance from others, so little hath it been considered, tho' it be of the
highest importance in education.

The character of that true philosophy, which alone hath produced, and
only can produce patriots, truly good and great members of society, is
strongly painted out to us by Tacitus in his account of Helvidius Priscus,
and the education to which he owed his eminent abilities and virtues. "In-
genium illustre altioribus studiis juvenis admodum dedit: non ut plerique,
ut nomine magnifico segne otium velaret, sed quo firmior adversus for-
tuita, rempublicam capesseret. Doctores sapientiae secutus est, qui sola
bona quae honesta, mala tantum quae turpia; potentiam nobilitatem, cae-
teraque extra animum neque bonis neque malis annumerant, &c."[63]

---

63. Hist. lib. 4. circa initium. [Tacitus, *Histories,* 4.5: "In his early youth Helvidius
devoted his extraordinary talents to the higher studies, not as most youths do, in order
to cloak a useless leisure with a pretentious name, but that he might enter public life
better fortified against the chances of fortune. He followed those teachers of philosophy
who count only those things 'good' which are morally right and only those things 'evil'
which are base, and who reckon power, high birth, and everything else that is beyond
the control of the will as neither good nor bad" (Loeb translation by Clifford H.
Moore).]

This was the philosophy that prevailed in Greece and Rome, while these countries produced those glorious names, which, being an honour to human nature, so greatly adorn their histories; as indeed it is the only philosophy that can inspire or support virtue, and keep men firm to duty in spite of all temptation from the side of danger or of pleasure: The philosophy, that by accustoming one to regard the rectitude of actions, more than external loss and suffering, or pleasure and advantage, enables him to disdain whatever comes into competition with virtue, with the *honestum*, and steadily to prefer untainted integrity to all that can be gained by prostitution of honour. How elegantly is it described by Lucan in his soul-rouzing character of Cato?

> ———*Hi mores, haec duri immota Catonis*
> *Seca fuit, servare modum, finemque tenere,*
> *Naturamque sequi, patriaeque impendere vitam,*
> *Nec sibi, sed toti genitum se credere mundo.*
> *Justitiae cultor, rigidi servator honesti:*
> *In commune bonus, nullosque Catonis in actus*
> *Subrepsit, partemque tulit sibi nata voluptas.*
>
> LUCAN. l. 2. v. 300.[64]

So Socrates, as we learn from Plato and Xenophon, always described the truly great and brave man. And how delightfully, how warmingly do we find Cicero combating the contrary philosophy, in proportion to the spreading and prevalence of which, hath public virtue ever declined, as it manifestly did among the Greeks and Romans: That philosophy which set up pleasure as the sovereign good, and taught men that selfishness is wisdom, and that they were chiefly to consult external ease and conveniency, and not solely the dignity of human nature, or the eternal and immutable

---

64. [Lucan, *The Civil War*, 2.380–83, 389–91: "Such was the character, such the inflexible rule of austere Cato—to observe moderation and hold fast the limit, to follow nature, to give his life for his country, to believe that he was born to serve the whole world and not himself . . . he worshipped justice and practiced uncompromising virtue; he reserved his kindness for the whole people; and there was no act of Cato's life where selfish pleasure crept in and claimed a share" (Loeb translation by J. D. Duff).]

rules of moral rectitude, in their choices and pursuits.[65] "Were ever, saith he, the names of Lycurgus, Solon, Leonidas, Epaminondas, and other such heroes, who made public good the sole or chief measure and standard of their conduct mentioned in the schools of Epicurus, where pleasure was painted out in regal pomp, beautifully arrayed, and sitting upon a magnificent throne, with the virtues attending her like waiting-maids, who had no other employment but to receive and execute her orders, and whispering her in the ear only to take care to do nothing rashly, or that might bring pain after it. 'Nocet empta dolore voluptas.'[66] The disciples of Epicurus painted this tablature elegantly enough in words: But can you, Torquatus, look into your own mind, and seriously consult your own honest heart, and the noble pursuits to which it generously stimulates you, without being ashamed of this picture? Can you bear the servile language and air he gives to the virtues?—Can such principles animate and excite men to truly laudable and heroic actions? Can such philosophy produce public spirit, love of mankind and true magnanimity? In truth Torquatus, you must either quit the defence of indolence and voluptuousness, or give up all our patriots, heroes and deliverers for fools.—To bring the enjoyments of sense, and the satisfactions of our superior powers of reason and judgment under the denomination of pleasure, is a plain receding from the common notion of the word, and a mere shift and collusion. They do not deal fairly or candidly with us, who in their grave lectures admit that for pleasure, which, at an ordinary time, and in the common practice of life is so little taken as such. The mathematician who labours at his problems and theorems, the bookish man who fatigues his body and mind by severe studies and profound researches, the artist who voluntarily endures the greatest toils and hardships, none of these are said to follow pleasure, nor will those who call themselves the only men of pleasure admit them of their number. The satisfactions of the mind, which are purely mental, and consist solely in sentiment and thought, are too refined for them who are so taken up with pleasures of a more substantial kind. They who are so

---

65. [Turnbull is paraphrasing Cicero, *De Finibus Bonorum et Malorum,* esp. 2.21.]
66. [Horace, *Epistles,* 1.2.55: "pleasure bought with pain is harmful."]

captivated by the idea of sensitive gratification, can have but little relish for the more spiritual and intellectual sort. But this latter, however, they cry up and magnify upon occasion, to avoid the ignominy which may redound from an open avowance of the former; and this done the latter may take its chance, its use is presently at an end. For it is observable, that when men of this sort have recommended the enjoyments of the mind under the title of pleasure, when they have thus dignified the word, and comprehended in it whatever is mentally good and honest, they can afterwards suffer it contentedly to slide back again into its own genuine and vulgar sense, whence they raised it only to serve a turn. When pleasure is called in question and attacked, then reason and virtue are called on to her aid, and make principal ingredients of her constitution. A complicated form appears, and comprehends streight all which is generous, beautiful and honest in human life. But when the attack is over, and the objection is once dissipated, the spectre vanishes; pleasure returns again to her former shape, and she may even be pleasure still, and have as little concern with dry virtue, and sober reason, as in the nature of the thing, and according to common understanding, she really has. If virtue be an empty name, if there be no distinction between moral rectitude and turpitude of actions, then 'tis no matter how one lives, or what he does, if he can but save himself from pain.—But if there be any dignity belonging to human nature, as adorned with intelligent and active powers:—Or if there be any rule of action, then the first and essential question to be asked on every occasion is, whether the thing proposed be virtuous, whatever it may cost, or be not base whatever advantage it may bring with it. And men consequently are to be taught to postpone and undervalue every gratification on the one hand, and every pain or danger on the other, in comparison of an untainted heart and life." Thus does Cicero often argue, or this language, at least, does he put often in the mouth of his advocate for virtue against the Epicurean doctrine.

But to proceed more regularly in this present enquiry, we shall fix before our view a short definition of the philosophy which ought to be the chief object and scope of education given us by an admirable author, in whose words, as near as I can remember them, I have given you these reasonings in Cicero de finibus, concerning virtue and true philosophy. "To philosophize, says he, in a just signification, is but to carry good-breeding a step higher. For the accomplishment of breeding is to learn whatever is decent in company, or beautiful in arts; and the sum of philosophy is to learn what is just in society, and beautiful in nature, and the order of the world."[67] True philosophy teaches the order of nature, and the order of human life. And therefore tho' languages ought not to be neglected, this philosophy ought to be the chief employment of youth every day from their earliest years; that they may timeously learn to delight in searching into the wisdom and goodness of nature, and to love and imitate its all-perfect former and ruler. Lead pupils through air, sea and earth, and teach them to observe the chief properties of these elements, and their final causes, or the infinitely various uses to which they minister, with relation to all the immense diversities of perceptive beings with which they are so richly peopled, that in reality there is no chasm, no blank in nature, but perfection rising above perfection so gradually, from the lowest to the highest, as to leave no room to doubt that any possible or imaginable species of life is wanting in it. Teach them why all matter hath gravity, and why, in the proportion, that gravity takes place near the surface of our earth: Shew them how and why all matter attracts and is mutually attracted, and set before them various effects of this universal law: Let them be taught to observe what an infinite diversity of qualities arises from various textures of bodies, and to what excellent uses all these serve or may be employed: Explain to them the law according to which fluids press; and why fluids, as well as solids, have different specific gravities, and the manifold advantages of these laws: Point out to them the elasticity of the air, and the advantages arising from thence: Explain respiration, flying, swimming, and sailing to them: Carry them into the fields and gardens, and entertain them with the riches of nature that there displays itself, and with the laws of vegetation: Dive with them into the bowels of the earth, and develop to them the treasures of useful minerals and metals which lie hid there: Let not the structures of animals be neglected, but shew them how each species is furnished and adapted for its proper element and peculiar

67. [Shaftesbury, *Characteristicks*, III:99.]

manner of life: And far less let the wonderful instincts implanted by the Author of nature in every tribe of animals, so suited to each particular oeconomy, be overlooked: Travel over our whole earth with them, and shew them how and where it was first peopled, and into what various climates and soils it is divided: Explain to them the source of light and heat, these genial powers of nature whence proceeds all life and motion; the diurnal and annual revolutions of the earth round the sun, and in consequence thereof, the regular succession of day and night, and of the seasons departing and returning at their appointed times: Mount with them to the heavens, and unfold to them our mundan system, and the laws of central and centrifugal forces, which retain our earth and its companion planets in their orbits, while they roll round, at so well proportioned distances and periods, their common enlivener: Unfold to them the various uses of the moon to our earth; and then acquainting them with the fixed stars, teach them to consider them as so many suns of like utility with ours: Teach them not to be startled at eclipses, nor at storms and earthquakes, but to trace them to their causes: Learn them to admire the simplicity and consonancy of all nature's laws: Shew them how nature never deviates from her purpose, never errs or is deficient; but that in a system compounded of such immense variety, some laws must unavoidably be sometimes thwarted by other laws of equal advantage in the whole, hence all her seeming irregularities or deviations: In fine, guide them gradually through all of nature philosophers have yet been able to understand and explain: And teach them to observe how nature can only be understood or unfolded, and how general properties or powers, and laws of powers are inferred from particular experiences by induction: And take every opportunity that offers of recommending to them that study of lines, figures and proportions, which hath been of so great use in unraveling nature, and explaining her operations, and in the invention of beneficial arts. For so soon as they have any idea of the utility of geometry in this respect, viz. as a key to the works of the great Geometrician, who doth all things according to weight and measure, they will be desirous of being initiated into it; and a little daily practice in it will wonderfully enlarge and invigorate their minds. But let not researches into nature stop here, but proceed yet higher to its nobler parts, viz. to the contemplation of the human mind, and the

various capacities with which it is endued, to be improved by proper culture to very high perfection; till they clearly perceive what constitutes good
order within the soul, and consonancy thereby with the universal Mind,
whose workmanship our thinking and reasoning powers and all things
that exist, are, and what makes good order in human society, or maintains
and upholds public happiness. The transition from facts and final causes
of the one kind, to those of the other, is exceeding natural and easy; and
all the while the student is entertained with real harmonies, the knowledge
of which qualifies for real usefulness in the world. 'Tis strange that any
should imagine that enquiries into the structure of the mind, or its powers,
and their laws and connexions, are to be carried on in any other way than
researches into the qualities of bodies and their laws, i.e. by careful attention to what experience teaches, and just reasoning from experience; or
that these enquiries should be imagined to have no affinity or relation the
one to the other. How can facts be known but by experience; external facts
but by the testimony of our senses, or internal ones but by inward sensation or consciousness? And what things can be more closely or intimately
blended and connected than our bodies are with our minds, and by consequence, the laws of the material world with those relating to our moral
powers? In the knowledge of these two consists the whole of real science;
the science which enables either for self-government, or for beneficialness
in human society; beneficialness to society, whether with respect to the arts
of policy, or the mechanical arts, on the advancement of which the conveniency and comfort of human life so greatly depend. Contemplation is
the proper employment, the proper food of the understanding; and the
contemplation of the beautiful order and wise final causes of nature in all
her laws and productions, hath a delightful influence on the temper of the
mind, by inspiring into it the love of order in the heart, and in outward
manners, and by wonderfully harmonizing the soul, and all its affections
and motions. And indeed, as it is in itself an exceeding pleasing employment, for which man is the only creature within our cognizance that is
fitted by his frame, whether of body or mind; so it must be considered by
all who believe a future more spiritual existence of our souls, in which their
principal business and happiness are to consist in the intelligent contemplation and admiration of the divine works and government, as a very nec-

essary preparation to capacitate for such exercise. For they who are acquainted by practice with searching into established connexions and
general laws of nature, and their good ends here, are by such use qualified
for continuing the same research, however new the objects may be;
whereas, on the other hand, one who is an utter stranger to such enquiries,
must enter into a future state, very unprepared for that which is justly supposed to make so considerable a part of the employment and entertainment of a future more intellectual and refined existence. But this is not all;
for even confining our views entirely to our present state, all the interests
of human life require large insight into the laws of the natural and moral
world. Nothing can be done for the furtherance of human happiness without it. And in proportion to the advancement of moral and natural knowledge, are men qualified for all the nobler purposes and uses or advantages
of human life. All the practical arts, whether of the moral or natural kind,
from which any benefit to society can be brought, presuppose this knowledge: They cannot precede, prevent or surpass it, but must owe their advancements to its improvements, and do indeed proportionably advance
with it. In every regard therefore, it is the business of education to acquaint
youth early with the method of studying nature, and with the pleasure and
advantage of such study: It is not merely necessary on this account, that
they may be able, when men, to amuse themselves agreeably, and without
making the least step towards vice in hours of retirement and solitude: But
it is absolutely requisite, in order to qualify them for serving their country
when they enter into the world, and capacity for action is reasonably expected from them: From all, of some kind, and of the highest sort from
those whose birth and fortunes afford them time and means of high improvement: For no man is born for himself alone; and consequently a happier situation for improving one's mind, is in reality a proportionably
stronger obligation to take due pains to fit one's self for the most important services to society. If every man be under obligations to mankind, to
his country in particular, the bond, the tie must bear proportion to, and
grow with the means and power one's rank and place, by the allotment of
providence, gives him. In this wise and just light ought youth, exeemed by
an advantageous birth from drudgery to their backs and bellies, to consider this their good fortune. But in vain would they be called upon to

enforce this noble sentiment upon their minds, if they were not at the same time initiated into the knowledge, which alone can qualify them for acquitting themselves of this obligation. Moral and natural philosophy, sciences, which tho' distinguished by different names, are indeed, in their nature, as nearly allied as their objects, soul and body, ought therefore chiefly to enhance the time of youth, whom we would prepare for living either agreeably or usefully in the world, either for solitude or for active life: And languages are only necessary as means of getting into acquaintance with the knowledge of those who went before us, or who speak different languages from our own; or for the sake of communicating what we know to others; and are therefore but a subordinate part, which should have but a subordinate share of their time and application. Let youth be early led through several parts of nature, and from them to the consideration of the Author of all things, whose perfections shine so conspicuously in every law and effect of nature. Let some part of this study be their daily employment, so soon as they can, by the properest care, be rendered capable of it, which, if proper means and methods be used, will be found to be much sooner than we are apt to imagine; and can never be, without taking fit ways for engaging them in it, and making them like it. Much, very much may be done, as we shall see afterwards, to gain this effect, without the formality of lessoning, by conversation. But let even their earliest lessons be of this kind chiefly. Nor will this be difficult for masters who are themselves acquainted with this study, considering the helps they may have from several excellent writings, in which natural phenomena are reduced to their general physical laws, and others in which the final causes of these laws are pointed out. Yet it is to be wished that some system of physics were compiled out of such writings for the use of youth, in which effects were ranged into a more simple and natural order than any I have yet seen, in which final causes are not entirely overlooked. For, generally speaking, the explication of effects, and the doctrine of final causes are sejoined: at least, in the treatises of physics wrote for the instruction of young students, little or no notice is taken of the uses and ends of the laws of nature. Sir Isaac Newton, who may be justly called the light of the natural world, since a great part of it was utterly involved in darkness, utterly unknown till he was able to penetrate into it and unfold it; but more especially, since the nature of light itself, by which all things are rendered visible, was first laid open and explained by his accurate profound researches and reasonings.—This truly marvellous genius, as Socrates in ancient times, with good reason blames[68] "Latter philosophers for banishing the consideration of the first cause out of natural philosophy, feigning hypotheses for explaining all things mechanically, and referring other causes to metaphysics; whereas the main business of natural philosophy is to argue from phaenomena, without feigning hypotheses, and to deduce causes from effects till we come to the very first cause, which certainly is not mechanical; and not only to unfold the mechanism of the world, but chiefly to resolve these and such like questions: What is there in places almost empty of matter, and whence is it that the sun and planets gravitate towards one another, without dense matter between them? Whence is it that nature does nothing in vain; and whence arises all that order and beauty which we see in the world? To what end are comets, and whence is it that planets move all one and the same way in orbs concentric, while comets move all manner of ways in orbs very excentric; and what hinders the fixed stars from falling upon one another? How come the bodies of animals to be contrived with so much art, and for what ends are their several parts? Was the eye contrived without skill in optics, and the ear without knowledge of sounds, &c?" To treat physics in another manner, is to leave out the most pleasing and useful part of that science, with respect to the habit and temper of the mind. For repeated views of harmony, wisdom and goodness in all the works of nature rivet firmly upon the mind a fixed conviction, that all is under the administration of a general Mind, as absolutely remote from all malice as from all weakness, whether in respect of understanding or power, than which nothing can have a more sweetning influence upon the mind. A bad opinion of the Author and Governor of the universe must not only sour the mind, but provoke to like malignity as far as our power reaches. "And, according to the hypothesis of those who exclude an universal Former and Father of the world, it must be con-

---

68. [Isaac Newton, *Opticks*, bk. III, pt. I (Chicago: Encyclopaedia Britannica Great Books, 1952), 528–29.]

fessed there can nothing happen in the course of things to deserve either our admiration and love, or our anger and abhorrence. However, as there can be no satisfaction at the best, in thinking upon what blind chance and atoms produce, so upon disastrous occasions, and under calamitous circumstances, 'tis scarce possible to prevent a natural kind of abhorrence and spleen, which will be entertained and kept alive by the imagination of so perverse an order of things. But (continues the same excellent moralist) on another hypothesis (that of perfect Theism) it is understood, 'That whatever the order of the world produces, is in the main both just and good.' Therefore, in the course of things in this world, whatever hardship of events may seem to force from any rational creature, a hard censure of his private condition or lot, he may, by reflection nevertheless, come to have patience, and to acquiesce in it. Nor is this all. He may go further still in this reconciliation, and from the same principle, may make the lot itself an object of his good affection, whilst he strives to maintain his generous fealty, and stands so well disposed towards the laws and government of his higher country. Such an affection must needs create the highest constancy in any state of sufferance, and make us in the best manner support whatever hardships are to be endured for virtue's sake. And as this affection must of necessity cause a greater acquiescence and complacency with respect to ill accidents, ill men and injuries, so of course it cannot fail of producing still a greater equality, gentleness and benignity in the temper. Consequently, the affection must be truly a good one, and a creature the more truly good and virtuous by possessing it. For whatever is the occasion or means of more affectionately uniting a rational creature to his part in society, and causes him to prosecute the public good, or interest of his species with more zeal and affection than ordinary, is undoubtedly the cause of more than ordinary virtue in such a person. This too is certain, continues the same author, that the admiration and love of order, harmony and proportion, in whatever kind, is naturally improving to the temper, advantageous to social affection, and highly assistant to virtue, which is itself no other than the love of order and beauty in society. In the meanest subjects of the world, the appearance of order gains upon the mind, and draws the affection towards it. But if the order of the world itself appears just and beautiful, the admiration and esteem of order must run higher, and the elegant passion or love of beauty, which is so advantageous to virtue, must be the more improved by its exercise in so ample and magnificent a subject. For 'tis impossible that such a divine order should be contemplated without extasy and rapture, since in the common subjects of science and the liberal arts, whatever is according to just harmony and proportion, is so transporting to those who have any knowledge or practice in the kind." These are excellent reasons for instructing youth early in the harmony and good order of the world. In truth virtue hath not, it cannot have its full force, unless it be considered as imitation of, and conformity to the temper of the universal Mind, that framed and governs all things, and therefore as absolutely requisite to recommend to his favour. Virtue is not only not complete, when due affection is wanting towards the infinitely perfect Parent of nature, but where this is wanting, there can neither be the same benignity, firmness or constancy; the same good composure of the affections, or uniformity of mind, as where the settled persuasion of perfect administration is daily comforting the mind in its adherence to virtue, and exciting to more and more extensive benevolence, in emulation of such an amiable character, and through desire of his approbation and love. Natural philosophy, or instruction in the wisdom and goodness of the works of creation and providence, is therefore the first step in teaching and recommending virtue. The moral lesson should proceed thus, viz. by inferring from every fresh instance of good order and wise contrivance, the perfection of the universal Mind, and his liking to virtue, which is nothing else but serious affection to publick good, subduing and ruling all our other affections. Thus virtue comes upon the mind with all its collected force, with all its charms and obligations; and therefore cannot fail of taking fast hold of it, and of bringing, by repeated considerations of this kind, all our appetites and passions into due and regular subordination to it. Instances of wise final causes, duly explained, will easily lead at once to a clear view of the nature of virtue, or of rational perfection, and of all our obligations to it. For they will lead to this evident truth, which renders the cause of virtue quite triumphant; namely, "That God, who is perfect wisdom and virtue, must approve and love those who are at due pains to improve in wisdom, and what he loves and delights in he will make happy." Indeed every evidence of the wisdom and benignity of the Author of the universe, is an incontestible proof of his sincere and thorough regard to virtue; and consequently, that the truly good will be well taken care of under his administration. For perfectly wise and good administration must mean such government as is adapted to the promotion, improvement, encouragement and honour of virtue. These are equivalent propositions; or at least the one is involved in the other. And as nothing can be more preservative of virtue, more comfortable or strengthening to it than this delightful persuasion; so the proper way of confirming and fixing it upon the mind, in such a manner as to render it an active principle, is to be daily inculcating it upon youth, from such instances or examples of wisdom and goodness in the works of nature, as set the moral perfection of the Creator and Governor of the universe beyond all doubt. But for this effect, natural philosophy must not stop short at natural phenomena, properly so called, that is, the effects of matter and motion, but consider also the moral powers, faculties and affections with which human minds are adorned, and the noble improvements to which they may be exalted by due culture. And indeed here final causes lie yet more open and obvious to all who will be at any pains to enquire into them, than in physiology. For how many glorious instances doth history, nay even present times, afford of the perfection of knowledge to which human reason, and the perfection of benignity to which human hearts may be improved, which loudly upbraid the folly, perverseness or indolence of all who fall short of them! Not one power or affection can be named in the human soul which may not be cultivated into some very noble perfection or virtue. Take away our understanding or our activity, and we become mere passive beings; but with these faculties, how great a dominion may men acquire, even on earth, and what noble and glorious deeds may they do? Take away our appetites and passions, and men will not indeed be in danger of several vices: But on the other hand, where will there be place for temperance, fortitude, generosity, and all the brighter virtues, which are the greatest ornaments of human nature? These powers and affections therefore are given us for very noble ends, however we may corrupt, abuse or pervert them: Even to make us truly great and good, to enable us to rule, and to give us subjects to rule and keep in good order and subjection, to afford us means of spiritual or moral dominion. In teaching the philosophy of the natural world, and of the hu-

man mind more especially, in order to lead to just conceptions of providence, and of human duty, frequent occasions will present themselves of
taking off all the difficulties about providence which are apt to disturb the
virtuous in their gloomy hours, or have ever afforded any plausible subter-
fuge to the professed disbelievers of a deity and a future state. For virtue,
which is the best possession, as well as highest ornament of the rational
nature, and into competition with which nothing can come, if there really
be an after-life; or if the souls of men be really immortal, is a purchase in
every man's power. The vigorous persevering efforts of the mind to improve in knowledge, and every moral excellence, never prove abortive, but
are ever rewarding themselves by fresh acquisitions, in which conscience
triumphs with an undisturbable joy, no riot of sense amidst the greatest
affluence or grandeur can equal. And as for external goods, how obvious
is it, that they are upon the most equal footing imaginable with respect to
all men, since it is industry or toil that procures them? They are by the
establishment of nature its rewards: And therefore they are falsely said to
be distributed by the Author of the world with partial respect of persons.
In truth to demand that riches and health, and outward advantages,
should never fall to the share of the vitious, but into the hands of the good
and upright alone, is absurdly to demand, that honesty alone should be
able to put forth the hand or move the limbs: It is to demand, that all the
properties of air, fire and water, in one word, all the laws of mechanism,
should shift and change, according to the intentions of human agents. But
nature works not in so desultory a manner, but steadily and uniformly,
that intelligent industry may be as successful as the laws of matter and motion, upon which the whole order of our corporeal system depends, permit, being never crossed or disappointed, but in consequence of the uniform operation of some very useful law. For did not nature produce
external effects, according to the same unvarying laws and connexions,
men would not be able to comprehend nature, nor consequently to imitate it, or to produce any effect by counsel and art; and being thus divested
of all power, dominion or activity in the natural world, man would be a
most ignoble, inglorious creature, in comparison of what his reason and
active powers now render him. There lies therefore no objection against

providence on account of the law of industry, by which external purchases or advantages are obtained, according to the appointment of nature. And much less do inequalities in the partition or division of outward happiness, arising from the want of benevolence amongst mankind, or the bad constitutions and administrations of civil governments, afford any ground for arraigning the frame of mankind, or the government of the world, since man is furnished with powers by his Author, improveable into so noble a capacity for promoting public good and happiness; and the partition or circulation of happiness must greatly depend upon the forms and administrations of civil societies, in consequence of man's being framed for society and union: Because, in order to be framed for society, men must have been made mutually dependent, or in other words, common happiness must exceedingly depend upon right or proper confederacy to promote it. This is the case with regard to outward advantages, and necessarily too, in some measure, with regard to internal ones. But still a virtuous habit of mind is the truest felicity of man: And it is in every one's power who will set about it in earnest to obtain this best of goods, even under the greatest outward disadvantages. For if we look into nature and transfer our view from thence inwardly into our own minds, we shall quickly find, that the supreme Author of the universe hath bound nature fast in the chains of his fixed decrees, laws or ordinances, which all corporeal things steadily obey; but he has left the soul of man absolutely free, so that every one may be what he wills, a Titus or a Caligula. Our power to form our minds, to subdue our passions, and to establish reason in our breasts as our legislator and ruler, is as evident to our feeling and consciousness as our existence: That within certain bounds we have power, dominion, or liberty, is as indisputable as our being. Now what remains to render this idea of human life absolutely consistent with the most perfect administration, if, consistently with these things above mentioned, we consider our present state as our first step into being, our entrance upon rational life; and consequently, as intended to be what such a state should be, a proper school of education, discipline and trial, for forming, cultivating, and bringing to perfection all the glorious virtues of which our moral powers and affections are naturally capable, to be succeeded by a state in which improved moral faculties shall be properly placed, i.e. so situated as to have proper exercise and employment about objects suited to them, and in consequence thereof, high and noble happiness. For if we look upon human life in this light, not only adversity but prosperity ought to be considered as designed to be a trial, a school to virtue for its exercise; and the vicissitudes with which this world is chequered, have, over and above the final cause already mentioned, this further moral fitness, even that they render this world a proper theatre for forming and bringing forth into action several noble truly glorious virtues. Some are tried by adversity, and some by prosperity, or rather all have their successions of both, not only that human nature may be diversified, and appear in various lights, and thus be a school to the thinking for acquiring moral knowledge, but that all may have their opportunities of fixing and invigorating in their minds all the active virtues and graces in their turns. To this we may add, that tho' none are destined to be vitious, merely to give occasion to the wise and virtuous to display their wisdom and goodness, yet the vices into which so many wilfully plunge themselves, do in fact afford opportunities for the wise and good to exert several excellent qualities, for which there would otherwise be no room. For were there no infirmities, deficiencies, errors or vices, to supply, redress, correct, oppose, or reform, how would there be place for compassion, generosity, wisdom, valour, patience, magnanimity, patriotism, and a meek forgiving temper? It is in difficulties or struggles that virtue exerts all her excellence, and shines out with her fullest lustre.

This view of human life is at once consonant to the idea of the beginning of rational life, as ours plainly is, and to the perfections of the Creator of the world. Nay, perfect providence hath indeed no meaning, if we conceive otherwise of it. For what doth that universal pursuit of the greater order and good, which all researches into nature are daily confirming by fresh discoveries of beautiful and good contrivance mean, if rational powers, capable of eternal progress and exercise, are made to be destroyed, just after by great care and assiduous culture they are brought to a capacity for truly noble employments, instead of being removed into a situation proportionated and adapted to their acquired excellence, as this is to their cultivation and improvement? Where is there in nature any trace or mark of such waste and destruction, not to say cruel malignity? But having elsewhere insisted at great length[69] upon these important truths, it is sufficient to observe here, that it is only by inculcating them early upon youth, that virtue can be taught or fully recommended and endeared to them. And therefore, unless virtue be an empty name, this is the proper, the essential lesson in education. Now the way to teach and confirm this doctrine, and all its excellent comfortable consequences, is to lead youth daily thro' various instances of wisdom and order in the world, and from thence to the consideration of the human mind, and the perfection it is capable of; and to shew them how these marks of wisdom and benignity confirm a divine providence, universally pursuing the greater good, and therefore particularly interested in favour of virtue, the supreme excellence of the rational nature, and therefore God's image. But in order to carry on moral philosophy to its due perfection, together with natural philosophy instead of stated lectures upon the faculties and affections of the human mind, and the virtues belonging to them, a better method is to read daily with them some piece of history. I have already taken notice, that it is proper to begin with reading and discoursing to them upon select characters or actions, such as those singled out by Mr. Rollin; but after their minds are a little opened and enlarged by this practice, it will be proper to read history with them in chronological order, that thus they may have a view of the progress of human affairs. There, 'tis known, fit examples will ever be presenting themselves for unfolding human nature, all the springs and movements by which we are actuated, all the vices into which mankind may degenerate or be perverted, and all the temptations by which men are misled or corrupted, and all the glorious virtues of which men are susceptive, and the means by which they are strengthened, tried and perfected. Lectures have but little force without examples, and it is better that examples should give occasion or rise to the lectures, than that the latter should seem to haul in the other, as it is better in natural philosophy, that a simple narrative of the facts should precede the conclusions they lay a foundation for. Let the first lessons aim at nothing higher than fixing useful facts upon the memories of youth, which are very tenacious of whatever is agreeably rep-

69. Principles of moral philosophy.

resented or told to them, and giving them a general notion of the excellence of virtue and the deformity of vice. But let not, however, such lessons stop short at mere generals: But let youth be often practised in giving their opinion of actions and characters, and resolving questions about fit and unfit, just and unjust, that they may have by this practice clear and distinct ideas of just and unjust, generous and mean, in every particular circumstance of life, and may thus lay up in their minds sound judgments, confirmed by examples for the direction of their conduct in all the various cases, relations, businesses, or incidents of human life, which shall ever afterwards be ready for use. For it is not enough to have a general notion of virtue: One to be prepared for life must be able to judge readily what virtue requires in almost every particular situation or circumstance. No doubt order requires, that teachers begin with the simpler cases, and proceed gradually to those which require accurate attention to more circumstances; but neither wisdom nor virtue are a ready stock at full command, till by frequent practice in judging, duty immediately presents itself, supported by the solid reasons which render it such, when decision or action is requisite. The great lesson to be inculcated is the excellence of virtue, or unblemished integrity, by steady impervertible adherence to truth and right. And the most important work of education, in order to produce this incorruptible disposition, is to fortify youth early against all the allurements of vice, on the one hand, and all base or mean terrors on the other. Now, for these lessons or instructions, history will ever and anon be furnishing expert masters with very proper and natural opportunities. And to proper examples of greatness of soul, in preferring public good, or truth and moral rectitude in any case to private interest, or of baseness of mind in yielding to any vice, either through voluptuousness or cowardice, it will be fit to add the most beautiful energetic passages in poets, describing or celebrating such true virtue, and stigmatizing with eternal infamy the opposite vices. Let this be done in our own language, till the students have made considerable progress in the learned languages. For maxims, precepts, principles or examples, written in harmonious numbers, both strike the reason more strongly at first, and are more easily retained by it afterwards. And surely instructions in virtue and duty ought not to be postponed to languages. Let all the force of reasoning be confirmed by examples, and all the charms of poetry and eloquence be likewise employed to rivet upon young minds abhorrence of every vice, and sincere love to virtue, and to teach them to look down with disdain upon wealth and outward grandeur, in comparison of the inward independency and liberty of an unpolluted heart. What requires the greatest caution of teachers, when they read history with young pupils, is to take care lest the splendor of the external pomp and magnificence of very wicked men, or the renown with which very inhuman atchievements have been most unjustly honoured, should dazle and mislead them into a false notion of glory. Let care therefore be taken, in the earliest part of their education, to inure them first to enquire into the justice and equity of actions, and to raise their aversion against all cruelty, all violence, all ungenerousness, from a full conviction of the essential difference betwixt right and wrong. But these things are obvious, and therefore need not be further enlarged upon. Teaching moral knowledge and virtue by history, tho' it must begin, as we have said, yet it must not rest here, but proceed gradually, taking occasion, as the minds of pupils enlarge, to point out to them all the laws of natural equity with regard to the conduct of one sovereignty or civil state towards another in matters of negociations, commerce, war and peace, and to distinguish them from certain polite formalities, which tho' they have been generally received amongst the more civiliz'd nations from very ancient times, because of their use, are not however founded on the same solid, unchangeable principles of justice. The one are to the other what in private life between man and man the forms of good-breeding or politeness are to the immutable rules of integrity. For in reality, tho' the law of nature be distinguished, for the sake of order and method, from the law of nations, we are not to imagine that there is one law of equity and rectitude for the regulation of private men in their mutual commerce one with another, and another quite different for the regulation of states, or of those who hold the sovereignty in civil states, towards one another. Violence, injustice, ingratitude, infidelity, falshood, dissimulation, are the same hateful vices in the one case as in the other. And between nation and nation, as well as between man and man, truth, integrity, candour and generosity are the same virtues, and have the same indelible obligation: A state is but a greater one. If these laws of war and peace, as they are generally called, war and peace being the two principal articles to which all the affairs of nations or states may be reduced, are carefully attended to in reading history, youth will soon be prepared for reading with judgment and intelligence Pufendorff, Grotius, Heineccius,[70] (an excellent introduction to this most important study) or any other of the celebrated doctors of the laws of nature and nations. And indeed it is very preposterous to begin reading or explaining these authors to youth till they are pretty well acquainted with history, since such lectures cannot stir one step without bringing examples, which, without previous acquaintance with history, cannot be sufficiently understood, but must rather be an embarassment. Another thing that ought not to be omitted here is, that before students can read the authors above mentioned, or any writer upon these subjects, or indeed fully draw all the information they otherwise might, from the best Roman authors, or fully relish them, it is necessary that they should be pretty well acquainted with the Roman law. And therefore I have always thought, that so soon as students have formed clear notions of justice, and of the end of civil government, or rather, in order to perfect their notions of them, Justinian's institutes should be read with them, and they be practised in strictly examining the Roman laws and usages by principles of natural equity. It is well known, that the language of the writers on the laws of nature and nations is taken from the civil law; and besides, the principles of justice can never be so clearly or fully comprehended from mere general propositions and precepts, without the help of examples, as by taking to task, so to speak, a particular body of laws, and observing their agreements and disagreements with natural law, their deficiencies in respect of it, or their departures from it, and strictly canvassing the reasons of these diversities, with careful attention to the difference there must always be between the extent of natural and civil laws, and to the coherence there ought to be amongst the laws of any state, and the agreement they should have with the temper of the people for whom they were made, and their

---

70. Heineccius's methodical system of the laws of nature and nations, englished by Dr. Turnbull, with remarks added by the translator, and a discourse on the origin and spirit of moral and civil laws. [J. G. Heineccius, *A Methodical System of Universal Law,* trans. George Turnbull, 2 vols. (London: Noon, 1741).]

particular polity. Now the Roman laws are the best example for this purpose, for from them are the writers on natural equity ever borrowing their
examples: No body of law, perhaps, recedes less from the law of nature:
And in proportion as classical learning is reputed or valued, will acquaintance with the Roman laws and usages be necessary on this very account,
that knowledge of them is indispensibly requisite to a thorough understanding of the best Roman authors, the best of their poets not excepted.
Entrance upon this kind of study requires very considerable preparation.
But however much reading the laws of nature and nations may be neglected in education, it is certainly necessary, if a thorough intelligence of
equity be so; for it means nothing else. And if it be necessary, this is the
regular manner of setting about and pursuing it. There is no other road to
it. How can persons be qualified for making, reforming, or applying laws,
which is the business of the highest civil stations in societies, without a
thorough acquaintance with natural justice, and all the best fences for liberty and property, and with the interests of their country, which its laws
and courts of justice ought to be adapted to promote or secure? With what
conscience can any who are ignorant of these matters, thrust themselves
into the important trusts which require profound acquaintance with
them? And if the study be really of such evident utility, nay necessity, how
unaccountable is it that it should not make a principal part in education?
One who cannot judge of equity, and the interests of a country, whatever
his birth may entitle him to, excludes himself from such a trust, by his
neglect to fit himself for the momentuous charge: For if he adventures,
unprepared, to undertake any such high commission, he boldly tramples
under foot the most sacred rights of mankind, in respect of which crime
that of any other who professes what he does not understand, or is not able
to perform well, however high it be, is proportionably less, as the scope of
every other profession is of inferior moment to this highest of trusts, pro-
viding for the public welfare and good, by redressing grievances, changing
or reforming statutes, laying on taxes, and deciding fairly in ambiguous
contests about property. Let me therefore call upon our young nobility
and gentry seriously to consider what is their proper study, and upon all
who are concerned in education, to reflect how unqualified they leave their
pupils for the great business providence calls them to, however loaded they

may go from them with other erudition, or however bedecked with merely ornamental accomplishments, if they are strangers to the nature and end of civil government, and the design and spirit of civil laws, and have not well digested notions of natural equity in its utmost extent, enabling them to discharge with equal dignity to themselves, and advantage to their country, the duties of judges, magistrates, or representatives; for otherwise they are not qualified for the great duty and business of their life. May I not add here a famous saying of Socrates, "That it is very strange that all the world should agree, that the arts of judging and governing are the most important of all arts, and yet every inferior profession should be thought to require an apprenticeship to fit for it, and this none at all. Who thinks of trusting a physician that is not known to have taken due pains to qualify himself for the business? And can birth or wealth give one a right to oc-cupy the most momentous employments in the state, upon the skilful honest discharge of which all the interests of the public so greatly depend, whether he hath studied the arts of government, and thoroughly under-stand public good, and the intention of laws and magistracy, or not?"

Reading Justinian with young people, is necessary to acquaint them with the more useful part of Roman antiquities: And in general, it is fit that the books they read, in whatever language, should, so soon as possible, be such as are conversant about things of moment, the laws and customs of countries, and their foundation in reason, or the public interest of their country in particular: Such as are properest to give them a turn towards the fittest studies for them, and to qualify them to pursue these studies in the best manner. I am not for neglecting any branch of knowledge or sci-ence. But certainly, these of the highest and most extensive utility ought to be chiefly minded. And what can be more useful than expertness in judging of civil orders, laws and constitutions? Now to prepare for the reading and study which this requires, nothing more is necessary than just notions of good and fit, and their contraries in private life, or between man and man, and a strong sense of our natural indispensible obligations to the pursuit of public good: To this first part of education the other properly succeeds, as a continuation of the same study towards its perfection. But by what steps one ought first to be led to the notion of public good, and of the obligations we lie under to pursue it, hath been already observed. If

natural philosophy, and the history of mankind so divide the time of
youth as to make their principal work, and yet leave room for progress in
languages, and exercises and diversions, youth may, by inculcating on their
minds, upon proper occasions, these studies will plentifully afford to skilful masters for that purpose, a just idea of the frame and government of
the universe, and this well-grounded hope the sincerely virtuous may comfort themselves with, in consequence of a divine providence administring
all things to the best, "That in a state which is to succeed to our present
one of trial and education, not to correct or amend, but to compleat and
perfect this present system, well-improved moral powers shall be fully dignified and honoured, by being placed in circumstances adapted to their
improvements, and affording them suitable employments, and by that
means happiness of the noblest and most perfect sort the rational nature
is capable of; happiness the same in kind with that of the divine Being,
which appears evidently from his works, to consist in the perpetual exertions of his infinite power, under the direction of unerring wisdom and
compleat benevolence, in communicating or spreading happiness and perfection as far and wide as omnipotence can reach, by the wisest and
benignest management."—By inculcating this proper lesson upon youth,
on every occasion, they will soon be qualified for determining what virtue
requires or forbids, in whatever particular cases and circumstances, insomuch that after some gradual practice in comparing and examining cases
of right and wrong, the most complicated will become easy to them.

In truth, where this kind of education hath no place, youth are daily
employed in things much more intricate, perplexed and difficult. And till
it can be proved not to be the most necessary branch of education for private happiness or public service, it ought certainly to have the principal
share in the instruction of youth, whatever may be thought the fittest
method of teaching it. But what can be a more natural, easy, or pleasant
method, what can answer the main end better, which is recommending
virtue by a full view of all its charms and obligations, than that which hath
been pointed out, I cannot conceive. For till virtue is apprehended as conformity to the character, temper and will of the Author of the universe, as
what he likes and approves, and will in proper time sufficiently dignify,
honour and reward, by placing it in a state which will afford it high and

noble entertainments and exercises, after it is qualified for them by inferior employments, in its first state of schooling and probation. Till virtue is thus conceived of, all its excellence, all its strength, all its obligatory force is not understood or felt: And it is only from the nature of the divine works, which may be called his actions, that we can judge of the divine disposition, character or government, even as we can only judge of other beings by their conduct. We may indeed draw some few certain conclusions from the nature of a first cause, considered as such; and when we have found reason to infer the wisdom and goodness of the first independent mind, the source of all the beauty, excellence and perfection that are so largely dispersed through the universe, from his works and government, we may draw several necessary consequences from these his perfections, of the highest moment with relation both to our conduct and comfort. But 'tis from samples or specimens of wisdom and goodness alone that we can be fully satisfied with regard to the moral qualities of the first and universal Cause. And these indeed carry an irresistible conviction along with them; an evidence equally forcible and pleasing to the mind. Here therefore the first lessons concerning virtue ought to begin. And let it be considered by the by, how such instruction and study will qualify for the most agreeable of all entertainments in retired hours, whether forced or voluntary. None who are acquainted with such delightful, uncloying researches, and with the benign, generous emotions they excite and keep alive in the mind, with the sweetness, cheerfulness, and complacency they diffuse through the whole soul, will ever complain of the dulness, the insipidity, the tiresome circle of human life, as many of those who are called men of pleasure are forced to do, amidst the most redundant affluence. 'Tis no wonder that strangers to all enjoyments but those of sense and voluptuousness, should be so often out of humour with themselves, with all about them, with the world in general, and be constantly pursuing happiness and ever disappointed, as they plainly appear to be, by their splenetic fretting, by their flying from themselves, and choosing to live in a perpetual hurry, and their changing and shifting their pleasures as often as their sickly peevish imaginations can present them with new fancies, and thereby raise new appetites. The mind of man must have business or exercise. But the pleasures of mere sense bear no proportion to the large capacity, or the active and refined nature of our rational faculties. But who ever tired of useful study; of enquiring into nature's wisdom, order and goodness, or of imitating the Author of the world, by giving all diligence to improve his mind, and by exerting himself to the utmost of his power in doing friendly and generous offices? When did truth or virtue ever cloy, or leave remorse or disgust behind them? And the reason is, because rational are our properest, our best employments: Knowledge and virtue are the perfection of the reasonable nature: And it must hold universally true throughout all nature, whether in the material, animal, or moral world, that the most perfect state of a being is its soundest and happiest: To divide the perfection of a being from its happiness, is to separate a thing from itself: These two can no more jar than the essence of a being can differ from itself.

It cannot be expected that in a treatise of this kind, we should dwell long upon all the useful lessons that ought to be inculcated upon youth from history read in order, and which may indeed be much better taught and enforced from characters, actions and events, developing the inward springs of human conduct, and the different consequences of actions, whether with respect to private or public good, than by abstract philosophical lectures. In order to do this, it would be necessary to give some specimens of the instructions that may be drawn from a few select parts of history, by a kind of lectures upon them. But in truth, not to mention any of the ancient historians, one need only look carefully into Mr. Rollin's abridgment of ancient history, to see that the records of human affairs which are transmitted to us, however defective they may be in several respects, will, however, afford sufficient opportunities of discoursing upon, and explaining at great length, of pointing out in examples, as in a glass, all the passions of the human heart, and all their various workings in different circumstances, all the virtues, and all the vices human nature is capable of, all the snares, all the temptations, all the vicissitudes and incidents of human life: Nor is it less evident, that history will give occasion for explaining not only all the rules of prudence, justice and integrity in private oeconomy, but likewise all the rules of justice, equity and decency relative to civil states, in their transactions one with another, i.e. all the laws of nature and nations, as they are commonly called, or more properly speaking, all the laws of natural reason with regard to independent nations or governments: 'Tis in history likewise that we may best see the necessity of good civil government, in order to the greatest happiness of mankind, the terrible effects of bad or ill-constituted government; and all the various springs and causes of changes and revolutions in governments of every sort. 'Tis therefore the best political as well as moral master. The bishop of Meaux[71] and Mr. Rollin, not to name any other, have clearly pointed out every thing that ought chiefly to be attended to in history: And indeed there is hardly any truth in morals or in politics, which one may not learn from their works, with the assistance of a master acquainted with mankind, and with the ancient originals from which they have taken their remarks, as well as their facts. These authors teach us not only to attend to the moral and political facts above mentioned, but likewise to the regular succession and suite of human affairs, plainly demonstrating the superintendency of infinite wisdom, to the progress of religion in particular: In fine, they teach us to connect human affairs, and to take an united view of God's moral providence. And indeed without this direction, one must needs be lost and bewildered in the moral world, in much the same manner, as he is in the natural, who rambles from part to part, without considering all as making one whole closely joined together, i.e. without any idea of the general laws into which all the variety of phenomena in it are reducible, and their excellent final causes. The instructive writers just mentioned are (I say) so full and distinct upon the uses of history, and the profitable lessons that may and ought to be derived from it into young minds, by a skilful teacher, in an equally pleasing and useful manner, that I shall here only take notice, that I have known very young men, without having neglected languages, very well acquainted with ancient and modern geography, and such perfect masters of the more remarkable successions and changes of empires, as they are delightfully delineated to us by the bishop of Meaux in a very narrow compass, as to be able thoroughly to understand, nay feel the important affecting truths these facts demonstrate, which can't be better described than by briefly recounting a noted story of

71. [Jacques Bénigne Bossuet (1627–1704). Turnbull had in mind his *Discours sur l'histoire universelle* more than his other theological and historical works.]

Scipio Africanus, whose character, in consequence of the excellent turn proper care about his education had early given him, ought frequently to be set before the eyes of youth, to excite them who would qualify themselves early for public service, to copy after his noble example. The story is shortly this:[72] "When Scipio saw the famous city of Carthage, which had flourished seven hundred years, and might have been compared to the greatest empires, on account of the extent of its dominions both by sea and land, its mighty armies, its fleets, elephants, and riches, and that the Carthaginians were even superior to other nations by their courage and greatness of soul, as that notwithstanding their being deprived of arms and ships, they had sustained for three whole years, all the hardships and calamities of a long siege: Seeing this city entirely ruined, historians relate, that he could not refuse his tears to the unhappy fate of Carthage. He reflected that cities, nations and empires are liable to revolutions no less than particular men; that the like fate had befallen Troy, antiently so powerful, and in later times the Assyrians, Medes and Persians, whose dominions were once of so great an extent: And lastly the Macedonians, whose empire had once been so glorious throughout the world. Full of these mournful ideas, he repeated the following verses of Homer.

The day shall come, that great avenging day,
Which Troy's proud glories in the dust shall lay,
When Priam's pow'rs, and Priam's self shall fall,
And one prodigious ruin swallow all.

POPE Il. IV. 164.[73]

Thereby denouncing the future destiny of Rome, as he himself confessed to Polybius, who desired Scipio to explain himself on that occasion. He foresaw what must be the inevitable fate of Rome, if wealth should beget impatience of discipline, and in the room of ancient virtue introduce corruption, venality and dissoluteness of manners. How he came to be thus early, so knowing, both in political and military affairs; and withal so

72. [Scipio's reflections upon the defeat of Carthage, repeated throughout the eighteenth century, were originally taken from Polybius, *The Histories,* bk. 39.]
73. [Alexander Pope, trans., *The Iliad,* bk. 4, line 164.]

thoroughly generous and virtuous, as the whole of his conduct shews him to have been, we may learn from the accounts that are given of him and his education by history. Scipio, the destroyer of Carthage, was son of the famous Paulus Aemilius who conquered Perseus the last king of Macedon, and consequently grandson to that Paulus who lost his life in the battle of Cannae. He was adopted by the son of the great Scipio Africanus, and called Scipio Aemilianus, the names of the two families being so united, pursuant to the law of adoptions. Our Scipio supported with equal lustre the honour and dignity of both houses, being possessed of all the exalted qualities of the sword and gown. The whole tenor of his life, says an historian, with regard to his actions, his thoughts or words, was conspicuous for its great beauty and regularity. He distinguished himself particularly (a circumstance seldom found at that time in persons of the military profession) by his exquisite taste for polite literature and all the sciences, as well as the uncommon regard he shewed to learned men. It is universally known that he was reported to be the author of Terence's comedies, the most polite and elegant writings which the Romans could boast. We are told of Scipio, that no man could blend more happily repose and action, nor employ his leisure hours with greater delicacy and taste: Thus was he divided between arms and books, between the military labours of the camp, and the peaceful employment of the cabinet, in which he either exercised his body in toils of war, or his mind in the study of the sciences. By this he shewed, that nothing does greater honour to a person of distinction, of what quality or profession soever he be, than the adorning his soul with knowledge. Cicero speaking of Scipio, says, that he always had Xenophon's works in his hands, which are so famous for the solid and excellent instructions they contain, both in regard to war and policy. He owed this exquisite taste for polite learning and the sciences, to the excellent education which Paulus Aemilius bestowed on his children. He had put them under the ablest masters in every art, and did not spare any cost on that occasion, tho' his circumstances were very narrow. Paulus Aemilius himself was present at all their lessons, as often as the affairs of government would permit, becoming, by this means, their chief preceptor. The strict union between Polybius and Scipio finished the exalted qualities, which, by the superiority of his genius and disposition, and the excellency of his education, were already the subject of admiration. Polybius, with a great number of Achaians, whose fidelity the Romans suspected during the war with Perseus, was detained in Rome, where his merit soon attracted the eyes, and made his conversation the desire of all persons of the highest quality in that city. Scipio, when scarce eighteen, devoted himself entirely to Polybius, and considered as the greatest felicity of his life, the opportunity he had of being instructed by so great a master, whose society he preferred to all the vain and idle amusements which are generally so eagerly pursued by young persons. Polybius's first care was to inspire Scipio with an aversion for those equally dangerous and ignominious pleasures to which the Roman youth were so strongly addicted, the greatest part of them being already depraved and corrupted by the luxury and licentiousness which riches and new conquests had introduced into Rome. Scipio, during the first five years that he continued in so excellent a school, made the greatest improvement in it; and despising the levity and wantonness, as well as the pernicious examples of persons of the same age with himself, he was looked upon, even at that time, as a shining model of discretion and wisdom. From hence the transition was easy and natural to generosity, to a noble disregard of riches, and to a laudable use of them, all virtues so requisite in persons of illustrious birth, and which Scipio carried to the most exalted pitch, as appears from many instances of this kind related by Polybius, and highly worthy of being set before youth, to teach them where true dignity consists, and inflame them with a generous ambition to attain to it. It was at Scipio's return from Macedon, that he met with Polybius in Rome, and contracted the strict friendship with him, which was afterwards so beneficial to our young Roman, and did him almost as much honour in after ages as all his conquests. We find by history that Polybius lived with the two brothers, and this incident, well worth our notice, is handed down to us. One day when Scipio and Polybius were alone, the former vented himself freely to him, and complained, but in the mildest and most gentle terms, that he, in their conversations at table, always directed himself to his brother Fabius, and never to him. 'I am sensible, says he, that this indifference arises from your supposing, with all our citizens, that I am a heedless young man, and wholly averse to the taste which now prevails in Rome, because I do not plead at the bar, nor study the graces of elocution. But how should I do this? I am told perpetually, that the Romans expect a general and not an orator from the house of the Scipio's. I will confess to you, pardon the sincerity with which I reveal my thoughts, that your coldness and indifference grieve me exceedingly.' Polybius, surprized at these unexpected words, made Scipio the kindest answer, and assured the illustrious youth, that tho' he always directed himself to his brother, yet this was not out of disrespect to him, but only because Fabius was the eldest; not to mention (continued Polybius) that knowing you possessed but one soul, I conceived that I addressed both when I spoke to either of you. He then assured Scipio, that he was entirely at his command: That with regard to the Sciences, for which he discovered the happiest genius, he would have opportunities sufficient to improve himself in them from the great number of learned Grecians who resorted daily to Rome: But that as to the art of war, which was properly his profession and his favourite study, he might be of some little service to him. He had no sooner spoke these words, but Scipio grasping his hand in a kind of rapture: 'Oh! when, says he, shall I see the happy day, when disengaged from all other avocations, and living with me, you will be so much my friend, as to improve my understanding and regulate my affections? It is then I shall think myself worthy of my illustrious ancestors.' From that time, Polybius overjoyed to see so young a man breath such noble sentiments, devoted himself particularly to our Scipio, who for ever after paid him as much reverence as if he had been his father. However, Scipio did not only esteem Polybius as an excellent historian, but valued him much more, and reaped much greater advantages from him, by his being so able a warrior and so profound a politician. Accordingly he consulted him on every occasion, and always took his advice, even when he was at the head of his army, concerting in private with Polybius all the operations of the campaign, all the movements of the forces, all enterprizes against the enemy, and the several measures necessary for rendering them successful. We have already observed, that Scipio had never given into the fashionable debauchery and excesses to which the young people at Rome so wantonly abandoned themselves. But he was sufficiently compensated for this self-denial of all destructive pleasures, by the vigorous health he enjoyed all the rest of his life, which enabled

him to taste pleasures of a much purer and more exalted kind, and to perform the great actions that reflected so much glory upon him."

'Tis such education that alone can produce so glorious a pattern of
every great and amiable quality. And so soon as youth are able to enter into
the excellency of such a character; they will have an example fixed on their
minds that will at once give their ambition a very laudable turn, and direct
them how to satisfy it. It was instruction in human affairs, knowledge of
mankind, deep insight into all the movements of the human breast, and
all the operations of moral causes, gathered from facts, that qualified
Scipio very timeously for serving his country with such prudence and dignity, whether as a statesman or as a general. And therefore history, applied
to these equally substantial and delightful uses, ought to make a main part
in the institution of youth. Let it not however be imagined, that I would
have any of the sciences, any part of philosophy overlooked in education.
As for natural philosophy, it hath been already observed, that it ought to
go hand in hand with moral history: And as for the other sciences, a little
reflection upon the scope and uses of them, will soon shew every thinking
person that one cannot on the one hand be qualified for them, till he is
pretty well acquainted with the history of mankind, and hath treasured up
in his judgment several of the more important truths it teaches, and it
alone can confirm. Moral philosophy may be divided into the preliminary
and more general part, which explains the constituent properties or powers of human nature, and their various motions or operations; all the faculties, powers, appetites and affections implanted in the breast of man,
and their objects, tendencies, connexions, bearings and effects, and all the
perfections or imperfections, virtues or vices belonging to them. But how
abstruse, how abstract, dry and laborious will lectures of this kind be, till
youth have been led by real examples to the knowledge of moral facts and
their causes? And how easy and pleasant, on the other side, will such reading or study be to those, who having often seen the chief properties of human nature reflected on them by examples, as it were, in several mirrors,
can immediately recal to their memories pregnant authorities for all that
true philosophy can teach concerning mankind? As for the other subsequent and more particular part, which first of all classes under proper gen-

eral heads the dictates of reason with relation to all the affairs of war and peace, and then enters into an accurate examination and comparison of different forms of civil government, and the maxims of policy, can it proceed solidly one step without historical examples; or can one be at all prepared for it till he hath carefully read the history of different nations and governments, and is considerably versed in the public affairs of states, which are at once the subjects of this philosophy, and the experiments from which alone it can draw any certain conclusions? It is highly necessary that the best writers on the laws of nature and nations, and upon politics, both ancient and modern, should be carefully read and well understood by all who would be duly prepared for the higher stations and services in their country: We are far from excluding such study from education: On the contrary, we regret that it is so much neglected. The question now under consideration is not whether it ought to have place, but when and what previous reading and instruction is requisite to it. And that very considerable acquaintance with history, and practice in drawing moral or political inferences from history is necessary to qualify for this study, seems to be indisputable, seeing it is from facts or experiments that moral doctrines must be deduced, as well as physiological truths. Every one is ready, now at last, to own that physical explications or rules, not founded upon and inferred from real facts in nature, are mere romance. But certainly it must be no less true with regard to morals and politics, that explications of effects, or rules for private or public conduct, not founded in and deduced from real truths or facts relative to mankind and human societies, are also mere vision. And which of the two is the most dangerous delusion we may leave to any considering person to decide. For all that is to be determined in this point is briefly, whether mistakes in mechanical or in moral attempts are likely to be of the most fatal consequence. Let youth in an orderly regular manner be instructed in the progress of human affairs, and inured to draw proper conclusions from them, first moral, and afterwards political ones, in proportion as their minds open and strengthen: And let the books put into their hands for teaching or improving them in languages, be such chiefly as have human affairs and duties for their subjects, such as Cicero's books of laws and offices, &c. and after them Justinian's institutes, and we shall soon find youth qualified to read with understanding, any of the best writers on natural law or on politics. But carry them without such preparation directly to systems of morals and politics, and you will find them sadly embarassed and difficulted, and proportionably displeased and fretted. The sciences have their natural order, and in vain do we attempt to get up to the top but by the gradual steps of nature's appointment. There is indeed a science[74] which bears very nearly the same relation to morals (by which let me be understood to mean the whole of philosophy relating to human nature and human affairs) that mathematics bear to natural philosophy, because, as the latter consists in investigating or demonstrating what properties of lines, figures, surfaces, solids, &c. may, must, or cannot co-exist [as when it is proved that a triangle or a circle must have such and such other properties] so the former consists in investigating or demonstrating what moral qualities may co-exist, what must co-exist, and what are absolutely incompatible: And therefore, as the one is a key to the natural world, so will the other, in proportion as it is cultivated, prove a key to the moral world. In other words, moral philosophy duly prosecuted, must be a mixed science, consisting of facts, and reasonings from facts, and abstract truths of the nature above mentioned conjointly, in like manner as physiology is a science mixed of observations or experiments, and reasonings from them, and mathematical truths conjointly. But having no orderly systems of these moral abstract universal truths for our assistance in moral enquiries, as we have of mathematical ones, to help us in physical researches, it cannot be introduced into the schools formally. The science we are now speaking of is widely different from that wild, pedantic jargon that hath long had too great a share in some schools and universities, under the name of metaphysic or ontology, of which we have already had occasion to speak our sentiments. But since we have as yet no system of the kind, it is needless to debate here what place it ought to have in education. Any one, however, who has any notion of what it must mean or propose to do, will immediately perceive,

---

74. My lord Verulam calls this science, *philosophia prima & universalis*, primary and universal philosophy; and from him may we learn the nature and use of it, and the way of improving, carrying it on, and applying it to the other sciences. [Francis Bacon, *The Advancement of Learning*, 2.3.1.]

that it is not a study for novices, or raw unexperienced minds, but requires a large stock of distinct ideas, and a solidity of judgment, which must be the fruit of large acquaintance with nature, with human nature in particular. And indeed one of the best lessons that can be given to youth, whether with regard to progress in science, or to conduct in life, is to teach them to receive maxims, aphorisms, or general canons with great deliberation and caution. But, by the by, they are much mistaken who think, that whatever use even true maxims may be of in demonstrating truths after they are found out, they can be but of very little use to help invention. Were this the proper place for it, it might be easily made appear, that one of the best exercises for the improvement of invention, and the augmentation of science, is attentive practice in comparing and developing maxims of the truth of which we are sure. For upon a narrow scrutiny into any axiom of importance, it will be found to contain many truths in it which were not perceived when it was at first found to be true: When we begin to lay it open and spread it out, treasures that before lay hid in it gradually appear. There are in reality, as a great philosopher has well observed, but a very few truths in the world which make totally separate or distinct propositions. The greater part of every science is but one single maxim or two, diffused or spread out. To prove this, many moral maxims which are readily admitted and appear very simple, might be named, which, if duly attended to, would quickly put a period to several very warm disputes, and many very prevailing falshoods; as for instance, "that the knowledge of creatures must be progressive, or that moral experience must precede knowledge of rules that can only be deduced from many experiences": "Habit or propensity presupposes not only a known object but repeated acts": "Affections must have objects, or cannot be exercised without them": But however that may be, the point in question remains indisputable, namely, that the best way of instructing in the affairs of mankind, is to begin with reading history, and drawing proper conclusions from the examples history furnishes; and to proceed to the profounder treatises on morals, after youth are very well acquainted with reasonings from facts, and have their minds richly stocked with clear ideas of human affairs, conveyed to them by examples. This certainly is the proper and natural order, if ideas can only be got from experience, and if we must have clear ideas before we can reason about them.

As for mathematics, it hath been already hinted, that some time should be allotted for regular instruction in that science, so far as is necessary at least for understanding the principles of mechanism, and comprehending the use of this science, as a key to nature, for the investigation of unknown natural causes, or the resolution of effects into known causes. And another reason hath likewise been suggested for making instruction in this science an early part of education, which is the natural tendency that a little practice in this elegant orderly science has to beget a habit of attention, to form the reasoning habit, and a taste of and liking to order and method. Now the only part of philosophy that remains to be considered, is logic; and of it we have had occasion elsewhere to say enough to shew that it is absurd to think of teaching it till youth have not only very well furnished minds, but have been pretty well practised in all the different species of reasoning. Let it only be added here, that the nature and degrees of moral, probable, or historical evidence, tho' left out of what is commonly called logic, or but very superficially treated of in it, is, if not the most essential part of a science that merits to be called the art of reasoning, at least a very useful science in itself: And it can never be more successfully taught than in reading history, by leading students to consider and examine attentively and accurately the evidence of particular facts, and the assent due to various degrees of historical evidence, in proportion to the foundation each degree has in the general principles of probability. Plato considered logic as the finishing science in education. He illustrates the nature and use of it, by representing it as designed to give youth, after practice in various sciences, and all the different kinds of reasoning, demonstrative and probable, as from a summit, a view of the unity of the sciences: And as for that part of it which teaches disputing, or rather wrangling, he calls it teaching young people to delight in barking at one another like young whelps; and he pronounces it most pernicious in its tendency, in consequence of the dogmatical temper, or the itch of puzling, confounding, and perplexing by subtleties, it naturally has an influence to beget. Some may think we have been too long in delineating the sciences, which ought to make up liberal education: And others may think we have not been particular enough in our description of some of them. But the objection I am surest of meeting with is, How can there or will there be place for all these things? And therefore, tho' some reply hath been elsewhere made to this objection, let me add here. 1. That what I have represented as the main instruction youth ought to have in view, is, in reality but one coherent lesson, that does not consist of many separate independent parts, but of two branches only, which are in their nature very closely united, the knowledge of the laws of our material system, and their final causes; and the properties of human nature and their laws. 2. Whatever be gained or neglected, if youth be not instructed in nature so far as to be able to carry on the study of it with equal understanding and pleasure, in proportion as they have leisure for it, when they leave the schools; and so far instructed in the nature, duties and rights of mankind, as to be fit, not only for private life, but for advancing by themselves in that knowledge without great perfection in which they must be absolutely unfit for public service, the most important point in education is not accomplished. 3. That while the sciences we have mentioned are left out in education, nothing but mere words can be minded, for there remains nothing else to mind; and to say that mere words should make the principal, or indeed more than the lowest scope in education, is directly to prefer words to things, i.e. pedantry, if there be any such thing, to real knowledge. 4. In the last place, it is contrary to many known facts or experiments, to say that a few hours a-day are not sufficient, if wisely managed from their tenderest years, to advance pupils very considerably in the knowledge of languages. And what is to be done with the rest of their precious time?

To proceed: It surely can't be objected that we have left out religion. For we have endeavoured to shew, that even natural philosophy, if not employed to lead youth to a just notion of the perfections of the one Lord of the universe, and of our duties resulting from thence, falls far short of its best aim and noblest use, and is indeed little better than what is justly called in contempt cockle-shellship. The great design for which we have recommended instructing youth early in natural philosophy, i.e. in the laws of nature and final causes, is the moral use that may be made of this science, together with the improvement or extension of human power, which can only be brought about by advancing or cultivating the knowledge of nature. Youth ought to be taught and inured to ascend from instances of perfect wisdom and goodness in the creation, to the first Author of all beauty and good, and to pay the worship of heart that is due to such a Being: But above all, to inculcate upon themselves their obligations, arising from their relation to him, and from their interest, in consequence of his all-perfect government, [which must be in favour of virtue, and by consequence proportionably to the disadvantage of vice, in the sum and final result of things], to imitate the perfections of the Creator in wisdom and goodness; or to give all diligence to improve their moral powers, and to do good as they have opportunity, for this is the sum of religion, virtue and human duty. Now a mind thoroughly convinced of these truths, and deeply affected by them, is well prepared for instruction in the excellence of the Christian revelation. 1. For such a one will attend to it without prejudice, and consequently will soon see, that all the obligations Christianity represents as moral, all the duties it requires, whether with respect to God, our fellow-creatures, or ourselves, are perpetually binding, as resulting necessarily from the very nature of God, and our relation to him and to one another: And consequently, that were it possible to refute the external evidence with which the Christian revelation is accompanied, yet we could not shake off our obligation to these duties. Good men will not easily be induced to disregard a pretence to revelation which lays the stress of our acceptance with God where reason itself places it, i.e. where it must lie, in consequence of the divine immutable perfections: And whatever encouragement Christianity gives to those, who having long continued in their vitious courses, may, through their awful apprehensions of the divine rectitude and justice, despair of recovering the divine favour even by a change of life, it gives no ground of hope or comfort to any but those who become sincere lovers of virtue, and accordingly give due pains to advance and improve in it. This none of its enemies have dared to say: Nor can they, so strict, so pure are the morals Christianity teaches and commands, as the will of God for our salvation in a future state. 2. Those who have just conceptions of God, and the moral obligations resulting from thence, cannot have any objection against the glorious hopes Christianity sets before us, of rewards to duly improved moral powers, in a future state to succeed to this our present state of discipline and culture, by placing or employing them suitably there. For this is the very doctrine reason teaches us to infer from the divine rectitude. And it is in vain for vitious men to think of eluding severe suffering or punishment in a future state, for their neglect or prostitution of their moral powers, under the government of a Being who is infinitely perfect: Since an administration by which vice will suffer in the sum of things, in proportion to its demerit, is, in reality but another expression for an administration in favour of virtue, or in which men shall be treated according to their advancements in moral perfection. 3. And one who is well fixed in these principles, which are the foundations of religion, that is, without which there can be no religion, and it is absurd to talk of revelation, will not quarrel with Christianity on account of the positive duties it requires. One who is persuaded of the utility in respect of the public, and of the fitness in the nature of things, of public worship, will not find fault with Christianity for setting apart a stated time for cessation from labour to the brutes and the working part of mankind, on which God may be decently worshipped, and all ranks of men may have opportunity of fixing and enforcing their common duties upon their minds, and of being instructed in them. This Christian ordinance, if not absolutely a moral command, is so near a-kin to moral laws, that it is evidently in its nature a very proper mean of keeping alive in our minds a sense of divine providence, and all moral obligations. Nor are the other two positive rites or ordinances of Christianity more remote from moral duties, being likewise excellent means of improvement in virtue. Is not baptism a very proper mean of representing to parents their duties towards their children, and of bringing them under a known or declared public obligation to the diligent performance of them? And the Lord's supper being nothing else but a serious grateful commemoration of all the blessed doctrines, i.e. all the blessed and glorious hopes set before us by Christianity thro' Jesus Christ, who came to call us to virtue and glory, that we being made partakers of the divine nature, through holiness, might be qualified to dwell with God for ever, in the happy state he hath purchased, and is gone to prepare for the sincerely good, what can be more conducive, either to the improvement or comfort of Christians? of reasonable agents? It is an act of grateful praise, than which nothing in itself can be more joyous; and it is naturally a strong way of enforcing upon the minds of those who believe the truth of Christianity, a lively sense of all the obligations they lie under to the sedulous practice of true piety and virtue? All these therefore, which are the only institutions of Christianity that can be called positive, are indeed, in a true view of them, if not precisely of the same class with moral duties, yet very nearly allied to them, as moral means of improvement to every good affection or disposition of the soul.

4. He who is persuaded of the intrinsic excellence of the Christian institution, will not hesitate long about giving his assent to the external evidence it offers of its divine authority. For the works Jesus Christ wrought and gave his apostles power to work, bear the same relation to his doctrines that experiments have in natural philosophy to the doctrines or conclusions inferred from them, or which they are brought to prove, i.e. they were specimens or samples analogous in kind, and commensurate in quantity or moment to the knowledge and power he pretended to as a superior teacher, authorised by God to instruct mankind in several important truths relating to God, providence, virtue, vice, and a future state. By his works are meant the extraordinary cures he performed upon the sick and diseased of all sorts, his healing the lame, the dumb, and the blind, his instantaneously changing men's tempers and dispositions, his insight into men's most secret thoughts, his predictions of future events, his command over air, and sea, and every element, and above all, his raising the dead, and his rising from the dead himself the third day, as he had foretold, his ascension into heaven, and sending down miraculous gifts and powers upon his apostles, who were to be employed in propagating his gospel, as he had promised, to qualify them for that important business, and support them in it, and gain them credit. These works have been shewn to have the closest connexion with the truth of Christ's doctrines, and together with the evidences he gave of his piety and integrity, to make a natural, proper and full evidence of his mission.[75] And as for the credibility of

---

75. See a philosophical enquiry into the connexion between the works and doctrines of Jesus Christ, by G. T. LL. D. [George Turnbull, *A Philosophical Enquiry Concerning the Connexion Betwixt the Doctrines and Miracles of Jesus Christ* (London: Willock, 1731).]

the histories recording the works and doctrines of Christ and his Apostles, they stand on the same footing with other histories, and have indeed been so often proved to be above all scepticism, if historical evidence be at all admitted, that the disputers against Christianity do not choose to attack it on that side. In fine, the rational instruction of children in the genuine principles of Christianity, cannot be neglected by Christian parents or preceptors, without sinning against what they know and believe to be their indispensible duty: But certainly sound instruction in the principles of natural religion is a necessary preparation for it. And history will at least afford frequent proper occasions of shewing the utility, the absolute necessity of a public religion, and of evincing the excellence of true Christianity above all other religions that have ever been heard of in the world. That the persuasion of a divine providence, and a future state of rewards and punishments, is one of the strongest incitements to virtue, and one of the most forcible restraints from vice, can hardly be doubted of: And that public worship is necessary to support a general sense of religion, or of God's providence, and a future state of rewards and punishments is very evident: Nor is it less so, that there can be no public worship without some received form and some established external rites: 'Tis as absurd to talk of public religious service without some settled manner and method of expressing or performing it, as to talk of languages without words. But what cult that ever obtained in the world under the notion of religion, except the Christian institution, when kept free or reformed from all the abominable corruptions with which it hath been and still is in some countries depraved, was not rather hurtful to society, than suited to the ends for which public religion is requisite to society? Or what can be pointed out on the one hand as wanting in true Christianity to make it a useful, a perfect public belief and worship; or on the other, as burdensom, superfluous, or liable to superstitious perversion? Christianity abounds with motives to encourage to virtue, and to deter from vice; nay none stronger can be added to them. And as its positive rites or ordinances are but few, so none can be imagined that are less liable to superstitious abuse? History will furnish frequent opportunities of illustrating and confirming these important observations to young students. And from the truths of natural religion and true morality, which it is the chief design of education to teach and inculcate, the transition to the doctrines and precepts of Christianity is very easy and natural: For as Christ himself, and all his apostles tell us, love must be the fulfilment of all divine laws, whether natural or revealed: These two commandments, saith Christ, love God with all your heart and all your soul, and love your neighbour as your self, are the sum of religion: Upon these two hang the law and the prophets. He that dwelleth in love, saith one apostle, dwelleth in God, for God is love: And charity, saith another, is the bond of perfectness, and endureth for ever. Christianity is indeed nothing else but the religion or law of nature carried to its utmost perfection. Christ came not to destroy, void or commute this eternal unchangeable law, but to compleat, to fulfil it, by rescuing it from the subtle evasions and distinctions with which it had been rendered a mere form of godliness by the Jewish casuists, without the power, the reality thereof, by pointing out its full spiritual extent; by shewing, in particular, that tho' it is injustice alone, that civil courts can conveniently punish, and tho', in a certain sense, justice is of anterior and more perfect obligation by the law of nature than benevolence, yet without benevolence reigning in the heart, and by consequence actuating the life, and keeping all other passions and appetites in due subordination to it, no man can be acceptable to God, or pleasing in his sight, God being perfect benevolence, guided by unerring wisdom in the exertions of his unbounded, uncontroulable power. Indeed, in respect of the stress Christianity lays on benevolence, it is Christ's new and peculiar law.

In short, there is no moral or political truth, which a judicious reader of history with young people may not find frequent opportunity of explaining and confirming to them. And so much am I persuaded that we ought to be very well acquainted with facts or examples, before we are carried by our teachers to systems, that I think it were to be wished that even our systems of physiology begun with the facts or experiments, and ended with the doctrines, instead of formally laying down the truths to be proved, and then bringing experiments to prove them. The method we recommend in both philosophies would inure one from the beginning to the only true way of getting real knowledge, which is by searching into facts, without prepossession in favours of any particular hypothesis or system; a fatal obstacle to science, not yet entirely banished from amongst enquirers into nature, as clear as Lord Verulam hath long ago made it, and as generally confessed as it now is, that there is no other way of developing nature, or of learning rules of arts or of conduct from her, but by attending carefully, and without any biass to her operations and effects. Neither mechanical nor moral truths will yield to our fancy or caprice, but will remain inflexibly what they are, whatever we may imagine or dream them to be: And it is as absurd to think of executing moral ends, otherwise than by the means, and according to the order of nature's appointment, as to think of working upon water, air, or any other body, in a way repugnant, or not suited to its properties and laws. Let youth therefore be inured to study mankind in real life or history, and be cautioned against attempting to form theories, whether of moral or natural things by the force of imagination, or otherwise than by endeavouring, by a close and accurate unbiassed scrutiny into facts, to find out the real qualities and laws of the Author of nature's establishment, by which all his works are governed, each agreeably to its nature and kind. Be not afraid of shewing mankind to youth in the worst colours they have ever appeared. 'Tis long indeed since there was just ground for the Roman Satyrist's complaint and exclamation.

> Sed jam serpentum major concordia: parcit
> Cognatis maculis similis fera. Quando leoni
> Fortior eripuit vitam leo? Quo nemore unquam
> Expiravit aper majoris dentibus apri?
> Indica tigris agit rabidâ cum tigride pacem
> Perpetuam: saevis inter se convenit ursis.
> Ast homini ferrum lethale incude nefandâ
> Produxisse parum est, &c.[76]

---

76. [Juvenal, Satires, 15.159–66: "But in these days there is more amity among serpents than among men; wild beasts are merciful to beasts spotted like themselves. When did the stronger lion ever take the life of the weaker? In what wood did a boar ever breathe his last under the tusks of a boar bigger than himself? The fierce tigress of India dwells in perpetual peace with her fellow; grim bears live in harmony with bears. But man finds it all too little to have forged the deadly blade on an impious anvil."]

Yet human nature is well constituted for society: There is no pleasure we are capable of, which does not some way *lean or hearken to our kind,* as our own admirable poet tells us.

The same Roman satyrist gives us, in the same satyr, a very true description of the social sense and propension, deeply interwoven with our frame and constitution.

> ——— ——— ——— *Mollissima corda*
> *Humano generi dare se natura fatetur,*
> *Quae lacrymas dedit. Haec nostri pars optima sensûs.*
> *Plorare ergo jubet causam lugentis amici,*
> *Squalloremque rei, pupillum ad jura vocantem*
> *Circumscriptorem, cujus manantia fletu*
> *Ora puellares faciunt incerta capilli.*
> *Naturae imperio gemimus, cùm funus adultae*
> *Virginis occurrit, vel terrà clauditur infans,*
> *Et minor igne rogi. Quis enim bonus, & face dignus*
> *Arcanâ, qualem Cereris vult esse Sacerdos,*
> *Ulla aliena sibi credat mala? Separat hoc nos*
> *A grege mutorum, atque ideò venerabile soli*
> *Sortiti ingenium, divinorumque capaces,*
> *Atque exercendis capiendisque artibus apti*
> *Sensum à coelesti demissum traximus arce,*
> *Cujus egent prona, & terram spectantia. Mundi*
> *Principio indulsit communis conditor illis*
> *Tantùm animas, nobis animum quoque; mutuus ut nos*
> *Affectus petere auxilium, & praestare juberet,*
> *Dispersos trahere in populum, migrare vetusto*
> *De nemore, & proavis habitatas linquere sylvas;*
> *Aedificare domos, laribus conjungere nostris*
> *Tectum aliud, tutos vicino limine somnos*
> *Ut collata daret fiducia; protegere armis*
> *Lapsum, aut ingenti nutantem vulnere civem;*

Communi dare signa tubâ, defendier iisdem
Turribus, atque unâ portarum clave teneri.

JUV. Sat. 15.[77]

As savage, ferocious, or cruel as men have, or may become, nothing is wanting in our frame to draw us to friendship and society, or impel us to compassion and benevolence. Even revenge itself is a social passion in its origin and rise, being nothing else but indignation roused by wrong or injury. Shew youth what a large share communication and participation have in all our enjoyments, or how largely all our pleasures partake of something relative to others. To be made for society is to be made for mutual giving and receiving. And the abilities and wants of men are so dispersed as to lay a necessary foundation for mutual assistance and intercourse. As it is the difference of products in different regions and climates that gave rise to external commerce, and makes it necessary; so universally in every district of mankind, men have different talents and powers, that they might mutually stand in need one of another, and have each something to give and something to receive.—Many united labours are necessary to make any one live tolerably happy in the world: And nothing gives pleasure or satisfaction to the human mind, equal to that which accom-

77. [Juvenal, *Satires,* 15.131–58: "When Nature gave tears to man, she proclaimed that he was tender-hearted; and tenderness is the best quality in man. She therefore bids us weep for the misery of a friend upon his trial, or when a ward whose streaming cheeks and girlish locks raise a doubt as to his sex brings a defrauder into court. It is at Nature's behest that we weep when we meet the bier of a full-grown maiden, or when the earth closes over a babe too young for the funeral pyre. For what good man, what man worthy of the mystic torch, and such as the priest of Ceres would wish him to be, believes that any human woes concern him not? It is this that separates us from the dumb herd; and it is for this that we alone have had allotted to us a nature worthy of reverence, capable of divine things, fit to acquire and practice the arts of life, and that we have drawn from on high that gift of feeling which is lacking to the beasts that grovel with eyes upon the ground. To them in the beginning of the world our common maker gave only life; to us he gave souls as well, that fellow-feeling might bid us ask or proffer aid, gather scattered dwellers into a people, desert the primeval groves and woods inhabited by our forefathers, build houses for ourselves, with others adjacent to our own, that a neighbour's threshold, from the confidence that comes of union, might give us peaceful slumbers; shield with arms a fallen citizen, or one staggering from a grievous wound, give battle signals by a common trumpet, and seek protection inside the same city walls, and behind gates fastened by a single key."]

panies a sense of love and esteem, merited by well employed power.—
Nature hath abundantly furnished mankind with the means of happiness,
but hath left it to be their own purchase by united skilful industry: For
industry is the purchaser of every good in life; but single industry can go
but a very little way.—Finally, the equal regular circulation of happiness
greatly depends upon the manner in which neighbourhoods or districts of
men unite and confederate together for mutual relief, support and furtherance. Now this is to be made for society: And to what a noble height of
happiness and grandeur do not well constituted and well regulated societies arise? Or what, in fine, is wanting to render any part of the earth
happy, but good constitutions or orders equitably executed, i.e. good civil
government? Nature, we may see, from the history of mankind in all ages
of the world, hath laid a necessity of society in human nature, and pointed
out by its lines the proper kind of it: For mankind are, and always have
been an aristocracy, consisting of the few able to consult, debate and direct, and the many able to execute by their labour and strength; ever ready
and willing to put and keep themselves under the direction of the former,
while they consult and pursue the common good, but impatient of op-
pressive servitude, and prone to spurn and kick when they are despised or
maletreated. History will afford opportunity of observing how the first
governments were formed, and of attending to what may properly[78] be

78. Property is the natural foundation of power, as wisdom and virtue are of authority. Hence the natural foundation of every civil government is laid in the distribution
of the lands or territories belonging to it, to the several members of it. If the prince is
proprietor of the lands, as in some eastern governments, such princes will be absolute;
for all who hold the lands, holding them of the prince, and enjoying them at his will
and pleasure, are so subject to his will, that they are in a condition of slaves, not of free
subjects. *They hang on him by the teeth.* If the property is divided among a few men, the
rest holding of them, and under them as vassals, the power of government will be in the
hands of those few men, as a nobility, whatever authority may be lodged in the hands
of one or more persons, for the sake of unity in counsel and action: But if the property
be generally divided near equally among all the members of the society, the true power
of such government will naturally be in all the members of that society, whatever form
of union they may have, for the direction of the whole as a political body.

See this political truth of great moment and extent fully confirmed and illustrated
by historical examples in Mr. Harrington's Oceana, and his other political tracts. See
likewise a most ingenious dissertation by Mr. Lowman on the civil government of the

called the generative principle of empire, the progress of industry and property. Readers of history can't indeed be too often put in mind to observe how enlargement of, or changes in property, create, enlarge, fix, or change dominion.—But above all, let youth be taught to consider, that however much the regular distribution or circulation of human happiness must, in the nature of things, depend upon the constitution and administration of the political bodies into which men of the same regions coalesce; yet the best form of civil government is a lesson that cannot be learned without long experience, from many changes and revolutions in human affairs. Experience must precede every art, because it is experience alone that can lead to any art. But the art of government is at the same time the most important and the most difficult of all arts, or that which requires the longest previous experience and the profoundest thinking to compleat it; nor can it be otherwise: For arts must be difficult or remote from invention, in proportion as they are complex, and depend on the knowledge of many springs and causes. But what is more complex than the right formation and modelling of civil society, in order to gain and secure all the noble purposes of civil union? The political science can no more be perfected without long and attentive observation of human nature in various appearances and situations, than the theory of the moon, for instance, can be compleated, without long and careful attention to her revolutions and appearances. 'Tis no wonder, therefore, that it is so long before we see any thing in the history of the world approaching to a perfect form of civil government; especially, if we add to this the other consideration just mentioned, viz. That dominion will always be proportionable to property and vary with it. Let youth carefully attend to all the different forms of government that have ever been known in the world; their establishments, their changes and revolutions, the diseases they fell into, and their decays, ruins, or deaths; and hence let them form to themselves sure and solid maxims concerning civil polity.[79] But let not the course of

---

Hebrews, and Turnbull's remarks upon the chapters about government, in Heineccius's system of the laws of nature and nations.

79. 'Tis a usual piece of vanity (says a very ingenious writer) in the historians of every nation to represent the original constitutions of their respective states, as founded on

historical reading stop, till it comes gradually to modern times, and brings youth home into their own country, and shews them the various changes it has gone through, and explains to them its present constitution, laws and interests, and they are able to apply to it all the political truths and rules they had previously learned from more ancient histories. "It would be strange (says a most judicious author, whom we have often quoted in this essay)[80] to suppose an English gentleman should be ignorant of the law of his country. This, whatever station he is in, is so requisite, that from a justice of the peace to a minister of state, I know no place he can well fill without it. I do not mean the chicane, or wrangling and captious part of the law: A gentleman whose business is to seek for the true measure of right and wrong, and not the arts how to avoid doing the one, and secure himself in doing the other, ought to be as far from such a study of the law, as he is diligently to apply himself to that wherein he may be serviceable to his country. And to that purpose, I think the right way for a gentleman to study our law, which he does not design for his calling, is, to take a view of our English constitution and government, in the ancient books of the common law; and some more modern writers, who out of them have given an account of this government. And having got a true idea of that, then to read our history, and with it join in every king's reign the laws then made. This will give an insight into the reason of our statutes, and shew the true ground upon which they came to be made, and what weight they ought to have." By careful instruction in true politics from ancient history, one will be soon prepared for reading the history of his own country with intelligence: Prepared for examining into the excellence or defects of its government, and for judging of the fitness or unfitness of its orders and laws.

---

deep laid systems and plans of policy, in which they imagine that they discover the utmost reach of human wisdom; whereas in truth they are often the effects of downright chance, and produced by the force of certain circumstances, or the simple dictates of nature itself, out of a regard to some present expediency, and with little providence to the future. Such was the original of the celebrated Gothic government, that was formerly spread all over Europe, and tho' much defaced by time, is still distinguishable here (Britain): Let not this important observation which history abundantly confirms, be overlooked.

80. [Locke, *Education*, §187.]

It is not so proper to begin with it, because one will better learn the true maxims of politics from distant histories, in reading which he is not in so much danger from any false biass or prejudice: And he will then proceed with far greater advantage to the study of his own country's constitution, history and laws, when he hath got a measure or standard, the justness of which he is fully convinced of by repeated proofs and trials, to compare and judge them by.

But it is in vain to attempt pointing out all the noble lessons that may be best taught from history. Let me therefore only add once more, That the first and last, the great point to be aimed at from reading history with youth, is to fix upon their minds just notions of true worth, true greatness, and solid happiness; or to teach them to place merit where it only lies, not in birth, not in beauty, not in riches, not in external shew and magnificence, not in voluptuousness, but in a firm adherence to truth and rectitude or virtue; in an untainted heart, that would not pollute or prostitute its integrity in any degree, to gain the highest worldly honours, or to ward off the greatest worldly misery. This is true magnanimity: And he alone can be truly happy, as well as truly great, who can look down with generous contempt upon every thing that would tempt him to recede in the smallest degree from the paths of rigid honesty, candour and veracity.

> *Es modicus voti, presso lare, dulcis amicis;*
> *Jam nunc astringas; jam nunc granaria laxes;*
> *Inque luto fixum possis transcendere nummum;*
> *Nec gluto sorbere salivam Mercurialem?*
> *Haec mea sunt, teneo, cum verè dixeris: Esto*
> *Liberque ac sapiens, Praetoribus ac Jove dextro.*
> *Sin tu, cum fueris nostrae paulò ante farinae,*
> *Pelliculam veterem retines, & fronte politus*
> *Astutam vapido servas sub pectore vulpem;*
> *Quae dederam suprà, repeto, funemque reduco.*
> *Nil tibi concessit ratio: digitum exere, peccas,*
> *Et quid tam parvum est? Sed nullo thure litabis,*

Haereat in stultis brevis ut semuncia recti.
Haec miscere nefas: ——— ———

PERSEUS, Sat. 5.[81]

The great lesson in life is, that virtue alone is true honour and solid durable happiness: It is not till this persuasion is deeply rooted in the heart, that one can be said to be well instructed, educated or formed. Our senses rush up fast to maturity, and their objects are ever assailing them. And therefore it is the business of education early to fortify and strengthen reason, that it may timeously be able to bear head against all the allurements of sense, all the specious promises and sollicitations of vice. But he alone can do so, who daily looks narrowly into his heart and life, and calls his appetites and conduct to a strict account, and seriously inculcates upon himself this lesson, which were it not true, 'tis indeed no great matter what else be true or false, That worth, merit and happiness are proportionable to one's ability and disposition to do good. By ability, I mean not the external abilities which depend not upon us, but upon providence; but moral abilities, absolutely in our power to acquire, the ability of knowing what virtue or the public good requires, in whatsoever circumstances of life, and readiness and firmness to pursue it in our sphere, and to the utmost of our power, through whatever opposition, and in spite of whatever temptations from the side of pleasures, or whatever menaces and dangers. This lesson, in other words, amounts to this, That virtue is its own reward. By which saying is not understood, that virtue is to have no other reward but the

---

81. [Persius, *Satires,* 5.109–22: "Are you moderate in your desires, modest in your establishment, and kindly to your friends? Can you now close your granaries, and now again throw them open? Can you pass by a coin sticking in the mud, without gulping down your saliva in your greed for treasure? When you can truly say, 'Yes, all these things are mine,' I will call you a free and a wise man, under the favour of praetors and of Jupiter; but if, after having been but a little ago of the same stuff as ourselves, you hold to your old skin, and though your brow be smooth, still keep a crafty fox in that vapid heart of yours, I take back what I have just granted you and pull in my rope. Not one point has reason granted you; put out your finger (and what can be a slighter thing than that?) and you go wrong: not all the incense in the world will win leave from the Gods that one short half-ounce of wisdom may find lodgment in the head of a fool! To mingle the two things is sacrilege."]

pleasing consciousness of acting a worthy part that accompanies it here; no reward in another life: But that there are no satisfactions equal to, or comparable with virtuous or rational exercises; and that virtuous dispositions, or well improved moral powers, cannot be rewarded, cannot receive happiness or enjoyment suited, proportioned to their nature, but from their exercises and employments about proper objects: And that as virtue gives pleasure here in proportion to the improvements it makes, far beyond all that mere sense can yield, in the most advantageous circumstances of outward enjoyment; so in a state to come, it shall be so placed as its improvements require, i.e. be placed in circumstances that shall afford it business or employment proportioned to its capacity, and by means thereof the highest satisfaction. This is the only happiness a virtuous mind can imagine for itself, or fix its desires and hopes upon: All other enjoyments are low and mean in one's view, in proportion to the strength and excellence of his virtue. And this is the happiness true philosophy and true religion promise to virtue: It is with this glorious hope it feeds, comforts and strengthens itself. In keeping the precepts of moral rectitude, the precepts of God, who is perfect virtue, there is a high present reward, that animates and supports virtue, as being a presage of the higher rewards awaiting it in another world, when it is become qualified by proper culture here, for higher employments there, or a more exalted sphere of activity. The glory that grace or virtue aspires, and only can aspire after, is grace or virtue made perfect, and suitably placed for exerting all its benignity and excellence. If this be not true, 'tis no matter what is, or is not truth; for unless this be true, religion, virtue, reason, public good and obligations to it, are empty names, and there is nothing truly desirable in existence: All nature is by the opposite opinion laid under a most horrible gloom, that men intoxicated by gross pleasures may forget, but that thinking will only increase and thicken. Let therefore the excellence of virtue, and the glorious hopes which virtue naturally calls up in every mind where it dwells, and gradually invigorates as itself grows and improves, be the subjects of the principal instructions given to youth. Nor will any one who is acquainted with the almost infinitely various ways in which this comfortable lesson hath been illustrated by ancient and modern writers, be afraid of surfeiting youth with it. In truth, the beauty of virtue never palls upon its admirers, but on the contrary, the more they consider and examine it, the more they see of its worth and truth: It gains approbation at its first appearance, but to discover all its charms and excellencies, requires deep and profound searching. And indeed all the ingenious arts, when they depart from or forsake virtue, become nauseous or insipid: It is in ministring to virtue, or setting forth her real beauty, that their dignity and value chiefly consists: Or rather, it is some just view of some part of the excellence of virtue, or of the deformity of vice, that makes what is called truly beautiful art, whether in writing or painting, or whatever other ingenious composition. Throughout all nature, and by consequence, throughout all the arts which imitate nature, virtue is the supreme beauty, the supreme charm. And therefore, let all the arts be called upon in education, to conspire in exhibiting the true beauty, which needs only be seen and known to be thoroughly and seriously admired and beloved. Some characters and actions of virtuous men we meet with in history, set forth the charms of integrity in their full lustre: And we must be very well acquainted with history, to be able to judge whether fiction be natural or not; but fiction, when it is probable, hath at least as much force as real history.

We have been recommending history as the best basis for building moral instructions upon, yet other arts, which can be rendered subservient to virtue, ought by no means to be neglected. And how proper fables (by which I would be understood to mean, not barely such Aesopic tales as are properly so called, but all fables, allegories, visions, every specious fiction, in short, by which any moral truth may be conveyed into the mind under the ingenious and agreeable semblance of aiming at nothing higher than mere amusement) are to attract the minds of youth, and gain their attention to useful instruction, the unanimous consent of the wisest instructors in all ages of the world, in the use of them, sufficiently demonstrates? In a collection of essays, which abounds with most excellent fables and allegories, this subject is thus discoursed of:[82] "There is nothing which we receive with so much reluctance as advice. We look upon the man who gives it as offering an affront to our understanding, and treating us like children or

---

82. [Joseph Addison and Richard Steele, *The Spectator*, nos. 512 and 183.]

ideots. We consider the instruction as an implicit censure, and the zeal which any one shews for our good on such an occasion as a piece of presumption or impertinence. The truth of it is, the person who pretends to advise, does in that particular exercise a superiority over us, and can have no other reason for it, but that in comparing us with himself, he thinks us defective, either in our conduct or our understanding. For these reasons, there is nothing so difficult as the art of making advice agreeable: And indeed all the writers, both ancient and modern, have distinguished themselves among one another, according to the perfection at which they have arrived in this art. How many devices have been made use of, to render this bitter portion palatable? Some convey their instructions to us in the best chosen words; others in the most harmonious numbers, some in points of wit, and others in short proverbs. But among all the different ways of giving counsel, I think the finest, and that which pleases the most universally is fable, in whatever shape it appears. If we consider this way of instructing or giving advice, it excels all others, because it is the least shocking, and the least subject to those exceptions which I have before mentioned. This will appear to us, if we reflect in the first place, that upon the reading of a fable we are made to believe we advise ourselves. We peruse the author for the sake of the story, and consider the precepts rather as our conclusions than his instructions. The moral insinuates itself imperceptibly; we are taught by surprize, and become wiser and better unawares. In short, by this method, a man is so far over-reached as to think he is directing himself, while he is following the dictates of another, and consequently is not sensible of that which is the most unpleasing circumstance in advice. In the next place, if we look into human nature, we shall find that the mind is never so much pleased, as when she exerts herself in any action that gives her an idea of her own perfections and abilities. This natural pride and ambition of the soul is very much gratified in the reading of a fable: For in writings of this kind, the reader comes in for half of the performance; every thing appears to him like a discovery of his own; he is busied all the while in applying characters and circumstances, and is in this respect both a reader and a composer. It is no wonder therefore, that on such occasions, when the mind is thus pleased with itself, and amused with its own discovery, that it is highly delighted with the writing which is the occasion of it. This oblique manner of giving advice is so inoffensive,

that if we look into ancient histories, we find the wise men of old very
often chose to give counsel to their kings in fables: Fables were indeed the
first pieces of wit that made their appearance in the world, and have been
still highly valued, not only in times of the greatest simplicity, but among
the polite ages of mankind. Jotham's fable of the trees is the oldest that is
extant, and as beautiful as any that have been made since that time.
Nathan's fable of the poor man and his lamb is likewise more ancient than
any that is extant, besides the above mentioned, and had so good an effect,
as to convey instruction to the ear of a king without offending it, and to
bring the man after God's own heart to a right sense of his guilt and his
duty. We find Aesop in the most distant ages of Greece; and if we look into
the very beginnings of the commonwealth of Rome, we see a mutiny
among the common people appeased by a fable of the belly and the limbs,
which was indeed very proper to gain the attention of an incensed rabble,
at a time, when perhaps they would have torn to pieces any man who had
preached the same doctrine to them in an open and direct manner. As fables took their birth in the very infancy of learning, they never flourished
more than when learning was at its greatest height. To justify this assertion, I shall put my readers in mind of Horace, the greatest wit and critic
in the Augustan age; and of Boileau, the most correct poet among the
moderns; not to mention La Fontaine, who by this way of writing, is come
more into vogue than any other author of our times. The fables I have here
mentioned, are raised altogether upon brutes and vegetables, with some of
our own species mix'd among them, when the moral hath so required. But
besides this kind of fable, there is another in which the actors are passions,
virtues, vices, and other imaginary persons of the like nature. Some of the
ancient critics will have it, that the Iliad and Odyssey of Homer are fables
of this nature; and that the several names of Gods and heroes are nothing
else but the affections of the mind in a visible shape and character. Thus
they tell us, that Achilles, in the first iliad represents anger, or the irascible
part of human nature. That upon drawing his sword against his superior
in a full assembly, Pallas is only a name for reason, which checks and advises him upon that occasion; and at first appearance touches him upon
the head, that part of the man being looked upon as the seat of reason.
And thus of the rest of the poem. As for the Odyssey, I think it is plain
that Horace considered it as one of these allegorical fables, by the moral

which he has given us of several parts of it. The greatest Italian wits have applied themselves to the writing of this latter kind of fables: As Spencer's Fairy Queen is one continued series of them from the beginning to the end of that admirable work. If we look into the finest prose authors of antiquity, such as Cicero, Plato, Xenophon, and many others, we shall likewise find, that this was their favourite kind of fable. I shall only observe farther upon it, that the first of this sort that made any considerable figure in the world, was that of Hercules meeting with pleasure and virtue; which was invented by Prodicus, who lived before Socrates, and in the first dawnings of philosophy. He used to travel through Greece by virtue of this fable, which procured him a kind reception in all the market-towns, where he never failed telling it, as soon as he had gathered an audience about him." To these recommendations of fables, as one of the best means of insinuating moral lessons agreeably into the minds of all, the young more especially, I have nothing to add; but that the politest of writers, Horace himself, never pleases so much, or conveys his lesson or reproof either more agreeably, or more forcibly, than when he introduces a fable, tale or story. And there is indeed no moral truth, even the most abstract, nor no moral counsel or reproof that may not be conveyed in this elegant manner of instruction. Those therefore who are concerned in the education of youth, ought to make themselves acquainted with all the best fables by which ancients or moderns have illustrated moral truths; and to exercise their wit in contriving or inventing proper ones, that they may have always at hand some apposite fable to confirm and set off any truth they would impress upon young minds, but chiefly for conveying their admonitions and reproofs in the least provoking, and, consequently, the most successful manner: A preceptor skilled in this art, would seldom or never be obliged to reprimand in the austerer way; and would be able to render all his lessons equally pleasing and instructive.

And this leads to observe, that teachers of youth must not trust entirely to their grave and formal lectures, but take frequent opportunities of instructing their pupils by conversation, by entertaining them sometimes with a fable, and sometimes with a piece of real history; by leading them to ask questions, and by guiding them to the discovery of truth, in the Socratic way, by acting the midwife to their thoughts, as Socrates himself called his manner of instructing, by a series of questions issuing naturally one from another, till the truth to be confirmed shewed itself, as it were, of its own accord, to the person instructed, or rather till he was brought as it were to start it himself, and then seize it as his own discovery. We are indeed at a great deal of pains to load the memories of youth; but very little is done to exercise their judgments or inventions: And yet it is by suitable exercises only, that judgment or invention, as well as memory, can be quickened or strengthened. Youth, whatever science they are taught, ought to be inured to speak out what they have learned, not by rote, in consequence of servilely mandating what they have read, but easily and in their own words, from their judgments and not from their memories. They ought also to be practised in resolving questions belonging to the science they are learning, for the solution of which they have already laid up sufficient data: This ought universally to be the practice of masters in teaching all the sciences, mathematics, natural philosophy, or morals and politics; in teaching the latter more particularly: For here it is of great moment, that youth be early able to judge both quickly and solidly concerning right and wrong, just and unjust: But to this perfection in the moral science they can never attain by the help of general rules alone, without practice in pronouncing concerning characters and actions, and in determining particular cases.[83] In order to qualify masters for all these methods of

83. 'Tis worth while to copy here what is said upon this important part of education, Spectator 337. [The third in a series of four letters on education (along with nos. 307, 313, and 353) written to *The Spectator* by Eustace Budgell.]

If I had not been hindered by some extraordinary business, I should have sent you sooner my farther thoughts upon education. You may please to remember, that in my last letter, I endeavoured to give the best reasons that could be urged in favour of a private or public education. Upon the whole, it may perhaps be thought that I seemed rather inclined to the latter, tho' at the same time, I confessed that virtue, which ought to be our first and principal care, was more usually acquired in the former.

I intend therefore in this letter to offer at methods, by which I conceive boys might be made to improve in virtue, as they advance in letters. I know that in most of our public schools, vice is punished and discouraged, whenever it is found out; but this is far from being sufficient, unless our youth are at the same time taught to form a right judgment of things, and to know what is properly virtue.

To this end, whenever they read the lives and actions of such men as have been famous in their generation, it should not be thought enough to make them barely under-teaching; and more particularly, for instructing by familiar conversation, they ought to be close studiers of the Socratic dialogues, that are preserved to us by the disciples of that great master, from whom all the different families or sects of ancient philosophers sprung, as all the different species or forms of poetry did from the first father of that art Homer; those particu-

---

stand so many Greek or Latin Sentences, but they should be asked their opinion of such an action or saying, and obliged to give their reasons why they take it to be good or bad. By this means they would insensibly arrive at proper notions of courage, temperance, honour and justice.

There must be great care taken, how the example of any particular person is recommended to them in gross; instead of which they ought to be taught, wherein such a man, tho' great in some respects, was weak and faulty in others. For want of this Caution, a boy is often so dazled with the lustre of a great character, that he confounds its beauty with its blemishes, and looks even upon the faulty part of it with an eye of admiration. I have often wondered how Alexander, who was naturally of a generous and merciful disposition, came to be guilty of so barbarous an action as that of dragging the governor of a town after his chariot. I know this is generally ascribed to his passion for Homer; but I lately met with a passage in Plutarch, which, if I am not very much mistaken, still gives us a clearer light into the motives of this action. Plutarch tells us, that Alexander in his youth had a master named Lysimachus, who, tho' he was a man destitute of all politeness, ingratiated himself both with Philip and his pupil, and became the second man at court, by calling the king Peleus, the Prince Achilles, and himself Phaenix. It is no wonder if Alexander having been thus used not only to admire, but to personate Achilles, should think it glorious to imitate him in this piece of cruelty and extravagance.

To carry this thought yet further, I shall submit it to your consideration, whether instead of a theme, or copy of verses, which are the usual exercises, as they are called in the school phrase, it would not be more proper that a boy should be tasked once or twice a week to write down his opinion of such persons and things as occur to him in reading; that he should descant upon the actions of Turnus and Aeneas, shew wherein they excelled, or were defective, censure or approve any particular action, observe how it might have been carried to a greater degree of perfection, and how it exceeded or fell short of another. He might at the same time mark what was moral in any speech, and how far it agreed with the character of the person speaking. This exercise would soon strengthen his judgment in what is blameable or praiseworthy, and give him an early seasoning of morality. Next to those examples which may be met with in books, I very much approve Horace's way of setting before youth the infamous or honourable characters of their contemporaries. That poet tells us, this was the method his father made use of to incline him to any particular virtue, or give him an aversion to any particular vice, &c. Xenophon's schools of equity, in his life of Cyrus the great, are sufficiently famous: He tells us, that the Persian children went to school, and employed their time as diligently in learning the principles of justice and sobriety, as the youth in other countries did to acquire the most difficult arts and sciences, &c.

larly which Xenophon hath transmitted to us with his inimitable simplicity. No method certainly is so proper, whether for instruction in truth, or for refuting error, and disentangling from prejudices and difficulties. It is not so properly instruction, as the art of leading to truth, and enabling one to instruct himself. Never was a philosopher or teacher so much followed and beloved: Never were lessons so greedily attended to and sought after as his; and never had any mere man more success in recommending and teaching virtue and true knowledge than Socrates, as is plain from his history: And this is an irrefragable argument of the peculiar excellence of that method of instructing or reproving, which takes its name from him who was the first inventer, or at least made the greatest use of it. And in all probability, one of the chief reasons why schools and lectures so soon disgust youth in modern times, at all that bears the name of erudition or scholarship is, that masters seldom or never descend from their austere

---

The method which Apuleius tells us the Indian Gymnosophists took to educate their disciples is still more curious and remarkable. His words are as follow: "When their dinner is ready, before it is served up, the masters enquire of every particular scholar how he has employed his time since sun-rising: Some of them answer, that having been chosen as arbiters between two persons, they have composed their differences and made them friends; some that they have been executing the orders of their parents; and others, that they have either found out something new by their own application, or learn'd it from the instruction of their fellows. But if there happens to be any one among them, who cannot make it appear, that he has employed the morning to advantage, he is immediately excluded from the company, and obliged to work while the rest are at dinner."

It is not impossible, that from these several ways of producing virtue in the minds of boys, some general method might be invented. What I would endeavour to inculcate is, that our youth cannot be too soon taught the principles of virtue, seeing the first impressions which are made on the mind are always the strongest. The Archbishop of Cambray makes Telemachus say, that tho' he was young in years, he was old in the art of knowing how to keep both his own and his friends secrets, &c.

There is hardly any virtue which a lad might not early learn by practice and example.

In short, nothing is more wanting to our public schools, than that the masters of them should use the same care in fashioning the manners of their scholars, as in forming their tongues to the learned languages. Wherever the former is omitted, I cannot help agreeing with Mr. Locke, That a man must have a very strange value for words, when preferring the languages of the Greeks and Romans to that which made them such brave men, he can think it worth while to hazard the innocence and virtue of his son for a little Greek and Latin.

magisterial manner, into the familiar way of conference, but rather affect to banish from philosophy, as too sprightly and gay, all the arts of illustrating and sweetening moral lessons by fables, allegories, and other such ingenious and agreeable embellishments, with which we find the best ancient sages, Socrates in particular, ever adorning and begaying, so to speak, their lectures. But we need not insist longer upon explaining or recommending instruction in the Socratic way: Its nature and excellence can only be understood by examples; and a little acquaintance with the authors above mentioned, will soon satisfy every thinking person, that tho' it be an art that cannot easily be acquired, yet some degree of dexterity in it is absolutely necessary to qualify for the knack of rendering teaching agreeable: And that without having frequent recourse to it, 'tis hardly possible to improve the invention or imagination of youth.

Before I leave this article, in which teaching youth from history hath been so earnestly urged, it is proper to take notice, That history will afford the properest occasions of explaining to young people ancient customs and rites, civil, political or religious, and consequently, all that is commonly called antiquity; and of pointing out to them, in good prints, at least, all the remains of ancient sculpture or painting, that preserve representations of them to us: 'Tis in historical lessons, as usages of these kinds happen to be mentioned in history, that coins, pictures, statues, bas-reliefs, &c. properly have their place; the chief use of them being, either to confirm history, or to give us clear representations of customs that can hardly be fully understood from mere verbal descriptions; and to shew, at the same time, the progress and decline of these very ingenious and useful arts themselves. Nothing can be more dry than a course of lectures upon antiquities, without such monuments before the teachers and scholars: And a regular course of antiquities, even with such proper helps, cannot be so entertaining, or be so well retained, as when customs and manners are taken notice of, just as they occur in history, and are then explained from the coins or other monuments, which exhibit them to our eyes. Thus things succeed or mix as they ought; and the one serves at the same time to diversify and to enlighten the other.

It is the same, in a great measure, likewise with respect to rhetoric. 'Tis by pointing out to youth the beauty of sentiments and of expressions, and of order and arrangement in the charming speeches that we meet with in ancient historians, and by inuring them to translate, imitate, and repeat them, that the art of speaking, and a just notion of oratory is best taught: And by frequent lessoning and practice of this kind, they will soon be prepared for examining, or tracing to their foundations in human nature, and in order and harmony, all the rules and precepts of oratory: All the rules concerning stating and unfolding the truth or fact to be confirmed, and concerning proving and establishing it, or concerning refuting the contrary opinions and suppositions, and amplifying and enlarging the point to be proved and enforced, and working up and interesting the passions of the hearers in favour of what we would recommend to them or persuade them of. Rules are best understood, when examples that confirm them and point out their fitness or necessity, naturally lead one, as it were by the hand, to take notice of them. One who is persuaded and moved by a speech, and heartily admires its force and beauty, will with pleasure enter into a critical examination of its excellencies; and willingly lay up in his mind the rules of rhetoric such an example of eloquence plainly suggests. But to teach rules abstractly, or without examples, and before the agreeable effects the observance of them tends to produce, which are in reality their reason or foundation, have been felt, is exceeding preposterous. It is here as it is in natural philosophy, after we are well acquainted with causes, having been led to them by their effects, we may compute what their influences or effects would be in given circumstances, or how they should be applied, and how they would operate: But we must begin with effects, and learn causes and rules or general laws from particular specimens or examples of them, i.e. in short, we must first be very well acquainted with effects before we can understand causes, or their applications, and draw any conclusions from them. The case is the same both in natural philosophy and rhetorick. For what are general rules of rhetorick, but rules collected from effects, for gaining certain effects upon the mind. But it is by means of specimens only that rules can be shewn to be fit means for accomplishing such or such ends; nor could they ever have been known to have been fit rules, were not certain effects resolvable into them: In other words, 'tis only by analyzing effects into them, that they can be demonstrated to be good or true rules, in much the same manner as it is by reducing effects in nature into a cause or law that accounts for them, by which alone certain other phaenomena can be accounted for, that we can only collect with any certainty the general laws of nature, whether for the explication of natural appearances, or for the direction of mechanical arts.

Another reason for making history, and the truths it affords, proper occasions of explaining and confirming a principal branch of education is, that as such reading will take in the progress of all arts and sciences, and give opportunity of discoursing of their rise, improvement, and uses, it must prove a very proper means of trying different genius's, and exciting them to disclose and shew themselves. The instructor will by this means have an opportunity of observing what kind of observations, or what kind of arts, most strike some, and what others. For the natural biasses of minds towards particular studies and pursuits, want but invitations to bring them forth, and make them declare themselves, and cannot appear 'till they are properly tried. While education proceeds in one beaten uniform rout, it is impossible to discover different talents or turns of pupils; tho', in all probability, each mind hath a particular one; because as affections so genius never puts itself forth, till its proper objects call upon it. There is a book written by *Juan Huartes,* a *Spanish* physician, entitled, *Examen de ingenios,* wherein he lays it down as one of his first positions, that nothing but nature can qualify a man for learning; and that without a proper temperament for the particular art or science which he studies, his utmost pains and application, assisted by the ablest masters, will be to no purpose.[84] He illustrates this by the example of *Tully's* son *Marcus. Cicero,* in order to accomplish his son in that sort of learning which he designed him for, sent him to *Athens,* the most celebrated academy at that time in the world, and where a vast concourse, out of the most polite nations, could not but furnish the young gentleman with a multitude of great examples, and accidents that might have insensibly instructed him in his designed studies: He placed him under the care of *Cratippus,* who was one of the greatest philosophers of the age, and he himself composed books on purpose for

84. [The quote found on p. 375 of this book, from "an excellent writer of our own" (*The Spectator,* no. 307), actually begins here.]

his use. But notwithstanding all this care, history gives us no great character of *Marcus;* nature (who it seems was even with the son for her prodigality to the father) rendered him incapable of improving, by all the rules
of eloquence, the precepts of philosophy, his own endeavours, and the
most refined conversation in *Athens.* This author therefore proposes, that
there should be certain triers or examiners appointed by the state to inspect the genius of every particular boy, and to allot him the part that is
most suitable to his natural talents. To confirm this, he adds, that *Plato,* in
one of his dialogues, tells us, that *Socrates,* who was the son of a midwife,
used to say, that as his mother, tho' she was very skilful in her profession,
could not deliver a woman, unless she was first with child, so neither could
he himself raise knowledge out of a mind, where nature had not planted
it. Accordingly, the method the philosopher took of instructing his scholars by several interrogations or questions, was only helping the birth, and
bringing their own thoughts to light. The *Spanish* doctor abovementioned, as his speculations grow more refined, asserts, that every kind of
temperament has a particular science corresponding to it, and in which
alone it can be truly excellent. As to those genius's, which may seem to
have an equal aptitude for several things, he regards them as so many un-
finished pieces of nature, wrought off in haste. An excellent writer of our
own, after quoting these remarks from the Spaniard, adds the following
reflexions. "There are indeed but very few to whom nature has been so
unkind, that they are not capable of shining in some science or other.
There is a certain bent towards knowledge in every mind, which may be
strengthened and improved by proper application. The story of Clavius is
very well known: He was entered in a college of Jesuits, and after having
been tried at several parts of learning, was upon the point of being dismissed as an hopeless blockhead, till one of the fathers took it into his head
to make an essay of his parts in geometry, which, it seems, hit his genius
so luckily, that he afterwards became one of the greatest mathematicians
of the age. It is commonly thought, that the sagacity of these fathers in
discovering the talents of a young student, has not a little contributed to
the figure which their order has made in the world. How different, continues the same author, from this manner of education, is that which prevails
in our own country? Where nothing is more usual than to see forty or fifty

boys of several ages, tempers and inclinations, ranged together in the same class, employed upon the same authors, and enjoined in the same tasks? Whatever their natural genius may be, they are all to be made poets, historians, and orators alike. They are all obliged to have the same capacity; to bring in the same tale of verse, and to furnish out the same portion of prose. Every boy is bound to have as good a memory as the captain of the form. To be brief, instead of adapting studies to the particular genius of a youth, we expect from the young man, that he should adapt his genius to his studies. This I must confess, is not so much to be imputed to the instructor, as to the parent, who will never be brought to believe, that his son is not capable of performing as much as his neighbour's, and that he may not make him whatever he has a mind to." After which this author adds: "If the present age is more laudable than those which have gone before us in any single particular, it is in that generous care which several well disposed persons have taken in the education of poor children; and as in these charity schools, there is no place left for the overweaning fondness of a parent, the directors of them would make them beneficial to the public, if they considered the precept which I have been thus long inculcating. They might easily, by well-examining the parts of those under their inspection, make a just distribution of them into proper classes and divisions, and allot to them this or that particular study, as their genius qualifies them for professions, trades, handicrafts, or service by sea and land."

Education in our schools is too narrow and confined, and therefore not at all calculated for this very important purpose to society; early to discover different genius's, in order to give to each betimes its proper improvements. All with us are educated in the same manner; a few classics is all they see or hear of, except it be a little of arithmetic and a little dancing: How therefore can masters discern different turns and abilities of youth? What is done to draw out each particular genius and make it shew and exert itself? Yet at a very small cost to the public, this very momentous end might be gained, by furnishing our schools, as the *Instituto* at *Bologna* is, by the care and direction of the Count Marsigli, and originally at his private expence. There are in that academy schools or apartments for all the sciences, properly adorned or rather fitly furnished. The chamber of painting and sculpture is replenished with antique busts and statues, some good pictures, and many very good drawings and prints; the mechanical chamber, with models of engines of various sorts; the chamber of mathematics and fortification, with maps and models of fortified towns, and with the more necessary pieces of artillery and instruments of war; the astronomical school with telescopes, globes, quadrants, and other proper utensils for observing the heavenly bodies: And there is a large gallery furnished with minerals, metals, fossils, plants, flowers, and other natural curiosities, so elegantly and properly disposed, that by visiting this apartment now and then with attention, one can hardly fail of becoming pretty well acquainted, in a little time with natural history: There are masters for the learned languages: and lectures are given upon drawing, fortification, all the parts of mathematics, and upon mechanics and the other sciences, at such regular well distributed hours, that all the students may attend them, without neglecting their language-lessons. Now, in schools or colleges thus furnished, there would be proper means for employing geniuses, and alluring them to appear and exert themselves: But even where that is not, or cannot be done, reading history with youth in such a manner as to take every proper occasion to discourse of every science and art, its end, use, origin, progress, and improvement, would in a great measure serve this momentous purpose of schools and education, viz. finding out early the natural bent, genius, and talents of youth, in order to cultivate and improve them to the best advantage, and avoid forcing nature, as must happen when education is carried on in the same beaten uniform train, without any proper attempts to discern natural geniuses, or to suit education to them. And in truth, the same methods which are necessary to gain this end, are of admirable use to enlarge and open every mind: It is true, one in order to be useful in life, ought to apply himself to one study, business or profession chiefly, and to choose that for which nature has best disposed and qualified him: But before one betakes himself to any of the more liberal professions for life, it is very fit that he should have had a very large view of men and things, and have, for that effect, been assisted in looking with intelligence into many arts and sciences: So much ought one to know of all, in order to succeed in any one well, as is necessary to give him a view of the strict union, connexion, and dependance of all the sciences, and enable him to discern what helps and assistances any one of them may, or rather must derive from the rest. And indeed there is no other remedy or antidote against the narrowness, stiffness, and pedantry which are so often complained of by men of large and liberal minds, as accompanying, more or less, all the learned professions; but this more enlarged institution in the public schools, or under private tutors, we are now recommending. We have already had occasion to observe the good effects of it amongst the ancient Greeks and Romans. And may we not appeal to experience, and ask what it is that forms or produces the truly liberal scholar, the man of thorough good taste and equal politeness, the large, open-minded, easy, as well as knowing and learned gentleman, no less fit for public business than for private company, equally useful and entertaining and agreeable wherever he is, or about whatever he is employed.—What else is it but extensive large views, deep insight into men, comprehensive knowledge of the world, and such an acquaintance with all human affairs and arts, as preserves him on every occasion from embarassment, being sufficient, at least, to direct him into the proper train of informing himself more fully concerning whatever occurs.—And to what else can this perfection be owing; or how else can it be brought about, but by an education which leads one in a natural proper order through all human affairs; and instead of confining him to one narrow spot, teaches him to extend and widen his views, and gather in acquaintance with every part of nature, by looking with attention into the methods of carrying on every study or science, and into its chief discoveries and improvements. This may at first sight appear cutting out a task for education that is more than enough for human life. But every seeming difficulty, every objection against the manner of education which hath been inculcated in this chapter, will immediately evanish, if one will but consider that there are but two subjects of human enquiry or real knowledge; the laws or order of the material world, and human nature, which two have a very near, a very intimate connexion: And all therefore that is required to render education full and complete, is to divide the time of youth between these two; every other study besides, as we shall see more fully afterwards, comes properly under the notion of languages, or arts of expressing or communicating knowledge. Now, if youth went from schools or tutors well acquainted with these two sciences, what study, what profession or business would they not be at least well prepared to pursue by themselves, in a manner that could not fail of success? But on the other hand, while they are ignorant of these sciences, however full their heads may be crammed with words and terms of art, what are they fit to do, or apply to of any use to mankind, of any relation to society or real life? Suppose them masters of several grammars, capable of construing readily several books of different languages, and of giving English words or phrases for every word or phrase in the abstrusest Latin or Greek authors, yet if they have no notion of natural philosophy, no notion of the method of cultivating that science, and of the uses that have and may be made of it for the extention and enlargement of human power, and are utter strangers to moral philosophy, to human nature, and human rights and duties, for what service to society are they prepared; what science are they capable by themselves to pursue; into the elements or first principles of what profession are they yet initiated; or can they as yet be said to have only so much as a tolerable notion of any of the enquiries which best befit and most concern mankind; any idea of what is most worth our knowing, or most worth our pursuing? In fine, what authors in any language really worthy of our study are they qualified to enter into and understand? For books absolutely remote from these subjects, what are they at best but innocent amusements? And to understand books which have any relation to the order of nature, or to human affairs, more instruction surely is necessary than merely instruction in words or grammars? It was undoubtedly owing to the large and rational education of the Greeks in their better days, that their great men made so shining a figure in various capacities and situations, and that in the very beginning of what is called manhood: It could have been owing to nothing else; and to this alone do historians ascribe it. And indeed what advantages the Grecian youth had for opening, enlarging, and strengthening their minds betimes with extensive knowledge, not only by means of their schools, in which all the arts and sciences were taught them, and words were far from being their only employment, but in another way, quite unknown in modern times, is well worth our observation. Plutarch divides the life of statesmen into three ages. In the first he would have them learn the principles of morality and government; in the second reduce them to practice in the actual service of their country; and in the third instruct others. He applies, on this occasion, the custom used in Rome, where the vestals spent the first ten years in learning their office, and this was a kind of novicate; the next ten years they employed in the exercise of their functions; and the last ten in instructing the young novices in them. Now this is not so much a description of the duty of good citizens, or men capable of serving their country in the more important offices of society, as it is a real and true account of the manner in which the ancient Greeks divided their lives in the best times of that renowned country. For thus did Aristides and other great men in and about his time lay themselves out. Aristides, says Plutarch, was not always in office, but was always useful to his country. For his house was a public school of virtue, wisdom and policy. It was open to all young Athenians who were lovers of virtue, and these used to consult him as an oracle. He gave them the kindest reception, heard them with patience, instructed them with familiarity, and endeavoured, above all things, to animate their courage and inspire them with confidence. It is observed particularly, that Cimon, afterwards so famous, was obliged to him for this important service. This was also the practice at Rome in the best days of that republic, as hath been already remarked in the short account we have given, from a very good author, of Cicero's education. And who will not own, that it would be of great advantage to a state, if those who excel in professions of every kind, would take pleasure, and make it their duty to fashion and instruct such youths as are remarkable for the pregnancy of their parts and goodness of disposition? They would thereby have an opportunity of serving their country even after their death, and of perpetuating in it, in the person of their pupils, a taste and inclination for true merit, and the practice of the wisest maxims.

ʝʘʝ CHAPTER V ʝʘʝ

Of instruction in poetry and her sister arts, painting, sculpture, music and architecture; and the place which these arts of design ought to have in liberal education, in order to form elegant taste, which is one of the best preservatives against luxury, being naturally assistant to, and corroborative of virtue.

The more ordinary course of education hath obliged us to take a great deal of pains to prove a very plain truth, "That science, or real knowledge, and not mere words, ought to be its principal object and scope." And we have sufficiently shewn what we mean by the science or real knowledge which qualifies for usefulness, whether to one's self, or to society. The science of nature, which at once teaches men how they may employ material things for their benefit and advantage, and unfolds to them the character of the supreme creator and governor of all things, in conformity to whose will our dignity and happiness must consist: And such a clear and full knowledge of human rights and duties, as that we may be able, in every circumstance of life, however complicated, easily to discern what virtue and public good, and by consequence, the laws of our Maker for our conduct, require at our hands, and oblige us to do, if we would act a truly worthy and right part, and approve ourselves to him who is perfect rectitude. The great art of education therefore lies in contriving and employing proper methods for engaging the young early in the love of these studies, and for early instilling the more important truths belonging to these sciences into their minds, and impressing them deeply upon them. I may perhaps be thought to have taken language in a very uncommon sense in the former chapter, when I hinted, that all that can belong to education may be reduced to these two general heads, science and languages. But that I have used language in its justest, as well as most comprehensive meaning, will be obvious to every one who but reflects, that there can be but two objects of human enquiry; truths themselves, i.e. real connexions in nature or facts, and the various manners of making truths understood and felt. Under science then we comprehend all truths or facts relating to the natural world, or to human nature, which can be discovered by experience or inferred from experiments, and by comparing properties known by experience one with another. So that we may divide science into natural and moral, and both into experimental and abstract; experimental which infers facts and rules from experiences; abstract, which shews what properties may, must, or cannot co-exist. Besides these, there plainly remains no other subject of enquiry to us, but the different methods of expressing, embellishing, or enforcing and recommending truths discovered by either these ways in either kind: And such methods we call in one word languages; under this idea, the didactic stile, oratory, poetry, and likewise all the arts of design, statuary, sculpture, painting, plainly fall. And therefore, if right education ought to teach and instruct first of all, or chiefly in truths, but next in the various good methods or arts of expressing or conveying truths into the mind, no sooner is a pupil led into the discovery of any truth, than he ought to be employed in comparing and examining several different ways, by which it may be unfolded, explained, cleared up, proved, adorned, beautified, or enforced, and recommended by oratory, poetry, or painting. For to apply this general observation to painting, which at first sight appears, and is commonly reckoned so remote from philosophy, nothing is more evident, than that pictures, which neither convey into the mind ideas of material laws, and their effects and appearances, nor moral truths, i.e. moral sentiments and corresponding affections, have no meaning at all; they convey nothing, because there is nothing else to be taught or conveyed. But on the other hand, such pictures as answer any of these ends, must for that reason speak a language, the correctness, strength, purity and beauty of which it must be well worth while to understand as a language, especially, since such a language is, as far as it can go, an universal one, the signs it uses being universal signs of nature's establishment, the meanings of which never vary, but remain in all countries, and always the same.

The chief and most early care in education ought to be, to form good habits or dispositions in young minds: For unless the mind be, by previous discipline, pure from vice, and regular, docile, and well-disposed, instruction instead of having success, will be quite lost or thrown away upon it. And in this part of education, the principal thing to be aimed at is, to fix or settle early in young minds the considerative temper, or the habit of comparing and computing, before they choose or act: Indeed when patience of thinking, or the deliberative habit is gained, the chief and most difficult point is gained, whether with respect to advancement in science, or with regard to right practice in life. For he who can once settle and fix himself to think, will find no lesson very difficult; far less will he find the most important lessons such, those, to wit, which relate to duty or right conduct. It will be very easy to lead young minds to just and clear conceptions of the rules of life, and thus to furnish them with a measure or standard to judge by, if we can but once rivet in their breasts the love of instruction, and an attentive thinking habit. 'Tis certainly pleasure and pain that move us: Nothing can be the object of aversion and dislike but pain; or on the other hand, the object of affection or desire but pleasure. Pleasures of sense, of contemplation, of sentiment, of self-approbation, and their opposites, are all of them but so many different sorts of pleasures and pains. Let metaphysicians subtilize and wrangle as long as they will, this must be true, and be no more than an identical proposition, That what is pleasing is pleasing, and that pleasure alone can be pleasant. But it is reason's business to compute and ballance pleasures and pains of all kinds, the more remote as well as those that are nearer; and those that are likely to follow as well as the absolutely certain: And then is reason well-educated, or formed into a really useful, because into a governing principle, when the mind hath acquired the habit of deliberating and computing before it chooses; and is qualified for computing readily as well as truly; which habit or temper can only be attained by inuring the mind betimes to think and reason before it acts, i.e. to compare, weigh, and ballance pleasures and pains in fair and accurate scales, before it determines and gives the preference. It is by this temper that one becomes master of himself, and able to resist all the most inviting specious promises and sollicitations of objects, till their pretensions have been thoroughly tried and canvassed. This disposition is what is properly called virtue or strength of mind: Without it one must be feeble and unsteady, unable to act firmly and regularly a reasonable or becoming part in life: Nay, he must be the sport of contradictory passions and appetites. It is by it alone that one can attain to that harmony and consistency of affections and manners which create peace within, and command trust, love and reverence from all around, even from the most dissolute and vitious: For human nature can never be so depraved as to be rendered quite insensible to the beauty and authority of wise and good conduct.

This temper makes one truly free: It gives us the truest, the most satisfactory and durable power, dominion or independency. Now, in forming this habit of acting with judgment, and in furnishing the minds of youth for judging well, there are two things chiefly to be taken care of. One is to inure youth to reason and compute from experience only, that is, from facts ascertained by observation, and not from abstract imaginary theories and hypotheses. The other is, to inure them to employ their reason chiefly about those objects and connexions in nature, which have the nearest relation to human life and happiness. In order to both which, it is manifest, that they ought to be early taught to take a just view of human nature, and to consider man as he really is, neither as a merely sensitive being, nor as a merely intellectual or moral one, but as a compound of moral and sensitive powers and affections. For in the human composition, those two different sorts of powers and affections are so intimately blended, that it is impossible to avoid errors concerning man's duties or interests, if any one class of them be considered separately and independently of the other. Conclusions deduced from moral powers and affections considered apart from sensitive ones, cannot make human morality, if man really be a sensitive as well as a moral being, i.e. a being invested with certain moral powers and affections mingled with sensitive ones, both of which are intimately related to and connected with the laws of the sensible world. An exact theory of human morals can only be formed from a full and accurate review of the various natural principles, or natural powers and dispositions of mankind, as these stand related to one another, and to surrounding objects.

It were easy to point out several absurdities or mistakes, which take their rise from dividing those constituent parts of our frame from one another, that are really inseparable in the nature of things. I shall only mention one here, that there will be more occasion for attending to in the subsequent part of this chapter than any other: Hence, I think, it is, that some moralists have railed in such a vague, undetermined manner against luxury, as if all sensible pleasures ought to be despised by good and wise men, and therefore banished human society, but those that are absolutely necessary to our subsistance. In the more general, confused way of declaiming against luxury; all the pleasures of imagination, and all the ornamental arts, are damn'd as absolutely superfluous, nay, as inconsistent with reason and virtue. Cleanliness, not to say elegance, is condemned and interdicted, as if nature had given man eyes, ears, and other senses, with a natural taste of proportion, beauty, order and harmony in material objects, to no purpose. One happy consequence of inuring youth to reason from experience alone; and to employ their reason first and chiefly about those things that have the nearest relation to life, and with which therefore it is our interest to be early acquainted, would be, that the natural desire of knowledge, which is implanted in us on purpose to compel us to seek after that science, which is as necessary to guide our conduct in life, as light is to shew us our road, would not be misled into a way of gratifying itself by enquiries quite remote from the practice and business of the world, or that have no relation to human affairs and duties, as it too often is: For I am apt to imagine, that more are ignorant of life, and quite strangers to the world, and the affairs of human society, in consequence of employing their minds about objects that have little or no concern with men and things, than through mere stupidity or want of capacity. It is false learning that is the most dangerous enemy to the true, or that most effectually supplants it. Nothing therefore is of greater importance in education than to render youth betimes capable of distinguishing useful enquiry from those that ought only to have the place of amusements, like a game at chess or piquet. And for that reason, it would be of more consequence to exercise young people in often reviewing with attention a well-calculated table of arts and sciences, in respect of their different values or degrees of utility, than any other categories or arrangements of ideas whatsoever, that are called logic in the schools, tho' such likewise may have their use.

But having sufficiently discoursed of instruction in science, teaching of words being generally well enough understood, and the fault with regard to that matter lying chiefly in this, that Latin and Greek words engross too much of the care of masters, to the exclusion, for too long a time, of real knowledge; I now proceed to consider instruction in what we have called above languages, viz. the arts of expressing, explaining, proving, embellishing or enforcing truths. The didactic stile ought to be clear, perspicuous and full, diffuse, or duly diversified, i.e. teachers, or those who write upon any science, in order to lead, as it were, by the hand, the raw and unexperienced gradually from truth to truth, till having opened their minds, and strengthened their reason and judgment, they are able to understand a conciser manner of instruction, should deliver their sentiments in the neatest and plainest manner, and endeavour to set what they would establish and inculcate in a great variety of lights, all concurring at once to illustrate or set off to advantage, and to confirm the points in question, and above all, they ought to study the method and order of beginning and proceeding by proper steps from the more simple to the more complex, and from the first and most obvious principles to those that lie next to them, or follow most immediately from them, which will be best learned by familiarity with the ancient geometricians: This didactic art will be learned of course by scholars at the same time that knowledge itself is conveyed to them in that way, if their masters excel in it; and yet more especially, if youth, after they fully understand any truths, are not only accustomed to speak or express them, but employed in teaching them to others but just beginning to learn: The art of teaching or speaking clearly, and of laying open and explaining known truths to others, by a regular progress, i.e. step by step, like all other habits, can only be acquired by practice: And nothing will be found more improving to youth, than to practise them in instructing others in what they have learned and thoroughly understand: Nor can masters, indeed, as will be found by experience, impose a more agreeable task upon scholars: It is a very proper way of rewarding their success; a proper way of honouring and distinguishing them, that will wonderfully flatter a very laudable vanity or ambition. Masters cannot enough study this art themselves, since it is only in proportion to their ability in it, that they can succeed as teachers, however freighted they may be with knowledge: And indeed, as easy an art as it may appear to those who never tried it, the expert teacher will, however, be daily finding new difficulties in it, so various are the turns and casts of human minds, and so imperfect, deficient, or equivocal and ambiguous are many phrases, names or words, in the best, the most improved and refined languages.

But there is an eloquence of another kind that ought not to be neglected in the formation of youth, and that would soon be attained by them, were but this one rule observed in education, viz. to inure students, after they have been led to the knowledge of any truth in the didactic way, to find out the properest methods of expressing it strongly and concisely, or of giving a convincing and emphatical view of it in few words. This last would be teaching them the language in which men ought to speak to men about the same points or truths, which can only be conveyed into the raw unformed, in a more slow and tedious manner. After young people understand any truth, it would neither be unpleasant nor unprofitable, but on the contrary, a very pleasing and useful exercise, to shew them in what different manners or lights different authors have represented it, each according to his own genius, or in order to adapt it to some particular cast of understanding; and then to make them try to find out other ways of expressing the same truth with due force, elegance and perspicuity. But we commonly begin in education with words, as if there were any other way of trying or judging words and phrases, or signs of any kind, but by comparing them with other expressions of the same truths they are intended to signify, and considering which are best, in respect of the sole end of language, which is to convey sentiments with perspicuity and force. The chief thing indeed is to have just or true sentiments, i.e. to have right apprehensions of the connexions in nature, material or moral, well disposed or digested by the judgment, and so ready at hand for use, on every proper occasion: For Horace's rule will ever hold true,

> ———— *Cui lecta potenter erit res,*
> *Nec facundia desoret hunc, nec lucidus ordo.*
>
> Art. Poet.[85]

85. [Horace, *Ars Poetica*, lines 40–41: "Whoever shall choose a theme within his range, neither speech will fail him, nor clearness of order."]

But that knowledge may take fast hold of our minds, dwell with us, and afford us variety of delight, and that we may be capable of imparting it to others, so as to render it the source of manifold entertainment, as well as of information to them, various proper ways of proving, embellishing, and enforcing truths, ought to be studied. And therefore, in proportion as one acquires knowledge worth communicating, he ought likewise to be made acquainted with all the better ways of evincing and impressing any truths upon the minds of others, and to be practised in speaking, arguing, proving and enforcing; more especially, in giving equally clear and strong views of them in concise speech: For that is the language in which men ought to speak to men, or the improved: Diffuse discourse is proper only for the instruction of novices: It will please them as it lets in upon them light and knowledge altogether new, that wonderfully exhilerates and enlarges their souls: But as for the more advanced, it will be tedious to them, because unnecessary; or rather it will fret and provoke them, because it is a way of addressing them that does not acknowledge their improvements, but treats them upon the same level with the more ignorant and uninstructed. In discourses, and indeed in all kinds of composition designed for them, Cicero's rule holds true, that the *parum* is less offensive than the *nimium*.[86] The way to please such is to say just enough to light up their understandings, or warm their fancies, and so guide them to the subject treated of, as that by means of what is said, they may immediately be set a thinking about it in such a manner, as soon to be able to form a very full notion of it, which they shall take to be their own discovery, and think themselves obliged to the author for, only on account of the hints or direction he gave to their own understandings or imaginations, with regard to it. In truth, the great perfection of writing consists in so engaging the reader's attention, and setting his mind so to work, that he can flatter himself with discovering, by means of the author more than the author intended, or at least all he intended, and much more than he has expresly or particularly spoke. And happy indeed is he who hath this talent, and can

86. ["Too little . . . too much."]

be short, substantial and concise, without obscurity; the common error the affectation of brevity leads into being darkness.

> *Decipimur specie recti: brevis esse laboro;*
> *Obscurus fio:* ———
>
> Hor. Art. Poet.[87]

But the principles and rules of oratory, both as to what regards stating and proving a point, and what regards the movement of the passions, have often been so fully explained, that I need not dwell longer upon this subject than just to add, 1. That when pupils have once felt the power of some excellent speeches, their beauties will be easily understood by them; and then it will be very proper to read with them the principal passages in Cicero or Quintilian themselves, rather than in any modern copists from these authors; the chief maxims concerning proposing, developing, disintangling, establishing, confirming, amplifying a subject, and interesting the passions of the auditors in it. And 2. That in teaching the rules of oratory, if they are taught as they ought to be, philosophy is not deserted; for they all have their foundation in human nature, by nothing else but arts of moving and leading human affections, which must be deduced from their natures and dependencies; and consequently, to explain them aright, is indeed to lay open the human breast, and the avenues which lead into it, or the means by which its most secret principles of action are bestirred and agitated. For eloquence, as Plato observes, is only the art of directing the minds of people at will: And therefore the chief excellency of this art consists in moving seasonably the various passions, whether gentle or violent, which being to the soul what strings are to a musical instrument, need only be touched by an ingenious and skilful hand, to produce their effects. Now, in order to know how to move the strings of the human heart, its texture must be thoroughly understood: And teaching the arts of moving the affections, must be in effect teaching human nature: These arts can only be inferred from the nature of the human passions: They are

---

87. [[Horace, *Ars Poetica,* lines 25–26: "[We] deceive ourselves by the semblance of truth. Striving to be brief, I become obscure."]]

nothing else but certain methods of working upon them, which, on the one hand, cannot be known without deep insight into human nature, and without the knowledge of which, on the other hand, human nature is but very imperfectly understood. In one word, oratory being an art which enables us to move and draw forth and lead the passions of others at our pleasure, it is a part of our moral power or dominion, acquirable only in the same way as any branch of our power in the material world is, to wit, by a thorough knowledge of its object: And therefore in a tree of the sciences, representing their dependencies and their unity, oratory would be placed among the practical arts issuing from the knowledge of human passions, and as such, among the arts of government. For of such power is eloquence, especially in free states, (indeed in absolute governments it will always be discouraged, and never come to any perfection, unless we can admit fulsome panegyric to be the chief part of it) that what Valerius Maximus says of Pericles may be applied to many others in the same and other such like ancient states, that there was scarce any other difference betwixt Pisistrates and him, except that the one exercised a tyranical power by force of arms, and the other by the strength of his eloquence, in which he had made a very great progress under Anaxagoras. And let it just be suggested by the by, that a table or tree of all the sciences, representing them springing from the same root, and mutually depending one upon another, would be of no inconsiderable use to young beginners in philosophy, but make a very proper subject for their initiatory lessons. The schoolmen probably meant some such thing, by their trees of science and their categories in their logic. Indeed I have found in practice, a general map of the sciences, shewing them issuing from the same trunk and root, and from one another, and intimately connected together, of great use to open the minds of young people, to inflame their curiosity and desire of knowledge, and above all, to keep for ever in their eye the real unity of all the sciences, into whatever different tribes and classes they are divided. And it is easy to conceive how such a tree may be delineated, since from natural experience, or knowledge of the laws of the material world, immediately and naturally sprout all the mechanical arts, and from moral experience as naturally and immediately sprout all the moral arts, among which the more considerable are politics, oratory and poetry, and all these have evidently a very close reciprocal connexion and dependence.—But not to make too long a digression from our subject: The rules of oratory being founded in human nature, to develop them is certainly to unfold a considerable part of human nature: It therefore coincides with, or makes a part of moral philosophy, and ought to be taught like the other parts of it, in proportion as examples occur in history, of its power and excellence, which exemplify or point forth the dispositions of the human mind, on which it depends, or which lay a foundation for it. Accordingly Aristotle's book on rhetoric is really a very profound treatise on the human passions, in order to shew what rules an art that would move them must observe. And of the same kind is his short art of poetry, and all the better commentaries of moderns upon it. For the principal end of poetry being to touch the heart, or to move some passion, pity or fear in particular, what hath been just now said of teaching aright the foundations of oratorical rules, must likewise hold true of poetical rules and maxims. It is impossible to teach or explain them well, without entering very deep into the contexture of the human mind, and the various turns, bearings, connexions and dependencies of our passions. But this subject also having been often very fully and well explained, we shall content ourselves with the few following observations upon it. 1. Plutarch in his excellent discourse upon hearing or reading the poets with young scholars (for that is evidently the design of his treatise, entitled, *concerning hearing the poets*) has some admirable observations upon the caution with which the poets ought to be read with young people, that well deserve the attention of all concerned in the education of youth. He shews that the philosopher may make a very happy use of good poetry, in teaching human nature and human duties: And that philosophers ought to make it a part of their business in the institution of youth, to point out to them the true design and the real excellency of that art. Two things which he remarks upon this subject particularly deserve our notice. In the first place, he says, that in reading the poets with young people, they ought early to be informed, why it is that poetry feigns lies, or contrives fables, and how it ought to feign or lie, namely, agreeably to nature, or with probability, and always in order to give a just view of some part of human na-

ture, and to recommend some virtue or dissuade from some vice. He does
not give the name of poets to all versifiers, but only to the writers of agreeable and useful fables in verse: And as the poet's art chiefly consists in lying
speciously or probably, in order to convey pleasantly and forcibly into the
mind some useful and instructive lesson, so youth ought early to be taught
and inured to consider poems as fictions copied from nature, or as imitations of nature, not taken indeed from any particular facts, but from the
general laws and rules of nature. For thus they will learn to consider poems
in their true light: Thus they will learn to look upon characters as pictures,
and to consider whether they are well drawn or not, and so be led by characters into the examination of human nature itself, the original from
which they are taken: And there will thus be no danger of their mistaking
the poet, as if he intended to recommend every character he paints out to
the life, or to instruct his hearers in every art of intrigue, dissimulation or
cunning, for example, he describes, when his design is really no more than
to exhibit such characters to view in their true light, and is indeed rather
to create aversion against them, than to beget a liking to them. Another
thing he observes is, that in order to lead youth to a just notion of poetry,
moral poetry in particular, which imitates human life and manners (for it
is that species he seems chiefly to have in view) teachers would do well to
inure youth to consider poems as pictures, and for that reason, to shew
them the strict natural relation or close affinity there is between these two
arts, both with respect to their best, their only laudable aims, and the
methods of accomplishing them. The pleasure, says he, the poet intends
to give by drawing the character of any villain, or of any particular vice, is
the same the painter proposes by portaiting the image of any ugly or monstrous creature, to please, to wit, by hitting of likeness, and to entertain
our mind by raising our horror or loathing to a degree that does not tor-
ment. For as truth in imitation pleases as such, so likewise do all the passions, all the emotions of the mind, give pleasure by their exercises, when
they are worked up by proper objects within certain bounds, especially by
fiction; for an object that would create a painful horror, were it really present, excites a pleasing one, when it is but only present in effigy or semblance. We find Aristotle, in like manner, often borrowing illustrations
from the art of painting in his discourse upon poetical imitation. And in-

deed the most successful way of giving a distinct notion of either of them, is to join them together in teaching, and to make them mutually illustrate one another.

2. It is certainly very proper in education to make use of dramatical poetry, and not only to read good comedies and tragedies with young people, but to carry them to see them well represented. It would be preposterous, as has been already observed, to think of explaining to youth the principles and rules of dramatical composition, till they had in several instances fully felt the effects of them. But having been frequently tried by good theatrical pieces, and having often experienced their pleasant and instructive influences, they will then easily understand a master, when he talks to them of their design, and represents them as imitations of human manners, and contrived for certain moral ends: They will then easily comprehend what Aristotle means by saying, the design of tragedy is to purge or refine our pity or our fear, and to work up gradually in the mind, an emotion that shall have in itself a very happy effect upon the temper: They will easily comprehend, that the rules for gaining such an end, must be fetched from human nature: And that pieces calculated to produce such effects, must be so conducted as that they shall be found, upon a critical examination, to be experiments or samples confirming some moral truths or maxims; and they will take pleasure in examining the progress of such pieces, the fable, the plot, and the unraveling, and by this exercise, they will at one and the same time, be learning human nature, and the rules resulting from thence for compositions, by which their authors would move the human heart, and agreeably agitate any of our affections: They will find such pieces to be an unanswerable proof of the sociality of the human mind, and the natural amiableness of virtue and deformity of vice; and will perceive, that such writing is not only an excellent moral school, but can indeed do more than merely teach, since by good performances of this kind, not only may very important truths relating to human nature and human affairs be demonstrated as by experiments, but by them the human mind is actually tried and exercised in such a manner, as hath immediately and directly a very salutary influence upon it.

So much for tragedy: And would a master effectually shew the ridicule of any vice, or strongly exhibit any character to his pupils, satyr and comedy, the latter more especially, are his properest instruments. None acquainted with human nature will doubt, that the best way of correcting any bad propension or habit in youth, is not directly to charge the young man with it, but to put some comedy in his hand, as it were by chance, that will shew him his fault, and the deformity and bad tendency of it in some well drawn character, as a mirror shews us the spots in our face.

3. The history of Greece will afford masters an opportunity of shewing their pupils the rise and progress of all the various species of poetry, the dramatical kind in particular. For there it was that these arts had their birth, or at least that they were brought to their perfection, and that chiefly by means of critics, who pursued a higher aim, than what in modern times assumes the name of criticism, and by laying open the truths poetical imitations ought to teach, and the salutary manners in which they ought to move our affections, and by consequence, all the springs and principles of motion in the human breast, from the workings of which these arts must derive their rules, taught poets how to model and conduct their fictions, agreeably to truth or nature, how to draw their characters and personages, in what circumstances to place them, what language to put in their mouths, conformably to their tempers and passions, and how to make them look and act, what moral ends they ought to propose to themselves, and what maxims and rules, in fine, they must observe in the whole contexture and process of their representations, to gain truly good, wholesome and praise-worthy ends. Thus was the taste of authors and auditors gradually refined and perfected.

4. Let it just be added, that there can be no objection against using Virgil, Homer, or Horace, merely for teaching the words and syntax of the languages in which they are writ, or to inure youth by reading them, to read and pronounce justly and with good grace: Yet these authors cannot be understood by boys quite unacquainted with the beauties of nature and with mankind; and therefore explaining upon them, ought to be delayed till students are by other proper studies qualified for entering into all their beauties, and all the truths they set in the most agreeable lights. But at whatever time they are read with pupils, we have a commentary upon one of them (Homer, to wit) in our own language, which shews what criticism

should propose and do, and what commentators and masters ought to aim at in their lessons upon such classics: I mean Mr. Pope's notes added to his admirable translation of Homer. He who hath read Homer with this help, so as to be able to discern all the beauties in his poems which these notes point out, will not satisfy himself with one reading, and is indeed capable of entering into the spirit of any author, or of comprehending any thing relating to human life and manners, or the design and rules of the highest kind of poetry. It could hardly be said before the English readers were obliged with this commentary on Homer, that we had any thing in any language upon any Greek or Latin authors, upon any poet at least, that answered the ends of true criticism, or that it was not really dangerous to put into the hands of youth, for fear of giving them the very worst of turns, a propension towards mere verbal criticism, which, if it be not pedantry, false erudition, empty, vain puffing up science, what can be so called?

It is indeed strange, that after all the just raillery by which men of true classical taste have exposed the ridiculousness of the pretended notes and commentaries with which ancient authors are encumbered; the vanity, impertinence and idleness, nay perniciousness to true learning and scholarship, of that which in certain countries hath long passed for polite literature, the learned world should still be pestered with, or which is worse, should still give encouragement to such dregs. For nothing certainly requires so little genius, nay, nothing so absolutely requires dullness and want of genius, as to compile large volumes under the name of notes or commentaries, like those of the celebrated Barmannus (for instance) with the help of indexes to classics, and a few dictionaries and books of mythology, without pointing out one beautiful sentiment in the authors that abound with them, or without suggesting any thing that can lead a scholar to think of learning any thing from books full of moral or political instructions, besides grammatical subtleties or various conjectural readings. Let the notes we have mentioned be compared with those upon the same author, or any other, by any of the Dutch or German commentators; and then let any one who does not prefer words, idle contentions about words, to solid and useful observations, decide who has best merited the name of a commentator, or by acquaintance with which of the two kinds, a young man is most likely to be led and formed into the best taste: Let them think which of the two kinds the original authors themselves would have preferred, or to which of them solid science is most indebted. The Casaubons, the Daciers, Gataker, and a few others, deserve praise: But yet never was there so perfect a commentary or critical survey of any author, as that of Homer by our excellent poet, or any system of notes so well adapted to initiate one into the right method of reading and considering an ancient poet: And it is indeed a pity that they are not translated into Latin, that foreign pedants might learn from that model how far their labours fall short of, nay how opposite they are to truly genuine and useful criticism. 'Tis plain from the notes this commentator has collected with so much judgment from the ancients upon his author, that he had learned the art of criticising and commenting from the best ancient critics: And we may judge of the extraordinariness of the genius he carried with him to that school, by the sublime height he hath carried almost every more useful kind of poetry in our language. Dictionary compilers, and other such collectors and explainers of words and phrases, are no doubt a useful set of labourers in the literary commonwealth: But is this a turn to be studiously given to youth, whose birth and fortunes call upon them to qualify themselves early for public service? Or is this the science, the learning that ought to be chiefly encouraged by the public, or by men in power, when it is so evident, that it is upon the promotion and cultivation of arts and sciences of a very different kind and rank, that the principal interests of the public depend; the knowledge of nature, and the knowledge of mankind and human rights and duties, and the best maxims of civil policy and government? For hence spring the arts, and hence alone can the arts spring that teach and enable nations to get wealth and power by commerce, and to employ wealth in an elegant, truly rational manner; the arts which teach subjects their rights, and magistrates their duties, and shew how a people may, and only can make themselves great and happy; how, in fine, a people may preserve, maintain, and secure that liberty without which a people are hardly men, and nothing indeed that is good, great or conspicuous in human life can subsist: For all history confirms what old Homer hath long ago sung.

Jove fix'd it certain, that whatever day
Makes man a slave, takes half his worth away.

Odyss. l. 17.[88]

So much for poetry: Let us now consider her sister arts, sculpture and painting, and the place they ought to have in education. Now, if these arts be languages by which useful truths, or agreeable ideas and sentiments may be conveyed into the mind, or may be pleasantly expressed, they are certainly worth our understanding as such, and instruction in them ought not to be neglected in truly liberal education. But that they are, will be very evident, if we consider that all these arts, painting in particular, can exhibit to us beautiful parts or effects of the visible world, of which kind are landscapes: And they can also represent moral actions and characters; and pictures of this kind are called history-pieces: And to these two classes, all paintings and sculptures may be reduced. Let us examine a little into the uses and rules of both these kinds.

In the first place, pictures exhibiting whether real views of nature, having been copied into the canvass from real appearances, or imaginary views, or such as tho' perhaps the painter never saw, but in his own imagination, yet being congruous to nature's laws, make beautiful as well as possible representations.—Landscapes of both these sorts are not only exceedingly entertaining to a well-formed eye and judgment, but they have a very near relation to, and are of very considerable use in natural philosophy: For they are samples or experiments of what the laws of light, shade and colours do or would produce in certain circumstances; and they are in this respect very proper for giving us a fuller idea of the nature, use and extent of these laws than we can learn from the more common course of nature, at least, without such assistance. As such pieces cannot, on the one hand, be painted without knowledge of light and shade, and of perspective, aerial perspective in particular, so it is scarcely possible to give beginners in the study of nature a just and clear notion of the manner in which nature herself paints various degrees of distances, more especially, and by means of light, shade, and various colouring, exhibites all the immense di-

88. [Alexander Pope, *The Odyssey of Homer,* 17.392–93.]

versity that constitutes the visible world, in such a manner as to render it a steady and sure guide to our touch, feeling, and motions, as it really is, in consequence of the established connexions between appearances to our eyes and our sensations by touch;—it is hardly possible, I say, to give young beginners in philosophy a clear apprehension of this so fundamental a truth in natural philosophy, that not to mention optics merely, scarcely any branch of it can be conceived of as it ought, or is not very difficult, without a just conception of it.—This is scarcely practicable, unless the teacher calls in pictures to his assistance, and teach his pupils to attend, how it is that the figures in them appear round and solid, and stand out; or how it is, on the other hand, that they retire and fly off; how, in fine, it is, that various grounds and distances are there represented: But by comparing good landscapes with nature, this matter soon becomes easy to be understood, familiar to the mind: And thus many difficulties that before perplexed the study of optics, more particularly, immediately evanish.

Now the same relation that landscapes bear to natural philosophy, do moral or historical paintings bear to moral philosophy. Such of them as represent ancient customs and usages, civil or religious, preserve clearer ideas of these usages and manners than can possibly be conveyed by words; and are therefore of great use for understanding ancient authors: And they properly have their place in education, when descriptions of them, or references to them in history, or allusions to them in poets occur, as hath been already observed. But such as exhibit any great man doing any great or heroic action; such as represent various passions moved in spectators of different ages, tempers, conditions and countries, by any action done, or any event happening in their sight—all such pieces are exhibitions of human nature, if they be agreeable to truth, and consequently are specimens or samples from which moralists may draw many very useful remarks: And accordingly we are told, that the ancient sages at Athens, where the porticoes, temples, and all public edifices were adorned with capital pictures, representing the characters and actions of their more remarkable heroes, and the more noted events that had happened in their state, often made such pictures the subjects of their moral lessons. Socrates himself often taught in this manner. One thing is very evident: They serve admirably to preserve the memory of great men and glorious actions: And hardly will any one call this use or benefit of them into doubt, who knows how much such monuments contributed, amongst the ancient Greeks, to support and promote public spirit and true courage: For that they may be most successfully employed to reward and encourage virtue is certain, since all ancient historians agree, that the statues, pictures, and other monuments erected by the Athenians, in favour not only of the commanders, but of the common soldiers, who had signalized themselves in the defence of their country and the public liberty, conduced exceedingly to enhance the merit of their valour, and of the services they rendered to their country, and to inspire the spectators with emulation and courage, and thus to cultivate and perpetuate a spirit of bravery and public zeal in the people, and render their troops victorious and invincible. Those that were slain in the famous battle of Marathon, had all the honour immediately paid to them that was due to their merit. Illustrious monuments were raised to them all, upon which their own names and that of their tribes were recorded, in the very place where the battle was fought. There were three distinct sets of monuments separately set up, one for the Athenians, another for the Platians, and a third for the slaves, whom they had admitted among their soldiers on that occasion. All the honour that was paid to Miltiades himself, the great deliverer of Athens and of all Greece, was, that in a picture of the battle of Marathon, drawn by order of the Athenians, he was represented at the head of the ten commanders, exhorting the soldiers, and setting them an example of their duty. Now Plato often makes it his business to extol the battle of Marathon, and is for having that action considered as the source and original cause of all the victories that were gained afterwards. And indeed on all important occasions, it was customary among them to put the people in mind of the monuments erected to Miltiades, and his invincible troop, that is, of a little army of heroes, whose intrepidity and bravery had done so much honour to Athens, and this motive wonderfully quickened and animated them. The picture of Miltiades was kept at Athens, in a gallery adorned and enriched with different paintings, all excellent in their kind, and done by the greatest masters, which for that reason was called $\pi οικιλη$,[89] signifying varied and diversified. The cele-

---

89. [Turnbull has included the translation of this word, within the same sentence, as "varied and diversified."]

brated Polygnotus, a native of the island of Thusos, and one of the best painters of his time, painted this picture, or at least the greatest part of it; and as he valued himself upon his honour, and was more attached to glory than interest, he did it gratis, and would not receive any recompence for it. The city of Athens therefore rewarded him with a sort of coin, that was more acceptable to his taste, by procuring him an order from the Amphictyons to appoint him a public lodging in the city, where he might live during his own pleasure. I need not say more to prove the moral uses pictures and sculptures are very proper to serve: Those who are acquainted with the history-pieces of the best painters, are already convinced of it: And as for others, there is no way of enabling them to conceive the power of pictures, to represent characters and actions, and thereby move the affections of spectators in a very beneficial and agreeable manner, but by presenting good pieces of the moral kind to them. Besides, I have elsewhere treated on this subject expresly at great length;[90] where I have shewed what good taste of painting means, and how it may be acquired; and wherein it differs from the mere virtuosoship that no less generally passes for good taste in painting, than mere verbal skill does for good taste in classical literature.

But in order to understand and relish painting, tho' much more be necessary than knowledge of drawing, even skill in human nature, and in the unity and truth of ordinance and disposition in imitating any action, in order to make a pleasing and beautiful consistent whole, yet intelligence in drawing is absolutely requisite. And indeed that skill is of such universal use in all the businesses and arts of life, that it certainly should, as Aristotle has recommended, and as it did amongst the Greeks, make an early part in the education of all sorts and ranks of people: In forming young gentlemen after they are taught to write, they should be taught to draw: For it is by such instruction, and by frequent practice in examining good pictures and drawings, or good prints of them, that the eye is formed to a just understanding and relish of proportion, harmony and beauty, in buildings, pictures, and all works of design. And why should not both the ear and

90. Turnbull on ancient painting, &c.

the eye be improved in education by proper exercises, till they are become truly intelligent, skilful, delicate and just? Hath nature given us eyes or ears capable of improvement, without intending that we should be at proper pains to teach, instruct, form or improve them? Nature hath given eyes and ears to all animals, but to man nature hath not given mere common eyes and ears, but hath joined with these senses in us, as Cicero hath observed, a relish or taste of harmony and proportion, by means of which they are capable of being qualified for enjoyments far above all the pleasures the gross senses of other animals can afford to them, for enjoyments truly rational and elegant. And are such excellent gifts of nature to be quite despised and neglected? to be quite overlooked in education, or are such valuable faculties to have no culture, no instruction bestowed upon them? Young gentlemen, who have higher business to mind, which requires much time and application, ought neither to throw away their precious time in learning to paint, nor to play upon musical instruments; but they ought to have their eyes so formed, by a little practice in drawing, and instruction in the principles of the art, as to be able to judge of and relish truth and proportion in drawing, and their ears so improved by instruction in the principles of music, and accustomance to music, as that they may be able to receive pleasure from sentiments well expressed, and set to proper music, when well performed by voices, accompanied with instruments: For music certainly is one of the best relaxations from severer studies and employments, when employed to excite wholesome affections, and not to inflame hurtful ones, and when good sentiments as well as sounds are conveyed. And accordingly in ancient education both these arts had early their proper share. In truth, what in one sense is called improving the eye and the ear, is more strictly and properly speaking, improving and forming the imagination. And surely none will say that education ought to leave this faculty quite uncultivated: None will say, that it is of no consequence whether youth are formed or not by proper care, to a just notion of the pleasures of imagination, and of the arts, by consequence, which have the entertainment of a well-formed imagination for their object and scope. If any one can make a question of this, let him read, for his better information, the admirable essays of Mr. Addison, in the sixth volume of the spectator, upon the pleasures and arts of imagination.[91] And there he will see, that the whole of what belongs to the discipline, improvement or culture of the imagination, is reducible into what may simply be called a just notion of truth, proportion and harmony, and is nearly allied to virtue: For a fine correct imagination is a fancy able to entertain itself with true and just images of beautiful or great objects, or able to draw to itself fine pictures worthy of contemplation, as well as to comprehend and relish good images or pictures, when set before it by an Author of taste, or an intelligent artist. Solidity is, properly speaking, a quality of the judgment; and good taste or genius, properly so called, is a quality of the imagination. The excellency or perfection of reason and judgment consists in distinguishing differences amidst resemblances, the discovery of which requires very close and accurate inspection into objects, and in discerning just and strict reasoning, in which every step naturally leads to that which follows, and the whole of which makes one closely connected chain from artful specious sophistry; or lastly, in accurately weighing and balancing probabilities, without missing or overlooking the minutest circumstance belonging to either side of the question: These are the principal offices and exercises of judgment: And in being able to perform these well, does its strength and virtue principally lie. On the other hand, the excellency and perfection of imagination consists in being quick and ready in finding out likenesses or analogies; and with regard to this faculty, the rule is, That as resemblances, when pointed out, please the more, the less they were expected, if they be true, and can abide examination; so it is by hitting of uncommon likenesses in such a manner, that all to whom they are discovered, wonder that such resemblances were never observed before that genius appears, or wit most shines, and best shews at once its fertility and correctness: Accordingly, the chief businesses of imagination are to bring ideas seemingly very remote from a subject, which dart an agreeable but surprizing uncommon light upon it; to be able to cloath intellectual or moral ideas with proper material forms and dresses; and to know how to bedeck or attire every truth in the garb most suited to it and best becoming

---

91. [*The Spectator,* nos. 411–21.]

it, or that sets it off to the best advantage. There are therefore two chief species of it; one which is dextrous in pointing out beauties; and another which excels in shewing the ridicule of follies and errors, or of vices and falshoods. These two talents seldom meet in the same person, being opposite turns of mind; yet to both belong a happy fertility in inventing metaphors and similitudes, and a just discernment or taste of their propriety and fitness. These are the natural instruments or weapons of wit in every kind of it. Now, as it will readily be owned to be the proper work of education to ripen, strengthen, and improve the judgment; so that, next to this, due care to enrich and correct imagination and taste, is the other main business of education, cannot be denied, whether we consider of what consequence it is with regard to private happiness to possess an imagination capable of entertaining itself in a variety of agreeable manners, all of them able to stand the test and trial of reason in every respect, instead of a dull, lifeless, insipid, or which is worse, a loose, impure, rambling and undisciplin'd one: Or whether we consider ourselves as social creatures, made for conversation and mutual commerce, and consequently, for reciprocally instructing and entertaining one another, by imparting our ideas, sentiments and knowledge to one another, in pleasing and agreeable lights? By the exercises and improvements of the intellect, one may become profoundly knowing; but if he be a stranger to the arts and exercises by which imagination is enriched and refined, he cannot communicate his science to others in a winning, agreeable way, because he will be unable to dress his sentiments and set them out as they ought to be, to attract attention and gain admittance, into polite company, more especially: He may indeed be useful to profound scholars, but he is not qualified for informing the ignorant, or alluring youth to the love of true wisdom. Besides, there is false wit as well as false reasoning; and is it not of consequence, to render youth capable of distinguishing false from true wit, and thus to fortify and guard them against all the deceitful arts of error or vice? To conclude, by plain, naked or simple reasoning, the understanding may be enlightened and convinced: But it is through the imagination only, that truth can find a passage into the heart, to move and interest our affections. For how else is it that oratory or poetry are able to agitate our minds, and lead our passions captive at their will, but by raising up in the imagination, warm, lively, moving pictures? The fancy is first not only struck but heated and briskly agitated, before any of our violent passions are inflamed? And in order to produce the soft and tender affections the same fancy must first be soothed and softened. If therefore we would qualify youth either on the one hand, for being suitably entertained and affected by just and proper addresses to their imaginations, and through it to their passionate part; or guard them, on the other, against all base, all misleading and corruptive impressions; in one word, if we would qualify them for relishing the beauties of poets or orators, it is of the greatest moment to bestow proper culture and improvement upon their imagination or fancy; a wonderfully active, busy and rich faculty, without which human life would indeed be very listless and insipid, in comparison of what its improvements render it; tho' on the other side, to its irregularities and extravagancies be owing a very considerable part of the vices and miseries of mankind. In truth, they must be great strangers to human nature, who know not of what moment it is to have a chaste well-regulated imagination formed to the love of order and proportion, and interested in favour of virtue, which is order in the affections, producing similar order and consistency in outward conduct: For if the fancy be not under due discipline, and hath not been taught to exert and entertain itself with true beauty and harmony, it will be tumultuous and irregular, and be ever rebelling against reason, and pursuing some equally false and pernicious species of beauty: The fancy cannot be without a Venus: "It will always be courting, says an excellent writer, a beauty, and pursuing a Venus of one kind or another. The species of fair, noble, handsome, great, will discover itself on a thousand occasions, and on a thousand subjects. The spectre still will haunt us in some shape or other; and when driven from our cool thoughts, and frighted from the closet, will meet us even at court, and fill our heads with dreams of grandeur, titles, honours, and a false magnificence to which we are ready to sacrifice our greatest pleasure and ease, and for the sake of which we become the meanest drudges and most abject slaves." Now how alone can the fancy be kept from false or pernicious pursuits; how alone can it be secured against error, deceit, or imposition of whatever sort, but by early giving it a right taste of the true *venustum* or *honestum*, and a strong propensity towards it, and the ideas of beauty, order and greatness, which are not only consistent with virtue, but assistant to and corroborative of it: A true taste of wit and ingenuity; a sound relish of order and decorum in ingenious compositions of every kind, or in all works of fancy; and that quick discernment of proportion, even in material objects, without which our senses of hearing and seeing are equally gross with those organs in the lowest kind of animals, and far from being improved and exalted to that superior pitch of perfection for which nature certainly intended them, by uniting with them in our contexture a sense of natural order, beauty and harmony, so nearly allied to our moral sense, that the one cannot reside where the other is not in some degree prevalent; and that he who hath a just notion of beauty and harmony of the first sort, if he be dissolute and irregular in his heart and manners, must live in downright contradiction to the principles from which he professes to derive his favourite entertainments. The truth of this will more fully appear from the following observation, which is the only maxim I shall at present mention with regard to teaching good taste in poetry, and in all the arts of design and fancy conjointly, having elsewhere discoursed very fully upon this subject. It is, that the main thing in instructing youth in the principles, foundations, and maxims of the polite arts, is to engage their attention to this sovereign, universal rule in nature, from which the imitative arts can never depart, without falling proportionably short of the harmony and truth which is their aim, and by which alone they can please, viz. "That what is beautiful is harmonious and proportioned, what is harmonious and proportioned is true, and what is at once both beautiful and true is of consequence agreeable and good." In other words, "Beauty, truth and utility are inseparably connected, or more properly speaking, are one and the same in nature, and therefore they cannot be disjoined in the arts which profess to imitate nature." Accordingly, beauty and truth are plainly joined with the notion of ability and conveniency in the apprehension of every ingenious artist; the statuary, the painter, the architect, the gardner: they do and know they must conform to this rule, because it is universally so throughout all nature. The same features which occasion deformity, create sickness and disease. The proportionate and regular state is the truly prosperous, sound and natural one in every subject. Health of the body is the just proportion, balance, and regular course of things in the constitution. And what else is health or soundness of mind, but harmony, or a just and equal balance of the affections? Or what else is it that produces deformity of the moral kind, but something that tends to the ruin and dissolution of the mental fabric? And in every ingenious art or composition, what is not useful, and strictly related to the whole, can never be beautiful: Ornaments which do not naturally rise out of the subject, and have not a due reference and subordination to the principal design, are not only superfluous and an incumbrance, but they are really noxious and hurtful with regard to the proposed end or effect of the whole, into which they are forced.

The Roman architect Vitruvius makes this observation with regard to all the arts, and applies it to his own, in particular, with great propriety and strength of reasoning. Quintilian has explained the same maxim, and unfolded its extent in a great variety of instances with his usual elegance: He thus concisely expresses the rule itself: "Nunquam veri species ab utilitate dividitur."[92] Cicero, whom he every where follows, had charmingly confirmed this truth long before in several beautiful passages of his writings on oratory: For he extends the rule to that art also, and lays it down as an essential one in it. One passage in particular, Orator. l. 3. c. 45, &c.[93]

---

92. [Quintilian, *Institutio Oratoria,* 8.3.11: "In fact true beauty and usefulness always go hand in hand."]

93. [Cicero, *De Oratore,* 3.45.178–81: "But in oratory as in most matters nature has contrived with incredible skill that the things possessing most utility also have the greatest amount of dignity, and indeed frequently of beauty also. We observe that for the safety and security of the universe this whole ordered world of nature . . . [Turnbull omits a geocentric description of the universe]. This system is so powerful that a slight modification of it would make it impossible for it to hold together, and it is so beautiful that no lovelier vision is ever imaginable. Now carry your mind to the form and figure of human beings or even of the other living creatures: you will discover that the body has no part added to its structure that is superfluous, and that its whole shape has the perfection of a work of art and not of accident. Take trees: in these the trunk, the branches and lastly the leaves are all without exception designed so as to keep and to preserve their own nature, yet nowhere is there any part that is not beautiful. Let us leave nature and contemplate the arts: in a ship, what is so indispensable as the sides, the hold, the bow, the stern, the yards, the sails and the masts? Yet they all have such a graceful appearance that they appear to have been invented not only for the purpose of safety but also for the sake of giving pleasure. In temples and colonnades the pillars are

is well worth pointing out to the reader.—"Sed in plerisque rebus incredibiliter hoc natura est ipsa fabricata: Sic in oratione, ut ea, quae maximam utilitatem in se continerent, eadem haberent plurimum vel dignitatis, vel saepe etiam venustatis. Incolumitatis, ac salutis omnium causa, videmus hunc statum esse hujus totius mundi atque naturae.—Haec tantam habent vim ut paulum immutata cohaerere non possint: Tantam pulchritudinem, ut nulla species ne excogitari quidem possit ornatior. Referte nunc animum ad hominum vel etiam caeterarum animantium formam & figuram. Nullam partem corporis sine aliqua necessitate afficiam, totamque formam quasi perfectam reperietis arte non casu. Quid in arboribus, in quibus non truncus, non rami, non folia sunt denique, nisi ad suam retinendam, conservandamque naturam? Nusquam tamen est ulla pars nisi venusta.—Linquamus naturam, artesque videamus. Quid tam in navigio necessarium quam latera, quam carinae, quam mali, quam vela, quam prora, quam puppis, quam antennae? Quae tamen hanc habent in specie venustatem; ut non solum salutis, sed etiam voluptatis causa inventa esse videantur. Columnae, & templa, & porticus sustinent. Tamen habent non plus utilitatis quam dignitatis. Capitolii fastigium illud, & caeterarum aedium, non venustas sed necessitas ipsa fabricata est. Nam cum esset habita ratio, quemadmodum, ex utraque tecti parte aqua dilaberetur: Utilitatem templi fastigii dignitas consecuta est: Ut etiam si in coelo statueretur, ubi imber esse non possit nullam sine fastigio dignitatem habituram fuisse videatur. Hoc in omnibus item partibus, orationis evenit, ut utilitatem ac prope necessitatem suavitas quaedam ac lepos consequatur." Compare the whole with what he says to the same purpose, Orator. c. 25. and concerning our senses, as they are distinguished from those of the brutes, by our

---

to support the structure, yet they are as dignified in appearance as they are useful. Yonder pediment of the Capitol and those of the other temples are the product not of beauty but of actual necessity; for it was in calculating how to make the rain-water fall off the two sides of the roof that the dignified design of the gables resulted as a by-product of the needs of the structure—with the consequence that even if one were erecting a citadel in heaven, where no rain could fall, it would be thought certain to be entirely lacking in the dignity without a pediment. The same is the case in regard to all the divisions of a speech—virtually unavoidable practical requirements produce charm of style as a result" (Loeb translation by H. Rackham).]

natural sense of beauty and harmony, which is united with them, de natura Deorum, lib. 2. c. 58, &c. For these passages furnish the proper materials for explaining the first principles and chief rules of all the ingenious arts. The chief excellence in them all is simplicity or frugality, and is therefore often called by ancient critics αφελεια:[94] For the arts which imitate nature must conform to her; and her beauty in all her works results from her simplicity, or her steady observance of this rule: "Natura nil frustra facit":[95] Arts, in order to be natural, and please as such, must be frugal and reserved as nature; like her, never profuse to any particular part, but bountiful to all in due proportion; never employing in one thing more than enough, but with exact oeconomy retrenching the superfluous, and adding force to what is principal in every thing, and thus managing all for the best. This is nature's method throughout all her infinitely various operations: And therefore the rule in imitating her, in whatever composition, is,

> *Denique sit quodvis simplex duntaxat & unum.*
> HOR. ART. POET.[96]

> *First follow nature, and your judgment frame,*
> *By her first standard, which is still the same:*
> *Unerring nature, still divinely bright,*
> *One clear, unchang'd, and universal light,*
> *Life, force, and beauty, must to all impart,*
> *At once the source, the end, and test of art.*
> *Art from that fund each just supply provides,*
> *Works without show, and without pomp presides;*
> *In some fair body thus the secret soul*
> *With spirits feeds, with vigour fills the whole,*

94. [Turnbull has included the translation of this word, within the same sentence, as "simplicity or frugality."]

95. ["Nature does nothing in vain."]

96. [Horace, *Ars Poetica*, line 23: "In short, be the work what you will, let it at least be simple and uniform."]

Each motion guides, and every nerve sustains,
It self unseen, but in th' effect remains.

POPE.[97]

We have said enough of poetry and oratory: And to form the eye and judgment to a just notion of drawing and proportion, nothing more is necessary than practice in drawing, and accustoming the eye to good drawings: And if we would form a just taste of painting, let youth be often assisted in attending to the disposition, ordonance and unity of pictures, and examining well composed ones, or good prints of them, by these and the like questions. "Is the subject worthy of being represented, and doth the representation excite a lively and just idea of it? To what end is the composition adapted, and what effect hath it upon the minds of attentive observers? Doth it fully fill and employ the mind? Have all the parts a just relation to the principal design? Or is the sight splitted, divided and perplexed by parts either not essential, or not duly subordinated to the whole? Is the colouring proper to the subject and design; and is it of a proportional consistent character throughout the whole, to that of the principal figure? Doth the same genius and spirit reign throughout all the work? Is there a sufficient and well chosen variety of contrasts? Is there too little or too much expressed? Of whatever kind it is, landscape or historical, doth it make a beautiful or a great whole? Is it a true and compatible choice of nature? Is there nothing repugnant to nature's laws and proportions? And above all, what influence hath it upon the mind? Doth it instil or call up great, uncommon, beautiful, or delightful ideas? Doth it light up the understanding, spread the imagination, and set the mind a thinking? Doth it shew a fine taste of nature, an exalted idea of beauty and grace, and raise the soul to the conception and love of what is truly great, beautiful and decent in nature and in arts?"

By these and such like questions, ought pictures as well as poems to be tried and criticised. And such an examination of either is a truly philosophical employment. There is indeed a false learning or taste with regard to the plastic arts, corresponding to pedantry, verbal criticism, or false taste

97. [Alexander Pope, *An Essay on Criticism*, 68–79.]

in classical learning, which is entirely occupied and taken up about names, and hands, and rarity or antiquity, without ever considering the meaning and design of pictures, or their contrivance and ordonance: But the best security against both is to teach and inure pupils to examine both poems and pictures, compositions, in fine, of all kinds, with a philosophical eye, and to seek first and above all, for sense, judgment and truth in them. This false taste is excellently described and chastised in an admirable Canto in imitation of Spencer, from which give me leave just to copy these lines.

> *Who aye pretending, love of science fair,*
> *And generous purpose to adorn the breast,*
> *With liberal arts, to virtue's court repair,*
> *Yet nought but tunes, and names, and coins away do bear.*

I shall just observe, before I quit this subject, that because the arts of design have been sadly perverted and abused to the worst of purposes, they have therefore been confounded with luxury, and misrepresented as rather pernicious than useful, or even ornamental to states. But according to this argument, must not poetry likewise be banished: For what hath been more abused and prostituted than the magic of numbers? According to this argument, what ought not to be called luxury? For hath not, not only wit, but philosophy, and even religion itself, been rendered by abuse exceeding mischievous, exceeding corruptive of honesty and good morals? At what, in fine, that is good or great does not this argument from the abuse of things strike as strongly as at the ingenious arts? In the times when oratory and poetry were at their highest perfection, painting and sculpture were also in their greatest glory: All the arts mutually lent aids, and charms and graces one to another.

> *Verse and sculpture bore an equal part,*
> *And art reflected images on art.*

POPE.[98]

These arts are dragged into the service of vice with no less reluctance

---

98. [Alexander Pope, *Epistle to Mr. Addison, Occasioned by His Dialogues on Medals.*]

than Homer beautifully describes poetry to yield to any vile prostitution of her powers and graces.

> *For dear to gods and men is sacred song,*
> *Self-taught I sing; by heav'n, and heav'n alone,*
> *The genuine seeds of poetry are sown;*
> *And (what the gods bestow) the lofty lay*
> *To gods alone, and god-like worth repay.*
> *That here I sung was force and not desire,*
> *This hand reluctant touch'd the warbling wire;*
> *And let thy son attest, nor sordid pay,*
> *Nor servile flattery stain'd the moral lay.*
>
> POPE'S Odyss. l. 22. v. 582.[99]

'Tis to virtue and truth alone they willingly impart their ornaments and charms. Indeed all the nobler ends and uses of poetry described by Theocritus in his delightful idyllion, Ἀεὶ τοῦτο Διὸς κουράις,[100] &c. or by Horace in his sublime ode in praise of poesy, *Donarem pateras,* &c. are likewise the ends and uses in which her sister arts most delight, and best shew their genuine force and beauty.

They are thus described by an admirable poet with great spirit and taste.

> *To softer prospect turn we now the view,*
> *To laurel'd science, arts and public works;*
> *That lend my finish'd fabric comely pride,*
> *Grandeur and grace. Of sullen genius he,*
> *Curs'd by the muses, by the graces loath'd,*
> *Who deems beneath the public's high regard,*
> *These last enlivening touches of my reign.*
> *However puff'd with pow'r, and gorg'd with wealth,*
> *A nation be; let trade enormous rise,*

---

99. [Pope, *The Odyssey of Homer*, 22.382–92.]

100. [Theocritus, *Idyl* 16, line 1: "This is ever the care of Zeus' maidens (i.e., the muses)."]

> *Let east and south their mingled treasure pour,*
> *Till swell'd, impetuous, the corrupting flood*
> *Burst o'er the city, and devour the land:*
> *Yet these neglected, these recording arts,*
> *Wealth rots a nusance, and, oblivious sunk,*
> *That nation must another Carthage lie.*
> *If not by them on monumental brass,*
> *Or sculptur'd marble, or the deathless page,*
> *Imprest, renown had left no trace behind.*
> *In vain to future times the sage had thought,*
> *The legislator plan'd, the hero found*
> *A beauteous death, the patriot toil'd in vain:*
> *Th' awarders they of fame's immortal wreath,*
> *They rouse ambition, they the mind exalt,*
> *Give great ideas, lovely forms infuse,*
> *Delight the general eye, and drest by them*
> *The moral Venus glows with double charms.*
>
>   THOMSON.[101]

In poor and indigent states, forced to toil and drudge for the necessaries of life, there is neither leisure nor spirit for cultivating ingenious, ornamental sciences and arts: It is only in opulent countries that men will think of applying themselves to what is not absolutely requisite to their convenient subsistence. Yet such, on the other hand, is the ordinary course of human affairs, that a people no sooner become rich, than they become wanton and sensual: Necessity begets industry, but so soon as industry has brought wealth into a nation, affluence and ease beget impatience of discipline and dissoluteness of manners, that quickly corrupt not only all the ingenious arts, but even philosophy itself: So true is this, that in no country where the polite arts have at any time flourished, did they ever begin to decline from their perfection, and to be prostituted to wicked uses, till philosophy itself had sadly degenerated into a very loose and profligate doctrine, unworthy of that sacred name; which signifies just ideas of the government of the world, and of good conduct in life, in conformity

---

101. [James Thomson, *Liberty, A Poem,* 5.374–99.]

to the character and will of the supreme parent of all things: This was the case both at Athens and at Rome. In the former republic, all the arts declined in proportion as false philosophy and corruption of manners gained ground: When their ancient virtue was gone, the spirit of tragedy went with it, and all the other arts soon gave way to shew, farce, effeminate music, or lascivious mimic-dances, horse-races, and such like trifling gaudy entertainments. In the latter, venality, luxury and voluptuousness were come to a very great height, before the polite arts were known in it; and for that reason, they never came to any considerable degree of perfection there: All the polite arts, according to the history of that state, after they had once been introduced into it, revived or faded, as liberty and virtue lift up their heads, prospered or declined. Under the wicked tyrants, after the dissolution of the commonwealth, whatever sumptuous works were carried on that are justly called by the best historians, "Ostentatio stultissima regum": and on account of which the taste of these princes is not celebrated, but they are set forth in their true light, as "*incredibilium cupitores,*" (so Tacitus speaks of Nero in particular) true taste sadly degenerated.[102] But under another race of good ones, it rose, as it were from the dead, and made considerable progress. Tho' the polite arts may, and often have been made in corrupt times incentives, panders to vice; yet they in fact have always soon evanished and disappeared, after they begun to be perverted to ends repugnant to their genius, and natural tendency and scope. This is the remark of one of the best ancient critics, who thus reasons the matter. "Quis inter haec literis, aut ullae bonae arti locus? non Hercule magis quam frugibus in terra sentibus ac rubis occupata. Age. Non ad perferendos studiorum labores necessaria frugalitas? Quid ergo ex libidine ac luxuria spei? Nam praecipue acuit ad cupiditatem literarum amor laudis. Num igitur malis esse laudem curae putamus?"[103]

---

102. ["The stupidest ostentation of kings," and "desirous ones of incredible things."]

103. [Quintilian, *Institutio Oratoria,* 12.1.7–8: "Amid such passions as these what room is there for literature or any virtuous pursuit? You might as well look for fruit in land that is choked with thorns and brambles. Well, then, I ask you, is not simplicity of life essential if we are to be able to endure the toil entailed by study? What can we hope to get from lust or luxury? Is not the desire to win praise one of the strongest stimulants to a passion for literature? But does that mean that we are to suppose that praise is an object of concern to bad men?"]

Carthage, sure, was not ruined by the prevalency of arts, absolutely unknown in that rich state: Nor could the arts which were totally excluded
from Sparta by its constitution have had any hand in its fall. The latter, as
well as the former, fell a sacrifice to the lust of power and avarice, as the
famous Pythian oracle is said to have foretold concerning Sparta. Cicero's
remark upon this subject deserves to be mentioned. "Nullum vitium te-
trius quam avaritia, praesertim in principibus & rempublicam gubernan-
tibus. Habere enim quaestui rempublicam non modo turpe est, sed sceler-
atum etiam & nefarium. Itaque quod Apollo Pythius oraculo edidit,
Spartam nulla alia re nisi avaritia perituram, id videtur non solum, Lace-
daemoniis sed & omnibus opulentis populis praedixisse."[104] The Persian
empire perished, as both historians and philosophers have observed,
through the bad education of their princes, and the gross voluptuousness
which soon spread itself over the whole body, after the union of the Persians with the soft Medes, and the vast conquests of Cyrus, who was indeed an awful instance of the truth of an ancient observation which a
Latin historian thus expresses: "Secundae res sapientium animos fati-
gant."[105]

A private man may throw away too much of his time, as well as of his
fortune, upon pictures, statues and coins, through a disproportioned admiration of these arts, which generally is not an intelligent one. But if any
one should object, for this reason, against giving proper encouragement to
the ingenious arts in a state, Horace furnishes us with the topic for a very
proper answer.

> *Insani sapiens nomen ferat, aequus iniqui;*
> *Ultra, quàm satìs est, virtutem si petat ipsam.*

---

104. [Cicero, *De Officiis*, 2.77: "There is . . . no vice more offensive than avarice,
especially in men who stand foremost and hold the helm of state. For to exploit the state
for selfish profit is not only immoral; it is criminal, infamous. And so the oracle, which
the Pythian Apollo uttered, that 'Sparta should not fall from any other cause than avarice,' seems to be a prophecy not to the Lacedaemonians alone, but to all wealthy nations as well."]

105. [Sallust, *Bellum Catilinae*, 11.8: "Even the wise have their temper tried by prosperity" (trans. Alfred W. Pollard, London: MacMillan, 1882).]

I nunc, argentum, & marmor vetus, aeraque, & artes
Suspice: cum gemmis Tyrios mirare colores:

HOR. Ep. l. 1. Ep. 6.[106]

The character to be recommended to the imitation of youth, in order to guard them against this folly, is that of Atticus in Nepos. "Elegans non magnificus, splendidus non sumptuosus, omni diligentia munditiam non affluentem affectabat. Supellex non modica, non multa, ut in neutram partem conspici possit."[107] Here elegance is well distinguished from luxury. And indeed so true is it, that good taste and true art were never able to subsist long, after affectation of magnificence and expence had spread from courts, corrupted with a false opinion of pomp and splendour, like a contagion over the land, that it quickly happens, every where in such cases, as Pliny the elder tells us it happened a little before his time in the Roman empire, viz. "That in statuary, painting, and architecture, nothing is admired but what is sumptuous and costly in the mere materials of the work. Precious metals, glittering stones, every thing that is merely shewy and glaring and *poisonous to art,* comes every day more into request, and are imposed upon masters as necessary materials to the ruin of good taste." Indeed, as our own poet happily expresses it,

'Tis use alone that sanctifies expence,
And splendour borrows all its rays from sense.

POPE.[108]

---

106. [Horace, *Epistles,* 1.6.15–18: "Let the wise man bear the name of madman, the just of unjust, should he pursue Virtue herself beyond due bounds. Go now, gaze with rapture on silver plate, antique marble, bronzes and works of art; 'marvel' at gems and Tyrian dyes."]

107. [Cornelius Nepos, "Life of Atticus," 8.5: "He was tasteful rather than magnificent, distinguished rather than extravagant; and all his efforts were in the direction of elegance, not of excess. His furniture was modest, not abundant, so that it attracted attention in neither direction" (Loeb translation by John C. Rolfe).]

108. [Alexander Pope, *Epistle to Richard Boyle, Earl of Burlington,* lines 179–80.]

A Pericles may have expended in superfluous buildings, and vain decorations, the treasury that was destined for carrying on a war in the defence of the common liberty of Greece: And Plato, who formed a judgment of things, not from outward splendour, but from truth, after his master Socrates, may have had reason to say of him, that with all his grand edifices and other works, he had not improved the mind of one of the citizens in virtue, but had rather corrupted the purity and simplicity of their ancient manners. A Verres may, without any taste or intelligence of the ingenious arts, have plundered and robbed cities and provinces, to adorn his own palace with pictures, statues, and antique vases. But still it will not follow from these or any other such examples, that a very proper use may not be made of these arts for promoting true virtue; or that monuments perpetuating the memory of great men, by just representations of their noble deeds, are not very becoming decorations for courts of justice, assemblies of the public states, colleges, schools, and all other public edifices, or that there is not an elegant way of laying out wealth, which is very opposite to gross voluptuousness, and indeed the best preservative against it: For order and proportion in buildings and gardens, and monuments that shew judgment, and have a virtuous meaning and tendency, are certainly the very reverse of tasteless waste, mere glare, idle unmeaning expence, and coarse sensuality; or reason, virtue, taste and judgment are empty names. The best things may be perverted; but surely the securest barrier against bad taste or corruption of any kind, is to form early, by proper education in young minds, a just sense of the excellency of virtue, and a thorough good taste of all the arts that may be rendered subservient to it, or from which men of easy fortunes may fetch amusements to themselves, without making one step towards vice; and an aversion from every abuse of them. And in order to gain this purpose, education must unite the ingenious arts and liberal exercises with philosophy, and by proper examples, teach her pupils what is beautiful in nature, or whence the beauty of nature proceeds; what is orderly and decent in the conduct of life; what produces and supports public order and happiness; and what is beautiful, elegant and decent in arts. Now all the parts of this lesson are strictly coherent: They cannot be severed without sadly maiming the true philosophy, and strangely stinting and confining young understandings, instead of expanding and enlarging them. For indeed, as Plato long ago observed, all the liberal arts and sciences which have any connexion with human affairs, or tendency to humanize the mind, have a strict and intimate affinity, and are bound together by a very close common bond, or natural relation.

Concerning Travelling

Every more important question relative to liberal education, hath (I think) been handled in this enquiry at great length; some questions, indeed, too minutely and particularly, were this treatise designed merely for such as only want hints. All therefore that remains to be treated of is travelling: And this indeed is a copious and important subject, that well deserves to be fully considered, and would require a volume by itself: We shall only suggest here a few observations upon it, which are indeed very obvious, but yet very little attended to in practice.

'Tis very plain that youth cannot be qualified for taking any advantageous notices of the state of learning in foreign countries, unless they be already very well acquainted with the chief branches of true learning, or the more useful sciences.

'Tis equally manifest, that without acquaintance with agriculture, manufactures and mechanical arts, they cannot be capable of making any useful observations for the benefit of their country upon these very important matters: And the same is likewise true with regard to commerce or trade.

'Tis no less evident, that they are not prepared for considering with intelligence the governments of foreign countries, their customs, manners, and maxims of policy, and the effects of different civil constitutions upon their respective subjects, till they have been considerably practised in reading history, and making political reflections: Unless they are well instructed in the nature of civil government in general, and the ends which laws and political orders ought to propose, they can no more profit by vis-

iting foreign states than one unacquainted with the principles of mechanism, can by seeing engines and machines.

'Tis fully as conspicuous, that raw unexperienced youth are not qualified for gathering information from the conversation of knowing men, or
for seeing into men's characters and dispositions.

And to conclude, without knowing the state of one's own country, none
can judge how other nations stand related to it, or wherein their interests
agree or jar and differ: Now it will readily be owned to be very dangerous
to send youth, for the sake whether of languages or exercises, abroad to
receive their first tincture, their first impressions and habits.—From these
considerations therefore it is obvious, who alone are qualified for travelling
to any good purpose, however promiscuously and indiscriminately all our
young people of birth and fortune may be sent to travel about seventeen
or eighteen years of age:—and what preparation, what qualifications are
necessary for travelling? The false, the very pernicious taste our young
travellers into France and Italy too often bring back with them, is strongly
painted out, and very justly satyrized in a beautiful canto in imitation of
Spencer, which travellers into these parts ought indeed to carry along with
them, as a preservative against the infection they are there so liable to be
tainted with. As to a proper directory for travellers, I know of none: some
such thing beginning with reflections upon our own government, and the
interest of our own country, and pointing out the ends which travellers
ought principally to have in their view, with proper instructions in the different manners, customs and governments of the foreign countries our
travellers more generally visit, is greatly wanting. But from Homer's Odyssey a young man may learn what should chiefly be attended to by those
who would learn the knowledge of men; for Homer certainly intended to
give us the character of a wise traveller, a sagacious inspector into men and
things, escaping many snares and temptations, and guiding himself
through various dangers by his prudence and virtue, and improving in
true wisdom by every incident in the person of Ulysses, as Horace twice
tells us.

> *Rursus quid virtus, & quid sapientia possit,*
> *Utile proposuit nobis exemplar Ulyssem:*

> *Qui domitor Trojae, multorum providus urbes*
> *Et mores hominum inspexit; latumque per aequor,*
> *Dum sibi, dum sociis reditum parat, aspera multa*
> *Pertulit, adversis rerum immersabilis undis.*
> *Sirenum voces, & Circes pocula nosti:*
> *&c.* —————— ——————
>
> Ep. 2. l. 1.[1]

And again,

> *Dic mihi, Musa, virum, captae post tempora Trojae,*
> *Qui mores hominum multorum vidit, & urbes.*
>
> Art. Poet.[2]

After one hath well digested Xenophon's Cyropoedeia, a careful reading of one of the best of modern books, Telemachus's adventures, will likewise be of great advantage; and to these the travels of Cyrus deserve to be added. But besides these, it will be proper, after acquainting themselves with the history, natural and moral, of the country they design to travel into, to read some books of travels, in which not merely buildings, pictures, or antiquities are described, tho' these should by no means be totally neglected, but the policy, the commerce, the religion, the manners of these nations or states are laid open: Such as Lord Molesworth's account of Denmark, Sir William Temple's account of the Netherlands, Busbequii epistolae, and several other such treatises, wrote by men capable of taking large and just views of men and things, and versed in public affairs. Above all, our travellers ought to begin at home, and be initiated, by the assistance of a qualified guide, in a journey through their own country, into the truly useful way of travelling. And they ought to lay themselves out to get all the

---

1. [Horace, *Epistles*, 1.2.17–23: "Again, of the power of worth and wisdom he has set before us an instructive pattern in Ulysses, that tamer of Troy, who looked with discerning eyes upon the cities and manners of many men, and while for self and comrades he strove for a return across the broad seas, many hardships he endured, but could never be o'erwhelmed in the waves of adversity. You know the Sirens' songs and Circe's cups."]

2. [Horace, *Ars Poetica*, lines 141–42: "Sing, Muse, for me the man who on Troy's fall / Saw the wide world, its ways and cities all" (the opening of the *Odyssey*).]

information they can about the countries they propose to see, by frequenting the conversation of those who have travelled into them, and made useful observations. In fine, we may safely venture to say, that till one is well acquainted with geography, ancient and modern, hath pleasure in reading history, and can draw solid instructions from it, and hath withal been accustomed to truly manly and useful conversation, he is not at all fitted for improvement by travelling: But if this be the case, then it is very evident what one must do to prepare and qualify himself for travel. On this subject, however, we did not propose to enter; and therefore we shall only add, that the education here delineated, is the proper one to prepare for travelling, and that travelling would indeed render it perfect.

F I N I S.

INDEX

Note: Page numbers followed by *n.* and a number indicate material in footnotes.

This book is set in Adobe Garamond, a modern adaptation by Robert Slimbach of the typeface originally cut around 1540 by the French typographer and printer Claude Garamond. The Garamond face, with its small lowercase height and restrained contrast between thick and thin strokes, is a classic "old-style" face and has long been one of the most influential and widely used typefaces.

Printed on paper that is acid free and meets the requirements of the American National Standard for Permanence of Paper for Printed Library Materials, z39.48-1992. ∞

Book design by Louise OFarrell,
Gainesville, Florida
Typography by Impressions Book and Journal Services, Inc.,
Madison, Wisconsin
Printed and bound by Edwards Brothers, Inc.,
Ann Arbor, Michigan